ORIGINS
LINKING SCIENCE AND SCRIPTURE

LINKING SCIENCE AND SCRIPTURE

ARIEL A. ROTH

REVIEW AND HERALD® PUBLISHING ASSOCIATION
HAGERSTOWN, MD 21740

This book was
Edited by Gerald Wheeler
Copyedited by James Cavil, William Cleveland, Jocelyn Fay
Designed by Willie Duke
Cover design by GenesisDesign/Bryan Gray
Typeset: Optima 10/14

PRINTED IN U.S.A.

02 01 00 99 98 5 4 3 2 1

R&H Cataloging Service
Roth, Ariel Adrien, 1927-
Origins: Linking science and scripture.

1. Religion and science. 2. Science—Philosophy. 3. Creationism. 4. Evolution. I. Title.

213

ISBN 0-8280-1328-4

DEDICATION

To Lenore,
Larry, and John;
all fine examples
of the work of the Creator

CONTENTS

CHAPTER #

THE AUTHOR

Ariel A. Roth was born in Geneva, Switzerland, and grew up in Europe, the Caribbean, and North America. Holding a master's degree in biology and a Ph.D. degree in zoology from the University of Michigan, he has taken additional training in geology, mathematics, and radiation biology at various campuses of the University of California.

Roth has held a number of college and university appointments and is a member of several learned societies. After serving as chairman of the Biology Departments at Andrews University and Loma Linda University, he was director of the Geoscience Research Institute at Loma Linda, California. For 23 years he has been editor of the journal *Origins.*

Roth has pursued research in invertebrate zoology and on fossil and living coral reefs in both the Pacific and Caribbean. There he has investigated the effects of light and pigment on the rate of coral reef growth. His research in various aspects of biology has been financed by several United States government agencies, including the National Institutes of Health and the National Oceanic and Atmospheric Administration.

Roth has been active in the evolution-creation controversy in the United States, serving as a consultant or witness to the states of California, Oregon, and Arkansas. He has conducted numerous paleontological and geological field trips in Australia, New Zealand, Europe, and North America in areas significant to the creation-evolution controversy. In addition, he has published more than a hundred articles in both scientific and popular journals, and has given many hundreds of lectures throughout the world.

PREFACE

Some consider an attempt to link science and Scripture an impossible task. This book challenges that "impossibility." It attempts to show that the dichotomy between science and Scripture is not what is often surmised and that a reasonable harmony exists between the two.

In the animated discussions about the truthfulness of science and Scripture, too often the focus is on one specialized topic, such as how life could arise by itself or the validity of the record of beginnings found in the Bible. However, the question of origins is comprehensive, dealing with the beginning of nearly everything. A broad question demands a broad base of evaluation. This book attempts to give an introduction to the wider picture. Often we trust the specialized experts who trust other specialized experts, all of whom have formulated their "worldview" on prevailing opinions without having had a chance to evaluate the larger picture that we so frequently take for granted. Too often we draw extended conclusions from a narrow database while being unaware that we are suffering from the bias of exclusion. A sociologist looks at a city from a different perspective than does an architect, yet both see a part of the total picture. This brief survey attempts to "specialize" in the more comprehensive view, evaluating various interpretations based on scientific data and on Scripture. While trying to cover the broad picture, practical constraints have forced me to select a limited number of topics for discussion. I have sought to choose the most important topics—namely, those that present the greatest challenge to Scripture and to science. The great questions of origins are approached from a variety of perspectives. Starting with the history of the conflict between science and religion, the book then considers biological, paleontological, and geological interpretations. Evaluations of science, of Scripture, and of views intermediate between the creation concept of Scripture and the evolutionary model of science then follow. Although I would have liked to address scores of other topics, alas, one cannot write about everything, and many readers will be grateful that I did not try!

One of the premises of this treatise is that truth ought to make sense. In other words, truth will bear up under investigation; however, that investigation should be comprehensive enough to be meaningful to the questions posed. One of the disappointing aspects of human nature is that more often than many of us are willing to admit, we believe what we want to believe, instead of what the data is saying. This is why it is so important in our search for truth to avoid relying on conjecture and to pay particular attention to the firmest anchor points we can find. As a practicing scientist, I take science extremely seriously. And as one who values meaning and religion, I also take the Bible just as seriously.

Many books have come off the presses recently to challenge creation, evolution, or related views. In this book, where possible, I have attempted a more constructive synthesis. This has been more feasible in the second half of the book. At the same time, I have tried to give special attention to critical evaluation. Most published discussions of this topic ignore geology. I have attempted to fill this gap with considerations from that neglected field.

This book often focuses on the intersection of science and religion. The reader will soon discover several possible uses of general terms, such as science or religion. This can be confusing, and precise understanding is important to the discussion. To clarify terminology, I have often identified specific uses in the text. Especially important are such terms as *science, naturalistic science, methodological science, religion, Scripture,* and *theology.* The glossary at the end of this book will define them.

A number of the conclusions I present are not mainline. I invite the reader to evaluate them on the basis of the data, not from preconceived perspectives. We cannot formulate new concepts by simply approving of old ones.

A few chapters (especially 4, 8, 10, and 14) cover rather technical topics. I have tried to simplify them as much as possible, but fear they might still be difficult to understand. They are important, but some readers may find it advantageous to read the conclusions at the end of these chapters and go on to easier topics.

Does this book represent a balanced treatment? Is it unbiased? Unfortunately, the answer in both cases is probably no. I have made special efforts to be fair to the data, paying special attention to the most reliable data, but who can claim complete freedom from bias? When it comes to interpretations of data, I make no claim to have tried to give every view an even voice. This book is not a survey of prevailing opinions. However, in a number of areas, our level of information is so meager compared to what we need for any final conclusions that I present several options to consider.

Whenever I look at a new book, one of the first things I do is glance at the final chapter to determine the author's perspective. Let me spare you that exercise, if you have not already done so. It is my conclusion that much more scientific information corroborates Scripture than most people have generally surmised. While a fair amount of scientific data is interpreted as favoring evolution, the evolutionary worldview is limited and leaves many questions, including the meaning of existence, unanswered. It appears to me that when we consider the total picture, creation explains more than evolution does. Views of origins that attempt to combine parts of creation and evolution (chapter 21) are not very satisfactory. They lack definition as well as scientific or scriptural authentication, or authentication from any other source of information.

I am aware that those whose views differ from mine may find my approach unpleasant. If this is the case, please accept my sincere apologies. I would urge such individuals to continue studying, communicating, and contributing to humanity's total fund of knowledge. We all have much to learn from each other.

Ariel A. Roth
Loma Linda, California

ACKNOWLEDGMENTS

The help of many friends with whom I have had extensive discussions over the years has been of immeasurable value. All the students in my classes, and especially my graduate students, have been a persistent source of illumination. I especially wish to thank Robert Brown, Arthur Chadwick, Harold Coffin, Jim Gibson, David Rhys, and Clyde Webster for their invaluable insights. Katherine Ching deserves special mention for her exceptional assistance with the seemingly endless bibliographical references. The support of the Geoscience Research Institute over the years is very much appreciated.

The following, who have given wise suggestions for the manuscript, or parts of it, deserve special mention: Earl Aagaard, John Baldwin, David Cowles, Paul Giem, Thomas Goodwin, George Javor, Karen Jensen, Elaine Kennedy, Glenn Morton, Bill Mundy, George Reid, William Shea, and Randy Younker. They bear no blame for any errors that might have crept into the final copy, nor for the views and prejudices expressed herein, for which I take full responsibility.

Since biological topics are the most common in this book, the reference format generally follows the guidelines presented in: Style Manual Committee, Council of Biology Editors. 1994. Scientific style and format: the CBE manual for authors, editors, and publishers. 6th ed. Cambridge and New York: Cambridge University Press.

THE QUESTIONS

A LINGERING QUESTION

It is one thing to wish to have truth
on our side, and another to wish
sincerely to be on the side of truth.
—*Richard Whately*[1]

The education committee of the state of Oregon's Legislative Assembly had convened a public hearing in the state capital, Salem. The large room overflowed, and the committee had to open four other meeting rooms to accommodate the crowd of interested onlookers. At issue was the teaching of creation in the public schools of Oregon. The general public overwhelmingly favored teaching both creation and evolution, and the legislature was considering a new law requiring balanced treatment of both views.

When I addressed the committee, I pointed out that the disagreements between creation and evolution were not over facts but over the *interpretation* of facts. Both evolutionists and creationists accept the data of science but place different understandings on them. For instance, evolutionists teach that the similarities in cell structure, biochemistry, and anatomy found among different kinds of animals and plants are the result of a common evolutionary origin, whereas creationists look at the very same data and interpret them as representing the imprint of a single designer, God.

After several hours of discussion the chair offered his concluding remarks. He pointed out that there really was no question at issue, because creation had lost to science more than 100 years ago. In his opinion the conflict had long been settled. His statements left some of us wondering why anyone had called a public meeting at all. As the keynote speaker for the creation viewpoint, I was impressed with how unsuccessful I had been! The entire meeting again reminded me of the strong emotional involvement we have in the basic philosophical issue of our origins. *Not* settled 100 years ago, it shows to this day little sign of abatement. Open conflict between scientific interpretations and the Bible has raged for two centuries. It is one of the greatest intellectual battles of all time. The instruments of battle are the pen and tongue, and the battlefield is the human mind. This question affects our basic worldview, our reason for existence, and our hope for the future. It is not an issue that we can easily lay aside.

A LINGERING QUESTION: WHICH IS TRUE, SCIENCE OR SCRIPTURE?

Science—probably humanity's greatest intellectual achievement—rightly commands a high degree of respect. When scientists make pronouncements, they may not be understood, but they are likely to be believed. Frequently courts of law and the advertising of commercial products appeal to scientific tests as the final word. Science in combination with technology has brought us computers, lunar modules, and genetic engineering. It has been almost more than successful.[2] We need not dwell long on the success of science.

The powerful scientific community generally endorses the evolutionary concept that the universe and life developed by themselves while at the same time questions or ignores the concept of a designer God. Such an approach brings the scientific community into conflict with those who believe the account of earth history given in the Scriptures (Bible). In this account, regarded by many as historical revelation, God is the Creator of all, and here the believer also finds some understanding and meaning to reality. By contrast, a naturalistic (i.e., no supernatural) evolution tends to reduce reality to mechanistic concepts and, in the words of Shakespeare, life becomes "a tale told by an idiot, full of sound and fury, signifying nothing."[3]

While science is powerful, the Bible is a book without peer in terms of influence.[4] By 1975 an estimated 2,500 million copies of the Bible had been printed, and yearly production is approximately 44 million. This record well surpasses the next contender, the "red book" compilation of quotations by Mao Zedong, which had an estimated circulation of 800 million copies. Other contenders on the more open market are *The Truth That Leads to Eternal Life* (more than 100 million), and the *Guinness Book of Records* (more than 70 million).[5] Current distribution of the Bible is more than 17 times that of any secular competitor. Often testaments or individual books of the Bible appear separately, further enhancing the Bible's dominance.

An important episode in the conflict between science and Scripture is the eighteenth-century Enlightenment, the period when intellectual activity freed itself from traditional religious beliefs and the Bible. The Enlightenment did not solve humanity's basic questions about its origins and the origin of everything else. Neither did it eliminate the Bible. During the past two centuries the battle over the Bible has sometimes raged openly, and sometimes it has been less noticed. But behind this conflict the Bible still remains the world's most sought-after book. If the Bible were entertainment, one might explain its popularity on that basis. But the Bible is hardly entertainment—at times it has some hard sayings. Its popularity derives at least in part on the confidence it engenders by its candor and meaningfulness.

In view of the public's broad acceptance of both science and the Bible and the contrasting views espoused by each, it is not surprising that we find controversy between the two. Many sincerely wonder which is the most reliable source of truth. We will discuss this question in a variety of ways in the chapters ahead.

Questions about ultimate origins such as the origin of the universe, or the origin of God are sometimes discussed, but with little evidence and few definitive answers. We will not dwell on these highly speculative questions which must at present remain moot. However, we will discuss at length the relative validity of both the evolutionary concept of naturalistic science and the creation concept described in Scripture. Much more evidence bears on these two models. Here our study has a greater potential for fruitfulness.

Sometimes we hear statements that both creation and evolution rest on faith—that we can prove neither. To a certain extent this is true, because both represent unique past events difficult to test and evaluate. But our faith is more secure if it is based on evidence. Yes, we all have to exercise some faith. We do it when we plant a seed or fly in an aircraft. Most of us have faith that the normal will prevail. But our faith derives from past experience. Likewise our answer to the questions about origins should not rest just on blind faith. We have a great deal of evidence available to us that bears on the question of which is true, science or Scripture.

THE CONTROVERSY[6]

While evolutionary concepts have been around for many centuries, a major turning point occurred in 1859, when Charles Darwin published his book *On the Origin of Species by Means of Natural Selection, or the Preservation of Favoured Races in the Struggle for Life*. The volume stressed evolution along with a suggested mechanism—natural selection—to produce more advanced forms of life. The reaction to Darwin's book was at first strongly mixed, but after a few decades a large number of scientists and some theologians began to accept some form of evolution. Some continued to oppose Darwin's ideas, especially among theologians and biologists, including a notable group at Princeton

University who adopted views intermediate between evolution and creation.

Although some organized resistance to evolution appeared in early twentieth-century England, the strongest opposition developed in the United States. The most influential creationist of that period was George McCready Price (1870-1963), whose many books challenged both evolution and the validity of the geologic column, a concept used to illustrate evolutionary progress.

During the 1920s a surge of public concern favored creationism, and several states passed laws forbidding the teaching of evolution in the public schools. One of them provided the basis for the famous Scopes trial[7] (sometimes called the "monkey trial") which attracted worldwide attention (Figure 1.1). A court found John T. Scopes, a biology teacher in the little town of Dayton, Tennessee, guilty of teaching evolution and later acquitted him on the basis of a technicality. Both sides declared a victory, and few minds changed. The usual sequel of books, plays, and motion pictures followed. Actually, the basic issue was more whether evolution or creation was true, rather than the legal concern of whether Scopes had violated the law. In 1968 the United States Supreme Court declared laws forbidding the teaching of evolution as

FIGURE 1.1

The crowded courtroom during the famous Scopes trial in Dayton, Tennessee (U.S.A.). Attorney Clarence Darrow is speaking.*

*Photo courtesy of Bryan College.

unconstitutional, not on the issue of whether evolution or creation was true, but on the basis of the United States Constitution requirement of the separation of church from the government. The United States has no official state religion, and the court argued that to forbid the teaching of evolution was to favor the establishment of religion by the state, thus violating a strict separation between church and state.

At about the same time some scholars foresaw the demise of traditional biblical views. The historian R. Halliburton, Jr., predicted in 1964 that "a renaissance of the [creation] movement is most unlikely."[8] Harvard theologian Gordon Kaufman wrote in 1971 that "the Bible no longer has unique authority for Western man. It has become a great but archaic monument in our midst. . . . Only in rare and isolated pockets—and surely these are rapidly disappearing forever—has the Bible anything like the kind of existential authority and significance which it once enjoyed throughout much of Western culture."[9] But the predicted demise of the Bible and creation did not materialize, certainly not in the United States.

Conservative evangelical churches grew rapidly in the 1970s and 1980s, while the more liberal mainline denominations lost members, sometimes by the millions. Creationism soon emerged stronger than ever because of a combination of factors: (1) Several government-financed, well-written secondary-level textbooks of biology that stressed controversial topics, such as sex education and evolution, angered parents because of what they considered to be an offensive approach. (2) A book by two creationists, John C. Whitcomb and Henry M. Morris, entitled *The Genesis Flood*[10] (based in part on George McCready Price's views) received wide circulation and strong support from religious conservatives. (3) Two influential housewives in southern California, Nell Segraves and Jean Sumrall, influenced the California State Board of Education to require that creation receive equal status with evolution. (The ruling was later modified.)[11] Since California is probably the most influential state in the United States, the publicity from this action encouraged a plethora of legislative attempts in other states to give equal consideration to both creation and evolution. During the following years state legislators introduced dozens of similar proposed laws.[12]

One of the major problems that fuels the fires of controversy is that science does not concern itself with morality, and many perceive evolution as challenging the Bible, which is highly concerned about moral standards. Because of this, many regard the teaching of evolution as an attack on traditional standards of conduct. This is not to say that scientists themselves are not moral. Many of them live highly moral lives, but morality is not a concern of either science or evolutionary theory, and parents become apprehensive when teachers present evolution in the classroom as authoritative over the Bible and its morality. A study of the coverage of creation and evolution in secondary-level biology textbooks in the United States from 1900 to 1977 shows a general increase in the presentation of both, although evolution dominates.[13] Adding to the public interest, the well-known creationist Duane T. Gish has been traveling throughout the United States, winning many debates against evolutionists before large university audiences.[14]

When the United States Supreme Court ruled that states could not outlaw evolution, creationists began to encourage the teaching of both creation and evolution, an approach also outlawed in 1987 by the United States Supreme Court, again on the basis of the same constitutional stipulation mentioned earlier that requires the government to remain neutral toward religious matters. The Court did say that public schools could legally present the scientific aspects of alternatives to evolution, as well as the scientific evidence against evolution. The ruling encouraged creationists to promote "scientific creationism," which deemphasized the religious aspects of creation. Evolutionists responded by declaring that creation is not science but religion and that the principle of separation of church and state should keep it out of the public schools, especially the science classes.

Over the years the argumentation has changed dramatically, being strongly influenced by the Supreme Court decisions. During the 1920s, when legislatures attempted to forbid the teaching of evolution, evolutionists appealed to the principle of academic freedom to encourage the inclusion of evolution. In the 1980s when creationists tried to have creation included, one heard little about academic freedom from the evolutionists, while the creationists promoted it. The battle has now moved from state legislatures to local school boards and the teachers themselves, who in the United States have considerable autonomy. Teachers often find themselves caught in a bind between parents who are ready to sue the public school system for teaching religion and those who do not want their children's religious beliefs destroyed by a secular science. One teacher reported that when he teaches evolution, he makes sure to collect all the student handouts so the parents won't know what he is presenting.[15]

At times the acrimony of the battle is almost beyond belief. Frequently creationists speak before checking the facts, presenting grossly erroneous information, including the imaginary story of Darwin's deathbed confession of the truthfulness of the Bible.[16] Evolutionists have bestowed deprecating terms on creationists, calling them "self-serving charlatans"[17] and many other equally pejorative descriptions. In debating a creationist, an Australian geologist donned insulating gloves and, taking a live electric wire, invited his opponent to electrocute himself.[18] The publicity generated by the controversy has helped spread creation to the far corners of the earth. It is no longer a phenomenon restricted to the United States or England. Creation societies have formed in dozens of countries, especially in Europe and eastern Asia, with some representation in Australia, South America, and Africa.[19]

Opinion surveys of the general public in the United States regarding human origins have produced results that surprised both creationists and evolutionists.[20] The academic community, especially scientists who broadly endorse evolution, discovered to its dismay that only about 10 percent of the general public followed the naturalistic science (no God) evolutionary model, while almost half believed in a recent creation less than 10,000 years ago, at least for humanity. Others followed intermediate views (Table 1.1). Some scientists wonder how it is that after more than a century of evolutionary education, so few accept the concept. I have heard scientists express concern about their poor sales ability and the need to improve their teaching. In my opinion, the problem is not sales ability. Scientists are good teachers, and excellent textbooks do a fine job of presenting evolution. The problem is that evolutionists have a product that is not easy to sell. Many find it difficult to believe that human beings and all the complex forms of life surrounding them, together with an earth and a universe that so adequately support it, all became organized by themselves. Also our ability to think, perceive, hope, and to have concerns, among many other attributes, all seem beyond a simple mechanistic evolutionary process. All of this fuels the battle over origins.

TABLE 1.1

ORIGIN	1982	1991	1993
God created human beings within the last 10,000 years	44	47	47
Humans developed over millions of years, but God guided the process	38	40	35
Humans developed over millions of years. God was not involved.	9	9	11
No opinion	9	4	7

Beliefs of adults in the United States regarding their origin. Figures represent percentages as obtained by Gallup polls taken in 1982, 1991, and 1993.

THE WARFARE OVER THE WARFARE

Does a war really exist between science and Scripture? After all, it is pointless to try to settle a nonexistent conflict. Opinions vary sharply over the issue. The question lies close to the lingering question of whether science or Scripture is correct. If you regard either as false, then you have no conflict. Some feel the problem is solving itself as they perceive religion retreating before the authority of science. Those who believe in a God whose Scripture is authoritative, of course, cannot accept such thinking. Some select parts of science and parts of Scripture to try to resolve the conflict. In so doing, they tend to deny the authority of both. Still others resolve the conflict by denying the validity or importance of both science and Scripture, believing they have little to say about the vital questions of existence and meaning.

Contrived argumentation and vague terminology confuse the issue. Stephen J. Gould, the eminent evolutionist of Harvard University, does not perceive a war between science and *religion* (not Scripture), which according to him do not conflict, because "science treats factual reality, while religion struggles with human morality."[21] The historian David Livingstone echoes his view: "This warfare model [between religion and science] has been dismantled with forensic precision by a squad of historical revisionists."[22] These historians often blame the warfare image on two important books that appeared about a century ago: *History of the Conflict Between Religion and Science,* by John William Draper (1811-1882), and *A History of the Warfare of Science With Theology in Christendom,* by Andrew Dickson White (1832-1918).[23]

Draper, who abandoned the religious faith of his family, produced a book that was immensely popular. It stressed how the church, especially the Roman Catholic Church, was the enemy of science. He emphasized the antagonism between religion and science, considering it highly important—in fact, "the most important of all living issues."[24] White also rebelled against his religious upbringing. As the first president of Cornell University, the first explicitly secular university in the United States, he faced strong religious opposition. White reinforced Draper's thesis that religion, and especially theology, smothered truth.

Both Draper and White strengthened their cases by pointing out that the medieval church had adopted a view that the earth was flat. Curiously, their accusation of the church's error was in itself an error. The medieval church did not believe that the earth was flat.[25] However, the charge that it did served to reinforce the impression that religion is wrong. Draper and White created "a body of false knowledge by consulting one another instead of the evidence."[26] The flat-earth fallacy has spread through many textbooks in the United States and even

England. Such sources portray Christopher Columbus as the hero who dared to fight church dogma by sailing on to discover America without falling off the edge of the flat earth. Fortunately, scholars are attempting to remove this error from historical accounts, but the popular fallacy continues to have many adherents.

Sometimes we comfort ourselves by musing over the mistakes of others. The famous European philosopher Ludwig Wittgenstein echoes this tendency for history in general: "One age misunderstands another; and a *petty* age misunderstands all the others in its own nasty way."[27] The "flat-earth" cliché about the past can let us think how superior our thinking is compared to that of past generations, but its use actually attests to our lack of information. Historian Jeffrey Burton Russell from the University of California at Santa Barbara insightfully comments that "the assumption of the superiority of 'our' views to that of older cultures is the most stubborn remaining variety of ethnocentrism."[28] In the evolution-creation controversy we need to keep in perspective the bias of the assumed superiority of our views. As Draper and White illustrate, our contempt for older ideas can lead us into strange and erroneous pathways. While I would acknowledge that our advancements in knowledge do represent progress, I would also warn that our proclivity for deprecating the past implies that the future may classify our own confidence in the present as itself foolishness. What seems to be progress (truth) today, future generations may very well interpret as error.

We return to the question of whether a warfare really exists between science and religion. Without a precise definition of terms we cannot resolve the warfare argument. A recent book entitled *Is God a Creationist?*[29] purports that God is not a creationist, because creation is not a biblical concept! Some who believe that God created life during long periods of time call themselves "creationists," but that is neither the biblical concept of creation nor the usual understanding of the term creationist. One can eliminate the warfare metaphor by altering the definition of terms. It is analogous to eliminating crime by legalizing it. But even after this is done, the crime problem still remains. Redefining terms can be superficial. You cannot bring unity between butchers and vegetarians just by giving them different names! Attempts to resolve the tensions between science and Scripture can employ the same terms in different and confusing ways. For instance, White thought one could reconcile science with religion but not with theology. Similarly, some individuals accept a form of religion but deny the validity of the Bible, even though the Bible has been the foundation of much of the religion of the Western world. The term *religion* can have varied meanings, ranging from the worship of God to a dedication to secularism. So far we find little consensus of precise terminology. But loose terminology cannot resolve a conflict that goes far beyond mere semantics.

While Draper and White were mistaken about the flat-earth concept, they were probably correct about a warfare between science and religion, and especially science and Scripture. History records numerous examples of such confrontations, and without question conflict occurs between the general evolutionary interpretations of science and the creation concept of the Bible. Much of this book addresses that conflict. William B. Provine, the historian of biology at Cornell University, who endorses evolution, has the following perceptive comments regarding some of the ramifications of this conflict as it has developed in the United States: "Scientists work closely with religious leaders to fight against the introduction of creationism into the classrooms of public schools.

"Liberal religious leaders and theologians, who also proclaim the compatibility of religion and evolution, achieve this unlikely position by two routes. First, they retreat from traditional interpretations of God's presence in the world, some to the extent of becoming effective atheists. Second, they simply refuse to understand modern evolutionary biology and continue to believe that evolution is a purposive process.

"We are now presented with the specter of atheistic evolutionists and liberal theologians, whose understanding of the evolutionary process is demonstrable nonsense, joining together with the ACLU [American Civil Liberties Union] and the highest courts in the land to lambast creationists, who are caught in an increasing bind. Evolutionary biology, as taught in public schools, shows no evidence of a purposive force of any kind. This is deeply disturbing to creationists. Yet in court, scientists proclaim that nothing in evolutionary biology is incompatible with any reasonable religion, a view also supported by liberal theologians and religious leaders of many persuasions. Not only are creationists unable to have their 'creation science' taught in the schools, they cannot even convince the court system that evolution is in any significant way antithetical to religion; thus the courts are effectively branding their religious views as terribly misguided. No wonder creationists (somewhere near half of the population!) are frustrated with the system and want equal time for their own views, or at least to be spared bludgeoning with evolution."[30]

Without question there is a conflict, often with evolutionists and liberal theologians on one side denying the validity of the biblical creation account and creationists and conservative theologians affirming it on the other side. Much revolves around the issue of which is more authoritative—science or Scripture? But that question quickly moves to more specific issues, such as: Is the biblical account of creation a myth? Is evolution just a theory? Are there alternative interpretations of the biblical creation narrative? Is compromise between creation and evolution possible? Succeeding chapters will address this complex set of questions from several perspectives.

WHAT DO WE MEAN BY CREATION AND EVOLUTION?

While many concepts will become clearer as we develop their details in succeeding chapters, some clarification of basic views should be helpful at this time.

The usual understanding of the term *creation* is the biblical model. In the creation account an all-powerful God prepares the earth for life and creates the various kinds of living organisms in six 24-hour days, each described with its own evening and morning. Traditional biblical chronologies imply that creation took place less than 10,000 years ago; however, the Bible does not address directly the question of a precise date for creation. Some creationists believe that God brought the whole universe into being during creation week, while others believe it existed long before that time and that God made only the livable world during creation week. The focus of the biblical account is more on the creation of life itself and on factors important to life, such as light, air, and dry land. Related to this creation is a worldwide catastrophe—the Genesis flood—that buried the many organisms found in the earth's fossiliferous layers. This flood accounts for the fossil record in the context of a recent creation and, as such, is an important element of the biblical creation concept.[31]

The term *evolution* has many meanings. Some equate it with the small changes in size, color, etc., that we constantly see in living things. However, both creationists and evolutionists recognize them as normal biological variability. The more general meaning of the term *evolution* refers to the advancement of life forms from simple to complex. The concept usually includes the origin of life and the development of the universe. It is a mechanistic approach to the questions of origins. Usually it does not involve God in any way as an explanatory factor. Development occurs naturalistically according to our understandings of ordinary cause and effect. In the evolutionary scenario, the universe formed by natural causes many thousands of millions of years ago. Simple life arose spontaneously on earth thousands of millions of years ago, and advanced forms of life evolved from simple ones, especially during the past hundreds of millions of years. Many variations exist of this general theme.[32]

Between the two major views of creation and evolution lies a variety of concepts that usually incorporate portions of both. They come under such designations as theistic evolution, progressive creation, or deistic evolution. Such models reject purely mechanistic views such as evolution. They endorse a progressive development of life that often involves the work of some kind of God, but they reject the biblical account of a recent creation. Chapter 21 discusses a number of these views.

THE CONFLICT AND ACCURACY

Probably the most colorful of the ancient Greek Cynic philosophers was Diogenes of Sinope. The imaginative, charismatic figure of the fourth century B.C. did much to promote the Cynic philosophy of virtue as the only good. Extreme asceticism, as exemplified in Diogenes' own life, often accompanied the basic philosophy. Many stories circulate about him. While some of them are doubtless apocryphal, they nevertheless serve to illustrate the enormity of the gap that sometimes exists between conventionality and ideals. Diogenes is reported to have discarded his final possession—his bowl—after watching a boy drink from his hands. He lived in a borrowed wooden tub, getting the idea from a snail with its shell. His often biting sarcasm came forth when Alexander the Great offered him anything he wanted (an offer that was less risky with Diogenes than with most!). His only request was that Alexander the Great move so that he would not block the sunshine. One of the most famous stories about Diogenes' activities is that of his trek, carrying a lighted lantern in broad daylight, in a futile search for an honest man.

Would Diogenes find honesty among creationists and evolutionists today? Dishonesty is difficult to evaluate because we cannot discern the motives of others. We all make unintentional errors, which we call honest mistakes. But when we are studying our own origin, the subject is so linked to our identity and emotions that we may have difficulty being objective. Our assumptions color our thought processes. We must, of course, be tolerant of other views, but so much misinformation has risen in this controversy that we should make sure that we are basing our analysis on correct information. Two accounts illustrate our need for careful evaluation.

Several years ago a number of newspapers and other public media publicized a story about a so-called missing day.[33] The account claimed that a group of scientists at the Goddard Space Flight Center in Greenbelt, Maryland, were studying planetary positions through time. They were unable to find exact agreement between ancient historical data and expected dates. As a result, the computer processing the data shut down. When the technicians made corrections for Joshua's long day described in the Bible,[34] the computer program obtained near-perfect agreement. When the operators made a second correction for when the sun moved backward 10 "steps" for King Hezekiah,[35] the data then produced perfect agreement.

Several individuals have attempted to trace the source of the story, but with disappointing results. The individual reporting the incident could not remember where he obtained the data from originally, and no one at the Goddard Space Flight Center seems to have been involved in any such incident. It appears that the event never took place. Some tried to exonerate those who perpetuated the incident by emphasizing the good purposes and intentions involved. Others pointed out that we should not take the incident so seriously, since a number of individuals who believed in the accuracy of the Bible did not accept the story. But the incident remains an embarrassment to defenders of the Bible.

During the second decade of this century Charles Dawson and Arthur Smith Woodward announced the discovery of the now-famous Piltdown human remains in Sussex County in southern England.[36] The Piltdown skull remained in more or less good standing for decades as one of the evolutionary intermediates between man and lower forms. The braincase was remarkably human while the jaw was more apelike, corresponding to the then-prevailing idea that the brain led the way in human evolutionary development. Some researchers also reported finding primitive features associated with the more modern cranium. About 40 years later three renowned anthropologists announced that the Piltdown skull was a hoax. The jaw had been stained and the teeth filed to make them match the cranium. Relative dating by the fluorine technique showed the jaw to be younger than the cranium.

Some have tried to excuse the incident by pointing out that a few had always questioned the validity of the Piltdown findings. However, at least for a while, the skull held a respected position on humanity's proposed evolutionary tree, and the incident remains an embarrassment to the defenders of evolution.

One hesitates to imply specific motives in either episode, but that they occurred and that for a time supporters of creation or evolution promoted the various arguments is both embarrassing and instructive. The incidents suggest that unreasonable zeal for what one believes to be true may lead to error. We must avoid this. Truth does not need the support of error. Furthermore, our private views may not be true. Truth is truth whether or not we like it.

Both stories are sobering: they can suggest that a modern Diogenes and his lamp could be destined for a long quest. The fact that some are willing to invent "data" to support their worldview witnesses to the intensity of the conflict. The way to avoid being deceived is not to be so gullible, but that is not always easy.

CONCLUSIONS

Science is one of humanity's most successful intellectual achievements.

Scripture also is highly respected, and the Bible is by far the most accepted book in the world. Secular scientists have proposed a slow evolutionary model of beginnings over a long time, while Scripture speaks of a recent creation by God. The quest to evaluate both models of beginnings has followed an interesting, contentious, and sometimes deceptive course. People have proposed a variety of schemas to reconcile these two basic models of origins, but such compromises have not worked well, and confusing definitions have confounded them. Many sincerely wonder whether we can find the ultimate truth concerning origins primarily in science or in Scripture. Such questions do not have a simple answer.

REFERENCES

1. Whately R. 1825. On the love of truth. In: Mencken HL, editor. 1960. A new dictionary of quotations on historical principles from ancient and modern sources. New York: Alfred A. Knopf, p. 1223.
2. This will be discussed at length in chapter 16.
3. Shakespeare W. Macbeth 5. 5. 26-28.
4. See chapter 18 for some further details.
5. Most figures are from Guinness: (a) McFarlan D, editor. 1990. Guinness book of world records 1990. 29th ed. New York: Bantam Books, p. 197; (b) Young MC, editor. 1994. Guinness book of records 1995. 34th ed. New York: Facts on File, p. 142. Also, information from Guinness Publishing, Ltd., and the American Bible Society.
6. The literature discussing the issue is almost endless. For a bibliographical introduction, see: (a) Livingstone DN. 1987. Evangelicals and the Darwinian controversies: a bibliographical introduction. Evangelical Studies Bulletin 4(2):1-10. A few others, among many good references, include: (b) Larson EJ. 1985. Trial and error: the American controversy over creation and evolution. Oxford: Oxford University Press; (c) Livingstone DN. 1987. Darwin's forgotten defenders: the encounter between evangelical theology and evolutionary thought. Grand Rapids: Wm. B. Eerdmans Pub. Co. (d) Marsden, GM. 1983. Creation versus evolution: no middle way. Nature 305:571-574; (e) Numbers RL. 1982. Creationism in 20th-century America. Science 218:538-544; (f) Numbers RL. 1992. The creationists: the evolution of scientific creationism. New York: Alfred A. Knopf; (g) Scott EC. 1994. The struggle for the schools. Natural History 193(7):10-13.
7. See chapter 19 for additional details.
8. Halliburton R, Jr. 1964. The adoption of Arkansas' anti-evolution law. Arkansas Historical Quarterly 23:271-283.
9. Kaufman GD. 1971. What shall we do with the Bible? Interpretation: A Journal of Bible and Theology 25:95-112.
10. Whitcomb JC, Jr., Morris HM. 1961. The Genesis flood: the biblical record and its scientific implications. Philadelphia: Presbyterian and Reformed Pub. Co.
11. For some further information, see: (a) Brand LR. 1975. Textbook hearing in California. Origins 2:98, 99. (b) Ching K. 1975. The Cupertino story. Origins 2:42, 43; (c) Ching K. 1977. Appeal for equality. Origins 4:93; (d) Ching K. 1978. Creation and the law. Origins 5:47, 48; (e) Dwyer BL. 1974. California science textbook controversy. Origins 1:29-34; (f) Ford JR. 1976. An update on the teaching of creation in California. Origins 3:46, 47; (g) Holden C, ed. Random samples: Alabama schools disclaim evolution. Science 270:1305.
12. Bailey LR. 1993. Genesis, creation, and creationism. New York: Paulist Press, pp. 202-204.
13. (a) Brande S. 1984. Scientific validity of proposed public education materials for balanced treatment of creationism and evolution in elementary science classrooms of Alabama. In:

Walker KR, editor. The evolution-creation controversy: perspectives on religion, philosophy, science and education: a handbook. The Paleontological Society Special Publication No. 1. Knoxville: University of Tennessee, pp. 141-155; (b) Skoog G. 1979. Topic of evolution in secondary school biology textbooks: 1900-1977. Science Education 63(5):621-640.

14. For samples of the argumentation, see: (a) Coffin HG. 1979. Creationism: is it a viable alternative to evolution as a theory of origins? Yes. Liberty 74(2):10, 12, 13, 23, 24 (rebuttal on pp. 24, 25); (b) Mayer WV. 1978. Creation concepts should not be taught in public schools. Liberty 73(5):3-7, (rebuttal on pp. 28, 29); (c) Roth AA. 1978. Creation concepts should be taught in public schools. Liberty 73(5):3, 24-27 (rebuttal on p. 28); (d) Valentine JW. 1979. Creationism: is it a viable alternative to evolution as a theory of origins? No. Liberty 74(2):11, 14, 15 (rebuttal on pp. 25, 26).
15. See: Scott (note 6g).
16. (a) Moore J. 1994. The Darwin legend. Grand Rapids: Baker Books; (b) Rusch WH, Sr., Klotz JW. 1988. Did Charles Darwin become a Christian? Norcross, Ga: Creation Research Society Books; (c) Roth AA. 1995. "Retro-progressing." Origins 22:3-7.
17. Frazier WJ. 1984. Partial catastrophism and pick and choose empiricism: the science of "creationist" geology. In: Walker, pp. 50-65 (note 13a).
18. (a) [Anonymous]. 1988. Evolutionist debater descends to all-time low. Acts and Facts 17(6):3, 5; (b) Numbers 1992, p. 333 (note 6f).
19. See: (a) Numbers 1982 (note 6e); (b) Numbers 1992, pp. 319-339 (note 6f).
20. For further details and interpretations, see: Roth AA. 1991. Creation holding its own. Origins 18:51, 52.
21. Gould SJ. 1992. Impeaching a self-appointed judge. Book review of: Johnson PE. 1991. Darwin on trial. Scientific American 267(1):118-121.
22. Livingstone (note 6a), p. 1. In his book *Darwin's Forgotten Defenders* (note 6c) Livingstone gives six references challenging the warfare image.
23. (a) Draper JW. 1875. History of the conflict between religion and science. New York: D. Appleton & Co.; (b) White AD. 1896. A history of the warfare of science with theology in Christendom. 2 vols. New York: Dover Publications, 1960 reprint. For background information regarding Draper and White, I am indebted especially to: (c) Lindberg DC, Numbers RL. 1986. Beyond war and peace: a reappraisal of the encounter between Christianity and science. Church History 55:338-354; (d) Lindberg DC, Numbers RL, editors. 1986. God and nature: historical essays on the encounter between Christianity and science. Berkeley and Los Angeles: University of California Press, pp. 1-18; (e) Russell JB. 1991. Inventing the flat earth: Columbus and modern historians. New York: Praeger Publishers, pp. 36-49.
24. Draper, p. vii (note 23a).
25. (a) Gould SJ. 1994. The persistently flat earth. Natural History 103(3):12-19; (b) Lindberg and Numbers 1986 (note 23c); (c) Russell, pp. 13-26 (note 23e).
26. Russell, p. 44 (note 23e).
27. (a) Wittgenstein L. 1980. Culture and value. Winch P, translator; von Wright GH, Nyman H, editors. Chicago: University of Chicago Press, pp. 86/86e. Translation of: Vermischte Bermerkungen. See also: (b) Kemp A. 1991. The estrangement of the past: a study in the origins of modern historical consciousness. Oxford: Oxford University Press, pp. 177, 178.
28. Russell, p. 76 (note 23e).
29. Frye RM, editor. 1983. Is God a creationist? The religious case against creation-science. New York: Scribner's.
30. Provine WB. 1987. Review of: Larson EJ. 1985. Trial and error: the American controversy over creation and evolution. Academe 73(1):50-52.
31. Chapters 10, 12, 19, and 21 discuss additional information on creation concepts.
32. Further discussion of the evolutionary concept can be found in chapters 4, 5, 8, and 11.
33. For some details, see: Hill H, Harrell I. 1974. How to live like a king's kid. South Plainfield, N.J.: Bridge Publishing, pp. 65-77.
34. Joshua 10:13.

35. 2 Kings 20:9-11.
36. Recent reviews of this much-discussed incident are: (a) Blinderman C. 1986. The Piltdown inquest. Buffalo: Prometheus Books; (b) Walsh JE. 1996. Unraveling Piltdown: the scientific fraud of the century and its solution. New York: Random House.

CHAPTER 2

FASHIONS IN THINKING

First it's absurd; then maybe; and at last we have known it all along.[1]

One of the ways in which human beings add variety to their existence is to change the style of their clothing. I recall when only narrow ties were fashionable. Later on, up-to-date ties had to be extremely wide; then a variety of widths became acceptable. Most have learned to keep their old ties so as to be prepared for the next whim. Ideas can also follow the same pattern. Certain views about diet, proper etiquette, or art are fashionable at one time, only to be replaced by others. Philosophical concepts show the same pattern. Different views have prevailed at various times and places. A few examples include: *naturalism,* the denial of the supernatural; *theism,* belief in God; and *agnosticism,* the idea that the answer to basic questions is "I don't know." We can add the concepts of *absolutism, animism, determinism, dialectic materialism, empiricism, pantheism, pluralism, rationalism,* etc. Each "school of thought" has or has had its adherents who believed in the truthfulness of its ideas. We should keep this pattern of group approval in intellectual pursuits in mind as we determine the weight of evidence of various concepts. Dominant ideas change, but they do not change truth. Three examples will illustrate the implications of fashions in thinking. We should also remember that the changing of human ideas over time is no excuse for abandoning our search for truth. Truth is there to be found, a fact that we will discuss further at the end of the chapter.

CONTINENTAL DRIFT

I remember listening to my professor of physical geology comment on the "jigsaw puzzle" match of the east and west coasts of the Atlantic Ocean. He

FIGURE 2.1

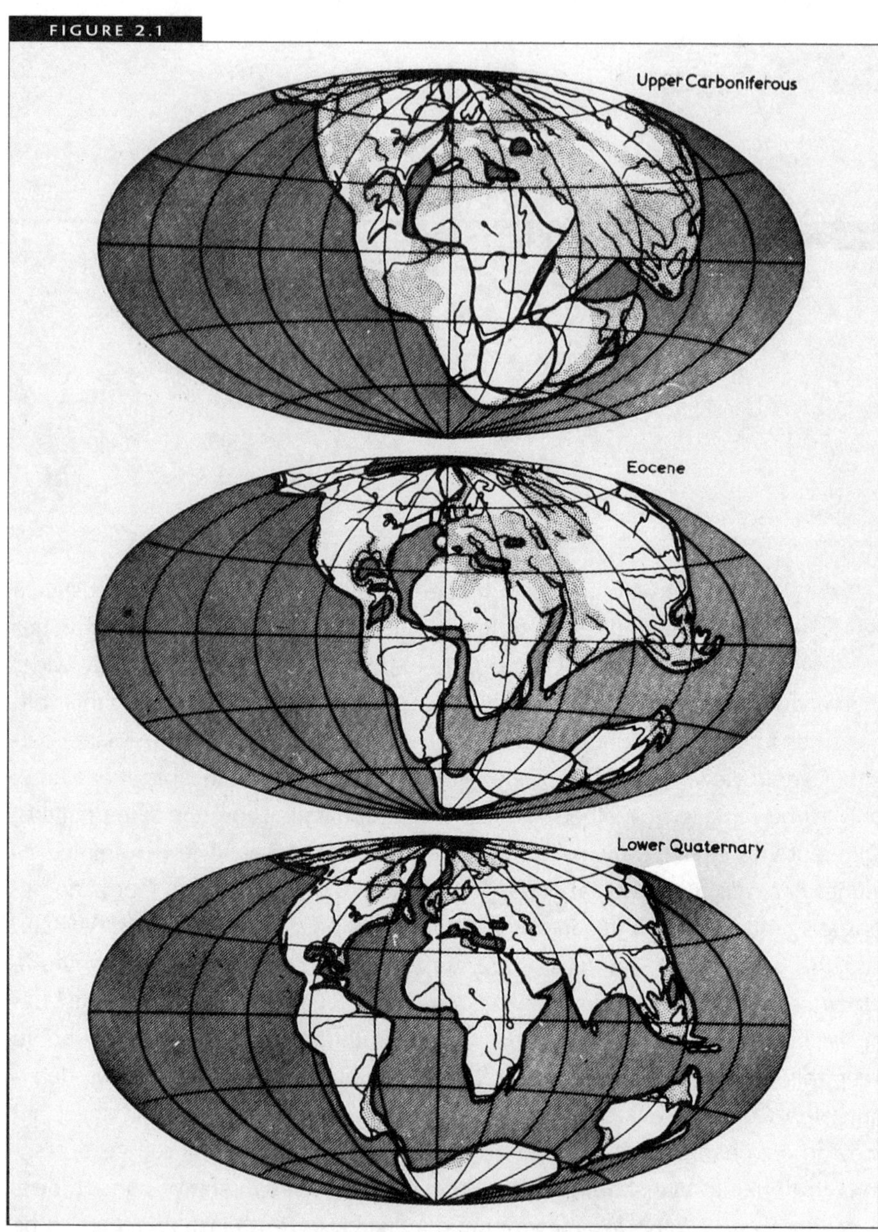

Pattern of movement of the continents of the world for three different periods as envisioned by Wegener. The lowest diagram represents the current arrangement. Darker regions are seas, dotted regions are shallow seas on the continents, while clear areas represent dry land. Newer concepts propose some modification in details, although the basic idea is well accepted.*

*From Wegener (note 2). Reproduced by permission of Methuen and Co.

mentioned that early in this century a man by the name of Wegener proposed that long ago North and South America had been next to Europe and Africa, and at that time no Atlantic Ocean existed in between. The continents had since moved apart (Figure 2.1). While the idea was interesting, my professor commented that no one paid much attention to it anymore. Little did he realize that within six years the geological community would have made a complete reversal from virtual rejection to almost total acceptance of Wegener's idea.

This "new" idea became a strong, unifying, and revitalizing factor in geological thinking, leading to new concepts for the formation of continents, mountain ranges, and the ocean floor. Scientists and educators had to rewrite geology texts. Living through this major shift in thinking was both exciting and sobering. Exciting because it generated so many new ideas and reinterpretations; sobering because it left one wondering which other major concept currently ridiculed would suddenly become accepted as dogma.

At the time that Alfred Wegener (1880-1930) suggested that the continents had moved, the prevailing, but not exclusive, idea was that in the past the earth had shrunk as it cooled, and mountain ranges resulted from lateral compression of our planet's surface layers, a process somewhat analogous to the ridges that form on the skin of an apple that shrinks as it dries up. Wegener outlined a number of evidences indicating that instead of the earth shrinking, the continents had been sliding over the surface of the earth.[2] Among his many arguments, he pointed out that the enormous lateral thrust of the huge and sometimes folded layers ("nappes") of the European Alps, which had traveled for scores of kilometers, were too great to be accounted for by mere shrinking. Also, one found some similarities of rock types on opposite sides of the Atlantic Ocean, implying their coasts may have been together in the past.

German-born Wegener's[3] main interest was not the movement of continents, although he published four editions of his book dealing with the idea. Primarily he was a meteorologist and Arctic explorer. The latter proved to be his undoing. Two of his colleagues, working near the center of the Greenland ice cap at an observation station called "Eismitte" ("mid-ice"), needed supplies for the winter. Against almost insurmountable problems, including breakdown of equipment, most of his companions giving up, and temperatures of -58° F (-50° C), he and two companions traveled 250 miles (400 kilometers) by dogsled from the west coast of Greenland, finally reaching Eismitte in the fall of 1930. However, it was without any supplies, which had to be left along the way. The team of three who stayed at Eismitte managed to survive the winter, but Wegener and a companion, who tried to return to the coast, lost their lives.

After one day of rest at Eismitte, the two left on November 1, Wegener's fiftieth birthday. Wegener's body was found the next spring, about halfway to the coast, carefully buried by his companion and well marked by Wegener's skis. The companion, who was only 22 years old, vanished completely. Wegener probably died in his tent of heart failure. His grave remains on the Greenland ice cap. Snow and ice long ago covered the six-meter (20-foot) cross that marked its location.

At the time of his death, Wegener's idea of moving continents had few supporters and a large retinue of opponents, especially in North America. His opponents often reacted with indignation and disdain toward his views. In 1926 an international symposium convened in New York to discuss the topic. Wegener attended it and faced general hostility to the idea. "The 'big guns' among American geologists fired full salvos in opposition,"[4] some accusing Wegener of ignoring the facts and of practicing autointoxication. The scorn bestowed on the idea of moving continents during the following years was severe enough that to show support for the idea could damage one's scientific reputation.[5] Perhaps the degree of attention and resistance the idea received actually indicated its value and strength. Worthless threats and meaningless hypotheses don't attract such attention.

During the late 1950s and 1960s researchers collected new data that fit well with the idea of moving continents, and some scientists even dared to promote Wegener's ideas. Especially important were new data suggesting that earth's wandering magnetic pole had reversed its north-south orientation many times in the past. Scientists could detect this reversal pattern because volcanic rocks had picked up the earth's magnetism as they cooled and formed huge ridges on the ocean floor. To accommodate the new data, geologists proposed that huge mobile plates cover the earth. They are generated from underneath along one edge at ridges, and are absorbed into the earth along trenches at the opposite side. Such plates travel slowly along earth's surface like huge wide conveyor belts. Their movement carries along the continents that ride on top of them.[6] Geologists call this the plate-tectonics model. Geology lacked a good mechanism for moving the plates, but surprisingly, after decades of resistance, the geological community embraced the idea with unusual speed and passion. Within five years anyone who did not believe in plate tectonics and the resultant movement of the continents risked being ostracized. But some opposition remained. Reviewing a book that supported the concept of plate tectonics, one geologist commented that he was not sure that the publisher should list the book as nonfiction![7] A reply suggested that in terms of distortion "the book cannot compete with the review"![8] But plate tectonics won. It is now the dominant view, questioned by only a small but persistent minority.[9] Geology no longer accepts the idea that the earth contracted,[10] but the idea that it might have actually expanded has limited support.[11]

Wegener has now become somewhat of a hero in science for being 30 to 40 years ahead of his time. It is unfortunate that he did not live to see many of his arguments accepted and the complete reversal of the scientific community's attitude toward him. Many have wondered why he seemed to have special foresight and why scientists did not accept him at first. Some suggest that the weight of evidence was not sufficient at that time,[12] which does not explain why the examples of his evidence that geology did later accept provoked such hostility for so long. Others have also suggested that his idea was too revolutionary for his time, given the unacceptability of major geologic changes, especially those caused by catastrophes. Furthermore, one could associate Wegener's hypothesized opening of the Atlantic with Noah's biblical flood, an idea that most geologists wished to avoid.[13] Several have mentioned that since Wegener was a meteorologist and not a member of the geologic community, professional elitism favored rejection of his views.[14] Most likely all of the above factors contributed. It is difficult to challenge established views, but as the history of the plate-tectonics model illustrates, when acceptance finally comes, it can occur rapidly.

ALCHEMY

Alchemy (Figure 2.2) offers another example of a widely accepted, dominant idea that has been later rejected.[15] Basically an attempt to liberate parts of the cosmos, alchemy had the practical application of trying to change base metals such as iron and lead into gold. Because alchemy now has a bad reputation, it is seldom appreciated that the basic idea had a respectable rational foundation. Since one could get pure iron out of crude reddish iron ores, one could reason that it should also be possible to extract gold from relatively crude substances such as iron or lead. Also, Aristotle had suggested that the four basic elements—earth, air, water, and fire—could be transformed into each other. Why not try to change lead into gold? In a sense the early alchemists were true scientists who were attempting to find out how to produce gold in the same manner they assumed nature had brought it into being in the past.

In time alchemy became associated with mysticism. The search was not only for gold but for that which might prolong life and even give immortality. One can divide alchemy into two parts—practical alchemy and esoteric alchemy. The latter engendered considerable speculation, sometimes to the

FIGURE 2.2

An alchemist and his laboratory.[†]

[†]Painting by David Teniers the Younger. Reproduced by permission of the Institut Collectie Nederland.

point of complete obscurity. Practitioners searched for an unknown substance or substances, called the "philosopher's stone" or the "elixir of life," which would produce gold and long life. This search became the consuming passion of many.

Alchemy enjoyed an enduring presence. In the Western world it appeared in the eastern Mediterranean region around the first century A.D. China had accepted the concept centuries earlier. It later showed up in India around the fifth century A.D., which is about the time that it declined temporarily in the Western world because of confusing mystical trends. The Arabs, who had a number of outstanding alchemists, pursued it for many centuries. In medieval times and later it spread to Europe, where it enjoyed a great deal of respect. Kings and nobles often supported both alchemists and well-equipped laboratories in the hope of increasing their resources. Probably the majority of the educated believed in the alchemical principle of transmutation of the elements. The theory's adherents included such notables as Thomas Aquinas, Roger Bacon, Albertus Magnus, Isaac Newton, the famous physician Paracelsus, and Emperor Rudolf II. Queen Elizabeth I employed several alchemists. Pope

Boniface VIII was a patron of alchemy, but Pope John XXII tried to ban it. The intellectual community accepted alchemy for nearly 2,000 years, even though no base metals were ever turned into gold during that entire period!

Fakers who enjoyed spreading tantalizing scraps of misinformation plagued the practice of alchemy. At the same time they risked eliciting the wrath of their patrons because they could not produce any gold. Occasionally their only safety was in flight. Too often they resorted to fraud and had a number of tricks, such as using a hollow, gold-dust-filled iron stirring rod plugged at the end with wax. When used to stir a hot potion in a crucible, the wax would melt and the gold dust inside the rod would appear as though it had been transmuted. Such fakers gave alchemy a bad name, and honest alchemists sometimes found themselves forced to work in secrecy.

In the seventeenth century the practice of alchemy eventually broadened to include the production of a variety of useful chemicals, while the search for the philosopher's stone dwindled. Many of the newer discoveries served as a basis for the development of modern chemistry. Ironically, transmutation is now a common process. Using particle accelerators and nuclear reactors, physicists have prepared numerous elements from other elements. However, making gold by such a process is too expensive to be worthwhile. The dominant idea of alchemical transmutation by ordinary chemical means—which enjoyed acceptance for nearly two millennia—is now dead. Alchemy demonstrates poor science, while the success of chemistry depicts good science.

WITCH-HUNTING

The pattern of dominant ideas does not restrict itself just to scientific pursuits. In 1459 a French congregation of devout worshipers who retired to go to solitary places at night to worship God faced accusations of collusion with the devil. Reports circulated that the devil appeared in their secret places to instruct them and give them money and food while the worshipers promised obedience.[16] The authorities arrested the worshipers, who included respected citizens along with some mentally feeble women. They subjected them to the excruciating pain of being stretched on a rack while the torturers demanded that their victims confess to the charges against them. A number admitted to the accusations and implicated others. Sometimes the newly accused individuals turned out to be the tormenters' personal enemies! The authorities hanged and burned the accused, although some managed to escape after paying large sums of money. Following an investigation 32 years later, the parliament of Paris declared the sentences invalid, but it was too late for most of the victims.

The incident occurred during the early stages of the witch-hunting mania, a most persistent and devilish idea that dominated in Europe for three centuries.[17] With fiendish fervor, society sought out anyone thought to have some kind of association with the devil and punished them. Many were burned alive, hanged, decapitated, or crushed to death. Any mishap, such as loss of crops, sudden death, and the Black Death (bubonic plague), which at times was rampant, was blamed on witches.

Once what seemed like apparently credible witnesses accused a group of women, some of them quite young, of participating in a witches' dance at midnight under an oak tree. Some of their husbands protested that their wives were at home with them at the time, but the authorities told the men that the devil might have deceived them, and that only the semblance of their wives remained at home. This confused the husbands. The authorities burned their wives.[18] Several individuals took on the mission of hunting down anyone who might be associated with the devil. One accuser reportedly bragged that he convicted and burned 900 witches in 15 years.[19] Not only were people involved, but pigs, dogs, many cats, and even a rooster were hanged or burned. It was difficult—if not impossible—to stop the mania. Any who denied the accusations underwent torture until they confessed. Few ventured to protest the practice, lest they be put to death themselves. The craze dominated in Germany, Austria, France, and Switzerland. It also spread to England, Russia, and even across the Atlantic to the United States. No one knows how many perished. Records are not complete. Some estimates run as high as 9 million.[20] Probably at least several hundred thousand lost their lives.

This wild idea illustrates both the subjectivity of some accepted concepts and their potential for harm. A wide gulf can exist between acceptance and correctness. We should not trust popular opinion to determine truth. Neither science nor Scripture are necessarily true because people accept them. We also need to use other factors in determining truth. No doubt psychological and sociological factors play a significant role in the development, popularity, and persistence of many ideas that human beings consider true.

PARADIGMS AND TRUTH

A common view of science is that it carefully and steadily destroys ignorance as it triumphantly wins battle after battle along the frontiers of knowledge. This view, somewhat encouraged by scientists themselves, ran into a major stumbling block in 1962 with the publication of Thomas Kuhn's *Structure of Scientific Revolutions*.[21] This highly influential book was immediately controversial. It challenged the authority and the "immaculate perception" of science.[22]

Kuhn proposed that science, instead of representing the accumulation of objective knowledge, is more the fitting of data under broadly accepted concepts "that for a time provide model problems and solutions."[23] He called such ideas *paradigms*. Paradigms are broad views that can be either true or false, but people accept them as true. As such they focus attention on those conclusions that will agree with the paradigm and thus restrict any possible innovation outside the paradigm. Examples include plate tectonics and catastrophism.[24] Such concepts set the constraints for what Kuhn calls "normal science," where scientists interpret data within the limits of the accepted paradigm. Sometimes we have a change in paradigm, leading to what Kuhn calls a "scientific revolution." The acceptance of plate tectonics represents a scientific revolution. Kuhn further emphasizes that if a scientist does not fit his conclusions within an accepted paradigm, other scientists will likely reject them as metaphysical or too problematic. This attitude tends to prolong the life of the paradigm. Paradigms also receive support by the fact that we feel more secure when we agree with prevailing opinion. In view of this, it may be well to remind ourselves of the dictum that if we always go by the majority, we have little chance for progress. Change from one paradigm to another is quite difficult since we have so much intellectual inertia to overcome.[25]

Kuhn did not endear himself to the scientific community by labeling a change in paradigm as a "conversion experience."[26] He also challenged the cherished idea of progress in science, stating, "We may, to be more precise, have to relinquish the notion, explicit or implicit, that changes of paradigm carry scientists and those who learn from them closer and closer to the truth."[27] In other words, a new paradigm can lead us away from truth.

While some have resisted it, scholars have widely accepted and applied the paradigm concept far beyond science, even into theology. The word "paradigm," which refers to an accepted dominant concept, has become a household word among the educated.

Kuhn's ideas have generated considerable agitation and even reform, especially in the history, philosophy, and sociology of science. Many sociologists see a strong sociological component governing both the questions and the answers that science generates.[28] The concept that the community of scientists regulates the kind of questions scientists ask as well as the answers they will accept does not fit with the image many scientists have of their field as an open search for truth, but the idea of sociological influence in science has gained considerable acceptance.

It is obvious that the grouplike behavior of the scientific community, when it works within or shifts from one paradigm to another, betrays a lack of independent thought on the part of the individual scientist. However, in general, science *does* progress toward truth. Many false paradigms may surface along the way, but eventually we should get closer to truth as we incorporate more of nature's data into developing concepts.

The saga of changing paradigms tells us that we need to dig deeper than prevailing opinion if we hope to secure truth. I would suggest two antidotes to prevent popular delusions from overwhelming us. (1) We should practice more independent thought. This may threaten our desire for social approval, but it will also reduce unproductive intellectual gregariousness. (2) In evaluating a paradigm, we would be well advised to determine the basis for its acceptance. There are good data and poor data, firm conclusions and speculative conclusions. And besides assumptions, there are assumptions based on assumptions. The task of evaluation is laborious, but it is necessary. In trying to determine which idea is correct, one must critically evaluate the foundation on which each competing view rests and not let the "climate of opinion" unduly influence us.

TRUTH—AN ENDANGERED SPECIES

A current fashion in thinking is to doubt almost everything, or to keep an open mind on most questions. Unfortunately, many an open mind has revealed mainly a vacuum. How often we hear about both sides of a question, but no conclusions! Too many in academic pursuits are satisfied with just presenting several possible opinions, often within a single broad paradigm, and fail to come to any final conclusions. Too often our research ends with a plurality of possibilities. Doubtless this forms part of the basis for the traditional and satirical "maybe" as the final conclusion of the typical doctoral dissertation. Recognizing the tentative nature of paradigms may encourage us to forgo necessary evaluation and resort to disbelief of nearly everything. We may just give up in our search for truth. But to do so is simplistic, lazy, unfruitful, and dull.

The famous French author Moliére wrote a comedy entitled "The Forced Marriage."[29] The play, written at the request of King Louis XIV, was an immediate success, and occasionally France's most opulent king even participated in its presentation. It addresses some of humanity's foibles in a humorous but instructive (and not so subtle) way. In the comedy a rich older gentleman wonders whether he should marry a young maiden primarily interested in his wealth. He seeks the advice of several individuals, including two philosophers. The first philosopher is Aristotelian and is so concerned about his own opinions, his philosophy, and the definitions of terms that the poor gentleman cannot communicate to him the reality of his practical problem. He departs disappointed and seeks advice from a skeptic philosopher. Introducing himself, he informs the second philosopher that he has come for advice, whereupon the philosopher replies: "Pray, change this mode of speaking. Our philosophy enjoins us not to enunciate a positive proposition, but to speak of everything dubiously, and always to suspend our judgment. For this reason, you should not say, I am come, but it seems that I am come." An extended discussion follows as to whether the man has really come or if it only appears that he has come! The philosopher keeps responding to the wealthy gentleman with such comments as "It may be so," or "It is not impossible," and "That may be." The philosopher refuses to address the gentleman's real question. Tension arises, and compelling reality suddenly appears when the exasperated "gentleman" kicks the philosopher, who responds with yells and vexed comments. Informing the gentleman that it is an insolence and outrage to beat a philosopher, he threatens to appeal to the magistrate. The gentleman answers appropriately, "Pray, correct this manner of speaking. We are to doubt everything; and you ought not to say that I have beaten you, but it seems I have beaten you." The gentleman replies to the philosopher with the same kind of uncertain statements he first received. The philosopher, who is positive that he has been beaten, rehears comments such as "It may be so" and "It is not impossible." Thus the gentleman proudly instructs the philosopher about the foibles of skepticism.

Our present intellectual milieu shares the same foibles of Molière's time. Too often relativism, agnosticism, and skepticism receive respect, while certainty and truth appear to be endangered. It is fashionable to question almost anything. Doubts are sometimes encouraged for their own sake, even when they have little to contribute except further doubts.

Relativism, agnosticism, and skepticism, which reduce truth to uncertainty, cannot claim any assurance of being correct. Their own tenets enjoin that we be uncertain about almost everything significant, which would include these propositions themselves. If you do not believe in anything, can you be consistent and still believe that you do not believe in anything? In the words of Pascal: "It is not certain that everything is uncertain."[30]

Obviously we can and should reject many ideas, and caution is a virtue as we evaluate many concepts. Also, there is room to suspend judgment legitimately because we do not have enough information to make a decision. As we work out truth, we should be reasonable and balance our acceptance of ideas with careful inquiry. Questioning has its place, but everything does not have to be questioned forever, and the all-important task of sorting out truth from error should never fall victim to fruitless skepticism. Sound scholarship can afford to make room for truth. We do not need to relegate ourselves needlessly to that realm of the "maybe," where everything seems, but nothing is.

Sometimes our doubting game comes face-to-face with the reality of plain cold facts, such as the collision between an iceberg and the *Titanic*. If someone steals our money, its existence and the concept of ownership become extremely real to us. Or if we are late and miss a plane, time becomes intensely real. The reality of having someone physically attack a skeptic philosopher can also jar our questioning! (Incidentally, in Molière's comedy the relatives of the young woman forced the rich man to marry her.) A divorce or the pardoning of a criminal can remind us that moral values, integrity, and forgiveness are also a part of reality. Most of us accept the existence of falsehood, but the acceptance of falsehood also implies the reality of truth. Sometimes in the midst of all our doubts reality confronts us and commands our respect. If there is reality, there is truth, but we will not find it by doubting everything. The one who doubts everything certainly does not have as much to offer as the one seeking truth.

The fact that we have dominant paradigms that change from time to time should not deter us from seeking truth based on firm information. Reality is there, truth exists, and a satisfying degree of certitude is possible. Truth is so important that we should diligently pursue it and actively protect its right to exist.

CONCLUSIONS

The history of human intellectual activity includes the acceptance of broad dominant ideas called paradigms. An example is the widely accepted idea that the continents drift across the surface of the earth (plate tectonics). Paradigms can come and go, and can be true or false. Their general acceptance does not guarantee their validity. Popular opinion is not a strong criterion for truth. As we search for truth, we can avoid letting ourselves be trapped by erroneous paradigms by practicing both independent thought and thorough investigation. We must always base our conclusions only on the firmest of data.

The fact that paradigms change should not detract from the certainty that truth exists and that careful study will help us find it.

REFERENCES

1. This aphorism, in various forms, has been attributed to a variety of authors, including William James, Thomas Huxley, and Louis Agassiz.
2. Wegener A. 1929. The origin of continents and oceans. Biram J, translator (1967). London: Methuen and Co. Translation of: Die Entstehung der Kontinente und Ozeane. 4th rev. ed.

3. I am indebted to the following references for a general review of his life: (a) Hallam A. 1989. Great geological controversies. 2nd ed. Oxford: Oxford University Press, pp. 137-183; (b) Schwarzbach M. 1986. Alfred Wegener, the father of continental drift. Love C, translator. Madison, Wis.: Science Tech, Inc. Translation of: Alfred Wegener und die Drift der Kontinente (1980); (c) Sullivan W. 1991. Continents in motion: the new earth debate. 2nd ed. New York: American Institute of Physics.
4. Sullivan, p. 14 (note 3c).
5. *Ibid.,* p. 19.
6. For some details, see Hallam, pp. 164-173 (note 3a).
7. Meyerhoff AA. 1972. Review of: Tarling D and M. 1971. Continental drift: a study of the earth's moving surface. Geotimes 17(4):34-36.
8. Cowen R, Green HW II, MacGregor ID, Moores EM, Valentine JW. 1972. Review appraised (letters to the editor). Geotimes 17(7):10.
9. For further comments, see chapter 12.
10. However, a recent publication in support of the contracting earth is: Lyttleton RA. 1982. The earth and its mountains. New York and London: John Wiley and Sons.
11. See chapter 12. See also: LeGrand HE. 1988. Drifting continents and shifting theories. Cambridge and New York: Cambridge University Press, pp. 251, 252.
12. Thagard P. 1992. Conceptual revolutions. Princeton, N.J.: Princeton University Press, pp. 181, 182.
13. (a) Giere RN. 1988. Explaining science: a cognitive approach. Chicago and London: University of Chicago Press, p. 229; (b) Rupke NA. 1970. Continental drift before 1900. Nature 227:349, 350. See chapter 12 for the problems with catastrophic interpretations.
14. (a) Giere, pp. 238, 239 (note 13a); (b) Hallam, p. 142 (note 3a); (c) Schwarzbach, p. xv (note 3b).
15. This brief account derives mainly from the following references: (a) Doberer KK. [1948] 1972. The goldmakers: 10,000 years of alchemy. Westport, Conn.: Greenwood Press; (b) Eliade M. 1962. The forge and the crucible. Corbin S, translator. New York: Harper and Brothers. Translation of: Forgerons et Alchimistes (1956); (c) Partington JR. 1957. A short history of chemistry. 3rd ed. rev. London: Macmillan and Co.; (d) Pearsall R. [1976?]. The alchemists. London: Weidenfeld and Nicolson; (e) Salzberg HW. 1991. From caveman to chemist: circumstances and achievements. Washington, D.C.: American Chemical Society; (f) Stillman JM. [1924] 1960. The story of alchemy and early chemistry. Reprint. New York: Dover Publications.
16. This account is from: Mackay C. [1852] 1932. Extraordinary popular delusions and the madness of crowds. New York: Farrar, Straus, and Giroux, p. 478.
17. (a) Dampier WC. 1948. A history of science and its relations with philosophy and religion. 4th ed. rev. Cambridge: Cambridge University Press, pp. 142-144; (b) Easlea B. 1980. Witch hunting, magic and the new philosophy: an introduction to debates of the scientific revolution 1450-1750. Atlantic Highlands, N.J.: Humanities Press; (c) Luck JM. 1985. A history of Switzerland. The first 100,000 years: before the beginnings to the days of the present. Palo Alto, Calif.: Society for the Promotion of Science and Scholarship, pp. 182, 183; (d) Mackay (note 16); (e) Monter EW. 1976. Witchcraft in France and Switzerland: the Borderlands during the Reformation. Ithaca and London: Cornell University Press; (f) Rosenthal B. 1993. Salem story: reading the witch trials of 1692. Cambridge Studies in American Literature and Culture, No. 73. Cambridge and New York: Cambridge University Press; (g) Russell JB. 1972. Witchcraft in the Middle Ages. Ithaca and London: Cornell University Press; (h) Tindall G. 1966. A handbook on witches. New York: Atheneum.
18. MacKay, pp. 482, 483 (note 16).
19. *Ibid.,* p. 482.
20. Tindall, p. 25 (note 17h).
21. Kuhn TS. 1962. The structure of scientific revolutions. Chicago: University of Chicago Press.
22. For some evaluations and discussions of Kuhn's work, see, among many references: (a) Cohen IB. 1985. Revolution in science. Cambridge, Mass., and London: Belknap Press of Harvard

University Press; (b) Gutting G, editor. 1980. Paradigms and revolutions: appraisals and applications of Thomas Kuhn's philosophy of science. London and Notre Dame: University of Notre Dame Press; (c) Laudan L. 1977. Progress and its problems: toward a theory of scientific growth. Berkeley and Los Angeles: University of California Press; (d) LeGrand (note 11); (e) Mauskopf SH, editor. 1979. The reception of unconventional science. American Association for the Advancement of Science Selected Symposia. Boulder, Colo.: Westview Press; (f) McMullin E, editor. 1992. The social dimensions of science. Studies in Science and the Humanities from the Reilly Center for Science, Technology, and Values, vol. 3. Notre Dame: University of Notre Dame Press; (g) Shapin S. 1982. History of science and its sociological reconstructions. History of Science 20:157-211.

23. Kuhn TS. 1970. The structure of scientific revolutions. 2nd ed. Chicago: University of Chicago Press, p. viii.
24. For a discussion of the catastrophism paradigm, see chapter 12.
25. Barber B. 1961. Resistance by scientists to scientific discovery. Science 134:596-602.
26. (a) Kuhn 1970, p. 151 (note 23). (b) Cohen, pp. 467-472 (note 22a) also refers to conversion experiences in science without implying religious significance, as the term "religion" is commonly understood.
27. Kuhn 1970, p. 170 (note 23).
28. For some recent opinions, see McMullin (note 22f).
29. Molière JBP. [1664] 1875. The forced marriage. In: van Laun H, translator. The dramatic works of Molière, vol. 2. Edinburgh: William Paterson, pp. 325-389.
30. Pascal. 1966. Pensées. Krailsheimer AJ, translator. London and New York: Penguin Books, p. 214.

PUTTING IT TOGETHER

This is man that great and true Amphibian, *whose nature is disposed to live . . . in divided and distinguished worlds.*

—Sir Thomas Browne[1]

In chapter 1 we referred to the lively discourse about the validity of science and the Bible. Such discussion has often become acrimonious, especially when focused on the specific issues of creation and evolution. Too often intellectual tribalism sets in. Creationists continue to emphasize the infamous Piltdown hoax once used to buttress concepts of human evolution, but long since discarded from humanity's evolutionary tree. Evolutionists never seem to tire of recounting the "horror story" of how the church persecuted Galileo Galilei (1564-1642) for teaching correctly that the earth rotates around the sun. The story has often been distorted. It appears that Galileo was somewhat of an aggressor himself, and although the threats he faced were ominous, the church never had him put in prison or physically abused.[2]

While the conflict between science and Scripture is genuine, does it have the fundamental irreconcilable differences so many assume? In this chapter we shall propose that, in the context of an open intellectual search for truth that includes a search for knowledge and understanding, both science and Scripture can work together and, indeed, need to work together. Unless designated otherwise, the term *science* as used in this chapter represents a methodology for finding any truth about nature. This methodological science is open to a broad variety of explanations, including the possibility of a designer. This is in contrast to naturalistic science, which excludes the concept of a designer in its search for truth. While it is not possible to reconcile naturalistic science and Scripture, it is possible to bring methodological science and Scripture together.

SCIENCE AND SCRIPTURE: NOT SUCH STRANGE COMPANIONS

In 1859 Charles Darwin published his famous *Origin of Species*, which had a dramatic effect on the philosophy of Western culture. A hundred years later several celebrations of that historic event convened around the world. One of the most important was held at the University of Chicago. In a speech delivered during that five-day convention, Sir Julian Huxley, the grandson of Darwin's defender, "bulldog" Thomas H. Huxley, stated, "The earth was not created; it evolved. So did all the animals and plants that inhabit it, including our human selves, mind and soul as well as brain and body. So did religion. . . .

"Evolutionary man can no longer take refuge from his loneliness in the arms of a divinized father-figure, whom he himself has created, nor escape from the responsibility of making decisions by sheltering under the umbrella of Divine Authority, nor absolve himself from the hard task of meeting his present problems and planning his future by relying on the will of an omniscient, but unfortunately inscrutable, Providence."[3]

He made his declaration at a special convocation held in the imposing Rockefeller Chapel. Curiously, Huxley uttered his statement only minutes after some 1,500 scientists from 27 countries had bowed their heads in prayer to "Almighty God."

Why would scientists celebrating Darwin's achievements pray to God? This should raise questions about our stereotyping of scientists. Many scientists are, in varying degrees, religious, and many base their religion on Scripture. This implies that there might not be such a fundamental dichotomy between belief in science and belief in Scripture. At present, naturalistic science has difficulty incorporating any religion into its explanatory menu, considering such explanations as unacceptable. But this was not the case a few centuries ago when Western society laid the foundations of modern science.

Without question major differences do exist between the basic approaches of science and Scripture. Science bases itself on observation of nature and concentrates on explanations, while Scripture claims to give authoritative information and focuses on God's activities and their resultant meaning. Science claims to be open to revision as new ideas develop, while the Bible has more of a tone of finality. However, as we will see in later chapters, scientists themselves can develop quite a posture of authority and finality, especially regarding the authority of science itself.

We find a number of similarities in the basic approaches used by both science and Scripture. Scientific observations and Scripture are more in the data mode, while scientific explanations and theology deal more with interpretation.

Scientific data and Scripture do not change, while interpretations of both can vary widely. Often we use the same basic rational process in interpreting both. Both science and Scripture overlap in limited ways and also complement each other. To find truth and meaning in the reality about us, we should not ignore either one. If a Creator exists at all, nature can give much information about its Creator. But if there is no Creator, science needs to explain the near-ubiquitous existence of complexity and religion.

THE BIBLICAL BACKGROUND OF SCIENCE

An intriguing idea promulgated during the past half century challenges the dichotomy usually implied between science and Scripture. The thesis is that science developed in the Western world especially because of its Judeo-Christian background. In other words, instead of science and Scripture being worlds apart, science owes its origin to the philosophy of the Bible. An impressive number of scholars support the thesis.[4]

The mathematician and philosopher Alfred North Whitehead, who taught at both Cambridge and Harvard universities, points out that the ideas of modern science developed as "an unconscious derivative of medieval theology."[5] The concept of an orderly world as deduced from the rational and consistent God of the Bible provided a basis for belief in the cause-and-effect concept of science. The pagan gods of other cultures were capricious, and this does not fit with the consistency of science. R. G. Collingwood, professor of metaphysical philosophy at Oxford University, also supports this thesis by pointing out that belief in God's omnipotence changed the view of nature from imprecision to the realm of precision,[6] a perspective that fits better with the exactitude of science. R. Hooykaas, professor of the history of science at the University of Utrecht, also emphasizes that the biblical worldview contributed to the development of modern science. Of special importance was the relative antiauthoritarianism fostered by the Bible that freed science from the authority of certain theologians.[7] One of the most important writers in this area is Stanley L. Jaki, a professor of physics and theology at Seton Hall University. Jaki argues that the Hindu, Chinese, Mayan, Egyptian, Babylonian, and Greek cultures all had, in varying degrees, starts in science that ended in stillbirths. He attributes it to their lack of confidence in the rationality of the universe. The Judeo-Christian tradition of the Bible provided the rationality necessary for the establishment of science.[8] Of interest is the more controversial Merton thesis,[9] which proposes that Protestantism, especially in seventeenth-century England, helped emancipate science through its antiauthoritarian stance against accepted dogma.

While we cannot unequivocally establish the broadly accepted thesis of a close relationship between Judeo-Christian tradition and science, the very existence of this thesis suggests that a strong dichotomy need not exist between science and Scripture.

RELIGIOUS COMMITMENT OF THE PIONEERS OF MODERN SCIENCE

The relationship that can exist between science and the Bible can be demonstrated by the strong religious commitment of the scientists who established modern science during the seventeenth and eighteenth centuries. Four examples follow:

Robert Boyle (1627-1691), sometimes called the father of chemistry, certainly was the father of physical chemistry. His major contribution to science was the overthrow of the classical idea of only four basic elements: fire, air, earth, and water. This innovative English scientist was a highly devout Christian who believed that God could directly move matter. He donated much of his wealth to religious causes in Ireland and New England.[10]

In France the brilliant mathematician Blaise Pascal (1623-1662) helped establish the principles of probability. He also stated that "the whole course of things must have for its object the establishment and the greatness of religion."[11] His famous wager to the skeptic—If God does not exist, the skeptic loses nothing by believing in Him; but if He does exist, the skeptic gains eternal life by believing in Him—reveals his religious commitment as well as his calculating mind. His conclusion is that one might as well believe in God.

The Swedish biologist Carl von Linné (1707-1778) was the foremost member of the faculty at the University of Uppsala. He is noted especially for establishing the significance of the genus and species level for the classification of organisms and for classifying almost everything he knew about. His fame attracted scholars from all over the world. Opposed to any ideas contrary to creation, he believed that "nature is created by God to His honour and for the blessing of mankind, and everything that happens happens at His command and under His guidance."[12] In his later life he modified his views about the fixity of species to allow for some small variation, a position now held by modern creationists.

Sir Isaac Newton (1642-1727), regarded by some as the greatest scientist who ever lived, was also a profound student of the Bible. Best known for establishing the principles of calculus and for discovering the laws of planetary motion, he still found time to write extensively on the biblical prophecies of Daniel and Revelation. Newton very much believed that God is the Creator and that nature gives us knowledge about God.[13]

We could cite scores of other similar examples to show that the foundations of modern science rose within a dominantly biblical atmosphere and that no fundamental antagonism need exist between science and Scripture. The difference appears to be more a matter of attitude. Our pioneer scientists did good science, and for them science was discovering the principles that God had already established in nature. Creation was the accepted and usually unquestioned presupposition about origins. Thus a religious atmosphere did not hinder the birth of modern science.

RELIGION AND CONTEMPORARY SCIENTISTS

One might argue that science developed in spite of religion, as suggested by the present independence of contemporary science. However, because of the weakening of a naturalistic philosophy among scientists, such an argument is certainly less valid now than it would have been a half century ago. The general acceptance of quantum mechanics (Max Planck, 1858-1947; Albert Einstein, 1879-1955; Niels Bohr, 1885-1962; Werner Heisenberg, 1901-1976) introduced a fundamental element of uncertainty into science. For instance, according to quantum mechanics theory, uncertainty exists in the simultaneous measurement of velocity and position, thus challenging the simple cause-and-effect of classical science. Together with other factors, it has stimulated an atmosphere of both humility and awe. While a number of scientists reject religion and Scripture, we still observe a definite contemporary component of thought, especially among some in the physical sciences,[14] favorable to the concept of some kind of God or organizer. I will mention three individuals as examples, all of whom have written extensively on this topic.

Paul Davies is professor of theoretical physics at the University of Newcastle upon Tyne in England. In his popular book *God and the New Physics* he ventures that "science offers a surer path to God than religion."[15] In a later book he comments on the "powerful evidence [that] there is 'something going on' behind it all."[16] He furthermore supports the thesis presented earlier in this chapter, that scientists can be religious: "Following the publication of *God and the New Physics,* I was astonished to discover how many of my close scientific colleagues practice a conventional religion."[17]

Arthur Peacocke is a biochemist and theologian having served at both Oxford and Cambridge universities. To him God creates through both His laws and by chance. Peacocke also expresses the view that the ultimate reality is God.[18]

John Polkinghorne had spent more than 25 years working as a theoretical-particle physicist at Cambridge University when he became an Anglican clergyman. He devoted himself to the study of the relationship of science to theology, but later became a college administrator at Cambridge. Among his theses is the proposition that God upholds and is active in the universe, and furthermore, that He facilitates our freedom of choice.[19]

These are only a minute sampling of an important group of scholars who are stating rather clearly that science needs to be integrated with religion. They have a fairly broad spectrum of views,[20] which, however, do not fit the usual image of either the naturalistic evolutionary scientists or the Bible-believing creationists. Such views do illustrate that scientific and biblical ideas are not opposite and irreconcilable.

THE IMPORTANCE OF A BROAD APPROACH

Discussions among scientists about religion are not unusual. Some of our leading scientific journals such as *Science* and *Nature* repeatedly participate, especially in the reader-response sections. Occasionally the correspondents conclude that science and religion do not conflict, since they represent separate domains. Others take an exclusively naturalistic stance, even suggesting that scientists should check in their brains along with their hats and coats when they enter the door of a church.[21] Still others argue that faith, something usually associated with religion, is indispensable for science. For Norbert Muller, a professor of chemistry at Purdue University, "Science simply cannot be done without religion," because a scientist must have "faith in the assumptions that make science possible."[22] Other scholars feel that religion has a rich contribution and indeed a responsibility to provide purpose and truth[23] and must be incorporated in any meaningful system of thought. Which line of thought should we follow?

A broad approach seems wisest in all intellectual pursuits. One of the tragedies of ignorance is that its victims do not realize their plight. We don't know what and how much we don't know. Truth needs to be sought, and it ought to make sense in all realms. Because truth is so broad, it encompasses all of reality or actuality, so should be our efforts to find it.

It is dangerous to form a worldview on the basis of a narrow field of inquiry. We may choose to look at only the mechanical world, as does naturalistic science, or mainly the thinking world, as does philosophy, but both of them, as well as all other perspectives, including humanity's spiritual dimension, are parts of a whole that we must always consider. Figure 3.1 illustrates the advantage of a broad approach. One circle can represent science and the other Scripture. In areas such as the nonoverlapping left and right parts, only science or Scripture can give us information. To form a worldview on the basis of either

FIGURE 3.1

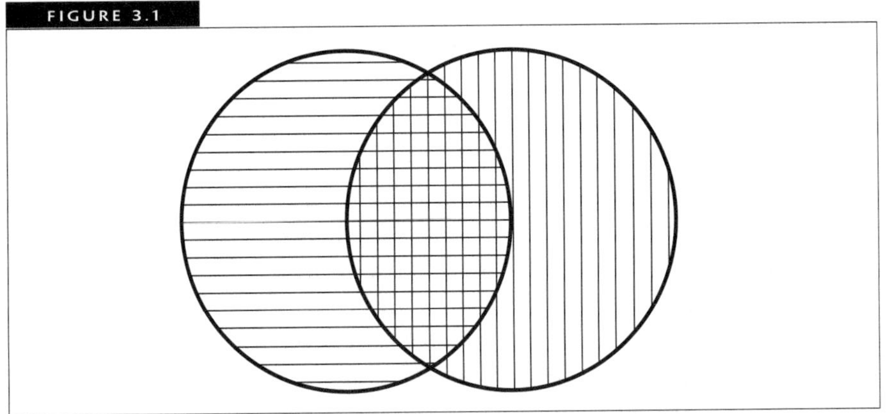

Diagram illustrating the advantage of a broad approach, such as combining science and Scripture. Either one alone can give us valuable information, as illustrated at the left and right ends. Richness of interpretation results when both are combined, as illustrated in the center portion.

alone seems unnecessarily restrictive. When we consider both, not only do we have a broader fund of information, but an abundance of richness and meaning. In asking the grand questions about origins, we can ill afford to look at only one narrow area of information.

An additional reason for a broad approach is the checks and balances that a multiplicity of perspectives can provide in testing and establishing truth. "Truth is eternal, and conflict with error will only make manifest its strength."[24]

It is not difficult to find evidence of the dissatisfaction caused by too narrow an approach to truth. Once I gave a seminar on creation in the Geology Department of the Riverside campus of the University of California. In my presentation I made four points:[25] (1) it is highly improbable that complex life could arise spontaneously, (2) the many missing links in the fossil record suggest that evolution from simple to complex did not occur, (3) science repeatedly changes its views, and (4) science and the Bible have a common, broad rational basis. I included the last point especially because the individual who requested my services informed me that the students had been complaining about being taught only evolution in their classes, and they wanted to hear the other side. They were dissatisfied with too narrow an approach. From this perspective, the lingering question—"Which is true, science or Scripture?"—is not a good question, although many ask it. A better question is: "What truth do I find after I have studied both science and Scripture?"

The cultural anthropologist David Hess emphasizes that the spiritualistic movement of the late nineteenth century, which sought communication with the dead, was "in no small degree" a response to the intellectual anxiety generated by discoveries in geology, biology, and astronomy, all of which tended toward pure naturalism. He ties spiritualism indirectly with the more recent New Age movement, which sometimes tries to synthesize non-Western wisdom with modern science.[26] The postmodern artistic and theological trends away from simple modernism also testify to an interest in a breadth of approaches. Human beings often want, and should seek for, the whole story. We are not easily satisfied with a narrow outlook.

Science by itself tends to be materialistic and void of meaning. Isolated religious pursuits can be prone to erroneous superstitions. Each can help the other. Albert Einstein reflected this when he stated, "Science without religion is lame, religion without science is blind."[27] All of this substantiates the need for a broad approach in asking the deeper questions about origins.

DEUS EX MACHINA

Human beings have used God to explain nearly everything. More than a century ago some held the opinion that only God could create organic compounds such as sugars, proteins, urea, etc. Such comparatively complex molecules were associated with living organisms and the mystery of life. Since that time, scientists have synthesized many thousands of different organic compounds, and God is no longer considered necessary for this process. In the cosmic realm, Sir Isaac Newton thought that God would occasionally have to adjust the universe to keep it operating properly. Few any longer take the idea seriously. Centuries ago some thought God created bedbugs to keep people from sleeping too much, and mice to teach human beings to put food away. Almost everyone has discarded such ideas. As science has advanced, the need for God as an explanatory factor has decreased, and some perceive that even if He exists, He is certainly not necessary.

Appealing to God whenever we encounter difficulties in explaining nature is often referred to as "God of the gaps," or "deus ex machina" ("God from the machine"). The latter term stems from the practice in Greek and Roman drama of having an actor representing a god come from the sky onto the stage to untangle major problems in the plot, an effect accomplished using a crane (the machine), hence the reference to the "God from the machine" concept for resolving scientific difficulties. Most usually treat the concept with disdain, implying that whenever we run into a problem, we invoke God to solve it, when given sufficient time, science would itself eventually solve the mystery. We should not use God to fill the gaps in our information.

Many scientists also feel concern about a powerful God who is able to manipulate nature at will and thus alter the consistency that makes science possible. In this respect they see a genuine conflict between God and science. But the conflict need not be that severe if, as believed by the pioneers of modern science, He Himself created the principles of science, and nature then reflects that consistency. In their thinking, God is the author of the principles that form the foundation of science. God can overrule the laws He has established, but only rarely does He do so. This permits science to work.

While the criticism of the "deus ex machina," or "God of the gaps," concept has some validity, to eliminate all of God's activities arbitrarily in this way is too simplistic. One needs to differentiate between the usual God of the gaps and a "God of necessary gaps."[28] For this latter case, God seems essential. The synthesis of organic compounds mentioned above would fit the "God of the gaps" concept, while the recent advances in molecular biology that make the possibility of the spontaneous origin of living things less and less plausible would support the concept of the "God of the necessary gaps." In the latter case it appears that God is actually becoming more essential as we discover more and more complex programmed biochemical relationships that could not possibly originate by themselves.[29] The same can be said for the fine-tuning of the universe, which involves extremely precise values for basic physical factors.[30] One should not use the fact that science has been able to duplicate some phenomena once attributed to God as an excuse to eliminate Him altogether, especially as we find nature to be more and more elaborate and precise.

IS CREATION SCIENCE, AND IS EVOLUTION RELIGION?

In 1981 the state of Arkansas enacted a law requiring that the students in public school science classes receive a balanced treatment of both creation and evolution. The American Civil Liberties Union (ACLU) opposed the law and brought suit against the state, and the Arkansas trial, sometimes called "Scopes II,"[31] followed.[32] "Scopes I" occurred in 1925 in Tennessee, with evolution in the legal defense position. In the Arkansas trial the final decision against creation did not rest on the basis of the intrinsic merits of creation or evolution. Presiding judge William Overton ruled the new law to be unconstitutional, on the basis of the United States' constitutional requirement for the separation of church and state. To establish that creation was religious, Judge Overton relied heavily on the testimony of Michael Ruse, a scientific philosopher at the University of Guelph in Canada. Ruse set up a narrow definition of science.[33] After the trial another scientific philosopher, Larry Laudan, of the University of Pittsburgh, devastated the restricted concept of science employed in the trial. Laudan is sympathetic to evolution, but, in referring to Judge Overton's decision, made such deprecating comments as "the ruling rests on a host of misrepresentations of what science is and how it works"; "this tale of woeful fallacies in the Arkansas ruling"; "perpetuating and canonizing a false stereotype of what science is"; and other qualifiers such as "altogether inappropriate," "anachronistic," and "simply outrageous."[34] Obviously, the definition of science is controversial. In addition, others have leveled a number of other criticisms at the judge's written opinion.[35] Overton argued that creation was religion, not science, and that such a classification disqualified it from public schools.[36]

The dispute over the definition of science[37] manifested at the Arkansas trial underlines the fact that we don't know how to define science. Evolutionists react rather negatively to the term *scientific creationism,*[38] arguing that such a thing cannot possibly exist. They have repeatedly succeeded in keeping creation out of the science classroom by arguing that creation is not science, but religion. Often they state that creation is not science because there exists no way to scientifically test a miracle like creation. However, they then turn about-face and write books such as *Scientists Confront Creationism,* and use science to try to disprove creation. Can evolutionists have it both ways?

Since there exists no accepted comprehensive definition of science, the issue of whether creation is science is really moot. If science is a truly open search for truth, science could accommodate "scientific creationism," and some of the pioneers of modern science described earlier in this chapter certainly qualify as scientific creationists. On the other hand, if we define science as a purely naturalistic philosophy that by definition excludes the concept of a creator, then scientific creationism cannot exist. As expected, evolutionists favor the latter interpretation. However, this interpretation also means that science is not an open search for truth, as often claimed.

We can also ask if science and/or evolution is a form of religion. The loyalty, passion, and fervor scientists exhibit at the many creation-evolution hearings and trials would certainly indicate that more than purely objective evaluation is involved. The book *Evolution as a Religion,* by Mary Midgley,[39] points out how science can function as religion in many ways. Other writers have also emphasized the religious aspects of evolution and Darwinism.[40] But in general, legal arguments to eliminate evolution from the classroom because it is a religion have not prevailed. The general perception is that evolution is some kind of science, and creation is religion. Actually, there is no sharp line of demarcation between science and religion. Both are comprehensive views with overlapping features.

THE MORE IMPORTANT QUESTION

At a public hearing before the California State Board of Education, I proposed that the scientific community should not be afraid of creation and should allow it to compete freely with evolution in the classroom. This would give the student the freedom to choose among various common options, thus favoring a degree of academic freedom.[41] Evolutionists argued that creation is not science. They have repeatedly taken refuge in certain definitions of what science is to try to keep creation out of the science classroom. However, as the French say: *"C'est magnifique, mais ce n'est pas la guerre!"* ("This is magnificent, but this is not the battle!") The real question is: Which is true, creation or evolution? Unfortunately, that question often gets buried under semantics, authoritarianism, and legal technicalities.

At that same public hearing I was impressed by the plea of a clergyman who pointed out that his parishioners were trying to inculcate in their children the moral principles and values of the Bible. These same parishioners had to send their children to schools supported by the parishioners' own taxes, only to find the science teachers destroyed the confidence the parents had sought to establish in the Bible and its principles. Such parents could hardly care less about various definitions of science or battles over academic turf. They were simply trying to nurture in their children morality and understanding based on the Bible, and the schools, they felt, were destroying this.

All of this brings into focus the need to associate science with the Bible. While they are complementary in certain respects, as we pointed out above, the two also have much in common in terms of a basic rationality.[42] Both receive wide respect, both have a unique contribution to make, and both are helpful in formulating worldviews.

CONCLUSIONS

The conflict between science and the Bible is not as deep as usually assumed. As a matter of fact, the rationality of the Bible may have been the foundation for the development of modern science. The devotion of the pioneers of modern science to the Bible also indicates an underlying compatibility between the two. As indicated in chapter 1, science and religion have parted ways, especially between naturalistic science and the Bible, but the rift seems to be based more on attitudes and interpretations than on more basic principles. In our search for truth, both science and the Bible can make good companions that complement and support each other. Because of this, the lingering question—"Which is true, science or Scripture?"—is not as good a question as: "What truth do I find when I look at both science and Scripture?"

REFERENCES

1. Browne T. n.d. Religio Medici I, p. 34. Quoted in: Mackay AL. 1991. A dictionary of scientific quotations. Bristol and Philadelphia: Institute of Physics Publishing, p. 42.
2. (a) Maatman R. 1994. The Galileo incident. Perspectives on Science and Christian Faith 46:179-182; (b) Shea WR. 1986. Galileo and the church. In: Lindberg DC, Numbers RL, editors. God and nature: historical essays on the encounter between Christianity and science. Berkeley and Los Angeles: University of California Press, pp. 114-135.
3. (a) This incident was reported in: [Anonymous]. 1959. Science: Evolution: a religion of science? Newsweek 54 (7 December):94, 95. (b) For the printed text of Sir Julian Huxley's speech, see: Huxley J. 1960. The evolutionary vision. In: Tax S, Callender C, editors. Issues in evolution: the University of Chicago Centennial discussions. Evolution after Darwin: the University of Chicago Centennial, vol. 3. Chicago: University of Chicago Press, pp. 249-261.
4. See for example: (a) Collingwood RG. 1940. An essay on metaphysics. Oxford and London: Clarendon Press; (b) Cox H. 1966. The secular city: secularization and urbanization in theological perspective. Rev. ed. New York: Macmillan Co.; (c) Dillenberger J. 1960. Protestant thought and natural science: a historical interpretation. Nashville and New York: Abingdon Press; (d) Foster MB. 1934. The Christian doctrine of creation and the rise of modern natural science. Mind 43 (n.s.):446-468; (e) Gerrish BA. 1968. The Reformation and the rise of modern science. In: Brauer JC, editor. The impact of the church upon its culture: reappraisals of the history of Christianity. Chicago and London: University of Chicago Press, pp. 231-265; (f) Gruner R. 1975. Science, nature, and Christianity. Journal of Theological Studies, New Series 26(1):55-81. This author does not support the thesis, but lists a number of other references that do (p. 56); (g) Hooykaas R. 1972. Religion and the rise of modern science. Grand Rapids: William B. Eerdmans Pub. Co.; (h) Jaki SL. 1974. Science and creation: from eternal cycles to an oscillating universe. New York: Science History Publications; (i) Jaki SL. 1978. The road of science and the ways to God. The Gifford Lectures 1974-1975 and 1975-1976. Chicago and London: University of Chicago Press; (j) Jaki SL. 1990. Science: Western or what? The Intercollegiate Review (Fall), pp. 3-12; (k) Klaaren EM. 1985. Religious origins of modern science: belief in creation in seventeenth-century thought. Lanham, N.Y., and London: University Press of America; (l) Whitehead AN. 1950. Science and the modern world. London: Macmillan and Co.
5. Whitehead, p. 19 (note 4l).
6. Collingwood, pp. 253-255 (note 4a).
7. Hooykaas, pp. 98-162 (note 4g).
8. Jaki 1974, 1978, 1990 (note 4h-j).
9. Merton RK. 1970. Science, technology and society in seventeenth-century England. New York: Howard Fertig.
10. (a) Boyle R. 1911, 1964. The skeptical chemist. Everyman's Library. London: J. M. Dent and Sons, pp. v-xiii; (b) Dampier WC. 1948. A history of science and its relations with philosophy and religion. 4th ed., rev. Cambridge: Cambridge University Press, pp. 139-141.
11. Pascal B. 1952. Pensées. Trotter WF, translator. In: Pascal B. 1952. The provincial letters; Pensées; Scientific treatises. M'Crie T, Trotter WF, Scofield R, translators. Great Books of the Western World Series. Chicago, London, and Toronto: Encyclopædia Britannica, p. 270. Translation of: Les lettres provinciales; Pensées; L'Oeuvre scientifique.
12. Nordenskiöld E. 1935. The history of biology: a survey. New York: Tudor Pub. Co., pp. 206, 207.
13. (a) Brewster D. 1855, 1965. Memoirs of the life, writings, and discoveries of Sir Isaac Newton. 2 vols. The Sources of Science, No. 14. New York and London: Johnson Reprint Corp.; (b) Christianson GE. 1984. In the presence of the Creator: Isaac Newton and his times. New York:

The Free Press; and London: Collier Macmillan Publishers; (c) Fauvel J, Flood R, Shortland M, Wilson R, editors. 1988. Let Newton be! Oxford, New York, and Tokyo: Oxford University Press; (d) Westfall RS. 1980. Never at rest: a biography of Isaac Newton. Cambridge: Cambridge University Press.

14. See first part of chapter 6.
15. Davies P. 1983. God and the new physics. New York: Simon and Schuster, p. ix.
16. Davies P. 1988. The cosmic blueprint: new discoveries in nature's creative ability to order the universe. New York: Touchstone; Simon and Schuster, p. 203.
17. Davies P. 1992. The mind of God: the scientific basis for a rational world. New York and London: Simon and Schuster, p. 15.
18. (a) Peacocke AR. 1971. Science and the Christian experiment. London, New York, and Toronto: Oxford University Press; (b) Peacocke AR, editor. 1981. The sciences and theology in the twentieth century. Northumberland, England: Oriel Press; (c) Peacocke AR. 1986. God and the new biology. San Francisco, Cambridge, and New York: Harper and Row; (d) Peacocke AR. 1990. Theology for a scientific age: being and becoming—natural and divine. Oxford and Cambridge, Mass.: Basil Blackwell.
19. (a) Polkinghorne J. 1991. God's action in the world. Cross Currents (Fall), pp. 293-307; see also (b) Polkinghorne J. 1986. One world: the interaction of science and theology. London: SPCK; (c) Polkinghorne J. 1989. Science and creation: the search for understanding. Boston: New Science Library, Shambhala Publications; (d) Polkinghorne J. 1989. Science and providence: God's interaction with the world. Boston: New Science Library, Shambhala Publications.
20. See chapter 21 for a discussion of some of their views.
21. Provine W. 1988. Scientists, face it! Science and religion are incompatible. The Scientist 2(16; September 5):10.
22. Muller N. 1988. Scientists, face it! Science *is* compatible with religion. The Scientist 2(24; December 26):9.
23. Reid GW. 1993. The theologian as conscience for the church. Journal of the Adventist Theological Society 4 (2):12-19.
24. White EG. 1946. Counsels to writers and editors. Nashville: Southern Pub. Assn., p. 44.
25. For additional discussion on the argumentation for these four points, see chapters 4, 11, 17, and 18, respectively.
26. Hess DJ. 1993. Science in the new age: the paranormal, its defenders and debunkers, and American culture. Madison, Wis.: University of Wisconsin Press, pp. 17-40.
27. Einstein A. 1950. Out of my later years. New York: Philosophical Library, p. 30.
28. Kenny A. 1987. Reason and religion: essays in philosophical theology. Oxford and New York: Basil Blackwell, p. 84.
29. See chapters 4 and 8.
30. See chapter 6.
31. Milner R. 1990. The encyclopedia of evolution. New York: Facts on File, p. 399.
32. For various accounts, see: (a) Geisler NL. 1982. The creator in the courtroom: Scopes II. The 1981 Arkansas creation-evolution trial. Milford, Mich.: Mott Media; (b) Gilkey L. 1985. Creationism on trial: evolution and God at Little Rock. Minneapolis: Winston Press; (c) La Follette MC, editor. 1983. Creationism, science, and the law: the Arkansas case. Cambridge, Mass., and London: MIT Press; (d) Numbers RL. 1992. The creationists. New York: Alfred A. Knopf, pp. xv, 249-251.
33. See Gilkey, pp. 127-132 (note 32b).
34. Laudan L. 1983. Commentary on Ruse: science at the bar—causes for concern. In: La Follette, pp. 161-166 (note 32c).
35. Bird WR. 1987, 1988, 1989. Philosophy of science, philosophy of religion, history, education, and constitutional issues. The origin of species revisited: the theories of evolution and of abrupt appearance, vol. 2. New York: Philosophical Library, pp. 461-466.
36. For a fairly accurate report of my testimony at this trial, see Geisler, pp. 461-466 (note 32a).
37. See chapter 17 for further comments on this complex question. Also see: (a) Roth AA. 1974.

Science against God? Origins 1:52-55; (b) Roth AA. 1978. How scientific is evolution? Ministry 51(7):19-21; (c) Roth AA. 1984. Is creation scientific? Origins 11:64, 65.

38. Godfrey LR, editor. 1983. Scientists confront creationism. New York: W. W. Norton and Co.
39. Midgley M. 1985. Evolution as a religion: strange hopes and stranger fears. London and New York: Methuen and Co.
40. E.g., (a) Macbeth N. 1971. Darwin retried: an appeal to reason. Boston: Gambit, Inc., p. 126; (b) Bethell T. 1985. Agnostic evolutionists. Harpers 270 (1617; February):49-52, 56-58, 60, 61.
41. For further discussion, see: (a) Roth AA. 1975. A matter of fairness. Origins 2:3, 4; (b) Roth AA. 1978. Closed minds and academic freedom. Origins 5:61, 62.
42. For a distinctive discussion, see: Murphy N. 1994. What has theology to learn from scientific methodology? In: Rae M, Regan H, Stenhouse J, editors. Science and theology: questions at the interface. Grand Rapids: William B. Eerdmans Pub. Co., pp. 101-126.

LIVING ORGANISMS

CHAPTER 4

WHERE DID LIFE COME FROM?

Of all the mysteries of biology, unquestionably the most baffling is the question of how life arose on earth.
—*Gordon Rattray Taylor*[1]

The surface of the earth literally teems with living organisms ranging in size from bacteria, with a diameter of $\frac{1}{2,000}$ of a millimeter, to the giant redwoods, reaching heights of 100 meters. In the animal kingdom great blue whales have lengths of 30 meters, which might be the heaviest animals that have ever lived on earth. A candidate for the largest "plant" might be an underground fungus in the state of Washington that covers an area of 600 hectares (1,500 acres). One of the great questions of all time is When, how, and where did this great variety of life originate?

In this chapter we will look at ideas about how life began on earth. Producing the necessary complex biological molecules, such as proteins and DNA, in a primordial setting seems extremely difficult, while making even a simple cell come spontaneously into being appears essentially beyond possibility.

HISTORICAL BELIEFS

In antiquity, and indeed, until fairly recently, few questioned the idea that various forms of life arose spontaneously from nonliving matter. It appeared to be an observational fact that fleas and lice appeared spontaneously on human and animal bodies, frogs generated from mud, pond water produced an almost endless variety of algae and small animals, moths formed in fog, and worms formed in fruit and plant galls. A variety of parasitic worms, such as tapeworms, were thought to arise spontaneously in human beings and animals. The pioneer chemist Joannes van Helmont (1579-1644) reported that he had himself seen scorpions develop from the herb basil crushed between two bricks. He also created a formula for manufacturing mice.[2] If you put old rags and wheat in a receptacle and hide it for some time in an attic or barn, it will eventually produce mice! The experiment is still repeatable now, with the same results. However, we interpret it differently. His experiment is one example of the many kinds of evidence that enabled the concept of spontaneous generation to thrive. The observations that supported the belief were highly repeatable. With time and effort you could find worms in apples and frogs in mud, etc. Science worked, and to question spontaneous generation was to question reason itself.

Nevertheless, some were skeptical, and from the seventeenth to nineteenth centuries the question was the subject of a heated conflict. One of the key players who invoked the experimental approach was Francesco Redi (1626-1697), a physician of Arezzo, Italy. People had long known that maggots—the larvae of flies—developed in decaying meat. Redi[3] experimented with a variety of animal remains, including those of snakes, pigeons, fish, sheep, frogs, deer, dogs, lambs, rabbits, goats, ducks, geese, hens, swallows, lions, tigers, and buffalo. The fact struck him that the same kind of flies emerged regardless of the kind of meat used. He was also aware that during the summer hunters protected their meat from flies with cloth, and he suspected that flies might be the source of maggots. To test the idea, he placed meat in closed jars and in open jars covered by fine gauze. Because maggots did not develop on the putrefying meat, he concluded that the meat did not produce the maggots spontaneously, but was only the breeding place for flies.

Redi's experiments did not resolve the question, however. The controversy raged for two more centuries. Other experiments gave mixed results. Researchers placed various interpretations on the same results, each side arguing from its own presuppositions. The idea of spontaneous generation became even more accepted in the early nineteenth century.[4] A major concern was how parasitic worms originated in their hosts. Some argued that God in His perfect creation would not do this—they must arise spontaneously. Few if any held the present opinion that such organisms generally represent degeneration from free-living forms.

The supposed "death blow" to the theory of spontaneous generation came from the hands of the famous French scientist Louis Pasteur (1822-1895). He became involved in the bitter quarrel while investigating microbes. Pasteur used flasks with contorted tubes that excluded dust but permitted access to air, then considered vital for spontaneous generation. Pasteur placed water and organic material as a culture medium in his flasks. Heating the flasks prevented the development of life, even though the culture medium had free access to air.

In his exuberant style Pasteur proclaimed: "Never will the doctrine of spontaneous generation recover from the mortal blow of this simple experiment!"[5]

Unfortunately, Pasteur was wrong, and the story does not end there. Microbiology textbooks in particular often display the colorful battle over spontaneous generation as an example of the triumph of science. That appears to be the case if the story concludes with Pasteur. However, at the same time that Pasteur was winning his battle, the concept of evolution and the related presupposition that life arose spontaneously on earth sometime in the distant past was beginning to receive some acceptance. This utterly confused the issue. On the one hand, the elegant experiments of Pasteur and others showed that only life begets life, while evolutionists proposed that life arose in the past from nonlife. In a sense, the problem for evolution was more severe. The earlier ideas of spontaneous generation often rested on concepts of life arising from dead organic matter (heterogenesis), while evolutionists suggested that life arose from simpler inorganic matter (abiogenesis). In 1871 Charles Darwin cautiously referred to this latter possibility as he suggested that "in some warm little pond" proteins might form and "undergo still more complex changes."[6]

A major step for the theory of spontaneous generation occurred in 1924, when the famous Russian biochemist A. I. Oparin gave details of how simple inorganic and organic compounds might gradually form complex organic compounds, and the latter form simple organisms.[7] Other scientists added supporting ideas, and the concept that life arose sometime in the past in a "soup" rich in organic compounds became a topic of serious consideration. Scientists often refer to the process as chemical evolution.

Decades later major questions developed. Biochemists and molecular biologists began recognizing some very complex molecules and highly integrated biochemical systems. The extreme improbability of the spontaneous generation of these complexities became a major challenge.

SIMPLE BIOLOGICAL MOLECULES (BIOMONOMERS)

The chemicals found in living organisms are often extremely complex. Some relatively simple organic molecules (biomonomers) combine to form complex biological molecules (biopolymers) such as proteins and nucleic acids (DNA). The biopolymers may contain hundreds to thousands of simpler molecules linked together. Amino acids (biomonomers) are the simple building blocks of proteins (biopolymers). Living organisms have basically 20 different kinds of amino acids in them. Several hundred of them can combine to form a single protein molecule. Nucleic acids (biopolymers) are even more complex,

FIGURE 4.1

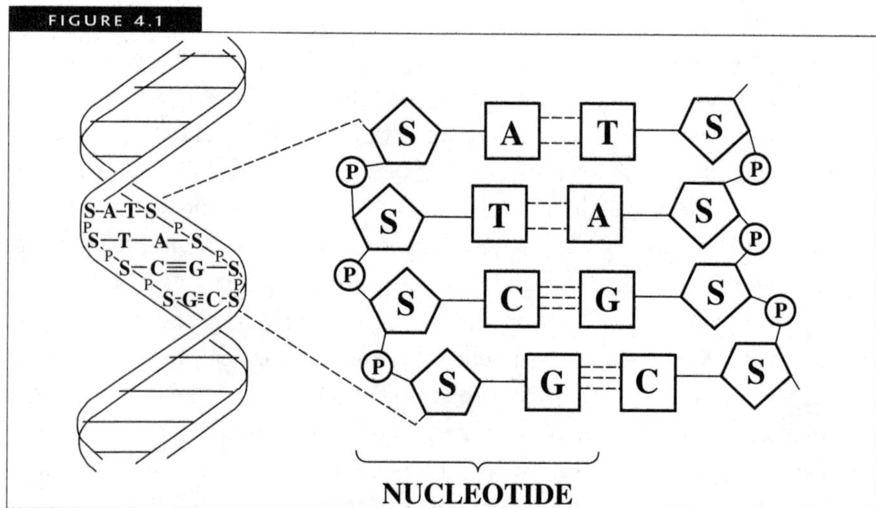

Schematic representation of the structure of DNA. The double coil is illustrated at the left. A nucleotide would be the combination of P, S, and one of A, T, G, or C. Human genetic information has about 3,000 million pairs of these in each cell. A, T, G, and C represent the bases adenine, thymine, guanine, and cytosine, respectively. S represents a sugar, and P is the phosphate. The two strands are joined together by hydrogen bonding (dashed lines in right diagram) formed between certain bases.

involving the combining of nucleotides (biomonomers) that themselves consist of a sugar, a phosphate, and a nucleotide base (Figure 4.1). (There are basically four different kinds of nucleotide bases.) Nucleic acids may contain millions of nucleotides. The basic hereditary and metabolic information of an organism is encoded in the sequence of the different kinds of nucleotide bases. Scientists refer to the nucleic acids as DNA (deoxyribonucleic acid) and RNA (ribonucleic acid). The difference between the two is that they have slightly different kinds of sugars.

In 1953 Stanley Miller published the results of a now-famous experiment on the synthesis of biomonomers.[8] Countless textbooks have described the experiment as a first step in understanding the spontaneous origin of life. While working at the University of Chicago in the laboratory of Nobel Laureate Harold Urey, Miller successfully produced amino acids under conditions that some scientists had postulated for a primitive earth. He accomplished this by using a closed chemical apparatus in which he exposed a mixture of the gases methane, hydrogen, ammonia, and water vapor to electrical discharges. Since then the experiment has been repeated many times and improved upon. Most of the biomonomers needed for proteins or nucleic acids have turned up in these types of experiments.

While researchers have synthesized many biomonomers with relative ease in the laboratory, relating these experiments to what might have occurred naturally on a primitive earth is fraught with questions. For instance, amino acids form in an alkaline environment, while that same environment is detrimental to sugars.[9] Yet both are essential in living organisms.

Another problem involves the configuration of the amino acids. Amino acids with the same number and kinds of atoms can exist in several different forms, depending on the arrangement of the atoms. We often identify an L (levorotary) form and a D (dextrorotary) form, depending on how the molecules rotate a plane of polarized light. The two forms are mirror images of each other, like a person's left and right hand (Figure 4.2). It turns out that living organisms consist almost exclusively of the L form of amino acid, while amino acids synthesized in the laboratory have equal amounts of the L and D form. How could a primitive "soup" containing an equal mixture of D and L molecules give rise to living organisms with only the L type?[10] It is difficult to imagine the different kinds of amino acids common to biological systems all happening by chance to be L forms before being incorporated into the proteins of the first life forms. Many suggestions have attempted to account for this. One recent set of experiments suggested that a magnetic field could produce nearly pure single mirror-image forms, but the report turned out to be a deception.[11] The problem of mirror images also applies to sugars.

FIGURE 4.2

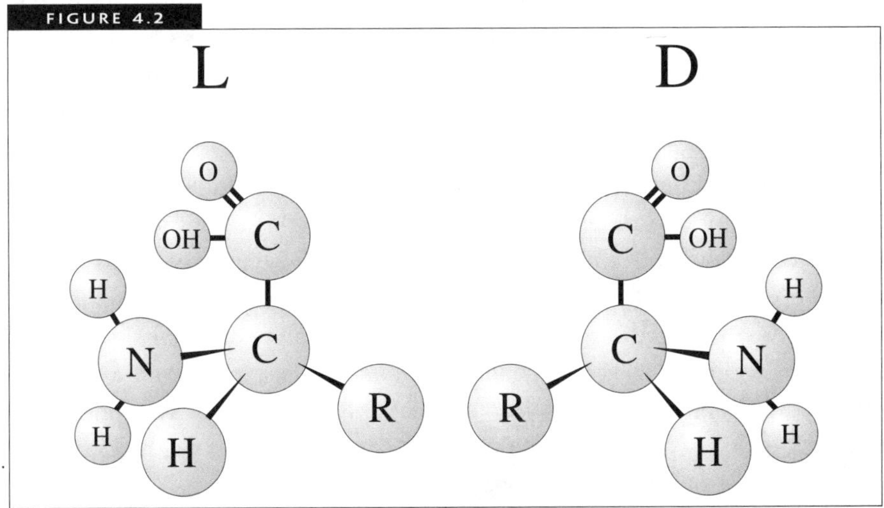

Optical isomers (D and L forms) of an amino acid. Letters represent the chemical elements of each atom. R is a radical that varies with different amino acids. Note that one form is a three-dimensional mirror image of the other.

Another question involves the lack of evidence in the earth's rocks for the assumed "primordial soup" in which all the molecules supposedly formed. If at one time in the distant past there existed an ocean rich with organic molecules in which life might by chance arise, the rocks do not show any sign of it. Rocks rich in organic matter are conspicuously absent in the deeper layers representing the time during which life supposedly evolved.[12]

Many questions have risen regarding the difficulty of getting a sufficient concentration of biomonomers together in the primordial soup to permit the synthesis of complex molecules known as biopolymers. Chemist Donald Hull, of the California Research Corporation,[13] gives an example using the simplest of amino acids, glycine, which has the formula NH_2CH_2COOH. He estimates that if glycine formed in a primitive atmosphere, 97 percent of it would decompose before reaching the ocean, and the remaining 3 percent would face destruction there. He also estimates that this amino acid would have a maximum concentration of less than $1/_{1,000,000,000,000}$ (10^{-12}) molar. He states: "But even the highest admissible value seems hopelessly low as starting material for the spontaneous generation of life." The problem he outlined above would be even more serious for the other more complex amino acids, which are more delicate. To get around these problems, some scientific models suggest concentrating and protecting the "soup" in caves. These require unlikely and highly specialized, limited, and fortuitous conditions.

Some investigators[14] have evaluated in detail another important question about chemical evolution. To what degree does the interference by the scientist bias the experimental results in favor of the desired outcome? It is one thing to have biomonomers formed in the laboratory using selected chemicals and sophisticated equipment, and an entirely different thing to have them produced spontaneously on a primitive earth. Some factors, such as using high concentrations of chemical reactants, can be used legitimately in the laboratory if they are corrected for by extrapolating the experimental conclusions to more dilute natural conditions, but shielding products from damaging energy sources, or using traps to isolate the product, as Miller did, or removing useless soup ingredients is considered illegitimate. The use of laboratory manipulations reflect more the kind of intelligent planning that one would expect from a Creator, rather than spontaneous activity on a lifeless prebiotic world. We should not use such experiments to illustrate chemical evolution unless we make proper adjustments for non-laboratory conditions.

COMPLEX BIOLOGICAL MOLECULES (BIOPOLYMERS)

Often textbooks report on the synthesis of biomonomers, but say much less about the origin of biopolymers. While the origin of biomonomers has its problems, they become many times more acute when we deal with nucleic acids and proteins, which are hundreds to thousands of times more complex. The proper functioning of the biopolymers requires correct sequences of their biomonomers. There is more involved here than merely using lots of energy to combine biomonomers. You can get a car to move by exploding a keg of dynamite under it, but the results would not be useful transportation! These complex molecules are highly organized, yet they supposedly appeared by chance. Nobel Laureate Jacques Monod, in his classic book *Chance and Necessity,*[15] describes the concept: "Chance alone is at the source of every innovation, of all creation in the biosphere. Pure chance, absolutely free but blind, at the very root of the stupendous edifice of evolution: this central concept of modern biology is no longer one among other possible or even conceivable hypotheses. It is today the sole conceivable hypothesis, the only one that squares with observed and tested fact." However, as many calculations have shown, the probability of functional complex biological molecules arising by chance is implausibly small.

We are all familiar with the fact that the chance of our obtaining a "heads" or "tails" in the tossing of a coin is 1 out of 2, or that the chance of obtaining a 4 when rolling a cubic die is 1 out of 6. If we have an urn containing 999 white beads and one red bead, the chance of picking out the red bead on the first try without looking is 1 out of 1,000. The chances of getting the right combination of biopolymers is infinitesimally smaller.

Living organisms usually contain many thousands of different kinds of proteins. Proteins usually consist of one to several hundred amino acids attached together in long chainlike structures, and as mentioned above, living organisms contain 20 different kinds of amino acids. Many amino acids have to be at a specific place along the chains in order for the protein to function properly. This arrangement is somewhat analogous to writing, in which the letters of the alphabet represent the amino acids, while the sentences—in this case usually 100 or more letters—represent the proteins. Some "spelling" errors are allowed at a number of positions along the amino acid chain. On the other hand, substitution of a single amino acid at a critical position can be lethal to the organisms. Diseases such as thalassemia, sickle-cell anemia, and some types of cancer result from the substitution of just one amino acid.[16]

Suppose we need a specific kind of protein. What are the chances that amino acids would show up in the specific order required? The number of possible combinations is unimaginably great, because there is the possibility of any one of 20 amino acids occupying each position. For a protein needing 100 specific amino acids, the number has been estimated at many times greater than all the atoms in the universe.[17] Hence the chance of getting a necessary kind of protein is extremely small. And what if we need two of them? The likelihood is much lower, too low to be plausible.[18] However, even the simplest form of life would need many specific kinds of proteins. One study[19] estimates the probability of getting 100 amino acids at the right place along the chain of amino acids of a protein. No substitutions (spelling errors) are allowed at these 100 specific points, although limited substitution is possible at other points between. To form such a protein, the specific amino acid has to be selected from 20 possibilities (probability $\frac{1}{20}$). The amino acid must be an L type (probability $\frac{1}{2}$), and it has to form a peptide chemical bond (probability $\frac{1}{2}$). In combining probabilities we have to multiply them. This one gets a chance of $\frac{1}{80}$ for the first amino acid, $\frac{1}{6,400}$ for two, etc. For 100 specific amino acids the chance of getting the right kind of protein is only 1 out of the number 49 followed by 190 zeros (4.9×10^{-191}). Other similar calculations yield numbers that are also beyond the realm of plausibility.[20]

The problem is not just getting the amino acids in the right sequence and having them unite chemically. We also have to select the right kinds of amino acids from a vast number of randomly produced organic compounds in a prebiotic soup. The spark-discharge experiments of Miller mentioned above produced more different kinds of amino acids that do not occur in living organisms than the 20 that do.[21]

Ironically, the very same year (1953) that Miller reported on the synthesis of amino acids and other biomonomers, J. D. Watson and Francis Crick published their Nobel Prize-winning discovery of the structure of nucleic acids (DNA).[22] They found that the cell's hereditary information is arranged in the now-famous double helix structure of DNA (Figure 4.1). To express its hereditary information, the cell requires a sequence of three nucleotide bases to code for one amino acid. Through a marvelous and complex system of information transfer and interpretation, the cell assembles protein molecules. A simple bacterium can have 4 million nucleotide bases in its genetic repertoire, while more complicated organisms such as human beings will have more than 3,000 million. Curiously some amphibians and flowering plants have more than 10 times the number of nucleotide bases found in human beings. The smallest independent (probably) living organism—a mycoplasma—has 580,000 nucleotide bases providing the code for 482 genes.[23] In advanced organisms the function of much of the DNA is still unknown. Some of it is obviously critical to life, such as directing the production of thousands of protein molecules serving as body structure or as enzymes. The enzymes facilitate chemical reactions such as the synthesis of amino acids and hundreds to thousands of other changes. Sometimes one enzyme molecule can direct the chemical change of thousands of molecules per second, but most changes are slower. Such complex enzymes, with many highly organized and essential portions and shapes, challenge any theory that their origin was spontaneous. More recently, some have suggested that life started with some kind of self-replicating molecules.[24] All such ideas ignore the need for sophisticated, complex, integrated information to direct hundreds of metabolic functions in living systems.

The improbabilities mentioned above for the assembling of amino acids into proteins are minor compared to those for assembling nucleotides into DNA. Could this all get started by chance?

In 1965 at two consecutive picnic lunches in Geneva, Switzerland, what has been described as a rather weird discussion generated a landmark study. Four mathematicians and two biologists were present. The mathematicians challenged the biologists by expressing their doubts about evolution from a probability standpoint. The heated debate ended with a proposition to study the disputed points in a more systematic way. That study culminated in a symposium held at the Wistar Institute in Philadelphia. The participants were primarily biologists, along with a few mathematicians who challenged the plausibility of evolutionary concepts. The almost-verbatim record of the symposium has been published,[25] and while complex, it is not dull reading! The biologists weren't too happy about the challenges to evolution. They insisted that the mathematicians did not understand evolution, but they did not provide any quantitative answers to the challenges.

As an example, Murray Eden, of the Massachusetts Institute of Technology, raised the question as to the probability of getting genes in order along the nucleic acid biopolymers (chromosomes) of the well-studied bacterium *Escherichia coli*. This organism is so small that we could put 500 end to end in one millimeter (12,500 per inch). But the bacterium has a number of genes arranged in exactly the right sequence in which they are used. How did they get from an original random origin into the right order by chance? Eden calculated that if one spread the bacterium over the earth's surface in a two-centimeter-thick layer, there is a chance that two genes would be brought into their proper position in 5,000 million years (a generous estimate for the length of life on earth). But even this long period of time gives no time for other genes to get in order, or for the genes to evolve—a much more complex process. Nor does it provide time for the evolution of other organisms, some of which are several hundred times more complex. Suffice it to say that the very long time postulated for the evolution of life on earth is far too brief when we examine the improbable events postulated. This landmark symposium helped accentuate a general dissatisfaction with contemporary explanations for the origin of life and encouraged some evolutionists to look for alternatives.

THE CELL

A still more complex problem for evolution is the difficulty of organizing biopolymers into functional units called cells. A cell (Figures 4.3 and 4.4) is a highly important unit, for it keeps the genetic information of the nucleic acids close to where the organism manufactures proteins, and in turn keeps these proteins close to the multitude of chemicals they act upon. The major gap between biopolymers and a functional cell is another of the great questions about the origin of life. A gradual evolutionary process to form a cell could be proposed, but until fully formed, many of the advantages of a cell would not exist.

FIGURE 4.3

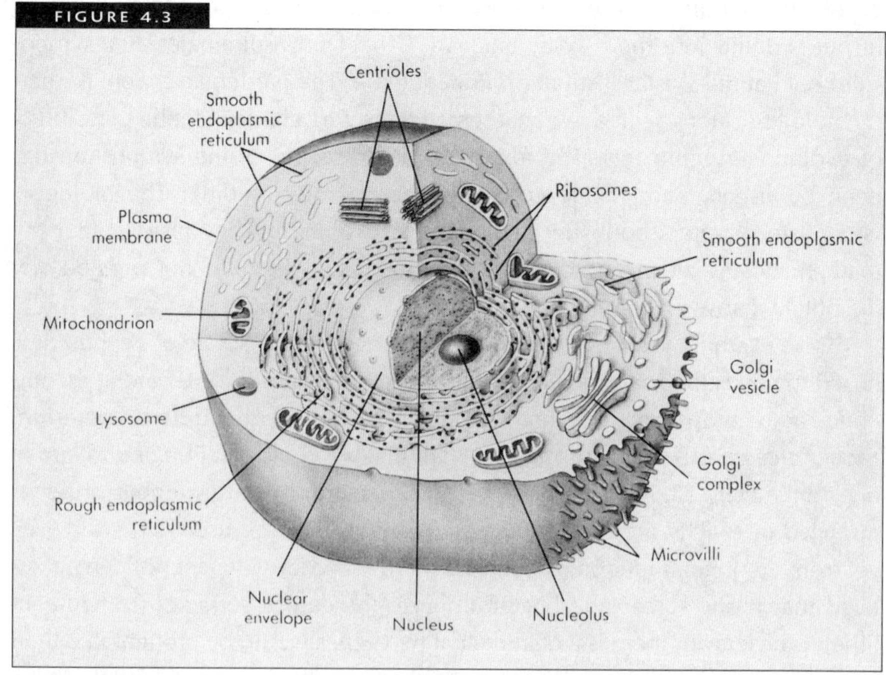

A typical animal cell.*

*From Raven PH, Johnson GB. Biology, updated version, 3rd ed.

In addition to getting the right proteins and DNA, cells need many other kinds of complex molecules, such as fats and carbohydrates. While it seems unreasonably fortuitous for the right kinds of chemicals to ever appear, it is even much less likely that they should all appear at the same time and place and then

FIGURE 4.4

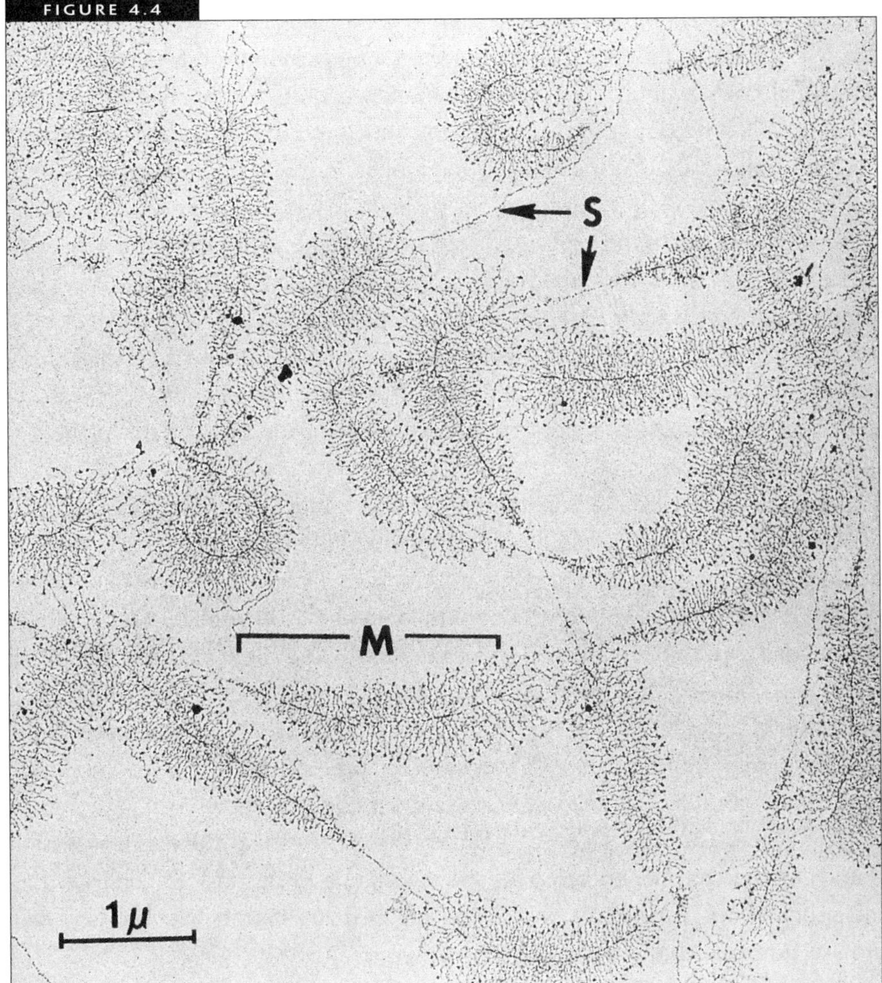

Electron micrograph of DNA strands coding for RNA. The DNA strands (S) are often covered with fine "branches" of RNA forming a cone-shaped matrix (M). The code of S is reflected in each branch of M as they are produced. The branch first starts out short and gets longer as they move along S, until they drop off when they are complete. Many special enzyme molecules (proteins) are involved in this complicated process. The 1μ scale unit is 1/1,000 of a millimeter.*

*From Miller OL, Beatty BR. Portrait of a gene, Journal of Cellular Physiology 74(2); Supplement:225-232. Copyright © 1969 Wistar Institute of Anatomy and Biology. Reprinted by permission of Wiley-Liss, Inc., a subsidiary of John Wiley and Sons, Inc.

be wrapped up in a cell membrane to start a living organism. Nevertheless, scientists have made some suggestions along this line.

One proposal suggests that some form of primitive cell called a protocell could have appeared spontaneously. Oparin[26] suggested that cells might form when large molecules combine together into spherical masses called coacervates. The chemist Sidney Fox[27] managed to get amino acids to combine eventually into spherical masses called microspheres. Such models, however, overlook the actual complexity of cells.[28] Commenting on both coacervates and microspheres, William Day, who still argues for some kind of biological evolutionary process, comments: "No matter how you look at it, this is scientific nonsense."[29]

It might be possible on a superficial level to equate protocells with real cells. Both are small and consist of organic molecules, but the similarity ends there. A living cell is an immensely complex structure that is a marvel of integrated chemical activity. Two molecular biologists have described the cell's formation from macromolecules as "a jump of fantastic dimensions, which lies beyond the range of testable hypothesis. In this area all is conjecture. The available facts do not provide a basis for postulating that cells arose on this planet."[30] Life is very special!

Harold J. Morowitz, using thermodynamics (the energy relationship between atoms and molecules), has calculated that the probability of the spontaneous organization of organic molecules to form a very small, simple microbe such as *Escherichia coli* is only 1 out of the number 1 followed by 100,000 million zeros ($10^{-10^{11}}$). For the smallest known free-living forms, the mycoplasma, which are about 0.0002 millimeter in diameter, he calculates a probability of 1 out of the number 5 followed by 1,000 million zeros ($10^{-5 \times 10^{9}}$). Not much of an improvement.[31] Many other such calculations indicate how complex life is and how highly improbable are the chances that it could arise by itself.

The Nobel Laureate George Wald once expressed the dilemma of evolution: "One has only to contemplate the magnitude of this task to concede that the spontaneous generation of a living organism is impossible. Yet here we are—as a result, I believe, of spontaneous generation."[32]

It is difficult to envision how a living system could have gotten started when we consider the complexity of even the simplest known organisms. A mandatory interdependent relationship exists between the components. For instance, the system for translating information from nucleic acids (DNA) to a finished protein product[33] requires at least 70, and probably as many as 200, different proteins.[34] The system will not work without the presence of each special protein. In addition, the proteins are necessary for the production of the nucleic acids, and the nucleic acids are required to produce the proteins. How did this interaction ever begin? Some have argued that RNA could get things started by self-replication (see below). Unfortunately, this does not explain how the RNA itself first appeared, and it is a big step from just RNA to the complex translating system found in living organisms. A gradual development is difficult to envision, since the system does not easily break down into separate functional units. It works largely as a whole, with most parts dependent on other ones.

Furthermore, a living system is not just a collection of biopolymers, etc., at normal chemical equilibrium inside a cell membrane. That would be a dead cell. The thousands of chemical changes occurring in a cell are at nonequilibrium, which is a basic requirement of the living process. In the origin of life, the metabolic motor has to get started. Biochemist George T. Javor illustrates this by comparing water in a container that is still (dead, or at equilibrium) to water flowing slowly from a source through a container (live, or nonequilibrium).[35]

But even this is not sufficient. One of the characteristics of living organisms is the ability to reproduce. Reproduction is a complex process involving precise replication of the most complex parts of the cell. Such a process must be programmed into the genetic repertoire of the cell. It is very difficult to think that all of this developed purely by chance.[36] Creationists sometimes face criticism for believing in miracles, but to believe that life arose spontaneously on earth without intelligent design appears to be even more of a "miracle."

OTHER IDEAS

While the scientific community generally accepts the concept that life developed spontaneously, the failure of probability studies to offer a plausible explanation for how it could happen in the postulated manner has resulted in a plethora of speculative alternatives. We will list six.

1. Some propose that elementary matter may have some special unknown properties that inevitably must have generated life. Scientists have called this the biochemical predestination model.[37] However, we have no evidence that the complex information such as is coded in nucleic acids exists in the chemical elements themselves.[38]

2. Another alternative is that life arose as a self-generating, interacting cyclic system of proteins and nucleic acids aided by the input of energy.[39] The model has such complex basic units that it is not very helpful.[40]

3. Possibly life originated in hot hydrothermal springs in the ocean.[41] Such an environment would offer some protection against certain adverse environmental effects. However, the heat could be lethal to delicate molecules, and it

requires that we account for the improbable development of complex life as we know it in a very limited and specialized environment.

4. It has been suggested that life did not originate as a cell type of structure, but on the surface of a solid such as a crystal of pyrite (fool's gold).[42] But we have no reason whatsoever to believe that the very simple arrangement of atoms in a pyrite crystal would provide the needed pattern for complex biological molecules.[43]

5. Another similar alternative is that the genes of life became organized using clay minerals as a pattern.[44] This model suffers from the same defect as the previous one. The simple orderliness of clay minerals contributes little to the high-grade specific complexity of proteins and nucleic acids.

6. Another suggestion is that the type of nucleic acid called RNA, which has some enzymatic properties of its own, could provide its own self-replication, thus starting life.[45] This idea has received a fair amount of attention recently. Researchers often refer to an ancient "RNA world"[46] and to "ribozymes," which are RNA molecules functioning as enzymes.[47] The model has many problems.[48] How did the first RNA originate? The RNA components are difficult to produce even under the best of laboratory conditions, let alone on a primitive earth. Discussing RNA replication, the Nobel Prize-winning biochemist Christian de Duve, who supports the concept of an RNA world, admits: "The problem is not as simple as might appear at first glance. Attempts at engineering—with considerably more foresight and technical support than the prebiotic world could have enjoyed—an RNA molecule capable of catalyzing RNA replication have failed so far."[49] Even if the right kind of RNA did somehow form, how does it acquire the comprehensive information necessary for guiding complex living systems? From the perspective of chemical evolution, the origin of the complexity of life remains an unresolved problem.

All these various ideas appear quite subjective, testifying to how far current explanations are from producing convincing evidence. Nobel Laureate Francis Crick candidly admits, "Every time I write a paper on the origin of life I swear I will never write another one, because there is too much speculation running after too few facts."[50] Stanley Miller reflects the same concern in expressing that the field needs a dramatic finding to constrain the rampant speculation.[51]

CONCLUSIONS

Pasteur demonstrated that only life begets life. Since that time an enormous amount of research has attempted to demonstrate how life could have arisen from nonliving material. Science has had some success in producing simple biomonomers in the laboratory. However, the relation of such experiments to what could have occurred on a raw prebiotic earth is suspect. Problems of concentration, stability, specific mirror image, and lack of geological evidence for a primordial soup make the scenario of chemical evolution extremely unlikely. Concerning the origin of highly organized biopolymers, the probability of their occurrence is too low to be given serious consideration for their accidental appearance. The problem further compounds when we consider the requirement for hundreds to many thousands of chemical changes working together simultaneously in a "simple" cell.

The problems associated with chemical evolution are resolved by some kind of creation. The data related to the origin of life favor the idea of a mastermind and a directed nonrandom process involved in the creation of life on earth. If we choose to eliminate the concept of a Creator, we have little choice but to accept some kind of chemical evolution, but the scientific data against such concepts are so compelling that reason would suggest that we explore other alternatives.

REFERENCES

1. Taylor GR. 1983. The great evolution mystery. New York and Cambridge: Harper and Row, p. 199.
2. See Partington JR. 1961. A history of chemistry, vol. 2. London: Macmillan and Co., p. 217.
3. Farley J. 1977. The spontaneous generation controversy from Descartes to Oparin. Baltimore and London: Johns Hopkins University Press, pp. 14, 15.
4. *Ibid.,* p. 6.
5. Vallery-Radot R. 1924. The life of Pasteur. Devonshire, Mrs RL, translator. Garden City, N.Y.: Doubleday, Page and Co., p. 109. Translation of: La vie de Pasteur.
6. Darwin F, editor. 1888. The life and letters of Charles Darwin, vol. 3. London: John Murray, p. 18.
7. Oparin AI. 1938. Origin of life. 2nd ed. Morgulis S, translator. New York: Dover Publications. Translation of: Vozniknovenie zhizni na zemle.
8. Miller SL. 1953. A production of amino acids under possible primitive earth conditions. Science 117:528, 529.
9. Evard R, Schrodetzki D. 1976. Chemical evolution. Origins 3:9-37.
10. A brief review of the problem appears in: Cohen J. 1995. Getting all turned around over the origins of life on earth. Science 267:1265, 1266.
11. (a) Bradley D. 1994. A new twist in the tale of nature's asymmetry. Science 264:908; (b) Clery D, Bradley D. 1994. Underhanded "breakthrough" revealed. Science 265:21.
12. (a) Brooks J, Shaw G. 1973. Origin and development of living systems. London and New York: Academic Press, p. 359; (b) Thaxton CB, Bradley WL, Olsen RL. 1984. The mystery of life's origin: reassessing current theories. New York: Philosophical Library, p. 65.
13. Hull DE. 1960. Thermodynamics and kinetics of spontaneous generation. Nature 186:693, 694.
14. Thaxton, Bradley, and Olsen, pp. 99-112 (note 12b).
15. Monod J. 1971. Chance and necessity: an essay on the natural philosophy of modern biology. New York: Alfred A. Knopf, pp. 112, 113.
16. Radman M, Wagner R. 1988. The high fidelity of DNA duplication. Scientific American 259(2):40-46.
17. Crick F. 1981. Life itself: its origin and nature. New York: Simon and Schuster, p. 51.

18. Erbrich P. 1985. On the probability of the emergence of a protein with a particular function. Acta Biotheoretica 34:53-80.
19. Bradley WL, Thaxton CB. 1994. Information and the origin of life. In: Moreland JP, editor. The creation hypothesis: scientific evidence for an intelligent designer. Downers Grove, Ill.: InterVarsity Press, pp. 173-210.
20. (a) Thaxton, Bradley, and Olsen, p. 65 (note 12b); (b) Yockey HP. 1977. A calculation of the probability of spontaneous biogenesis by information theory. Journal of Theoretical Biology 67:377-398.
21. Miller SL, Orgel LE. 1974. The origins of life on the earth. Englewood Cliffs, N.J.: Prentice-Hall, Inc., pp. 85, 87.
22. Watson JD, Crick FHC. 1953. Molecular structure of nucleic acids: a structure for deoxyribose nucleic acid. Nature 171:737, 738.
23. (a) Avers CJ. 1989. Process and pattern in evolution. New York and Oxford: Oxford University Press, Figure 4.24, pp. 142, 143; (b) Fraser CM, Gocayne JD, White O, Adams MD, Clayton RA, Fleishchmann RD, Bult CJ, Kerlavage AR, Sutton G, Kelley JM, and others. 1995. Science 270:397-403; (c) Goffeau A. 1995. Life with 482 genes. Science 270:445, 446.
24. (a) Dagani R. 1992. Synthetic self-replicating molecules show more signs of life. Chemical and Engineering News (February 24), pp. 21-23; (b) Reggia JA, Armentrout SL, Chou H-H, Peng Y. 1993. Simple systems that exhibit self-directed replication. Science 259:1282-1287.
25. Moorhead PS, Kaplan MM, editors. 1967. Mathematical challenges to the neo-Darwinian interpretation of evolution. The Wistar Institute Symposium Monograph No. 5. Philadelphia: Wistar Institute Press.
26. Oparin, pp. 150-162 (note 7).
27. (a) Fox SW, Harada K, Krampitz G, Mueller G. 1970. Chemical origins of cells. Chemical and Engineering News (June 22), pp. 80-94; (b) Fox SW, Dose K. 1972. Molecular evolution and the origin of life. San Francisco: W. H. Freeman and Co.
28. Thaxton, Bradley, and Olsen, pp. 174-176 (note 12b).
29. Day W. 1984. Genesis on planet earth: the search for life's beginning. 2nd ed. New Haven and London: Yale University Press, pp. 204, 205.
30. Green DE, Goldberger RF. 1967. Molecular insights into the living process. New York and London: Academic Press, pp. 406, 407.
31. Morowitz HJ. 1968. Energy flow in biology: biological organization as a problem in thermal physics. New York and London: Academic Press, p. 67.
32. Wald G. 1954. The origin of life. Scientific American 191(2)44-53.
33. Kenyon DH. 1989. Going beyond the naturalistic mindset in origin-of-life research. Origins Research 12(1, Spring/Summer):1, 5, 14-16.
34. Mills GC. 1990. Presuppositions of science as related to origins. Perspectives on Science and Christian Faith 42(3):155-161.
35. Javor GT. 1987. Origin of life: a look at late twentieth-century thinking. Origins 14:7-20.
36. Scott A. 1985. Update on Genesis. New Scientist (2 May), pp. 30-33.
37. Kenyon DH, Steinman G. 1969. Biochemical predestination. New York and London: McGraw-Hill Book Co.
38. Wilder-Smith AE. 1970. The creation of life: a cybernetic approach to evolution. Wheaton, Ill.: Harold Shaw Publishers, pp. 119-124.
39. Eigen M, Schuster P. 1979. The hypercycle: a principle of natural self-organization. Berlin, Heidelberg, and New York: Springer-Verlag.
40. Walton JC. 1977. Organization and the origin of life. Origins 4:16-35.
41. Corliss JB. 1990. Hot springs and the origin of life. Nature 347:624.
42. Wächtershäuser G. 1988. Before enzymes and templates: theory of surface metabolism. Microbiological Review 52:452-484.
43. Javor GT. 1989. A new attempt to understand the origin of life: the theory of surface-metabolism. Origins 16:40-44.
44. Cairns-Smith AG, Hartman H, editors. 1986. Clay minerals and the origin of life. Cambridge:

Cambridge University Press.
45. Orgel LE. 1986. Mini review: RNA catalysis and the origins of life. Journal of Theoretical Biology 123:127-149.
46. Gilbert W. 1986. The RNA world. Nature 319:618.
47. For recent reviews, see: (a) Maurel M-C. 1992. RNA in evolution: a review. Journal of Evolutionary Biology 5:173-188; (b) Orgel L. 1994. The origin of life on the earth. Scientific American 271(4, October):76-83.
48. (a) Gibson LJ. 1993. Did life begin in an "RNA World"? Origins 20:45-52; (b) Horgan J. 1991. In the beginning . . . Scientific American 264(2):116-125; (c) Mills GC, Kenyon D. 1996. The RNA World: a critique. Origins and Design 17(1):9-16; (d) Shapiro R. 1984. The improbability of prebiotic nucleic acid synthesis. Origins of Life 14:565-570.
49. De Duve C. 1995. The beginning of life on earth. American Scientist 83:428-437.
50. Crick, p. 153 (note 17).
51. Mentioned in Horgan (note 48b).

CHAPTER 5

THE SEARCH FOR AN EVOLUTIONARY MECHANISM

Ideas too sometimes fall from the tree before they are ripe.

—*Ludwig Wittgenstein*[1]

If you set 20 children free in a toy shop, something is certain to happen. Assuredly, the well-ordered stock of toys will become less organized. The longer the children revel in the store, the more mixed-up the stock will become. Active things naturally tend to mix. Molecules of perfume from an open bottle diffuse through the air—they do not collect from the air to become concentrated in a bottle. A hot iron brought into a room will warm up the room a little as the iron cools a lot and the heat becomes distributed more evenly. Pollution poured into the sea tends to disperse into earth's large oceans.

These crude examples illustrate the second law of thermodynamics. This physical law formalizes the well-observed phenomenon that naturally occurring processes tend toward randomness. Sometimes scientists use the word "entropy" to designate such randomness. Entropy is the equivalent of "mixed-upness." In other words, as things get more mixed up, entropy increases. This increase is illustrated almost daily on my desk as I try to find important items while letters, telephone messages, manuscripts, journals, faxes, E-mail, and advertisements pour in.

The trend toward "mixed-upness" in nature runs counter to evolution, which postulates changes from disorganized molecules to "simple" life (which is actually highly organized). Evolution is then assumed to form more complicated organisms with specialized tissues and organs. Some evolutionists suggest that the occasional self-organization of simple matter, such as we see in the formation of crystals, or the wave pattern that sometimes happens when chemicals migrate through solid matter,[2] might be a model for the self-organization of matter into living things. But a vast chasm exists between simple crystals and the complexities of living systems. Development toward functional complexity runs counter to the general tendency toward chaotic "mixed-upness." Here we observe one of the major problems of naturalistic evolution. While some have debated whether the second law of thermodynamics applies to evolution or not,[3] few would argue against a trend toward randomness in nature, or that evolution needs to explain why the opposite should happen at all.

Scientists have conducted a long and arduous search for a plausible evolutionary mechanism that would produce complex organized life from random events. In this chapter we shall look at the past two centuries of this search. Table 5.1 provides a summary of the proposed explanations.

LAMARCKISM

As I walked into Paris's famous park called the Jardin des Plantes, an imposing statue arrested my attention. The inscription at the base read in French: "Lamarck, founder of the doctrine of evolution." Having heard so many times that Charles Darwin was responsible for the theory of evolution, I mused about

TABLE 5.1

DESIGNATION AND DATE	MAIN PROPONENTS	CHARACTERISTICS
Lamarckism 1809-1859	Lamarck	Use causes development of new characteristics that become inheritable.
Darwinism 1859-1894	Darwin, Wallace	Small changes are acted upon by natural selection causing survival of fittest. Inheritance by gemmules.
Mutations 1894-1922	Morgan, de Vries	Emphasis on larger mutational changes. Natural selection not as important.
Modern Synthesis (neo-Darwinism) 1922-1968	Chetverikov, Dobzhansky, Fisher Haldane, Huxley, Mayr Simpson, Wright	Unified attitude. Changes in populations important. Small mutations acted upon by natural selection. Relation to traditional classification.
Diversification 1968-present	Eldredge, Gould, Grassé, Hennig, Kauffman, Kimura, Lewontin, Patterson, Platnick	Multiplicity of conflicting ideas, dissatisfaction with neo-Darwinism. Search for a cause for complexity.

EVOLUTIONARY MECHANISMS

the inscription and the attitudes we so often find associated with nationalistic pride. However, the French can justifiably take pride in their hero, because Lamarck had given a fairly comprehensive theory of evolution many decades before Darwin.

Jean-Baptiste Antoine de Monet, Chevalier de Lamarck (1744-1829)[4] believed in a Supreme Originator of existence, and that life diversified on its own over long periods of time. Impressed with the variety of life forms from simple to complex he observed in nature, he postulated a continuous evolutionary series. He attributed the common absence of intermediates between groups of organisms to gaps in human knowledge.

Lamarck is most famous for devising a mechanism for evolution based on his concept of use and disuse. He proposed that the use of an organ encouraged its development, and this improvement is passed on to the next generation. Thus characteristics accentuated by use in a parent appeared more strongly in the offspring. For instance, a deerlike animal needing to reach leaves on the highest branches of a tree would, after the stretching of many necks for many generations, acquire a longer neck and eventually emerge as a giraffe. Similarly, he declared that if one removed the left eye of children for a number of succeeding generations, eventually individuals would be born with only one eye. To Lamarck, the manner of life determined the eventual evolutionary development of organisms.

Science now considers Lamarck's mechanism for evolution as essentially invalid. Many years later the German evolutionist August Wiseman became notorious for cutting off the tails of mice. Though he did this for many generations, the mice continued to produce offspring with full-length tails. He concluded that his experiments proved that individuals cannot inherit acquired characteristics and thus Lamarck's mechanism of evolution was wrong.

However, the issue has not been resolved that simply. Many scientists have supported Lamarck to a limited degree, and a number of experiments suggest some inheritance of environmentally induced characteristics.[5] Nevertheless, in many biological circles Lamarckism is a pejorative term.

DARWINISM[6]

A few decades later Charles Darwin (1809-1882) and Alfred Russel Wallace (1823-1913), two avid naturalists in England, both studied an important paper on population by T. R. Malthus. Malthus proposed that population grows geometrically (by multiplication), while food for the population grows arithmetically (by addition), a much slower process. Obviously, food will eventually run out. This shortage served as a basis for the evolutionary mechanisms proposed by both Darwin and Wallace. In 1859 Darwin published his famous book *On the Origin of Species by Natural Selection, or the Preservation of Favoured Races in the Struggle for Life*. Darwin has usually received credit for the theory, although ideas about evolution had existed for centuries. In general, Wallace and Darwin supported each other, with Wallace taking a secondary place. It has been reported that Wallace also believed in spiritualism and testified in favor of the famous American spiritualist medium Henry Slade, who was on trial for fraud during one of his séances. Darwin was on the other side of the issue, contributing funds for Slade's prosecution.[7]

Darwin believed that variation occurred in living organisms, and that an overproduction of offspring results in both shortages and competition. Only the fittest of the new varieties will survive, and they in turn will produce similarly fit offspring. Thus the fittest, considered more advanced, endure through the process called natural selection. Darwin used this mechanism to explain evolutionary development despite the opposite tendency in nature.

He also stressed the broader theory of the evolution of organisms from the simplest to the most complex. Presenting this process, he placed special emphasis on the significance of minute changes, a concept that others soon challenged. The philosopher Marjorie Grene has delineated the problem: "By what right are we to extrapolate the pattern by which colour or other such superficial characters are governed to the origin of species, let alone of classes, orders, phyla of living organisms?"[8]

Charles Darwin developed his ideas before science had much information about genetics. In order to explain inheritance of new features, Darwin proposed a "pangenesis" model that had a strong component of Lamarckian inheritance of acquired characteristics. He suggested that the reproductive cells of organisms had "gemmules" that came from all over the body and passed on the individual's acquired characteristics to its offspring. Modern genetics has not found a basis for such a concept.

While many scientists accepted the general idea of evolution soon after the publication of Darwin's *Origin of Species*, others questioned many of Darwin's ideas and still challenge them today. The biological historian Charles Singer candidly states that Darwin's "arguments are frequently fallacious."[9] Among the most serious criticisms is the lack of survival value of small changes, changes that are not useful unless they can function in a complex whole that still has not yet evolved. For instance, in evolving a new muscle in a fish, what use would that muscle be until it had a connecting nerve so that it could contract? And what use would the nerve be until the brain had evolved a system to control that muscle's activity properly?[10] In addition, animals with useless but potential parts might actually be at a disadvantage. Such awkward or incomplete stages would probably not be able to survive and would get eliminated by the competition postulated by the model. Natural selection can serve in nature to eliminate aberrant types, but not to produce new complex structures that would not have survival value until all necessary parts have evolved to form a functional system.

The concept of "survival of the fittest" of itself has also faced severe criticism, possibly at times unfairly. Sometimes critics characterize it as a tautology (involving circular reasoning).[11] Darwinism proposed that organisms survive through the evolutionary process because they have gradually changed and become better fit, and the way one determines they are better fit is that they survive. In a sense the system is certain to work. Survival of the fittest does not demonstrate evolution, as sometimes claimed. Often it cannot be easily tested. That, however, is not the same as saying it is false. But obviously the fittest would survive whether they evolved or were created. Despite these flaws, Darwin's basic idea receives strong support from a number of evolutionists.[12]

MUTATIONS

Toward the end of the nineteenth century evolutionists began to ask serious questions about Darwin's mechanism of evolution. They had rediscovered the principles of genetics outlined by the Moravian monk Gregor Mendel, published 35 years earlier. His findings raised some questions about Darwin's views of inheritance. Prominent among the detractors of Darwinism was the Dutch botanist Hugo de Vries (1848-1935), who vigorously challenged the idea that small changes provided the basic evolutionary mechanism. He argued that such small changes meant nothing, and larger changes, called mutations, would be necessary to respond to the environment. De Vries found support for his views around Amsterdam, Holland, where the evening primrose imported from America had gone wild and some specimens became dwarfs. He considered the transformation to be a mutation.

De Vries conducted experiments by breeding thousands of plants, and he noted several major changes that he also attributed to mutation. He believed that such "new forms" acted as steps in a protracted evolutionary process. Unfortunately for de Vries' view, the changes were only the result of combinations of traits already present in the genetic makeup of the plants, and not new mutations.

Nevertheless, the concept of mutations as new hereditary information became accepted, largely because of the work of the American T. H. Morgan.

Experimenting with fruit flies, Morgan found new permanent changes that *bred true*. However, the examples he observed were largely degenerative instead of progressive, including loss of wings, bristles, and eyes.

The most commonly used illustration of evolution, the darkening of the English peppered moth, is not a mutation, although it has sometimes been described that way.[13] The moth population, which turned darker during the Industrial Revolution as soot blackened the environment, has been called a "striking evolutionary change."[14] Turning darker protected the moth from predation by birds as it matched the darkening color of its environment and thus could not be easily seen. The change, however, occurred through the manifestation of genes for darker color already present in the moth population. It was only a fluctuation in different kinds of genes and not new "permanent" genetic information, as we would expect from a mutation, a fact well acknowledged now.[15] As a result of modern attempts to control pollution and clean up the environment, the moth population is returning to a lighter color. However, the example does illustrate well the action of natural selection on simple gene fluctuation.

Evolutionary biologists still employ the concept of mutation, although explosive advances in modern genetics threaten the usefulness of such a general term. A mutation can refer to a variety of genetic changes, such as: a change in a nucleotide base on the DNA chain, an altered gene position, the loss of a gene, duplication of a gene, or insertion of a foreign genetic sequence. All of them represent more or less permanent genetic changes passed on to offspring. Researchers are also considering newer ideas, such as the heresy that the environment or the cell itself may stimulate the production of mutations.[16] We have only begun to find out about what appear to be extremely complicated biological mechanisms.

Living organisms show remarkable powers of adaptation through genetic changes. Flies become resistant to insecticides such as DDT, and our frequent use of antibiotics has created "supergerms" immune to most of them. The remarkable persistence of living organisms under varied and adverse conditions gives us hints that there may be systems for at least limited adaptation. On the other hand, thousands of laboratory experiments with bacteria, plants, and animals witness to the fact that the changes that a species can tolerate have definite limits. There appears to be a tight cohesion of interacting systems that will accept only limited change without inviting disaster. After decades or centuries of experimentation, fruit flies retain their basic body plan as fruit flies, and wool-producing sheep remain basically sheep. Aberrant types tend to be inferior, usually do not survive in nature, and, given a chance, tend to breed back to their original types. Scientists sometimes call this phenomenon genetic inertia (genetic homeostasis).[17]

Scientists have questioned for a long time the usefulness of mutations as an evolutionary mechanism. Favorable mutations are extremely rare, and most mutations are recessive—that is, they will not manifest themselves unless present in both parents. Furthermore, while mutations producing minor changes may survive, those causing significant modification are especially detrimental and unlikely to persist. Douglas Erwin and James Valentine, two evolutionists from the University of California, Santa Barbara campus, comment: "Viable mutations with major morphological or physiological effects are exceedingly rare and usually infertile; the chance of two identical rare mutant individuals arising in sufficient propinquity to produce offspring seems too small to consider as a significant evolutionary event."[18] The authors suggest changes in the developmental process of organisms as a means of producing major evolutionary changes, but experimental demonstration of this is only suggestive.

It would require many nonharmful mutations to produce the characteristics of a single useful structure. The problem is how to get such extremely rare events to occur simultaneously in an organism in order to produce a functional structure that might have some survival value. The evolutionist E. J. Ambrose has outlined the problem: "The frequency with which a single non-harmful mutation is known to occur is about 1 in 1,000. The probability that two favourable mutations would occur is 1 in $10^3 \times 10^3$, 1 in a million. Studies of *Drosophila* [fruit fly] have revealed that large numbers of genes are involved in the formation of the separate structural elements. There may be 30-40 involved in a single wing structure. It is most unlikely that fewer than five genes could ever be involved in the formation of even the simplest new structure previously unknown in the organism. The probability now becomes one in one thousand million million. We already know that mutations in living cells appear once in ten million to once in one hundred thousand million. It is evident that the probability of five favourable mutations occurring within a single life cycle of an organism is effectively zero."[19]

The noted French zoologist Pierre P. Grassé, who suggests another evolutionary mechanism, affirms some of the same concerns and states further that: "No matter how numerous they may be, mutations do not produce any kind of evolution."[20]

THE CREATIONIST VIEW OF MUTATIONS

Evolutionists often accuse creationists of believing that species do not change, a persistent and erroneous belief. But creationists actually recognize ample evidence for small variations in nature, as abundantly demonstrated in the breeding of dogs, in field observations of many organisms, and in laboratory experiments. The Creator may have designed species to produce a variety of colors, etc., and limited adaptations. Creationists do not feel that science has produced any significant evidence to indicate that nature changes much beyond this level. On the other hand, evolutionists propose that the process of small variation has produced all living things on Earth, organisms as different as an orchid and a walrus.

A frequent question is: "At which category of biological classification (species, genera, families) do such limited changes no longer show up?" The question is important to the evolution-creation debate, with evolutionists proposing much larger changes than creationists. But we have no definite answer. For one thing, classification of organisms is both subjective and tentative. Characteristics of classification groups, such as those of species, genera, family, etc., can be easily redefined. Sometimes the terms *microevolution* (small changes) and *macroevolution* (large changes), along with *micromutation* and *macromutation,* designate different levels of change. Creationists generally accept the first concept and reject the second. Unfortunately, scientists have used the term macroevolution in so many different ways[21] that it is hardly useful. Generally science defines macroevolution as change above the species level. But many creationists would recognize some genera and higher classification categories as representing changes since creation, especially when dealing with degenerate parasites. However, these are exceptions. In a creation context, one could say that in general the genus or family level probably represents an original created type. G. A. Kerkut of the University of Southhampton in England has proposed the expressions "special theory of evolution" and "general theory of evolution" to deal, when in an evolutionary context, with the issue of evaluating how much change has taken place. His terminology is meaningful to the discussion: "There is a theory which states that many living animals can be observed over the course of time to undergo changes so that new species are formed. This can be called the 'Special Theory of Evolution' and can be demonstrated in certain cases by experiments. On the other hand there is the theory that all the living forms in the world have arisen from a single source which itself came from an inorganic form. This theory can be called the 'General Theory of Evolution' and the evidence that supports it is not sufficiently strong to allow us to consider it as anything more than a working hypothesis. It is not clear whether the changes that bring about speciation are of the same nature as those that brought about the development of new phyla. The answer will be found by future experimental work and not by dogmatic assertions that the General Theory of Evolution must be correct because there is nothing else that will satisfactorily take its place."[22]

Creationists would agree with the special theory of evolution, but not the general one.

The minute changes proposed by Darwin or the larger ones advocated by de Vries seem inadequate to produce the major alterations necessary for the general theory of evolution, such as the transformation from a sponge type into a sea urchin type. Evolution faces its most serious challenge at the level of the major groups (orders, classes, divisions, phyla, and kingdoms). If evolution occurred as a gradual continuous process, why do such ubiquitous gaps exist between major groups of organisms, such as clams, earthworms, or pine trees? In fact, why do we observe any gaps at all?[23]

MODERN SYNTHESIS

As evolutionary thought developed during the early part of the twentieth century, several influential scholars helped shift the focus from mutations back to natural selection. The most important were S. S. Chetverikov in Russia, R. A. Fisher and J.B.S. Haldane in England, and Sewall Wright in the United States. This time the emphasis focused on the process of evolution within whole populations of organisms, rather than on individual organisms.

Fisher developed sophisticated mathematical models of the effects of mutations in extremely large populations. To him, small mutations were the important ones, since larger mutations have a more detrimental effect on the organism. He emphasized the natural selection of small favorable variations. Wright knew much about breeding, and, in contrast to Fisher, emphasized the usefulness of small populations in which a rare mutation would have a better chance to manifest itself. On the other hand, small populations are more likely to suffer from the deleterious effects of inbreeding. Wright introduced the concept of random changes in gene frequency within a population resulting from chance alone. The significance of this process, called *genetic drift,* has been and still is one of the more protracted and heated debates among evolutionists. Fisher and Wright strongly shaped the evolutionary thinking of the 1920s and 1930s[24] and provided significant underpinning for the full development of the "modern synthesis."

The modern synthesis combined the efforts of a number of brilliant evolutionists, including Theodosius Dobzhansky of Columbia University, biologist

Sir Julian Huxley in England, and Ernst Mayr and George Gaylord Simpson at Harvard University. The concept was dominant from the 1930s to the 1960s. The name "modern synthesis" originated with Huxley,[25] the grandson of Darwin's champion Thomas Huxley, as he lauded the "final triumph" of Darwinism.[26] Basically it combines variation by mutations with Darwin's concept of natural selection by survival of the fittest as applied to populations. Nevertheless, the modern synthesis is difficult to characterize, because attempts have been made to incorporate into it such varied disciplines as systematics (classification), biological variation, and paleontology (study of fossils).[27]

Many of the leaders of the modern synthesis stressed that by accumulating relatively small changes one could produce the major changes needed for macroevolution. However, the basic mechanism of evolution continued to elude researchers. The controversy between Fisher and Wright as to the optimal size for evolving populations also remained unresolved. The historian of biology William B. Provine (Cornell University) points out: "The primary mechanism of microevolution was still undecided. . . . Elucidation of the genetic mechanisms of speciation is not one of the great triumphs of the evolutionary synthesis."[28]

The modern synthesis may have been more an attitude of success than a precise synthesis. During 1959 a number of celebrations around the world commemorated the centennial of the publication of Darwin's *Origin of Species*. They encouraged confidence in the modern synthesis. I was privileged to attend one of the most important of the celebrations, held at the University of Chicago. There I listened to the leading architects of the modern synthesis, including Dobzhansky, Mayr, Huxley, and Simpson. Their knowledgeability impressed me, but at the same time their confident dogmatism puzzled me. Little did I realize that within a few years the unified spirit of the modern synthesis would be in disarray.

Meanwhile, the majority of evolutionists systematically ignored the disquieting voices of the paleontologist Otto Schindewolf in Germany and the geneticist Richard Goldschmidt in the United States. In contrast to the fairly small mutation changes suggested by architects of the modern synthesis, both were proposing rapid, large changes and different mechanisms. Schindewolf, who was familiar with fossils, suggested very sudden developmental jumps to bridge the large gaps between fossil types. Goldschmidt, professor of genetics at the University of California at Berkeley, completely disagreed with the idea that small changes within species could slowly accumulate and produce the major transformations needed for significant evolutionary progress. He considered awkward intermediate stages to be useless for survival and felt that natural selection would not favor them. Among the examples he cited are the formation of a feather, segmentation of body structure as seen in insects, the development of muscles, and the compound eye of crabs.

Goldschmidt advocated sudden major genetic changes producing what he called "hopeful monsters." Some of his detractors called them "hopeless monsters." Of course, even with the existence of one hopeful monster, there still remains the problem of finding a mate, "for who will breed with a monster, hopeful or otherwise?"[29]

Since Goldschmidt sharply disagreed with the promoters of the modern synthesis on the value of small changes,[30] they largely rejected his views. Later, as the modern synthesis was being dismantled, attitudes changed. The science writer Gordon Rattray Taylor, in referring to Goldschmidt, states: "Twenty years ago, students were encouraged to snigger at the mention of his name. Today, however, many biologists are coming round to the view that he was pointing to the right problem."[31] From a creation perspective, it appears that Goldschmidt was indeed raising an important question. For a number of evolutionists, the modern synthesis no longer seems tenable.

DIVERSITY

The embryologist Søren Løvtrup, who supports evolution, points out: "And today the modern synthesis—neo-Darwinism—is not a theory, but a range of opinions which, each in its own way, tries to overcome the difficulties presented by the world of facts."[32] New ideas appeared, some of them quite speculative.[33] Additional discoveries, especially in molecular biology and genetics, indicated that older, simpler genetic concepts were no longer valid. All of this contributed to a mosaic of thoughts that prevail to the present and could be collectively characterized as diversity. This stage—which we can call the *diversity period*—represents an assortment of new and often-conflicting ideas. Some of them we will discuss in detail in chapter 8. They revolve around such questions as: (1) Can one identify the evolutionary relationships of organisms? (2) Are evolutionary changes gradual or sudden? (3) Is natural selection important to the evolutionary process? and (4) How does complexity evolve? The search for an evolutionary mechanism continues.

THE NEED FOR CAUTION

While scientists generally agree that evolution is fact, they disagree on the details. Some of the most heated battles in evolutionary biology followed the modern synthesis. The well-known writer Tom Bethell emphasizes that "especially in recent years, scientists have been fighting among themselves about Darwin and his ideas."[34] The general public seldom hears of such disputes, much less understands them. A great contrast exists between the internal intellectual battles of the academic community, as found in the research literature, and the simple authoritative style of textbooks. Some simplification in textbooks may be helpful in facilitating learning, but laypeople and students should become more aware of the varied views in the evolutionary debate.

CONCLUSIONS

One can look with only a degree of respect at the dedicated efforts of evolutionists to find a plausible mechanism for their theory. Their perseverance is commendable. They have presented one theory after another during a period of two centuries. Their general failure, however, raises a sobering question: Is evolutionary thought more a matter of opinion than of hard scientific data? I would not discount the fact that some data may favor evolution and that creationists also have opinion problems and an abundance of persistence. But after such a long and virtually futile search for an evolutionary mechanism, it would seem that evolutionary scientists should seriously consider the possibility of creation by a Designer.

REFERENCES

1. Wittgenstein L. 1980. Culture and value. Winch P, translator; Wright GHv, editor (with Nyman H). Chicago: University of Chicago Press, p. 27e. Translation of: Vermischte Bemerkungen.
2. (a) Goodwin B. 1994. How the leopard changed its spots: the evolution of complexity. New York and London: Charles Scribner's Sons, pp. 1-76; (b) Kauffman SA. 1993. The origins of order: self-organization and selection in evolution. New York and Oxford: Oxford University Press; (c) Waldrop MM. 1992. Complexity: the emerging science at the edge of order and chaos. New York and London: Touchstone Books, Simon and Schuster.
3. Some argue that the second law of thermodynamics does not apply to evolution, and covers only isolated or systems in thermal equilibrium; e.g., see: Trott R. 1993. Duane Gish and InterVarsity at Rutgers. Creation/Evolution 13(2):31. This contention does not remove the obvious fact that most undirected activity tends toward randomness. Consequently, there is an intense effort to find a mechanism for evolution.
4. For a general review of Lamarck's accomplishments, see: (a) Nordenskiöld E. 1942. The history of biology: a survey. Eyre LB, translator. New York: Tudor Publishing Co., pp. 316-330. Translation of: Biologins historia; (b) Singer C. 1959. A history of biology to about the year 1900: a general introduction to the study of living things. 3rd rev. ed. London and New York: Abelard-Schuman, pp. 296-300.
5. For many examples, see: Landman OE. 1991. The inheritance of acquired characteristics. Annual Review of Genetics 25:1-20.
6. The discussions of Darwinism have been legion. For a recent review that explores the mechanisms of evolution, see: Provine WB. 1985. Adaptation and mechanisms of evolution after Darwin: a study in persistent controversies. In: Kohn D, editor. The Darwinian heritage.

Princeton, N.J.: Princeton University Press, pp. 825-833.

7. See: Milner R. 1990. Slade Trial (1876). The encyclopedia of evolution: humanity's search for its origins. New York and Oxford: Facts on File, pp. 407, 408.
8. Grene M. 1959. The faith of Darwinism. Encounter 13(5):48-56.
9. Singer, p. 303. (note 4b).
10. See chapter 6 for further discussion.
11. (a) Waddington CH. 1957. The strategy of the genes: a discussion of some aspects of theoretical biology. London: Ruskin House, George Allen and Unwin, p. 65; (b) Eden M. 1967. Inadequacies of neo-Darwinian evolution as a scientific theory. In: Moorhead PS, Kaplan MM, editors. Mathematical challenges to the neo-Darwinian interpretation of evolution. The Wistar Institute Symposium Monograph No. 5. Philadelphia: Wistar Institute Press, pp. 5-12; (c) Peters RH. 1976. Tautology in evolution and ecology. The American Naturalist 110:1-12.
12. See, for instance, (a) the symposium volume edited by Kohn (note 6). Also: (b) Mayr E. 1982. The growth of biological thought: diversity, evolution, and inheritance. Cambridge and London: Belknap Press of Harvard University Press, pp. 626, 627; (c) Maynard Smith J. 1989. Did Darwin get it right? Essays on games, sex, and evolution. New York and London: Chapman and Hall.
13. For example: Sagan C. 1977. The dragons of Eden: speculation on the evolution of human intelligence. New York: Ballantine Books, p. 28.
14. For example: Keeton WT. 1967. Biological science. New York: W. W. Norton and Co., p. 672.
15. Jukes TH. 1990. Responses of critics. In: Johnson PE. Evolution as dogma: the establishment of naturalism. Dallas: Haughton Pub. Co., pp. 26-28.
16. (a) Cairns J, Overbaugh J, Miller S. 1988. The origin of mutants. Nature 335:142-145; (b) Opadia-Kadima GZ. 1987. How the slot machine led biologists astray. Journal of Theoretical Biology 124:127-135. For another view, see: (c) MacPhee D. 1993. Directed evolution reconsidered. American Scientist 81:554-561.
17. (a) Edey MA, Johanson DC. 1989. Blueprints: solving the mystery of evolution. Boston, Toronto, and London: Little, Brown, and Co., pp. 125, 126; (b) Mayr E. 1970. Population, species, and evolution: an abridgment of *Animal Species and Evolution*. Rev. ed. Cambridge: Belknap Press of Harvard University Press, pp. 181, 182.
18. Erwin DH, Valentine JW. 1984. "Hopeful monsters," transposons, and Metazoan radiation. Proceedings of the National Academy of Sciences 81:5482, 5483.
19. Ambrose EJ. 1982. The nature and origin of the biological world. Chichester: Ellis Horwood, Ltd., and New York and Toronto: Halsted Press, John Wiley and Sons, p. 120.
20. Grassé P-P. 1977. Evolution of living organisms: evidence for a new theory of transformation. Carlson BM, Castro R, translators. New York, San Francisco, and London: Academic Press, p. 88. Translation of: L'Évolution du Vivant.
21. Hoffman A. 1989. Arguments on evolution: a paleontologist's perspective. New York and Oxford: Oxford University Press, pp. 87-92.
22. Kerkut GA. 1960. Implications of evolution. Oxford and London: Pergamon Press, p. 157.
23. For a comprehensive discussion, see: Wise KP. 1994. The origins of life's major groups. In: Moreland JP, editor. The creation hypothesis: scientific evidence for an intelligent designer. Downers Grove, Ill.: InterVarsity Press, pp. 211-234.
24. For further details, see Provine, pp. 842-853 (note 6).
25. Huxley J. 1943. Evolution: the modern synthesis. London and New York: Harper and Brothers.
26. Gould SJ. 1982. Darwinism and the expansion of evolutionary theory. Science 216:380-387.
27. *Ibid.*
28. Provine, p. 862 (note 6).
29. Patterson C. 1978. Evolution. London: British Museum (Natural History) and Ithaca: Cornell University Press, p. 143.
30. Goldschmidt R. 1940. The material basis of evolution. New Haven, Conn.: Yale University Press.
31. Taylor GR. 1983. The great evolution mystery. New York: Harper and Row, p. 5.
32. Løvtrup S. 1987. Darwinism: the refutation of a myth. London, New York, and Sydney: Croom Helm, p. 352.

33. See chapter 8 for details.
34. Bethell T. 1985. Agnostic evolutionists: the taxonomic case against Darwin. Harper's 270 (1617; February):49-52, 56-58, 60, 61.

CHAPTER 6

FROM COMPLEX TO MORE COMPLEX

There was never miracle wrought
by God to convert an atheist,
because the light of nature might have
led him to confess a God.

—*Francis Bacon*[1]

A modern paraphrase is: "God never performed a miracle to convince an atheist, because His ordinary works can provide sufficient evidence."

The cell is an incredibly complicated structure in which sometimes tens of thousands of different enzymes direct interdependent chemical changes. Most of us, unfamiliar with cells, easily dismiss them without realizing that "small" is not necessarily synonymous with "simple." Actually, in many ways it is easier to consider questions about the origin of familiar larger organs and organisms than elusive cells. Included in the mystery of life are such wonders as the echo-locating system of the bat (a sonar), the development of an adult elephant from a single microscopic cell, or the transformation of a caterpillar into a butterfly. One can also wonder about such aesthetic delights as the magnificence of the stars on a clear night or the iridescent colors and intricate patterns on Brazilian butterfly wings. Humanity has long pondered such questions, not only wondering how it all happened but also why. Is there purpose in the workings of nature? Could all of nature's peculiarities and specializations have occurred without guidance?

In this chapter we will consider questions about design in nature and related topics. Such questions come close to the "lingering question" mentioned in the first chapter, and especially the related issue of whether our universe has a designer.

THE ARGUMENT FROM DESIGN

The degree of orderliness and specialization we find in nature seems beyond the randomness that we would expect if there were not some kind of inherent design behind it all. Philosophers call this proposition "the argument from design," or "the argument to design." The universe, and especially the earth, appears to be especially ordered to support life,[2] and life itself especially suggests design.

Recently the argument from design has received special support from a number of physicists-cosmologists who find that the universe could not accommodate life if it were not for a most fortuitous set of circumstances. The universe appears to have been fine-tuned to extremely close tolerances. Stephen Hawking, the Lucasian professor of mathematics at Cambridge (a post once held by Sir Isaac Newton), comments: "The odds against a universe like ours emerging out of something like the big bang are enormous. I think there are clearly religious implications."[3] The problem to him is that if the energy of the postulated bang had been too large, stars and planets would not form.[4] On the other hand, if it had been too small, the universe would collapse into oblivion. Hawking comments further: "If the rate of expansion one second after the big bang had been smaller by even one part in a hundred thousand million million, the universe would have recollapsed before it ever reached its present size."[5] This illustrates the implausibility of even this widely accepted concept without some design behind it. In a similar vein, the nuclear strong force that binds the nucleus of the atom also appears to be at a very precise value to permit the formation of the elements.[6] Research has also shown a number of other factors, such as gravity and electromagnetism, to be extremely fine-tuned. A change in the strength of electromagnetism of only 1 part in 1 followed by 40 zeros (10^{-40}) could spell disaster.[7] Ian Barbour describes it well: "The cosmos seems to be balanced on a knife edge."[8] All this suggests design more than undirected random activity. Moreover, many wonder if there is not some special intelligent guiding force behind living organisms that makes them so different from the nonliving.

Some evolutionists have considered the need for a directive entity to originate all the complexities of both simple and complex organisms. Through the years scientists have proposed many different kinds of concepts as special unknown factors responsible for the intricacy, purposefulness, or design that everywhere seems so evident in living things.[9] They have used many terms to designate their concepts. Among them are: entelechy, emergence, finality, typostrophism, aristogenesis, elan vital, teleology, vitalism, homogenesis, nemogenesis, preadaptation, saltation, orthogenesis[10]—almost anything or everything except the God of creation. The abundance of terms reflects both the mystery and the need for a special explanatory factor. Unfortunately, various writers and disciplines define and use such terms in different and sometimes conflicting ways. We need not go into detail in this brief treatise. Besides, such a pursuit is quite boring. But it is important to note that although theologians, scientists, and philosophers all discuss these matters, it is difficult to find any common approach. For some, design need not imply a designer, and for others a proposed designer need not be the God of the Judeo-Christian tradition. To still others the question is not just one of any kind of design, but of how and why design originated. I shall simplify this chapter by addressing only the question of whether nature reflects intelligent design.

Human beings have discussed the idea of design in nature[11] for several millennia. It was well entrenched in mythology and early biblical manuscripts. Socrates (469-394 B.C.) expressed great interest in the concept of purpose, and Aristotle (384-322 B.C.) supported the argument from design. For him, the universe yearns toward the perfect form that is God. In the Western world the most influential medieval philosopher along these lines was Thomas Aquinas (1225-1274). Among his arguments for the existence of God was that the evidence of design in nature implies an intelligent designer. Several centuries later most scientists took design in nature for granted. Some, such as Sir Isaac Newton (1642-1727), actively promoted the concept. However, the Scottish skeptic David Hume[12] (1711-1776) did his best to destroy the argument, intimating that evidence for design did not necessarily point to the God of the Judeo-Christian (i.e., biblical) tradition. He did not provide a mechanism to answer the argument from design,[13] except to suggest an organizing force within nature itself.

Nevertheless, around the beginning of the nineteenth century, thinkers began to consider ideas that organisms might have formed by themselves. This stimulated[14] the English philosopher and ethicist William Paley (1743-1805) to publish in 1802 his famous book entitled *Natural Theology*, which went through many editions. Paley has become famous in the design debate for his example of the watch. He reasoned that if you should find a watch on the ground with all its specialized parts working together to tell time, you would infer that the watch must have had a maker. He then pointed out that the complexities in nature likewise must have had a maker and could not have arisen by themselves. Then he argued further that because such instruments as a telescope had a designer, the eye must likewise have a designer. Furthermore, small gradual changes are inadequate to produce such a structure. As an example of the inadequacy of gradual development over time, he cites the epiglottis, that indispensable structure that closes our windpipe when we swallow and keeps food and drink from entering our lungs. Paley argued that the epiglottis would have been useless during any gradual evolutionary development over many generations, because it would not close the windpipe to the lungs before it was fully formed.[15]

About a half century later Charles Darwin published his *Origin of Species.* It proposed that small random changes in combination with natural selection would over time enable simple organisms to evolve to more and more advanced forms, including human beings. Well aware of the argument from design, Darwin, in the very first edition of the *Origin of Species,* addressed the question of "organs of extreme perfection and complication." "To suppose that the eye, with all its inimitable contrivances for adjusting the focus to different distances, for admitting different amounts of light, and for the correction of spherical and chromatic aberration, could have been formed by natural selection, seems, I freely confess, absurd in the highest possible degree."[16] Darwin then invoked natural selection as the solution to his dilemma, but, as we will discuss below, many unanswered questions remain.

A number of Darwin's followers have employed his methodology in answering the problem of design. The historian Gertrude Himmelfarb outlines it: "Darwin was quick to see the problem, but not so successful in resolving it. His technique here, as elsewhere, was first to assume that by acknowledging the difficulty, he had somehow exorcised it; and second, if this act of confession did not succeed in propitiating his critics, to bring to bear upon the difficulty the weight of authority of just that theory which was being called into question."[17]

Although Darwin on rare occasions referred to the possibility of some kind of design, and in the last paragraph of editions 2 through 6 of the *Origin of Species* even mentioned the Creator[18] as originating life before it evolved, a review of his private letters indicates that he was "in great doubt about it." To him natural selection was the answer to evolution's problems.[19]

Both theologians and scientists are still discussing the origin of complex structures, although most theologians now tend to leave the study of nature to the scientists and concentrate on sociological or religious issues.[20] The basic problem is: How can purposeless random mutations,[21] accompanied by a natural selection that has no foresight, create organs of extreme complexity? Some evolutionists downgrade or eliminate the natural selection process, leaving evolution purely to chance. Furthermore, as we discussed in the previous chapter, only extremely rarely are mutations considered useful. An estimate of one beneficial mutation out of 1,000 is generous to evolution. Mutations are overwhelmingly detrimental and usually recessive in their manifestations, which means they will not express themselves in the body of an organism unless both parents have the mutation. How could a process beset with so many limitations ever put together a complex organ such as an ear or a brain? Many hail natural selection, which proposes survival of the fittest, as the solution, but it selects only for the immediate advantage. It does not have an "eye" to look into the future, while complex organs or systems would require long-range planning. Reason would suggest we look for other solutions. Most evolutionists disagree.

Richard Dawkins, of Oxford University, in referring to Paley's watch, indicates that the "only watchmaker in nature is the blind forces of physics," and that "Darwin made it possible to be an intellectually fulfilled atheist."[22] Some evolutionists would disagree with Dawkins, but they represent a minority view. The German zoologist Bernhard Rensch lists more than a dozen scientists, some of them leading authorities, such as E. Henning, Henry Fairfield Osborn, and Otto Schindewolf, who have been dissatisfied with the mutation and/or natural selection explanation and feel, as mentioned above, that we need some special, mysterious factor to add to the equation. Rensch points out that "it is by no means clear what sort of factors and forces these could possibly be."[23] Ernst Mayr, of Harvard, who himself supports the modern synthesis, lists still other scientists[24] who hold the opinion that we need more to explain the development of complex structures and organisms. Sharing the same concern, the eminent French zoologist Pierre Grassé states: "A single plant, a single animal would require thousands and thousands of lucky, appropriate events. Thus, miracles would become the rule." Furthermore, he emphasizes: "What gambler would be crazy enough to play roulette with random evolution? The probability of dust carried by the wind reproducing Dürer's *Melancholia* is less infinitesimal than the probability of copy errors in the DNA molecule leading to the formation of the eye; besides, these errors had no relationship whatsoever with the function that the eye would have to perform or was starting to perform. There is no law against daydreaming, but science must not indulge in it."[25]

The lack of a relationship between random mutations and complex biological structures presents a major problem for evolution.

INTERDEPENDENCE

The concept of design is especially significant to biological systems consisting of functionally interdependent parts. Such systems simply will not operate until all of the necessary parts are present and working together. For instance, a home burglar alarm requires (1) sensors for doors or windows, (2) wires connecting to a control center, (3) a complex control center, (4) a source of power, (5) wires connecting an alarm, and (6) the alarm itself. Unless *all* these basic components are involved and functional, the system will not operate. To suggest that such a system could arise gradually, with each stage being functional, would be unreasonable. We can raise the same kind of question about parts of a watch or interdependent components of complex biological systems. Can purely random mutations and a natural selection process with no foresight result in complex structures such as a lung or even a taste bud when the structure would have no survival value until all the necessary parts are present? A taste bud is useless without a connecting nerve cell to the brain, and that nerve cell cannot do anything without a brain function that interprets the impulse from the nerve cell as a taste. In such interdependent systems nothing works until everything works.

The multitude of simultaneous changes required to produce a functional system seems implausible from an evolutionary standpoint. When we consider a model of the gradual development of an interdependent system, we have to postulate the presence of useless parts waiting around until they eventually become useful through some final random mutation. According to evolutionary theory, we should expect to find many newly developing organs or organ systems, but as we look at more than a million kinds of living organisms over the world, we see virtually none, if any, such postulated organs. The problem of interdependent parts challenges both the evolutionist who believes in larger, sudden random changes and the one who advocates smaller, gradual changes. For the former, the problems include: (1) the extremely fortuitous set of complex and sudden changes needed to produce a new viable interdependent system or organ, and (2) the absence of any experimental evidence of such a thing ever happening. For the one who believes in small changes, the problems include: (1) the survival of many nonfunctional or awkward, useless, intermediate stages in the face of a natural selection that would try to eliminate them, and (2) the apparent absence of any such intermediates in current living organisms.

Evolutionists sometimes suggest that intermediate forms could have a useful function in themselves. For instance, an animal might use half a wing to glide in strong winds. It is not difficult to postulate some kind of purpose for almost anything. The satirical French writer Voltaire, in his always hopeful *Candide,* points out facetiously that "noses were made to wear spectacles; and so we have spectacles."[26] (My apologies to Voltaire for using his taunting remark in a different way than he may have intended!) Closer to reality is an incident reported by John C. Fentress when he was at Cambridge. While studying field mice he noticed what appeared to be good, protective behavior patterns. A species that lives in the field tends to scurry into hiding when an object moves overhead so it cannot be caught, while a species dwelling in the forest freezes so it cannot be seen. He consulted some of his zoologist friends about his observations. Except that as a special test he switched the data so that the field mice supposedly froze and the forest mice ran. He reports: "I wish I had recorded their explanations, because they were very impressive indeed."[27] So the problem is not so much whether we can find any explanation, but whether we can find the correct explanation. In our present context the question is whether intelligent design or the combination of usually detrimental random mutations associated with a foresightless natural selection can best explain the extreme complexities of nature.

THE SIGNIFICANCE OF SIMILARITIES

During an open discussion forum at a large university, I once heard an undergraduate student complaining that evolutionists call a muscle in one kind of animal by one name, give the same name to a similar muscle in a different kind of animal, and then call it evolution. Similarity of terminology does not demonstrate evolution, and the student appears to have had a valid complaint. On the other hand, many living things show a number of striking similarities, and evolutionists frequently use them to support their case. By default, they represent an argument against design.

Most basic textbooks of biology and other publications supporting evolution[28] use the similarity of the arrangement of bones in the forelimbs of vertebrates as evidence for evolution. The argument is that since there exists a basic pattern, they must have evolved from a common ancestor or from each other, thus perpetuating the pattern. In a variety of animals, such as salamanders, crocodiles, birds, whales, moles, and human beings, we find one long bone supporting the part of the forelimb closest to the body (the shoulder to elbow in humans) and two long bones in the next more distal section (elbow to wrist in humans). Evolutionists offer a number of other similarities as evidence of a common origin, including the universality of cells in living organisms, and hereditary information almost always based on the same genetic code.[29] Then we have the close similarity of comparable DNA sequences, such as we find in apes and humans. However, we should remember that in terms of our minds, a vast difference exists between humans and apes. More recently, biologists have found a striking similarity in special genes called homeotic genes. All these genes contain a DNA sequence called a homeobox. Homeoboxes consist of 180 nucleotide pairs and are associated with a variety of genes controlling some of the major developmental processes of organisms, such as where the body parts will form. In fruit flies a mutation in a homeotic gene will cause a fly to develop an extra set of wings, but the deformed fly can barely survive. The nucleotide sequence of homeoboxes is quite similar in a wide variety of organisms such as centipedes, earthworms, fruit flies, frogs, mice, and humans.[30] We could add a host of other biochemical similarities among living things to the list.

The argument from similarities offers only highly questionable support for an evolutionary model, since we can also argue that they represent a common design pattern. Why not use the same basic pattern, such as the bone arrangement of forelimbs that permits rotation of the extremity (hand in humans) in several kinds of organisms, especially if it works well? Cells make a good functional biochemical unit, just as a room makes a good functional unit for a variety of structures from small houses to skyscrapers. If a homeobox system works well in one organism, why not employ it in another? No law prohibits programmed creation patterns. A creator would not have to employ different systems for similar functions. Similarity need not indicate a common evolutionary origin any more than the proposition that all four-cylinder cars must have come from the same factory. Similarities can just as easily represent intelligent design using good workable systems.

THE EYE AND EVOLUTION

For two centuries the eye has been the focus of a discussion as to whether such a complex structure could result from evolution, or whether it would require intelligent design. While some evolutionists claim to have solved the problem,[31] others consider such a conclusion premature.[32] The problem is far from being resolved.

Many have compared the eye of vertebrates (fishes, amphibians, reptiles, birds, and mammals) (Figures 6.1 and 6.2) to a camera, but it is a highly sophisticated type of camera with millions of parts, and includes autofocus and autoexposure capabilities. On the other hand, invertebrates (sponges, worms, clams, spiders, etc.) have many different kinds of "eyes," including some extremely simple ones such as the microscopic light-sensitive eyespot of single-celled protozoa (protist). Earthworms have many light-sensitive cells, especially numerous at both its ends. Some marine worms have as many as 11,000 "eyes."[33] The marine limpet has a small cuplike eye, while many insects possess complex compound eyes as well as a few simple ones. The compound eye of insects (Figure 6.3) is an image-forming structure with many "light pipes" called ommatidia aimed in different directions, each contributing to the total picture. Dragonflies can have up to 28,000 ommatidia in their compound eyes. The largest known invertebrate

FIGURE 6.1

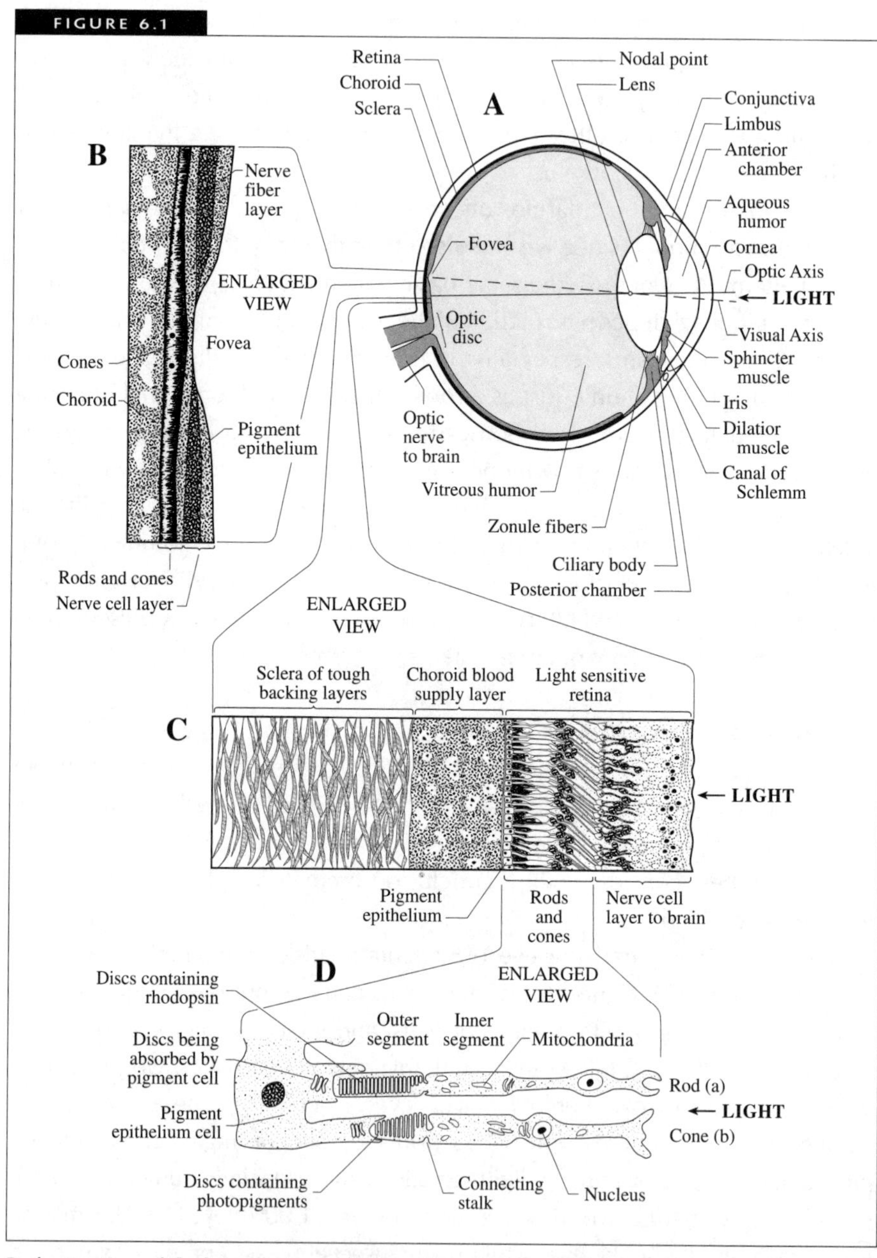

Basic structure of the human eye. A, cross-section; B, enlarged fovea region; C, enlarged wall of the eye; D, enlarged rods (a) and cones (b) of the retina. Note that for all diagrams light comes from the right and that disks are being absorbed into the pigment cell at the left end of D.*

*Based on (a) Berne and Levy, p. 143 (note 63); (b) Dawkins, p. 16 (note 13); (c) Newell, p. 29 (note 45a); (d) Snell RS, Lemp MA. 1989. Clinical anatomy of the eye. Boston, Oxford, and London: Blackwell Scientific Publications, p. 163; (e) Young (note 58).

is the giant squid, reaching a length of 21 meters. It also has the largest eye of any animal. A squid's eye, washed up on shore in New Zealand, had a diameter of 40 centimeters (16 inches), making Jules Verne's fantasy *Twenty Thousand Leagues Under the Sea* all the more realistic. The eye of man is only about 2.4 centimeters in diameter. While squids are very different animals from vertebrates, the basic structure of their eye is remarkably similar.

Also remarkable are some extinct fossil trilobites (organisms remotely similar to horseshoe crabs) that had compound eyes (somewhat similar to Figure 6.3) with many lenses made of the mineral calcite. Calcite is a complicated mineral with different refractive indices in different directions. In trilobite eyes the mineral formed in the right optical direction to provide the proper refractive index. Also, the lens was shaped in a complex way to relate to a second refractive medium and eliminate the problem of spherical aberration. It compares to sophisticated modern optical systems.[34]

A few animal phyla have no light-sensitive organs. Some eyes are so simple they can determine only the presence or absence of light, while others that are more complex can form an image. Image-forming eyes fall into three main categories. One is the pinhole type such as found in the chambered nautilus. In it light rays impinge directly on the light-sensitive retina through a small hole. A second type, such as we humans have and share with most vertebrates and

FIGURE 6.2

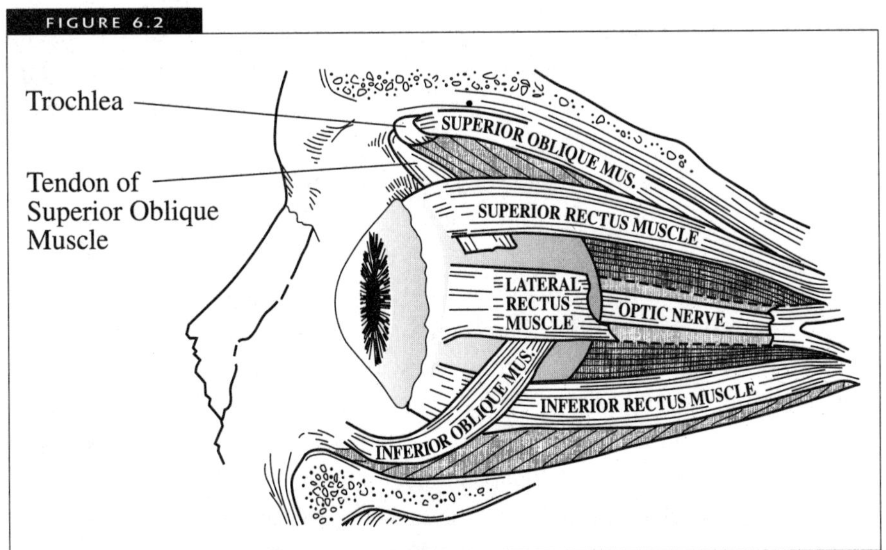

Side view of some of the external muscles of the eye of man. Note that the tendon of the superior oblique muscle threads itself through a pulley (the trochlea) on its way to the eye.†

†Based on Newell, p. 38 (note 45a).

FIGURE 6.3

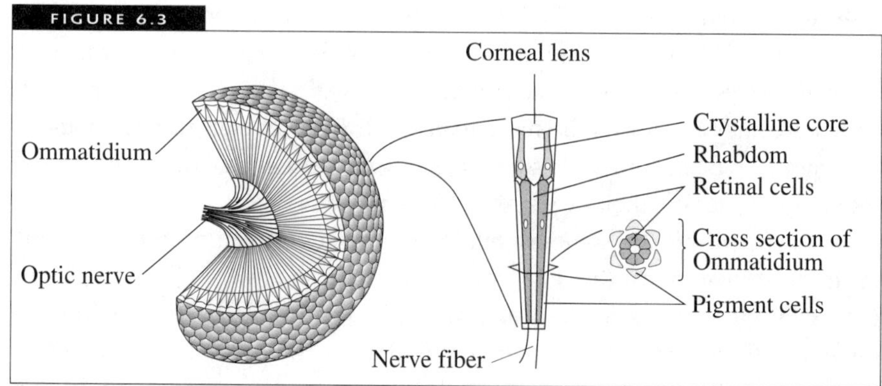

Compound eye of an insect.[‡]

[‡]Based on Raven and Johnson, p. 831 (note 28a).

squids, has a lens (Figure 6.1) that focuses the light on the retina. A third type, the compound eye of many insects, crabs, and trilobites, has, as described above (Figure 6.3), many light pipes creating a composite mosaic picture. A rare fourth type occurs in the planktonic crustacean *Copilia,* which apparently uses a vibrating lens to scan across the visual field and project light onto receptor cells. It is remotely analogous to how an image forms in a television tube.[35]

Several evolutionists have discussed the origin of the eye,[36] but understandably it is not a favorite topic.[37] Darwin, who was very aware of the problem, devoted several pages in the *Origin of Species* to it.[38] He pointed out that we can find a graduated range of eyes and proposed that starting from a simple organ, such as a nerve surrounded with pigment, natural selection could eventually produce even an eagle's eye.

A century later George Gaylord Simpson, at Harvard,[39] employed about the same argument. He noted that the variety of eyes in animals are all functional, and hence presumed that both simple eyes and more complex ones could survive through the evolutionary process. More recently Richard Dawkins,[40] at Oxford, again emphasized the variety of functional eyes currently existing and thereby concluded that other intermediates in the evolutionary process would also be functional. Both authors bypass the crucial questions of interdependent functional parts that face us when we consider the details of different kinds of eyes. The presence of functional simpler eyes does not demonstrate that advanced eyes evolved from them. The fact that we observe a variety of eyes does not of itself support their evolution. We can arrange many things in order of complexity. For example, when we look around a kitchen, we see simple spoons, more complex forks, then cups, kettles, and on up to stoves and refrigerators.

Such a sequence says little about their ultimate origin. The argument leading evolutionists have proposed for the origin of the eye is not very convincing.

Still more serious problems face evolution. We pointed out earlier that at least three to four systems exist to form images in advanced eyes. It is difficult to imagine how such different systems could evolve from each other and still remain functional in intermediate stages, since each type requires very different arrangements. Aware of the variety of basic kinds of eyes, some evolutionists have proposed that the different types must have evolved independently many times, instead of successively, perhaps even as many as 65 times.[41] On the other hand, based on the fact that a similar gene triggers eye development in a wide variety of animals, other evolutionists are suggesting a common origin.[42] None of this explains how a variety of basic eye types evolved, but it does illustrate how the evolutionary scenario can readily adopt the opposing views of similarity and difference. Furthermore, a common gene involved in eye development does little to explain the origin of the many other necessary genes associated with the development of the eye. It has been estimated that as many as 5,000 genes participate in the growth of the fruit fly eye.[43] A further problem arises from the distribution of kinds of eyes among animals, especially the invertebrates. The degree of sophistication does not follow any expected evolutionary pattern. In his comprehensive review of different kinds of eyes and their evolution, Stewart Duke-Elder points out: "The curious thing, however, is that in their distribution the eyes of invertebrates form no series of contiguity and succession. Without obvious phylogenetic [evolutionary] sequence, their occurrence seems haphazard; analogous photoreceptors appear in unrelated species, an elaborate organ in a primitive species [jellyfish] or an elementary structure high in the evolutionary scale [some insects]."[44]

From several perspectives the eye poses rather serious challenges to the evolutionary hypothesis.

THE COMPLEXITY OF THE EYE

Highly complex kinds of eyes, such as ours (see Figure 6.1 for details), are a marvel of coordinated parts working together to permit us to see.[45] The retina contains more than 100 million light-sensitive cells of two main types: rods and cones. Rods serve for viewing under dim light conditions, while three kinds of cones function in brighter light and provide color vision. The portion of each rod or cone directed toward the outside (back) of the eye contains up to 1,000 disks with light-sensitive pigment (Figure 6.1D). When light hits the pigment, it stimulates a multistep biochemical "avalanche" that in turn changes the electric charge of the rod or cone membrane. The electrical charge passes on to connecting nerve cells and eventually reaches the brain. An equally complex system reverses the biochemical avalanche in the rods as they again prepare for detecting more light.

We see most acutely in the center of our visual field, the region of the fovea (Figure 6.1A, B). This area, about a half millimeter in diameter, has some 30,000 cones and no rods. In front of much of the retina, outside the area of the fovea, is a complex of many kinds of nerve cells that start processing the information from the rods and cones. Nerve cells carry the visual information out the back of the eye through the 1.2 million fibers of the optic nerve leading to the brain. The millions of rods and cones and nerve cells have to be associated properly to develop a coherent picture in the brain.

Aside from the complex physical and biochemical changes in the rods, cones, and nerve cells of the retina, our eyes exhibit several other interdependent systems. The pupil (hole) through which light enters the eye gets larger and smaller according to the amount of light as well as in response to distance. This reduces spherical lens aberration and increases the depth of the visual field. In order to evolve a functional system to control the amount of light entering the eye, at least three components must be in place: (1) an analyzing system in the brain to control the size of the pupil, based on the amount of light received; (2) nerve cells that would connect the brain to the iris (the characteristically colored part of our eyes), which contains the muscles that control the size of the pupil; and (3) muscle cells themselves to effect changes in pupil size. Each part must be present and connected the right way. For instance, to connect some nerve cells intended to dilate the pupil to muscles that would contract it would, of course, be counterproductive. Actually the human system is even more complex, with several nerve cells in tandem for each connection between the brain and the eye. Still another system correlates the activity of both eyes so that they work together.[46]

A similar complexity involves the quick automatic focus system that changes the shape of the lens. We do not quite yet know how this system works,[47] but we do know that the brain controls it through a double system that involves a complex of nerve connections.[48]

On the sides and behind each of our eyes are six muscles that control eye movement, permitting us to look in different directions without moving our head (Figure 6.2). The same muscles also facilitate other visual functions,[49] including the ability to direct our eyes toward each other when looking at a close object so both eyes can center on the same spot. Should random mutations first produce a muscle that turns the eye to the left, it would be of little use, since we also need the opposite muscle to shift the eye back to the right, as well as nerves to stimulate the muscles and a control mechanism in the brain to coordinate the activity of both muscles.

The pathway of the superior oblique muscle of the eye also supports the concept of design. The tendon attached to it goes through a pulley system called the trochlea (Figure 6.2) to exert a sideways and forward pull (downward turn) on the eyeball. To simplify the case for evolution, one might assume that an already existing muscle would become modified into such a pulley system. But how would random changes produce anything functional, especially in a single step so as to provide survival value? It is analogous to the traditional chicken-and-egg problem—which came first? Did the tendon on the muscle first elongate so it would be long enough to go through the pulley, or did the pulley evolve first, or did a mechanism to thread the tendon through the pulley come first? Then the control system in the brain needs to be changed to accommodate the new direction of pull of the muscle. In addition, we need a mirror image of the system for the other eye. Unless all these factors are coordinated, the system cannot function properly. It is difficult to imagine that all this can fall into place accidentally without intelligent design behind it.

But this is only the beginning of the story. More complex and less understood is a system of many nerve cells in the retina (Figure 6.1B, C) that processes the information from the rods and cones. Even more intricate is the process whereby the brain transforms information from the retina, resulting in what we call seeing or visual perception.[50] We do not see directly from our eyes, although intuitively we may be inclined to think so. Information transferred from our eyes to the brain goes through complex processing to form a mental image. It appears that different parts of the brain take the millions of bits of information from the eyes, analyze different components separately at the same time, and put them together in an integrated picture.[51] The components include at least brightness, color, motion, form, and depth. The macaque monkey brain has more than 20 different major areas that function in seeing, and humans should have at least that many. The process of seeing is incredibly complicated and incredibly rapid. During the visual process the brain also integrates the information from both eyes. The back part of the brain contains numerous columns of cells in orderly arrangement, with every other column representing one eye. Some theoreticians working in this area comment that "the simplest visual tasks, such as perceiving colors and recognizing familiar faces, require elaborate computations and more neural circuitry than we have yet imagined."[52] It is also amazing that the entire process of visual analysis and synthesis goes on effortlessly, almost without our being aware of it. But seeing is only a start. Recognition and understanding of what we see are also integrated processes of daunting complexity.

In the evolution of the visual process we can ask which came first, the advanced eye or the advanced brain? The interdependent units are useless without each other. Looking at the details, we can also ask which came first, the ability to analyze images into their various color components or the ability to combine them into a single visual image? We could raise many similar questions. Such questions suggest that Paley and his ridiculed natural theology (argument from design) of 200 years ago might not be far from the truth.[53]

IS THE EYE WIRED BACKWARD?

One aspect of the eye that appears detrimental needs consideration. The rods and cones of vertebrate eyes seem to be turned backward, with the light-sensitive part (the disks) facing away from the incoming light. One would expect them to face the light. As depicted in Figure 6.1A-D (where in each case the light comes from the right), the light-sensitive part of the rods and cones (the disks) are located deep into the base of the retina (toward the left), and several nerve cells lie in the path of the incoming light. The light must go through all these cells before it reaches the disks. Responding to the concept of a designer, some evolutionists deride the idea of intelligent design and claim that the eye is wired backward. One claims that "in fact it is stupidly designed."[54] Others comment that "a camera designer who committed such a blunder would be fired immediately,"[55] or "Did God at the time of the 'Fall' turn the vertebrate retina inside out . . . ?"[56]

Actually, the eye appears to be very well designed. In the area of the retina called the fovea (Figure 6.1A), which is responsible for acute vision, the "interfering" nerve cells are almost completely absent and the nerve fibers radiate away from the central region, thus providing a much clearer visual area (Figure 6.1B).

There may be a very good reason for the orientation of the disk portion of the rods and cones toward the pigment epithelium, which lies toward the outside of the retina. The rods and cones are constantly replacing the visual pigment disks.[57] The old ones are discarded toward the outside, where the pigment epithelium cells (Figure 6.1D) absorb them. Were the disks to be disposed of toward the incoming light, we would soon expect a murky situation inside the eye. The rods and cones take no vacation, the disks are constantly being replaced throughout our lifetime. In the rhesus monkey each rod produces 80-90 new disks each day.[58] The rate is probably similar in human beings, and we have 100 million rods in each eye. (Parenthetically, we might note that this is slow compared to the 2 million red blood cells we produce in our bodies every second.)[59] The reason for renewal of the disks in the eye is not well understood, but some have proposed preventive maintenance and a way of providing a fresh supply of visually sensitive chemicals.[60] It appears important that the disks be absorbed at the end of the rods. Some rats have a genetic disease in which the pigment epithelium cells do not absorb the disks. Those rats form masses of debris (disks) at the ends of the rods, and under these conditions the rods degenerate and die.[61] A similar situation has not yet been confirmed in humans, but we are harder to study.[62] Should the disk end of the rods and cones be reversed in direction so as to face the light, as some evolutionists suggest they should, we would probably have a visual disaster. What would perform the essential function of absorbing the some 10,000 million disks produced each day in each of our eyes? They would probably accumulate in the vitreous humor region (Figure 6.1A) and soon interfere with light en route to the retina. If the pigment epithelium layer were placed on the inside of the retina so as to absorb the disks, it would also interfere with light trying to reach the rods and cones. Furthermore, the pigment epithelium, which is closely associated with the disk ends of the rods and cones, also provides them with nutrients for making new disks. The epithelium gets its nutrients from the rich blood supply in the choroid layer next to it (Figure 6.1C). In order for the pigment epithelium to function properly, it needs this blood supply. To put both the pigment epithelium and its choroid blood supply on the inside of the eye, between the light source and the light-sensitive rods and cones, would severely disrupt the visual process.

If in a Darwinian context the present arrangement of the rods and cones is so bad, why didn't natural selection, which originally formed the eye, change this long ago? Our eyes do not seem to be poorly designed, since they usually work very well. In view of science's recent findings about the eye, we could well revise Paley's classic example of a watch to: should we find a video camcorder on the ground, would we be more justified in thinking it was designed, or was it the product of some kind of random mutation/natural selection process?

OTHER EXAMPLES OF DESIGN

We could discuss many more examples of complex systems at length. Our brief survey permits us to list only a few others.

Many kinds of chemicals called hormones perform scores of regulatory functions in complex organisms. Their action and regulation involve intricate interdependence among cells and organs widely separated from each other in the body. Some hormones affect other hormones that in turn regulate or trigger still more hormones. Before one can have a functional system certain interdependent components must all be operating at the same time. For instance, the pancreas produces the hormone insulin, which regulates blood sugar and many other factors related to sugar metabolism. Insulin, whose basic amino-acid sequence is determined by the genetic information from DNA, goes through at least three maturation steps before it reaches a functional form. Furthermore, in order for it to be effective in the cells of the body, it has to attach to a more complex, but specific, protein receptor found on the surface of the cell. The configuration of the receptor is determined by a separate sequence of DNA, and it goes through two modifications before it is useful in helping insulin control different cell functions.[63] Without all these individual steps the system will not work.

Scientists have seriously discussed the evolutionary scenario of the transition from relatively simple nonsexual to complex sexual reproduction for decades.[64] Why should it have ever occurred? One problem is that it appears more efficient simply to divide to reproduce, as occurs in a few simple organisms, instead of requiring two parents, as is usually the case in complex organisms. Also, new evolutionary changes would more easily manifest themselves with just one parent instead of being diluted by another. Variation is what evolution needs, so why should the less-efficient system of sexual reproduction, which tends to suppress this, evolve and survive? One evolutionist has called the question "the queen of problems in evolutionary biology."[65] Evolutionists have a number of suggestions, including the advantage of providing genetic variety from two parents. However, one has difficulty envisioning just how random changes could bring about the involved interdependent processes of splitting the genetic information into equal halves. This special process (meiosis) produces the sperm and egg. Then it requires another complex mechanism to rejoin each during fertilization so as to produce a working, truly biparental reproductive system.

The ear is another marvelous organ. In human beings it has the ability to detect sounds transmitted as minute changes in air pressure at rates as fast as 15,000 per second. It then produces corresponding nerve impulses. The ear is quite small and complex. The information it generates goes through 200,000 fibers to a receptor region in the brain that interprets the sounds.[66] The simplest functioning ear would require at least a sound-detecting system (ear), a nerve, and a brain interpreting the sound, all providing a meaningful function.

Greater complexity appears in the sonar system of bats,[67] whales, dolphins, and shrews. Bats have a mechanism so finely tuned that they can separate their own echoes from those of multitudes of other bats in the vicinity and, using this echo-sounding system, can avoid flying into a wire less than one millimeter in diameter.

We can wonder about many other complex systems with interdependent parts. Human beings and advanced animal forms have hundreds of reflex actions, such as the control of our breathing, that require a sensor, a control mechanism, and nerves to muscles that will provide the appropriate response. The blood-clotting mechanism offers another example of an interdependent system difficult to explain except by intelligent design. In human beings the system requires at least 12 different kinds of complex molecules dependent on each other to produce a clot at the site of a wound. And about 12 other factors control clotting so our blood keeps flowing when we do not have an injury.[68]

Everywhere we investigate biological systems, we find complex interdependent systems in which nothing works until everything works. Human beings have an estimated 50,000 to 200,000 different genes, usually operating in harmony with each other. Could this all happen as a result of chance mutations and natural selection? Mutations, which are random, are almost always detrimental, while natural selection has no foresight and can give no advantage to parts of an interdependent system until the whole system is present and working. If one's mind is open to various options, the case would seem to favor some kind of intelligent design.

CONCLUSIONS

For centuries humanity has debated the question of whether nature reflects design. A cursory look that ignores details might allow one to think the answer is no. But an examination of the intricacies of living organisms reveals a multitude of complex interdependent parts that suggest the necessity of design. In the evolutionary scenario of natural selection, such interdependent components would have no survival value until all the parts began functioning. Strangely for evolution, when we look at nature, we don't seem to see new parts or organs evolving. Many examples, such as the eye and the ear, are so complex that it does not seem possible that they just happened by chance. These structures seem beyond the capability of an evolutionary mechanism of random mutations that are mostly detrimental, and a natural selection that has no foresight to plan ahead. Or according to some evolutionists, just accidental chance, without natural selection. The data favors some kind of intelligent design.

REFERENCES

1. Bacon F. 1605. The advancement of learning, Book II, Chapter VI, section 1. Reprinted in: 1936. The World's Classics, vol. 93: Bacon's *Advancement of Learning* and *The New Atlantis,* London, New York, and Toronto: Henry Frowde, Oxford University Press, p. 96.
2. For a comprehensive discussion, see: (a) Clark RED. 1961. The universe: plan or accident? The religious implications of modern science. Philadelphia: Muhlenberg Press, pp. 15-151; (b) Templeton JM. 1995. The humble approach: scientists discover God. Rev. ed. New York: Continuum Pub. Co.
3. See: Boslough J. 1985. Stephen Hawking's universe. New York: William Morrow and Co., p. 121.
4. Davies PCW. 1982. The accidental universe. Cambridge: Cambridge University Press, pp. 88-93.
5. Hawking SW. 1988. A brief history of time: from the big bang to black holes. Toronto, New York, and London: Bantam Books, pp. 121, 122.
6. Carr BJ, Rees MJ. 1979. The anthropic principle and the structure of the physical world. Nature 278:605-612.
7. For further discussion, see: (a) Leslie J. 1988. How to draw conclusions from a fine-tuned cosmos. In: Russell RJ, Stoeger WR, Coyne GV, editors. Physics, philosophy, and theology: a common quest for understanding. Vatican City State: Vatican Observatory, pp. 297-311. For other examples, see: (b) Barrow JD, Tipler FJ. 1986. The anthropic cosmological principle. Oxford: Clarendon Press, and New York: Oxford University Press; (c) Carr and Rees (note 6); (d) Davies P. 1994. The unreasonable effectiveness of science. In: Templeton JM, editor. Evidence of purpose: scientists discover the Creator. New York: Continuum Pub. Co., pp. 44-56; (e) de Groot M. 1992. Cosmology and Genesis: the road to harmony and the need for cosmological alternatives. Origins 19:8-32; (f) Gale G. 1981. The anthropic principle. Scientific American 245:154-171; (g) Polkinghorne J. 1994. A potent universe. In: Templeton, pp. 105-115 (note 7d); (g) Ross H. 1993. The Creator and the cosmos. Colorado Springs, Colo.: NavPress, pp. 105-135.
8. Barbour IG. 1990. Religion in an age of science. The Gifford Lectures 1989-1991, vol. 1. San Francisco: Harper and Row, p. 135.
9. For recent descriptions, see: (a) Davies P. 1988. The cosmic blueprint: new discoveries in nature's creative ability to order the universe. New York: Simon and Schuster. Davies still concludes that "the impression of design is overwhelming" (p. 203). For further discussion, see: (b) Waldrop MM. 1992. Complexity: the emerging science at the edge of order and chaos. New York and London: Touchstone Books, Simon and Schuster; (c) see also chapter 8.
10. For definitions, discussions, and/or references of these terms, see: (a) Barbour IG. 1966. Issues in science and religion. Englewood Cliffs, N.J.: Prentice-Hall, pp. 53, 132; (b) Barbour, pp. 24-26 (note 8); (c) Beerbower JR. 1968. Search for the past: an introduction to paleontology. 2nd ed. Englewood Cliffs, N.J.: Prentice-Hall, pp. 175, 176; (d) Bynum WF, Browne EJ, Porter R, editors. 1981. Dictionary of the history of science. Princeton, N.J.: Princeton University Press, pp. 123, 296, 415, 416, 439, 440; (e) Grassé P-P. 1977. Evolution of living organisms: evidence for a new theory of transformation. Carlson BM, Castro R, translators. New York, San Francisco, and London: Academic Press, pp. 240-242. Translation of: L'Évolution du Vivant; (f) Mayr E. 1970. Populations, species, and evolution: an abridgment of *Animal Species and Evolution.* Rev. ed. Cambridge: Belknap Press of Harvard University Press, p. 351; (g) Rensch B. 1959. Evolution above the species level. [Altevogt DR, translator]. New York: John Wiley and Sons, pp. 57, 58. Translation of the 2nd ed. of: Neuere Probleme der Abstammungslehre; (h) Simpson GG. 1967. The meaning of evolution: a study of the history of life and of its significance for man. Rev. ed. New Haven and London: Yale University Press, pp. 174, 175; (i) Simpson GG. 1964. This view of life: the world of an evolutionist. New York: Harcourt, Brace, and World, pp. 22, 144, 273.

11. For reviews of the argument, see: (a) Baldwin JT. 1992. God and the world: William Paley's argument from perfection tradition—a continuing influence. Harvard Theological Review 85(1):109-120; (b) Barbour 1966, pp. 19-91, 132-134, 386-394 (note 10a); (c) Barbour 1990, pp. 24-30 (note 8); (d) Kenny A. 1987. Reason and religion: essays in philosophical theology. Oxford and New York: Basil Blackwell, pp. 69-84.
12. Tweyman S, editor. 1991. David Hume: *Dialogues Concerning Natural Religion* in focus. Routledge Philosophers in Focus Series. London and New York: Routledge, pp. 95-185.
13. Dawkins R. 1986. The blind watchmaker. New York and London: W. W. Norton and Co., p. 6.
14 Baldwin (note 11a).
15. Paley W. 1807. Natural theology; or, evidences of the existence and attributes of the deity. 11th ed. London: R. Faulder and Son, pp. 1-8, 20-46, 193-199.
16. Darwin C. 1859. On the origin of species by means of natural selection, or the preservation of favoured races in the struggle for life. London: John Murray. In: Burrow J, editor. 1968 reprint. London and New York: Penguin Books, p. 217.
17. Himmelfarb G. 1967. Darwin and the Darwinian revolution. Gloucester, Mass.: Peter Smith, p. 338.
18. Peckham M, editor. 1959. The origin of species by Charles Darwin: a variorum text. Philadelphia: University of Pennsylvania Press, p. 759.
19. Himmelfarb, p. 347 (note 17).
20. For an exception, see the recent publication by the philosopher of religion Alvin Plantinga: Plantinga A. 1991. When faith and reason clash: evolution and the Bible. Christian Scholar's Review 21(1):8-32.
21. See chapter 7 for further discussion of mutations.
22. Dawkins, pp. 5, 6 (note 13).
23. Rensch, p. 58 (note 10g).
24. Mayr 1970, p. 351 (note 10f).
25. Grassé, pp. 103, 104 (note 10e).
26. Block HM, editor. 1956. Candide and other writings by Voltaire. New York: Modern Library, Random House, p. 111.
27. Fentress JC. 1967. Discussion of G. Wald's The problems of vicarious selection. In: Moorhead PS, Kaplan MM, editors. Mathematical challenges to the neo-Darwinian interpretation of evolution. The Wistar Institute Symposium Monograph No. 5. Philadelphia: Wistar Institute Press, p. 71.
28. E.g.: (a) Raven PH, Johnson GB. 1992. Biology. 3rd ed. St. Louis, Boston, and London: Mosby-Year Book, p. 14; (b) Diamond J. 1985. Voyage of the overloaded ark. Discover (June), pp. 82-92; (c) Committee on Science and Creationism, National Academy of Sciences. 1984. Science and creationism: a view from the National Academy of Sciences. Washington, D.C.: National Academy Press.
29. See chapter 8 for further discussion.
30. (a) Avers CJ. 1989. Process and pattern in evolution. Oxford and New York: Oxford University Press, pp. 139, 140; (b) Carroll SB. 1995. Homeotic genes and the evolution of arthropods and chordates. Nature 376:479-485; (c) De Robertis EM, Oliver G, Wright CVE. 1990. Homeobox genes and the vertebrate body plan. Scientific American (July), pp. 46-52; (d) Gehring WJ. 1987. Homeo boxes in the study of development. Science 236:1245-1252; (e) Schneuwly S, Klemenz R, Gehring WJ. 1987. Redesigning the body plan of *Drosophila* by ectopic expression of the homeotic gene *Antennapedia*. Nature 325:816-818.
31. (a) Dawkins R. 1994. The eye in a twinkling. Nature 368:690, 691; (b) Nilsson D-E, Pelger S. 1994. A pessimistic estimate of the time required for an eye to evolve. Proceedings of the Royal Society of London B 256:53-58. These reports suggest that the eye could have evolved incredibly rapidly, its shaping taking a mere 400,000 generations. But a vast difference exists between shaping an eye on a computer, as researchers did, and having a real working eye develop by itself. Notoriously absent from the computer model is the origin of the highly complex retina; the complex mechanisms for controlling the lens and the iris; and especially the evolution of visual perception. The eye would be useless, and developing

stages would have no survival value without an interpretation process in the brain recognizing the changes. To suggest that this incredibly simplistic computer model would evolve "the eye in a twinkling" is symptomatic of a serious problem in evolutionary thinking.

32. (a) Baldwin JT. 1995. The argument from sufficient initial system organization as a continuing challenge to the Darwinian rate and method of transitional evolution. Christian Scholar's Review 14(4):423-443; (b) Grassé, p. 104 (note 10e).
33. Duke-Elder S. 1958. The eye in evolution. In: Duke-Elder S, editor. System of ophthalmology, vol. 1. St. Louis: C. V. Mosby Co., p. 192.
34. (a) Clarkson ENK, Levi-Setti R. 1975. Trilobite eyes and the optics of Des Cartes and Huygens. Nature 254:663-667; (b) Towe KM. 1973. Trilobite eyes: calcified lenses in vivo. Science 179:1007-1009.
35. Gregory RL, Ross HE, Moray N. 1964. The curious eye of *Copilia*. Nature 201:1166-1168.
36. (a) Cronly-Dillon JR. 1991. Origin of invertebrate and vertebrate eyes. In: Cronly-Dillon JR, Gregory RL, editors. Evolution of the eye and visual system. Vision and visual dysfunction, vol. 2. Boca Raton, Fla., Ann Arbor, Mich., and Boston: CRC Press, pp. 15-51; (b) Duke-Elder (note 33); (c) Land MF. 1981. Optics and vision in invertebrates. In: Autrum H, editor. Comparative physiology and evolution of vision in invertebrates. B: Invertebrate visual centers and behavior I. Handbook of Sensory Physiology, Vol. VII/6B. Berlin, Heidelberg, and New York: Springer-Verlag, pp. 471-594. These references do not especially address the question of design, but take evolution for granted.
37. Grassé, p. 105 (note 10e).
38. Darwin C. 1872. The origin of species by means of natural selection or the preservation of favoured races in the struggle for life. 6th ed. New York: Mentor Books, New American Library, pp. 168-171.
39. Simpson, pp. 168-175 (note 10h).
40. Dawkins, pp. 15-18 (note 13).
41. (a) Salvini-Plawen LV, Mayr E. 1977. On the evolution of photoreceptors and eyes. Evolutionary Biology 10:207-263. (b) Land (note 36c) suggests that the compound eyes "evolved independently in three invertebrate phyla; the annelids, molluscs, and arthropods" (p. 543).
42. (a) Gould SJ. 1994. Common pathways of illumination. Natural History 103(12):10-20; (b) Quiring R, Walldorf U, Kloter U, Gehring WJ. 1994. Homology of the *eyeless* gene of *Drosophila* to the *small eye* gene in mice and *Aniridia* in humans. Science 265:785-789; (c) Zuker CS. 1994. On the evolution of the eyes: would you like it simple or compound? Science 265:742, 743.
43. Mestel R. 1996. Secrets in a fly's eye. Discover 17(7):106-114.
44. Duke-Elder, p. 178 (note 33).
45. For some details of the anatomy and physiology of the human eye, among many references, see: (a) Newell FW. 1992. Ophthalmology: principles and concepts. 7th ed. St. Louis, Boston, and London: Mosby-Year Book, pp. 3-98. Some other aspects of the complexity of the eye are given in: (b) Lumsden RD. 1994. Not so blind a watchmaker. Creation Research Society Quarterly 31:13-22.
46. Davson H. 1990. Physiology of the eye. 5th ed. New York, Oxford, and Sydney: Pergamon Press, pp. 758, 759.
47. *Ibid.*, pp. 777, 778.
48. Kaufman PL. 1992. Accommodation and presbyopia: neuromuscular and biophysical aspect. In: Hart WM, Jr., editor. 1992. Adler's physiology of the eye: clinical application. 9th ed. St. Louis, Boston, and London: Mosby-Year Book, pp. 391-411.
49. For further information on the complex arrangement and function of the external muscles of the eye, see: (a) Davson, pp. 647-666 (note 46); (b) Duke-Elder S, Wybar KC. 1961. The anatomy of the visual system. In: Duke-Elder S, editor. System of ophthalmology, vol. 2. St. Louis: C. V. Mosby Co., pp. 414-427; (c) Hubel DH. 1988. Eye, brain, and vision. Scientific American Library Series, No. 22. New York and Oxford: W. H. Freeman and Co., pp. 78-81; (d) Warwick R, reviser. 1976. Eugene Wolff's anatomy of the eye and orbit. 7th ed.

Philadelphia and Toronto: W. B. Saunders Co., pp. 261-265.

50. For an introduction to this complex and fascinating topic, see: (a) Gregory RL. 1991. Origins of eyes—with speculations on scanning eyes. In: Cronly-Dillon and Gregory, pp. 52-59 (note 36a); (b) Grüsser O-J, Landis T. 1991. Visual agnosias and other disturbances of visual perception and cognition. Vision and visual dysfunction, vol. 12. Boca Raton, Fla., Ann Arbor, Mich., and Boston: CRC Press, pp. 1-24; (c) Spillmann L, Werner JS, editors. 1990. Visual perception: the neurophysiological foundations. San Diego, New York, and London: Academic Press.
51. Lennie P, Trevarthen C, Van Essen D, Wässle H. 1990. Parallel processing of visual information. In: Spillmann and Werner, pp. 103-128 (note 50c).
52. Shapley R, Caelli T, Grossberg S, Morgan M, Rentschler I. 1990. Computational theories of visual perception. In: Spillmann and Werner, pp. 417-448 (note 50c).
53. Paraphrased from: Hoyle F, Wickramasinghe NC. 1981. Evolution from space: a theory of cosmic creationism. New York: Simon and Schuster, pp. 96, 97.
54. Williams GC. 1992. Natural selection: domains, levels, and challenges. New York and Oxford: Oxford University Press, p. 73.
55. Diamond (note 28b).
56. Thwaites WM. 1983. An answer to Dr. Geisler—from the perspective of biology. Creation/Evolution 13:13-20.
57. It was earlier thought that only rods shed their disks; however, the process has been well demonstrated in cones. See: Steinberg RH, Wood I, Hogan MJ. 1977. Pigment epithelial ensheathment and phagocytosis of extrafoveal cones in human retina. Philosophical Transactions of the Royal Society of London B 277:459-471.
58. Young RW. 1971. The renewal of rod and cone outer segments in the rhesus monkey. Journal of Cell Biology 49:303-318.
59. Leblond CP, Walker BE. 1956. Renewal of cell populations. Physiological Reviews 36:255-276.
60. Young RW. 1976. Visual cells and the concept of renewal. Investigative Ophthalmology 15:700-725.
61. (a) Bok D, Hall MO. 1971. The role of the pigment epithelium in the etiology of inherited retinal dystrophy in the rat. Journal of Cell Biology 49:664-682. For further discussion regarding the function of the pigment epithelium, see: (b) Ayoub G. 1996. On the design of the vertebrate retina. Origins and Design 17(1):19-22, and references therein.
62. (a) Bok D. 1994. Retinal photoreceptor disc shedding and pigment epithelium phagocytosis. In: Ogden TE, editor. Retina. 2nd ed. Vol. 1: Basic science and inherited retinal disease. St. Louis, Baltimore, Boston, and London: Mosby, pp. 81-94; (b) Newell, pp. 304, 305 (note 45a).
63. Berne RM, Levy MN, editors. 1993. Physiology. 3rd ed. St. Louis, Boston, and London: Mosby-Year Book, pp. 851-875.
64. (a) Eldredge N. 1995. Reinventing Darwin: the great debate at the high table of evolutionary theory. New York: John Wiley and Sons, pp. 215-219; (b) Halvorson HO, Monroy A, editors. 1985. The origin and evolution of sex. New York: Alan R. Liss; (c) Margulis L, Sagan D. 1986. Origins of sex: three billion years of genetic recombination. New Haven and London: Yale University Press; (d) Maynard Smith J. 1988. Did Darwin get it right? Essays on games, sex, and evolution. New York and London: Chapman and Hall, pp. 98-104, 165-179, 185-188.
65. Bell G. 1982. The masterpiece of nature: the evolution and genetics of sexuality. Berkeley and Los Angeles: University of California Press, p. 19.
66. Berne and Levy, pp. 166-188 (note 63).
67. (a) Dawkins 1986, pp. 22-41 (note 13); (b) Griffin DR. 1986. Listening in the dark: the acoustic orientation of bats and men. Ithaca and London: Comstock Publishing Associates, Cornell University Press.
68. (a) Behe MJ. 1996. Darwin's black box. New York: Free Press, pp. 77-97; (b) Berne and Levy, pp. 339-357 (note 63).

CHAPTER 7

HUMAN ORIGINS

What is man, that thou art mindful of him?
—Psalm 8:4

One writer hailed the 1971 discovery of the Tasaday tribe in the southern Philippines as the "most significant anthropological discovery of this century—and I think we could say centuries."[1] Characterized as ultraprimitive, lost, and "Stone Age," the 26 individuals, living in caves in a rain forest, pursued a Paleolithic lifestyle. They wore only leaves for clothing and knew nothing about hunting or agriculture. The tribe survived on berries, roots, and wild bananas, as well as crabs, grubs, and frogs. They said they were unaware of the existence of a large village just a three-hour walk away, or of the ocean 30 kilometers away, and reportedly even regarded themselves as the only people on earth. Their language was unique, although close enough to a known language used in the vicinity to permit translation.

Discovery of the Tasaday tribe attracted worldwide attention, and government agents closely regulated visits to the world's last two dozen Stone Age cave dwellers. The public media and about a dozen scientists received permission to view and interview the Tasaday through interpreters, but only for a few hours a day. While coverage to the general public was abundant, scientific reports were more limited. The National Geographic Society, whose journal has a circulation of 9 million, published two articles on the group. They and the National Broadcasting Corporation in the United States each prepared television programs shown worldwide. A book entitled *The Gentle Tasaday*[2] received wide circulation.

Three years later all communication with the Tasaday stopped, and it did not resume for 12 years, when major changes in the Philippine government altered the enforced isolation. It was then that a Swiss anthropologist-reporter made his way to the caves and discovered they were empty. He found the Tasaday wearing colored T-shirts, using metal knives, and sleeping on beds. One member of the group reported that they used to live in huts and had done some farming, but that government agents had forced them to live in caves so that they would be called cavemen.[3] A few days later some reporters from Germany also contacted the Tasaday and took pictures of one of the same individuals previously photographed by the Swiss reporter. This time the "caveman" had reverted to a garment of leaves. However, cloth underwear was showing under the leaves. These and other incidents led many to conclude that the Tasaday were a hoax. It also generated a major controversy in the anthropological community.

Returning to his homeland, the Swiss reporter who had discovered the Tasaday living under much more modern conditions immediately contacted the National Geographic Society, offering them his new information. They sent him a telegram the next day, indicating that they were not interested, and they did not reply to his follow-up letter. Two years later the *National Geographic* reported that the idea that the Tasaday were a hoax had been "largely discredited."[4] On the other hand, two television documentaries identified the Tasaday story as a deception. One was entitled "The Tribe That Never Was," and the other "Scandal: The Lost Tribe."

Many wonder whether the Tasaday are a genuine "Stone Age" tribe. Could such a group survive and remain isolated while living in such close proximity to more advanced groups? Most of the early anthropologists who saw the "tribe" support their primitiveness and authenticity. However, since it was suggested that the Tasaday might be a hoax, at least three international anthropological conferences have been convened regarding this challenging question. At stake are the propriety of the governmental agencies supervising the Tasaday, the integrity of the Tasaday, and the credibility of the science of anthropology.

Without question the Tasaday represent a unique group living under somewhat primitive conditions. There also seems to be a fair amount of agreement that they were coerced into orchestrating a cave-dweller show for publicity or economic reasons, sometimes referred to as the "rain forest Watergate."[5] It is also conceded that they could have undergone many changes between their discovery in 1971 and their rediscovery in 1986. Beyond that, many questions remain unresolved, a number stemming from differences between positions taken when they were discovered and newer interpretations.

One of the more important questions about the Tasaday is whether their language is sufficiently different to justify any claim of isolation for any length of time. Opinions among scholars vary. The Tasaday had three stone tools in 1971 that mysteriously disappeared before anyone had a chance to photograph them. They represented the only extant use of stone tools in the Philippines. Some substitute tools made by the Tasaday or their neighbors at the request of government authorities have been categorized as obvious fakes. Another controversy centers on the accuracy of the genealogical data collected by anthropologists. This has important implications regarding the degree of isolation of the Tasaday. Also much disputed is the question of the adequacy of the purported Tasaday diet. Some investigators believe that the forest in which the tribe supposedly secluded themselves could not have sustained them. Carbohydrates would be in especially short supply. Others disagree. We could list many other points of contention, but the above examples illustrate the diversity of the conflicting reports.[6]

As one attempts to evaluate the Tasaday controversy, one has to wonder how so many things could go wrong. The incident well illustrates the difficulty of correctly interpreting the past, and the ease with which we jump at conclusions based on preconceived ideas without making sure we have good supporting data. Such problems have especially afflicted the study of human origins. In this chapter we shall see that the information supporting human evolution is at best tenuous, and the suggested evolutionary origin of the human mind is even more of a mystery.

WHERE DID HUMANS COME FROM?

On a biological scale from simple to complex, *Homo sapiens* stands at the complex end. Human beings, the foremost of all organisms on earth, have advanced reasoning powers and the ability to accomplish such feats as painting the Sistine Chapel and traveling to the moon.

Although humans are small in size compared to whales, we cannot easily dismiss our biological complexity. Our bodies contain trillions of cells. Tucked in the nucleus of each cell are more than 3 billion DNA bases. If all the DNA in one nucleus were stretched out, it would be about one meter long. The DNA from all the cells in our body, if combined, could stretch from Earth to Jupiter and back more than 60 times. Though we admire the fine technology of computers with a few million transistors on a single flat chip a little more than one square centimeter in size, it is extremely crude compared to the nucleus of a cell, which can have 100 million times more information per unit volume than a computer chip.[7]

The question of human origin was one of the more sensitive issues raised by

Darwin's *Origin of Species*. The idea that animals and plants had evolved was tolerable. However, to suggest that human beings originated from a lower life form was a different matter. The idea contradicted the biblical statement that God created humans in His image. How do human beings' special powers of mind and spiritual values relate to an animal ancestry? A few years after the appearance of *The Origin of Species*, Darwin published another book entitled *The Descent of Man*, in which he more directly promoted his position on humanity's animal ancestry. He included in his argumentation some stories intended to soften the resentment against too close an association of humans with animals. Darwin told of a "true hero"—a baboon that risked its own life to save a younger baboon threatened with extermination by a pack of dogs. Later he recounted that a baboon had attacked a zookeeper, but a monkey, seeing "his friend" the zookeeper in peril, screamed and bit the aggressive baboon. In contrast, Darwin told about human "savages" he had seen near the southern tip of South America who tortured their enemies, practiced infanticide, and treated their wives like slaves. Darwin concluded that he would rather have descended from the heroic baboon or altruistic monkey than from a savage.[8]

Though Darwin's illustrations were certainly impressive, his argumentation illustrates selection of data. To contrast the worst acts of human beings with the kindest acts of animals is not very convincing. The heroic baboon that Darwin chose for comparison with human savages was not the baboon that attacked the zookeeper. Darwin did not mention humanity's parental and humanitarian gestures of love. Furthermore, in terms of basic intelligence, probably most of us would rather be associated with humanity than with monkeys and baboons.

The origin of the human race has been intensely debated, especially since Darwin's time. Many believe that humanity has a special purpose and destiny. On the other hand, classical evolutionary interpretation takes the position that human beings are the product of blind evolutionary processes. George Gaylord Simpson, of Harvard University, has stated that "man is the result of a purposeless and natural process that did not have him in mind."[9]

For many reasons the science of paleoanthropology (study of fossil humans) is fraught with controversy. The past 40 years, filled with major discoveries, have been especially tumultuous. The science writer and anthropologist Roger Lewin in his book *Bones of Contention* emphasizes that controversy is much more severe in this field than in other areas of science.[10] It has been humorously stated that you cannot get two anthropologists to agree on where to have lunch together! S. L. Washburn, an anthropologist from the University of California at Berkeley, once commented, "it is useful to regard the study of human evolution as a game, a game with uncertain rules, and with only the fragments to represent the long-dead players. It will be many years before the game becomes a science, before we can be sure of what constitutes the 'facts.'"[11]

David Pilbeam, from Yale and Harvard, reflects on the same problem: "I have come to believe that many of the statements we make about the hows and whys of human evolution say as much about us, the paleoanthropologists and the larger society in which we live, as about anything that 'really' happened."[12] And Roger Lewin adds that paleoanthropology is "a science that is often short on data and long on opinion."[13]

One reason for such dissension is the absence of the firm data needed to confirm proposed theories. Anthropologists debate endlessly about the relationships of the various fossil finds[14] and their validity as true species. A half century ago the problem was "bewildering,"[15] with more than 100 "species" of fossil humans to contend with. Revisions in classification have mercifully reduced the number to fewer than 10. However, the number is increasing again.[16] As a further illustration of the subjectivity involved in classification schemes, Louis Leakey redefined the genus *Homo,* to which we belong, to accommodate organisms like *Homo habilis,* which have smaller brains. The redefinition fits well with his theories.[17]

FOSSIL FINDS

Creationists have often referred to the scarcity of ancient human finds and the subjective reconstructions of skulls from just a few parts as weaknesses in the evolutionary model. While material continues to be relatively scarce, this argument has become less valid as the many finds in the past few decades have added significant information. Most of the fossil groupings now have good representation. A brief outline follows.

1. *Australopithecines*

At least four species belong to this group of small- to medium-sized apelike creatures that may have walked upright. Their remains have turned up in eastern and southern Africa. The braincase had a volume of approximately 350 to 600 cubic centimeters, which is in the range of some apes. Some notable examples are the Taung Child and Lucy. The latter may have been a male.[18] The evolutionary relationship among the various representatives to each other and to more advanced forms is obscure. Paleontologists have proposed at least six models.[19]

2. *Homo habilis*

This controversial "species," is called an "enigma" by some evolutionists.[20] Others comment that "some workers prefer to deny its existence."[21] Still others suggest that it should be two species.[22] First discovered in 1959 by Louis Leakey in the famous Olduvai Gorge in northern Tanzania, many consider it to be a crucial link between the primitive australopithecines and the human-like *Homo erectus*. The braincase is estimated to vary between 500 and 800 cubic centimeters. Paleontologists have recovered parts of more than two dozen specimens in Africa, but many questions remain. Some specimens might not belong to the group, and others not in the group might be included. Some specimens are reported to have human-like characteristics, while others are strongly apelike, and some appear to have characteristics of both.[23] It is not a well-defined category.

3. *Homo erectus*

This species had a stature close to that of modern humans and a cranial capacity of 750 to 1,200 cubic centimeters. It is represented by such classic finds of paleoanthropology as the Java and Peking fossils. A number of specimens have appeared in other parts of Asia, and Africa has provided a good number of specimens. Several European specimens are sometimes considered members of this species. Some anthropologists consider it to be a link between *Homo habilis* and modern humans, while others suggest it may be a variety of *Homo sapiens*.

4. Archaic *Homo sapiens*

This new grouping includes a large number of fossil finds considered closer to modern humans than *Homo erectus*. The average cranial capacity ranged from 1,100 to 1,750 cubic centimeters. Paleontologists have excavated specimens in Africa, Asia, Europe, and the Middle East. Usually included are the well-known Neanderthals, often characterized as primitive, with a low brow and stooped stance. This image,[24] based primarily on a specimen with severe arthritis, appears to be erroneous. After reinvestigating Neanderthal, two anthropologists comment that if a healthy Neanderthal "could be reincarnated and placed in a New York subway—provided that he were bathed, shaved, and dressed in modern clothing—it would be doubtful whether he would attract any more attention than some of its other denizens."[25] Neanderthals appear to have been fairly advanced. Their average cranial capacity is commonly reported as being larger than that of modern humans; e.g., 1,625 cubic centimeters, versus 1,450 cubic centimeters for modern humans.[26]

In a very general way the groups listed above that have smaller organisms, such as the australopithecines, also date older, but some of the major battles in paleoanthropology have raged over dating. An ash layer near Lake Turkana in Kenya was held to be 2.61 million years old, based on the potassium-argon method of dating.[27] The significance of this layer is that it dated an important *Homo habilis* finding. However, the date did not fit accepted views and was debated for years. Later redating by the same method yielded a more acceptable 1.88 million years.[28] Another controversy that has generated "intense skepticism"[29] relates to the origin of *Homo erectus.* Traditionally they are thought to have evolved in Africa about 1.8 million years ago. On the other hand, the *Homo erectus* from Java—assumed to have come from Africa about 1 million years ago—has given ages as old as 1.8 million years when dated with a modified potassium-argon system. Researchers report a similar date for early *Homo* from China.[30] This has raised the question of whether *Homo erectus* first appeared in Africa or Asia, along with the broader consequent question of whether according to evolution, humankind's origin centered in Africa or Asia.

Paleoanthropology does agree on some things. Newer discoveries show that several proposed evolutionary intermediates lived at the same time,[31] with considerable overlapping in time of different species. However, identification problems sometimes confound the data. Experts question the older idea of a linear stepwise evolution of humans from the primitive australopithecines through the more advanced species. Some data suggests that *Homo erectus* may have lived as recently as 27,000 years ago[32] and thus, according to evolutionary interpretations, would have been a contemporary of *Homo sapiens* for a half million years. The overlapping reduces the significance of many time relationships. Some also agree that we still have not found the early ancestors of the genus *Homo,*[33] and that the evolutionary relationship of earlier primates (apes and monkeys) is also unknown.[34] One major battle has been over whether some of the apelike australopithecines are part of human evolutionary ancestry, as endorsed by Donald Johanson,[35] or if some other yet-undiscovered organism is needed, as emphasized by Richard Leakey.[36] Several suggest that various humans may have evolved independently in different places.[37]

The comparison of similar complex organic molecules (biopolymers) in various primate groups (monkeys, humans, etc.) has played an important role in the study of human evolution. The closer the molecular similarity, the closer the assumed evolutionary relationship. Surprisingly, some of the tests based on estimated evolutionary rates of change infer that human types and apes separated from their common ancestor only 5 million years ago instead of 20 million years ago, as previously concluded from studies of the fossil record. This has sparked further debate.[38] Another problem is that hypotheses of evolutionary relationships based on molecular data differ from those derived from morphological (shape of bones) data as shown in Figure 7.1A-C. The figures should be read in an ascending direction. The lines diverge as assumed evolutionary separation takes place. The discrepancy between antibody, fossil, and molecular data indicates an inconsistent pattern for human evolution. Discrepancies between molecular data and morphological data have also turned up in a variety of nonprimate groups.[39]

Creationists also disagree over interpretations of the ape-human fossil types. Generally they seem to conclude that the small australopithecines are from an extinct created primate type. Neanderthal types, who have left good evidence of their existence in caves, are commonly thought to represent human migration since the biblical flood. The differences arise regarding the enigmatic *Homo habilis* and the more modern *Homo erectus* (Java and Peking fossils, etc.).[40] One commonly accepted interpretation is that created humankind includes the advanced human types *(Homo sapiens,* Neanderthal, archaic *Homo sapiens,* and *Homo erectus* groups). The enigmatic *Homo habilis* group is ill-defined and needs further study.

One further point deserves mention. It seems strange that if humankind *(Homo sapiens)* has been around for at least a half million years, the clear evidences of its activity seem so recent. History, writing, archaeology (including evidence of civilization such as cities, ancient travel routes, etc.)—all reflect only a few thousand years of activity. The basic data pose a question for evolution: If humankind has existed for a half million years, why should the truly compelling evidences of past activities appear so recently? And if humankind evolved gradually, why wait until the last 1 percent of that time for such advances?

Creationists sometimes wonder why the evidence for antediluvian humans, who, according to the biblical record, lived more than a thousand years between creation and the Genesis flood, is so sparse in the rock record. Evidences of fossil humans in the middle and lower parts of the fossil record are highly questionable. Firm evidence, such as good skeletal remains, seem to be limited to the uppermost part of the geologic column (Figure 10.1). Some suggested explanations within a creation context are: (1) Not that many humans may have lived before the flood, and the chance of finding them is remote. Reproductive rates as suggested in the biblical record for the period before the flood appear to have been much slower than at present. For instance, the Bible indicates that Noah had only three sons in 600 years, and the first sons of the preflood patriarchs were born on an average well after the patriarchs were more than 100 years

FIGURE 7.1

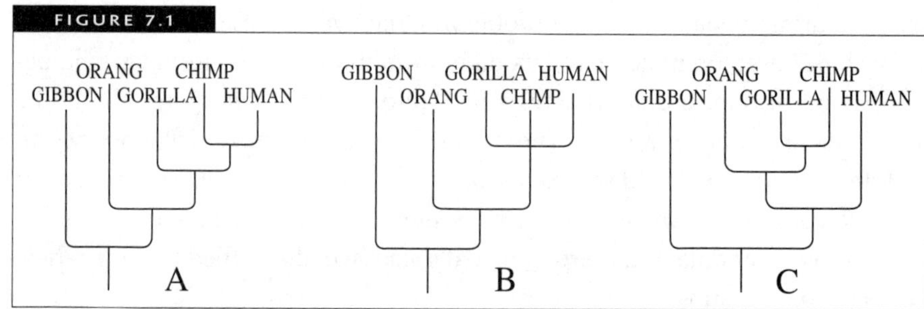

Reported evolutionary relationships of some higher primates based on different kinds of tests. A is based on similarity of DNA, B is deduced from antibody reactions, and C derives from the fossil evidence.*

*Based on Edey and Johanson, p. 367 (note 14c).

old.[41] (2) During the flood, humans above all other creatures would be expected to use their superior intelligence to escape to the highest regions. Once there, the chances of preservation by burial under sediments would not be good. (3) Before the Genesis flood, humans may have resided in the higher and cooler regions of the preflood earth, hence would not have been represented in the lower parts of the geologic column. (4) The activity of the floodwaters destroyed the evidence of preflood humans. The creationist difficulty of explaining the scarcity of humans for the short period before the flood is probably not as serious as the evolutionist problem of accounting for the sparsity of human remains and activity during at least a half million years of proposed human *(Homo sapiens)* evolution. Regardless of one's view, the fossil evidence for the past history of human beings is not good enough of itself to provide firm conclusions.

THE ORIGIN OF THE HUMAN MIND

The most complicated structure we know of in the universe is the human brain. This awesome organ is also the home of our mysterious minds. The complexity of the brain is difficult to envision. Each of us probably has at least 100,000 million nerve cells (neurons) in our entire brains.[42] About 400,000 kilometers of nerve fibers connect the cells together. The nerve fibers often branch repeatedly as they connect to other nerve cells. Changes in electrical charges conduct impulses along the fibers in a flurry of activity. At the connections between nerve cells at least 30 different kinds of chemicals, and most likely many times more that number, transmit information from cell to cell. Some of the larger nerve cells link to as many as 600 other cells, using some 60,000 connections. The brain has an estimated 100 million times a million (10^{14}) linkages. Such figures are too large to relate to ordinary experience. It may help to realize that in the external region of the largest part of the brain (cerebrum), where the nerve cells are less concentrated than in the hind brain, just one cubic millimeter of tissue will contain 40,000 nerve cells and probably 1,000 million connections. While these figures are only estimates, there is no question that we find it challenging to think about the complexity of the machinery with which we do our thinking.

Although the intricacy of our brains is difficult to encompass, the question of the mind (our thought processes) is even more obscure. Scientists are beginning to study the ineffable phenomenon of consciousness, the awareness we have of our existence. Related to this are attempts to produce artificial intelligence on computers that will make the machines conscious of their own existence.[43] Is the mind just a complex, self-aware machine that could have evolved from simpler machines,[44] or is it an entity on a higher level? We do not know enough about how the mind works to address that question effectively. Clearly, however, when thinking human beings make machines that think, that activity is more akin to the concept of creation by design than to an origin by evolution without any intelligent input.

A few animals show a degree of intelligence akin to that of humans.[45] Researchers have reported a limited form of symbolic communication in chimpanzees,[46] and dogs seem to show some understanding, although often less than their loyal masters claim. But the gap between animal and human intelligence is still enormous. One wonders how humankind could have evolved a mind that seems far beyond the requirement for evolutionary survival. Baboons have endured quite well without such complex brains. Alfred Russel Wallace (1823-1913), who along with Darwin developed the concept of natural selection, raised this question. He felt the need for something beyond the blind forces of nature to explain the mind. Some evolutionists still discuss the question. It is sometimes suggested that humans show that they have more mental ability than is good for their survival in that they are effectively destroying the very environment they need.[47] Referring to the expected increased reproductive rates of superior competitors (i.e., survival of the fittest), the evolutionist John Maynard Smith astutely and candidly comments that "few people have had more children because they could solve differential equations or play chess blindfold."[48] Perhaps we cannot explain humankind's special qualities by a simple evolutionary process.

Darwin, who lived in England, had a good friend and supporter in the United States, the botanist Asa Gray, with whom he shared many of his deeper thoughts. He once wrote to Gray: "I remember well the time when the thought of the eye made me cold all over, but I have got over this stage of the complaint, and now small trifling particulars of structure often make me very uncomfortable. The sight of a feather in a peacock's tail, whenever I gaze at it, makes me sick!"[49]

Why would the feather of a peacock make Darwin sick? I am not exactly sure I can answer that, but I suspect that few can reflect on the beauty of a peacock's iridescent tail feather without wondering if it is not the result of some kind of design, not simply because of its intricacy, but especially because of its beauty. Why do we appreciate beauty, enjoy music, and have that great wonder of existence? Such mental characteristics seem beyond the mechanistic level and above the requirements for survival expected from natural selection.

The origin of the mind is an enigma for any naturalistic explanation. As we look at the brain, we face the awesome fact that here in this 1.5-kilogram organ is the seat of "who I am." How did the multitude of connections get properly arranged so we can reason[50] (one hopes that most of us are thinking straight!), devise mathematical theorems, ask questions about our origins, learn new languages, and compose symphonies? Even more challenging to naturalistic theories of human origins is our power of choice and such characteristics as moral responsibility, loyalty, love, and a spiritual dimension. Both the physical complexities of the brain and the exceptional activities of the mind suggest a high level of intelligent design, and not a mechanistic evolutionary origin.

CONCLUSIONS

The study of human origins has been an especially contentious area of scientific inquiry. We can attribute this, at least in part, to the lack of firm data and the personal involvement of the scientist. The evidence for human evolution is sparse and subject to a variety of interpretations. The presence of the higher characteristics of the human mind, such as consciousness, creativity, free will, aesthetics, morality, and spirituality, all suggest that humans were especially designed as a higher kind of being and that they did not originate from animals by a purely mechanistic evolutionary process.

REFERENCES

1. Nance J. 1975. The gentle Tasaday: a Stone Age people in the Philippine rain forest. New York and London: Harcourt, Brace, Jovanovich, p. 134.
2. *Ibid.*
3. Iten O. 1992. The "Tasaday" and the press. In: Headland TN, editor. The Tasaday controversy: assessing the evidence. Scholarly series, Special Publications of the American Anthropological Association, No. 28. Washington, D.C.: American Anthropological Association, pp. 40-58.

4. McCarry C. 1988. Three men who made the magazine. National Geographic 174:287-316.
5. Berreman GD. 1982. The Tasaday: Stone Age survivors or space age fakes? In: Headland, pp. 21-39 (note 3).
6. For general references on the Tasaday, see: (a) Anonymous. 1971. First glimpse of a Stone Age tribe. National Geographic 140(6):880-882b; (b) Bower B. 1989a. A world that never existed. Science News 135:264-266; (c) Bower B. 1989b. The strange case of the Tasaday. Science News 135:280, 281, 283; (d) Headland (note 3); (e) MacLeish K. 1972. Stone Age cavemen of Mindanao. National Geographic 142(2):219-249; (f) Nance (note 1).
7. This is a conservative figure. It could easily run a hundred to a thousand times higher, but super chips are also becoming more and more refined.
8. Darwin C. 1874. The descent of man, and selection in relation to sex. Rev. ed. Chicago: National Library Association, pp. 116, 118, 643.
9. Simpson GG. 1967. The meaning of evolution: a study of the history of life and of its significance for man. Rev. ed. New Haven and London: Yale University Press, p. 345.
10. Lewin R. 1987. Bones of contention: controversies in the search for human origins. New York: Simon and Schuster, p. 20.
11. Washburn SL. 1973. The evolution game. Journal of Human Evolution 2:557-561.
12. Pilbeam D. 1978. Rethinking human origins. Discovery 13(1):2-10.
13. Lewin, p. 64 (note 10).
14. For a variety of proposed relationships, see: (a) Avers CJ. 1989. Process and pattern in evolution. New York and Oxford: Oxford University Press, pp. 496-498; (b) Bower B. 1992. Erectus unhinged. Science News 141:408-411; (c) Edey MA, Johanson DC. 1989. Blueprints: solving the mystery of evolution. Boston, Toronto, and London: Little, Brown, and Company, pp. 337-353; (d) Martin RD. 1993. Primate origins: plugging the gaps. Nature 363:223-233; (e) Wood B. 1992. Origin and evolution of the genus *Homo*. Nature 355:783-790.
15. Mayr E. 1982. Reflections on human paleontology. In: Spencer F, editor. A history of American physical anthropology, 1930-1980. New York and London: Academic Press, pp. 231-237.
16. E.g., (a) Leakey MG, Feibel CS, McDougall I, Walker A. 1995. New four-million-year-old hominid species from Kanapoi and Allia Bay, Kenya. Nature 376:565-571; (b) White TD, Suwa G, Asfaw B. 1994. *Australopithecus ramidus,* a new species of early hominid from Aramis, Ethiopia. Nature 371:306-312.
17. (a) Leakey LSB, Leakey MD. 1964. Recent discoveries of fossil hominids in Tanganyika: at Olduvai and near Lake Natron. Nature 202:5-7; (b) Leakey LSB, Tobias PV, Napier JR. 1964. A new species of the genus *Homo* from Olduvai Gorge. Nature 202:7-9; (c) Lewin, p. 137 (note 10).
18. (a) Häusler M, Schmid P. 1995. Comparison of the pelvis of Sts 14 and AL 288-1: implications for birth and sexual dimorphism in australopithecines. Journal of Human Evolution 29:363-383; (b) Shreeve J. 1995. Sexing fossils: a boy named Lucy. Science 270:1297, 1298.
19. (a) Grine FE. 1993. Australopithecine taxonomy and phylogeny: historical background and recent interpretation. In: Ciochon RL, Fleagle JG. The human evolution sourcebook. Advances in Human Evolution Series. Englewood Cliffs, N.J.: Prentice Hall, pp. 198-210; (b) Wood B. 1992. Origin and evolution of the genus *Homo*. Nature 355:783-790.
20. Avers, p. 509 (note 14a).
21. Stanley SM. 1981. The new evolutionary timetable: fossils, genes, and the origin of species. New York: Basic Books, p. 148.
22. Wood (note 14e).
23. (a) Bromage TG, Dean MC. 1985. Reevaluation of the age at death of immature fossil hominids. Nature 317:525-527; (b) Johanson DC, Masao FT, Eck GG, White TD, Walter RC, Kimbel WH, Asfaw B, Manega P, Ndessoia P, Suwa G. 1987. New partial skeleton of *Homo habilis* from Olduvai Gorge, Tanzania. Nature 327:205-209; (c) Smith BH. 1986. Dental development in *Australopithecus* and early *Homo*. Nature 323:327-330; (d) Susman RL, Stern JT. 1982. Functional morphology of *Homo habilis*. Science 217:931-934.
24. Boule M, Vallois HV. 1957. Fossil men. Bullock M, translator. New York: Dryden Press, pp. 193-258. Translation of: Les Hommes Fossiles.

25. Straus WL, Jr., Cave AJE. 1957. Pathology and the posture of Neanderthal man. Quarterly Review of Biology 32:348-363.
26. These figures are on display at the American Museum of Natural History in New York, as reported in: Lubenow ML. 1992. Bones of contention: a creationist assessment of human fossils. Grand Rapids: Baker Book House, p. 82.
27. See chapter 14 for a discussion of this method.
28. Lewin, pp. 189-252 (note 10).
29. Gibbons A. 1994. Rewriting—and redating—prehistory. Science 263:1087, 1088.
30. (a) Huang W, Ciochon R, Yumin G, Larick R, Qiren F, Schwarcz H, Yonge C, De Vos J, Rink W. 1995. Early *Homo* and associated artefacts from Asia. Nature 378:275-278; (b) Swisher CC III, Curtis GH, Jacob T, Getty AG, Suprijo A, Widiasmoro [n.a.]. 1994. Age of the earliest known hominids in Java, Indonesia. Science 263:1118-1121.
31. (a) Leakey R, Lewin R. 1992. Origins reconsidered: in search of what makes us human. New York, London, and Sydney: Doubleday, p. 108; (b) Lubenow, pp. 169-183 (note 26).
32. Swisher III CC, Rink WJ, Antón SC, Schwarcz HP, Curtis GH, Suprijo A, Widiasmoro [n.a.]. 1996. Latest *Homo erectus* of Java: potential contemporaneity with *Homo sapiens* in Southeast Asia. Science 274:1870-1874.
33. (a) Edey and Johanson, p. 352 (note 14c); (b) Wood (note 14e).
34. (a) Martin (note 14d); (b) Martin L, Andrews P. 1993. Renaissance of Europe's ape. Nature 365:494; (c) Moyà Solà S, Köhler M. 1993. Recent discoveries of *Dryopithecus* shed new light on evolution of great apes. Nature 365:543-545.
35. (a) Edey and Johanson, p. 353 (note 14c); (b) Johanson DC, Edey MA. 1981. Lucy: the beginnings of humankind. New York: Simon and Schuster, p. 286.
36. Leakey and Lewin, p. 110 (note 31a).
37. Aitken MJ, Stringer CB, Mellars PA, editors. 1993. The origin of modern humans and the impact of chronometric dating. Princeton, N.J.: Princeton University Press.
38. Edey and Johanson, pp. 355-368 (note 14c).
39. E.g., Patterson C, Williams DM, Humphries CJ. 1993. Congruence between molecular and morphological phylogenies. Annual Review of Ecology and Systematics 24:153-188.
40. For instance: DT Gish ([a] 1985. Evolution: the challenge of the fossil record. El Cajon, Calif.: Creation-Life Publishers, pp. 130-206) draws the line mostly above *Homo erectus,* while ML Lubenow ([b] p. 162 [note 26]) includes some *Homo habilis* types, and AW Mehlert ([c] 1992. A review of the present status of some alleged early hominids. Creation Ex Nihilo Technical Journal 6:10-41) apparently places *Homo erectus* with human beings.
41. Gen. 5; 7:11-13.
42. The estimate of the number of neurons in the brain varies greatly. The cerebellum has many more than the cerebrum. For details on these estimates, see: Williams PL, Warwick R, Dyson M, Bannister LH, editors. 1989. Gray's anatomy. 37th ed. Edinburgh, London, and New York: Churchill Livingstone, pp. 968, 972, 1043. Their figures can imply about 300,000 million in the cerebellum.
43. Davidson C. 1993. I process therefore I am. New Scientist (37 March), pp. 22-26.
44. (a) Calvin WH. 1994. The emergence of intelligence. Scientific American 271:101-107; (b) Penrose R. 1994. Shadows of the mind: a search for the missing science of consciousness. Oxford, New York, and Melbourne: Oxford University Press.
45. Reference can be made here to the debate over the evolution of altruism by kin selection, which gives an evolutionary basis for altruism, but which tends to deny the existence of free will. For some recent discussions, see: (a) Barbour IG. 1990. Religion in an age of science. The Gifford Lectures 1989-1991, vol. 1. San Francisco and New York: Harper and Row, pp. 192-194; (b) Brand LR, Carter RL. 1992. Sociobiology: the evolution theory's answer to altruistic behavior. Origins 19:54-71; (c) Dawkins R. 1989. The selfish gene. New ed. Oxford and New York: Oxford University Press, pp. 189-233; (d) Maynard Smith J. 1988. Did Darwin get it right? Essays on games, sex, and evolution. New York and London: Chapman and Hall, pp. 86-92; (e) Peacocke AR. 1986. God and the new biology. San

Francisco, Cambridge, and New York: Harper and Row, pp. 108-115.

46. (a) Lewin R. 1991. Look who's talking now. New Scientist (27 April), pp. 49-52; (b) Seyfarth R, Cheney D. 1992. Inside the mind of a monkey. New Scientist (4 January), pp. 25-29.
47. Edey and Johanson, pp. 371-390 (note 14c).
48. Maynard Smith, p. 94 (note 45d).
49. Darwin F, editor. 1887-1888. The life and letters of Charles Darwin, vol. 2. London: John Murray, p. 296.
50. For some attempted explanations that do not address the specific complexity needed for intricate thought patterns, etc., see: (a) Lee D, Malpeli JG. 1994. Global form and singularity: modeling the blind spot's role in lateral geniculate morphogenesis. Science 263:1292-1294; (b) Stryker MP. 1994. Precise development from imprecise rules. Science 263:1244, 1245.

CHAPTER 8

MORE BIOLOGICAL QUESTIONS

Everything from an egg.
—William Harvey[1]

The wonders of biology are almost endless. Scientists have now discovered that a tiny roundworm has 100 million nucleotide base pairs in the DNA of each of its cells. This DNA directs a wide variety of processes that enable the worm to be "alive." Similar information about a great variety of organisms has been emerging and is, to say the least, both fascinating and bewildering. The "diversity" period of evolutionary thought, referred to in chapter 5, is due in part to dramatic advances in molecular biology. We can hardly overemphasize that such discoveries have opened up vast and important biological vistas whose existence was unknown to us a few years ago. In this chapter we will consider several biological topics, beginning with some questions raised during the diversity period of evolutionary thought. We will continue with a brief look at some new complex discoveries and then consider the changes such questions and discoveries have produced in the thinking of some evolutionists.

TRADITIONALISTS AND CLADISTS

Evolution presupposes that all living organisms are related. Starting from a simple original form of life, and experiencing changes over billions of years, the organisms have finally evolved into their present-day variety. While the organisms are transforming into more and more complex forms, the number of species also has increased. An original species purportedly produced other species each of which evolved into other different species, and so on. This repeated process produced the typical evolutionary tree, with the original species at the base (trunk), more advanced types forming the branches, and currently living species forming the "leaves" of the tree (Figure 11.1).

The arrangement of the branches on evolutionary trees can vary considerably in configuration, since few species have the proper characteristics to represent the trunk or branches. Because plausible ancestors are so rare, hypotheses of evolutionary relationships take many arrangements.

The traditional evolutionary method has been to establish relationships by analyzing the overall similarities between organisms. The greater the similarity, the more recently the organisms are assumed to have evolved from each other. Some systematists (those who classify organisms) assign quantitative values to characteristics and calculate an index of similarities. Selecting which characteristics to evaluate, and determining the importance of each characteristic is quite subjective. Ernst Mayr, the prominent traditional evolutionist from Harvard, points out that classification of organisms is a kind of "art."[2] The lack of rigor and objectivity has stimulated another approach to systematics called cladistics. This term is not well defined.

Cladists, who have been highly influential, argue that general similarities tell little about evolution. Similarities can apply to many evolutionary pathways. They consider only *unique* shared similarities (synapomorphies) as important in determining relationships, but such traits are rare, and some cladists feel that they may never be certain of evolutionary relationships. We see the controversy between cladists and traditionalists illustrated by this quotation from a leading cladist, Norman Platnick, who studies spiders at the American Museum of Natural History. He outlines the problem as follows: "Evolutionary biologists have a choice to make: either we agree with Mayr that narrative explanations are the name of the game, and continue drifting away from the rest of biology into an area ruled only by authority and consensus, or we insist that wherever possible our explanations be testable and potentially falsifiable and that evolutionary biology rejoin the scientific community at large."[3]

Cladists believe in evolution, but to them it can be more a matter of faith than of assertion.[4] They are especially concerned about finding verifiable characteristics important in determining actual relationships between organisms.

GRADUALISTS AND PUNCTUATIONALISTS

Observation of nature indicates that even closely related species, such as two kinds of grasshoppers, may be quite distinct from each other. Neo-Darwinians propose that a slow, gradual process of minor changes eventually produces distinct new forms. They refer to this slow change as gradualism. As the changes accumulate, groups diverge, leaving a larger and larger gap between them. The only place where we might find intermediates abundantly is in the fossil record of past life. However, fossils show the same pattern of discontinuity. Some have attributed the missing evidence to the incompleteness of the fossil data because of lack of preservation or discovery.

In 1972 two prominent paleontologists, Niles Eldredge, at the American Museum of Natural History, and Stephen Jay Gould, at Harvard, proposed a different explanation for the discontinuities among fossils.[5] They suggested that evolution proceeds at an irregular pace, with long periods of stability between moments of rapid change. They called the new concept "punctuated equilibria." Punctuation refers to the changes, and equilibria denotes the periods of stability. The proposal "triggered an unusually hot debate"[6] that continues to the present. The idea, sometimes affectionately—and sometimes otherwise!—called "punk eck," proposes that significant evolutionary changes do not occur in large populations. If for some reason a small group of individuals becomes isolated, evolution should proceed more rapidly, because changes can become established more readily among the few members of a small population. Thus intermediates are rarely, if ever, preserved in the fossil record because relatively few ever existed.

Punctuated equilibria does not resolve the more serious evolutionary problem of the absence of entire series of intermediates between the larger major groups of living or fossil organisms.[7] It deals with small changes. Its proponents apply the concept at the species level. It does not address the critical question of an evolutionary mechanism capable of producing new classes, phyla, divisions, and kingdoms.

SELECTIONISTS AND NEUTRALISTS

Probably the most severe conflict in the diversified period of evolutionary thinking has been between selectionists and neutralists. It reminds one of the old debate over genetic drift, which developed early in the modern synthesis period. Selectionists emphasize the importance of natural selection. Neutralists conclude that evolution advances mainly by neutral mutations not selected by the environment. They believe that major evolutionary changes occur by the accumulation of such neutral mutations.[8]

In a 1968 article in the journal *Nature,*[9] Motoo Kimura emphasized the importance of neutral mutations. Soon thereafter the idea received support from two other molecular biologists, Jack Lester King and Thomas H. Jukes, who published in the journal *Science.*[10] Selectionists, unable to conceive of any genetic change not having some evolutionary significance, be it positive or nega-

TABLE 8.1

GROUPS		A	B	GROUPS		A	B
PRIMATES	Human	0	41	**FISH** (cont'd)	Carp	17	42
	Rhesus monkey	1	41		Dogfish	23	45
					Lamprey	19	45
OTHER	Pig, Bovine, Sheep	10	41				
				INSECTS	Fruit fly	27	42
MAMMALS	Horse	12	42		Screwworm fly	25	42
	Dog	11	41		Silkworm moth	29	42
	Gray whale	10	41		Tobacco horn		
	Rabbit	9	41		worm moth	29	44
	Kangaroo	10	42				
				PLANTS	Mung bean	40	45
BIRDS	Chicken, Turkey	13	41		Sesame	35	44
	Penguins	13	40		Castor	37	42
	Peking duck	11	41		Sunflower	38	43
	Pigeon	12	41		Wheat	38	42
REPTILES	Snapping turtle	14	44	**YEASTS**	*Candida kruses*	44	25
	Rattlesnake	13	44		*Debaryomyces kloeckeri*	41	27
					Baker's yeast	41	0
AMPHIBIA	Bullfrog	17	43				
				MOLD	*Neurospora crassa*	44	38
FISH	Tuna	20	43				
	Bonito	20	41	**BACTERIUM**	*Rhodospirillum rubrum* c_2	65	69

Percent difference of amino-acid sequence in the enzyme Cytochrome-C compared to humans (column A) and yeast (column B)*

*Data from: Dayhoff MO. 1972. Atlas of protein sequence and structure, vol. 5. Washington, D.C.: National Biomedical Research Foundation, p. D-8.

tive, sharply criticized the new concept. Since then, an abundance of conjecture has appeared on both sides of the issue.

We can better understand the controversy within the perspective of newer techniques in molecular biology that enable scientists to determine the specific nucleotide base sequence of DNA. Some of the genetic changes noted do not affect the physical makeup of the organism, hence would not be influenced by natural selection. Such unexpressed genetic changes fit better with the neutral mutation concept. Questions have also arisen as to how significant small changes are to survival (e.g., one extra bristle on the body of a fly). Neutralists, who usually do not entirely reject natural selection, propose that neutral changes spread by the random drift of genes in a population. Selectionists, however, doubt that this process can produce any significant changes without the help of natural selection. The issue remains unresolved.

THE MOLECULAR EVOLUTIONARY CLOCK

While the selectionist-neutralist discussion appears to be mainly an internal conflict within the evolutionary community, one aspect has important implications for evolution and creation: the question of the molecular evolutionary clock. Even before anyone postulated the neutral theory, it had been suggested that changes could be occurring in DNA at a more or less constant rate. This would cause the DNA-produced proteins to diverge in a pattern that would reflect the rate of evolutionary changes over time.[11] Some examples were noted in which protein differences among organisms seemed to form a pattern corresponding to that expected of their evolutionary relationships.

The molecular evolutionary clock rests on the assumption that the large molecules (biopolymers) change continuously over time. Therefore, the greater the differences noted, the more time implied for divergence from a common evolutionary ancestor. Table 8.1, Column A, compares the percent of difference of the amino acids in the ubiquitous enzyme cytochrome *c*, as found in a variety of organisms. Cytochrome *c* functions in electron transport during chemical energy release in the cell. One can see a general increase in difference as one compares human beings with simpler and simpler organisms, which evolutionary theory assumes to have diverged increasingly earlier. Column B shows the uniformity of the differences between other organisms and yeast cells which are regarded as having evolved very early. This consistency has been interpreted as indicating a highly uniform molecular clock in which we can estimate the length of time since divergence from the degree of molecular difference. Proponents of the theory consider cytochrome *c* to be one of the best clocks. Textbooks of biology and evolution often use this evidence to support the general theory of evolution. However the data may not reflect evolution. They may represent biological factors related to the degree of complexity of the various organisms.

A number of questions confront the molecular clock hypothesis. There is uncertainty regarding the effect of neutral mutations, the type most satisfactory for the molecular clock. If the changes are not neutral or only nearly neutral, then the theoretical basis for the molecular clock is not valid. Nonneutral changes controlled by natural selection would not work as a clock. They would reflect environmental influences, not time. Evolutionists have raised a number of other questions about the molecular clock, many of them stemming from the selectionist-neutralist controversy, with neutralists being more in favor of the clock.

While some studies of variation in the enzyme cytochrome *c* have given results consistent with the molecular clock, in other studies the rate of change can vary by as much as a factor of 10.[12] The enzyme superoxide dismutase, which alleviates the toxicity of oxygen in most living organisms, is notorious for giving erratic molecular clock results.[13] Researchers interpret the clock for apes and human beings as slowing down considerably.[14] Because of such differences, some have labeled the molecular clock as "episodic"[15]—that is, it has periods of slower and faster rates.

Table 8.2 compares sequence differences of the amino acids in the hormone insulin among vertebrates. According to the molecular clock hypothesis, all rodents should be approximately equivalent in their difference from humans since their ancestors would have evolved from each other at the same time. This is clearly not the case. Humans differ from the house mouse by 8 percent, but from the coypu (a South American rodent) by 38 percent. This latter figure is even greater than the difference between humans and several kinds of fish which would be expected to be much greater. In other comparisons of this hormone[16] the difference between a mouse and a guinea pig (35 percent), which are supposedly closely related, is greater than that between a mouse and a whale (12 percent), a human being and a rattlesnake (24 percent), a chicken and a bonito (fish, 16 percent), or many other distantly related organisms. The scientific literature has noted a host of similar inconsistencies.[17] We find little evidence of a constant rate of change on which the molecular clock must operate.

TABLE 8.2

ORGANISM	% DIFFERENCE	ORGANISM	% DIFFERENCE
Human	0	Chicken and Turkey	14
Rabbit	2	Duck	12
Spiny mouse	4	Rattlesnake	24
Mouse	8	Toadfish	34
Guinea pig	35	Cod	31
Coypu	38	Angler fish	29
Elephant	4	Tuna	29
Sheep	8	Bonito	22
Sperm whale	6	Atlantic hagfish	37

Percent difference of amino-acid sequence in the hormone insulin for various organisms as compared to human.[†]

[†] Data from Dayhoff MO. 1976. Atlas of protein sequence and structure, vol. 5, supplement 2. Washington, D.C.: National Biomedical Research Foundation, p. 129.

In view of the peculiarities we have just noted, it should not surprise us that amino acid sequence comparisons for different kinds of proteins offer conflicting evolutionary results. One such test, comparing the evolutionary relationship among several orders of mammals based on the amino acid sequence of four different kinds of proteins, gave "a general lack of congruence" among the four proteins used and only "moderate congruence" with relationships based on the general shape (morphology) of the various organisms.[18]

The so-called living fossils present another enigma for the molecular-clock hypothesis. Living fossils are species that are similar to fossil ancestors that supposedly lived hundreds of millions of years earlier. An example is the common horseshoe crab[19] of the east coast of North America. It appears nearly identical to fossil counterparts assumed to have existed at least 200 million years earlier. Could changes by the molecular clock process accumulate continuously for 200 million years without apparently affecting the organism?

The data of Table 8.1, Column B, are so uniform that they raise further questions about the molecular clock both within an evolutionary context and when we take other biological considerations into account. How could such results be so uniform when, as mentioned above, research has shown the cytochrome *c* clock to be so variable? Since changes in proteins (based on changes in DNA) are possibly facilitated by cell division, is it possible that there has been such constancy of mutation rate through all the varied pathways of evolution for all kinds of plants and animals? One has difficulty envisioning this, considering the evolutionary pathways sometimes involve mainly warm-blooded animals, while others only cold-blooded animals or various plants. Also some species reproduce very rapidly, others very slowly. Such uniform results for such assumed varied pathways of evolution can raise further questions about the assumptions of the molecular clock and suggest that we look for alternative explanations. Until we learn more about what makes the clock work—if there really is a clock—we should be cautious.

Science writer Roger Lewin has summarized the status of the molecular clock in an article entitled "Molecular Clocks Run Out of Time." He concludes that the one constant beginning to emerge concerning the ticking of the molecular clock appears to be variation in rate.[20] Siegfried Scherer, a biologist at the University of Konstanz, concludes "that the protein molecular clock hypothesis should be rejected,"[21] and biologist Jeff Palmer, at Indiana University, states that "it's all based on assumptions that the molecular clock is constant, when the more closely we look at molecular change, the more evidence we have that it is not."[22] Two molecular biologists, Lisa Vawter and Wesley Brown, are also emphatic, proposing "a robust rejection of a generalized molecular clock hypothesis."[23]

COMPLEXITIES REVEALED BY MOLECULAR BIOLOGY

A multitude of recent discoveries in molecular biology have contributed to the diversification of evolutionary thinking. They reveal features of life not conceived of 30 years ago. Many mysteries about genetic systems baffle the imagination of both evolutionists and creationists. Why should a sequence of only a few nucleotide bases be repeated about 100,000 times in the middle of a fruit fly chromosome? What is the function of the large amount of noncoding, or repetitive, DNA found in all but the simplest organisms? In humans this comprises possibly as much as 97 percent of our DNA. Those assuming it represents some kind of genetic garbage left from an evolutionary past call it junk DNA. Pseudogenes are another type of apparently noncoding DNA sequence. They appear similar to functional genes, but have portions that apparently prevent normal gene function.[24] However, we are not sure that noncoding sequences are really nonfunctional. Some have suggested that "junk DNA" is functional, and scientists are discarding the term. Other evolutionists wonder why it should survive with such "purity" if it does not have a function. One would expect mutations to alter it. Still others have proposed some kind of function for noncoding DNA, including a hidden language.[25]

The old idea of genes being strung along in lengthy chains of DNA, occasionally mutating and eventually producing new organisms, is far from what science is actually finding. Instead, genes appear to be organized in complex interacting systems, including some feedback mechanisms that would be difficult to develop by a gradual random evolutionary process because of a lack of survival value until the system is fully functional. A few examples follow.

1. **The Genetic Code**. The discovery of the genetic code has shown how the combination of four different kinds of nucleotide bases in code units of three bases each on the DNA chain (Figure 4.1) can dictate the order of any of the 20 different kinds of amino acids that form a protein. The cell uses information from DNA in its nucleus to manufacture thousands of different proteins through a complex coded system. How can a random evolutionary process produce a coded system? The system requires not only intricate coded information but also a code reading system. Otherwise nothing will happen.

2. **Gene Control System**. The process of manufacturing proteins from the information of the genes is complex and highly regulated. Genes must be turned on and off as needed. Researchers have discovered a number of gene control mechanisms,[26] some repressing the gene, others activating it. Some genes have

more than one control mechanism. The "*Lac operon*" system, discovered in a common bacterium, has become a classic example of a gene control system.[27] It regulates the production of three enzymes (proteins) employed in the metabolism of the sugar lactose. The three enzymes are coded next to each other on the DNA chain. Preceding the codes are four special regions of coded DNA necessary for regulating and producing the enzymes as needed. This basic kind of system, and more complex regulatory systems, also appear in higher organisms.[28] The vast numbers of chemical changes in cells have complex control systems.

3. **Error-correcting Systems**. Multicellular organisms produce many new cells as part of the normal maintenance and repair process. As each cell divides, it replicates millions to thousands of millions of nucleotide bases. In the case of humans, more than 3,000 million nucleotide base pairs form whenever the body makes DNA for a new cell. In the process of duplicating this information, errors can occur quite frequently. While some of the copying errors seem to make little difference, others can be lethal to an organism. The rate of error without the intervention of editing enzymes can be as high as 1 percent. This would result in thousands to millions of errors per cell division. Fortunately, the cell has efficient systems for preventing this. These elaborate mechanisms can improve the accuracy of copying by millions of times, so that very few errors remain.[29] The elegant correcting systems check for errors and repair any erroneous sections of DNA. Researchers have identified at least 15 enzymes involved in DNA repair in the bacterium *Escherichia coli,* and we still have much more to learn about such systems.[30] From an evolutionary perspective, certain questions arise when we consider this DNA proofreading system. For instance, how could an error-prone system be consistent enough to permit the evolution of a self-correcting mechanism? One researcher has described this difficulty as "an unsolved problem in theoretical biology."[31]

As they study DNA, molecular biologists are discovering a vast array of specialized functions that copy, cut, splice, edit, translocate, and invert DNA. A "fluid" DNA concept with programming capabilities is replacing the old idea of a simple DNA pattern dictating the development and function of organisms. J. A. Shapiro, of the University of Chicago, reflects the newer ideas when he states: "We need to think of genomes [DNA] as information-processing systems."[32] He further emphasizes "that many (perhaps the vast majority) of DNA alterations are not due to chance chemical events or replication errors. Rather, they result from the action of highly sophisticated biochemical systems which may be thought of as genome [DNA] reprogramming functions."

In molecular biology the search for truth has just begun.

EXTRAORDINARY EVOLUTIONARY CONCEPTS

The diversified period of evolutionary thought has generated more than the ordinary variety of ideas and conflicts. The failure to find any compelling explanation for evolutionary development has stimulated some unusual suggestions. I will mention only three or four as examples.

In England the chemist James Lovelock has promulgated the Gaia hypothesis. Lynn Margulis, a distinguished biologist at Boston University, has strongly supported him. The idea has gained significant popularity, but not among classical evolutionists. Gaia is the idea that the whole earth is a living organism in which life interacts harmoniously with the inanimate earth as a correlated whole.[33] Gaia involves more of a symbiotic process of organisms working together rather than competing for survival. Advocating his newer concept, Margulis states that neo-Darwinism "must be dismissed as a minor twentieth-century religious sect within the sprawling religious persuasion of Anglo-Saxon biology."[34]

Christopher Wills, of the San Diego campus of the University of California, has proposed that genes have evolved toward an increasing ability to facilitate their own improvement.[35] While he starts from an orthodox scientific perspective, Wills proposes that some of the complexities of advanced organisms result from the genes developing "wisdom" to manage more complex functions as evolution progresses. He provides little compelling evidence, but draws from a multitude of examples indicating that advanced organisms have highly integrated gene mechanisms. While living systems are unquestionably highly complex, the assumption that such "wisdom" developed all by itself does not have much support.

Along the same line of thought are computer studies attempting to discover how life could have organized itself. As mentioned earlier,[36] the second law of thermodynamics suggests that the universe has an inexorable tendency toward disorder. Evolution suggests the opposite, and these studies try to explain how this could happen.[37] In order to study this, the researcher creates a virtual biological world on a computer. Our familiar computer viruses contain some of the elements of this "artificial life." Programs note the effects of simulated factors such as variability, competition, and natural selection. Researchers hope that such studies can explain the self-organization expected of evolution. Those who work on this report some success, but there are many complicating factors even in this simplified "silicone universe."

The work has centered around the Santa Fe Institute in New Mexico, with specialists in several other research centers. They study the question of the origin of complexity in a broad perspective, including evolution, ecology, human systems, and Gaia. The search has been for some kind of universal explanation for the emergence of complexity. Some consensus has developed that complexity develops at the "edge of chaos." This is based on the fact that highly ordered and stable systems, such as crystals, follow a set pattern and do not generate anything new. On the other hand, completely chaotic systems such as a heated gas are too formless and mixed up to be significant. Hence complex systems should develop in between the two extremes, at the edge of chaos.

The work of the institute has received criticism from several perspectives. The hopes of a universal explanation for complexity are dimming.[38] Some biologists feel that natural selection alone is sufficient to explain complexity, and other explanations are not necessary.[39] Others express concern that simplification might bring comprehension at the expense of reality.[40] One prominent evolutionist, John Maynard Smith, characterizes this kind of artificial life as "basically a fact-free science,"[41] while the ecologist Robert May finds the work of the institute "mathematically interesting but biologically trivial."[42] One of the most serious criticisms comes from a logical perspective that points out that "verification and validation of numerical models of natural systems is impossible. This is because complex natural systems are never closed."[43] We can never be sure that we have all the information.

A different approach has come from the famous French zoologist Pierre Grassé, who has written an insightful volume entitled *Evolution of Living Organisms.*[44] Grassé, former president of the French Academy of Sciences and editor of a 35-volume treatise on zoology, is thoroughly familiar with living organisms. He is highly critical of some current evolutionary concepts and categorically denies the power of mutation and selection in evolution. To bridge the gaps between major groups of organisms, he suggests special genes and special biochemical activity, but agrees that evolution is a mystery about which little is, or can be, known. He concludes by stating: "Perhaps in this area biology can go no farther: the rest is metaphysics."[45]

WHERE IS EVOLUTION GOING?

A spate of books criticizing evolutionary theory have appeared during the past few years. Many of them have come from individuals who either believe in evolution or who at least do not believe in creation. Some examples follow.

1. Michael Behe, *Darwin's Black Box: The Biochemical Challenge to Evolution.*[46] A biochemist from Lehigh University who is not a creationist—certainly not in the traditional interpretation of the word "creationist"—gives many examples of what he calls "irreducible complexity" that he feels could not have

developed by a random process.

2. Francis Crick, *Life Itself: Its Origin and Nature.*[47] A Nobel laureate points out that the problems concerning the origin of life on the earth are so great that it must have originated from elsewhere in the universe and then been transferred here.

3. Michael Denton, *Evolution: A Theory in Crisis.*[48] This Australian microbiologist lightly dismisses creation as a myth, yet states, "Ultimately the Darwinian theory of evolution is no more nor less than the great cosmogenic myth of the twentieth century."[49]

4. Francis Hitching, *The Neck of the Giraffe: Where Darwin Went Wrong.*[50] Hitching rejects creation, but poses many serious problems for evolution.

5. Mae-Wan Ho and Peter Saunders, *Beyond Neo-Darwinism.*[51] Two academicians in England, both evolutionists, point out that "all the signs are that evolution theory is in crisis, and that a change is on the way."[52]

6. Søren Løvtrup, *Darwinism: The Refutation of a Myth.*[53] An embryologist from Sweden, Løvtrup accepts some form of evolution by major steps and states, "I believe that one day the Darwinian myth will be ranked the greatest deceit in the history of science. When this happens many people will pose the question: How did this ever happen?"[54]

7. Mark Ridley, *Problems of Evolution.*[55] An Oxford University evolutionist raises several questions about evolution, some of which he feels are minor, while others, such as how major evolutionary changes take place, are definitely problematic.

8. Robert Shapiro, *Origins: A Skeptic's Guide to the Creation of Life on Earth.*[56] A noted chemist from New York University raises many questions about evolution. He affirms his faith in science and hopes that it will be able to formulate a plausible model.

9. Gordon Rattray Taylor, *The Great Evolution Mystery.*[57] This knowledgeable British science writer affirms his belief in evolution, but referring to a possible mechanism for evolution, states, "In short, the dogma which has dominated most biological thinking for more than a century is collapsing."[58]

We should not interpret such a plethora of criticism as implying that scientists are giving up on evolution. This is not the case. It does suggest, however, of the fact that the latest findings of science are not providing anything approaching a workable model for evolution.

We don't know what lies ahead for evolutionary theory, but the winds of change are being felt. Despite the inadequacies and internal conflicts, however, scientists, teachers, and textbooks still usually represent evolution as a fact that needs no reevaluation. Richard Dawkins, of Oxford University, states that "today the theory of evolution is about as much open to doubt as the theory that the earth goes round the sun,"[59] while Ernst Mayr, of Harvard, comments that "there is no justification whatsoever for the claim that the Darwinian paradigm has been refuted and has to be replaced by something new."[60] Despite such optimistic pronouncements, a significant number of scientists are raising questions about the general theory of evolution.

CONCLUSIONS

One of the major problems evolutionists face is that the very science they espouse seems to be saying that no one has yet found a plausible mechanism for their theory. How did evolutionists get into this quandary? This is a most important question.[61]

At present, proposed evolutionary mechanisms seem to be more implausible than ever. Many biological systems appear too complex for a spontaneous origin by random events. Noteworthy examples include: (1) a system for protein synthesis that provides information through a genetic code, and then decodes it during synthesis; (2) complex gene-control systems; and (3) complex editing systems for correcting errors in DNA copying. We could give many more examples. All these systems appear to be intricate and highly programmed. It does not seem possible that they could arise spontaneously. We would not expect a preprogrammed computer to develop spontaneously on a desolate planet, nor should we expect the spontaneous origin of biological feedback systems. Besides origin, there is also need for reproduction. So these computers should also have the ability to reproduce themselves into thousands of duplicates. The creation alternative suggests that a variety of organisms with limited adaptability were purposefully designed. Creationists do not have all the answers, but the different opinions and the number of scientific problems for evolution can suggest that the creation model deserves serious consideration.

REFERENCES

1. Quoted in: Mackay AL. 1991. A dictionary of scientific quotations. Bristol and Philadelphia: Institute of Physics Publishing, p. 114.
2. Mayr E. 1976. Evolution and the diversity of life: selected essays. Cambridge and London: Belknap Press of Harvard University Press, p. 411.
3. Platnick NI. 1977. Review of Mayr's Evolution and the diversity of life. Systematic Zoology 26:224-228.
4. Bethel T. 1985. Agnostic evolutionists. Harper's 270(1617):49-52, 56-58, 60, 61.
5. Eldredge N, Gould SJ. 1972. Punctuated equilibria: an alternative to phyletic gradualism. In: Schopf TJM, editor. Models of paleobiology. San Francisco: Freeman, Cooper, and Co., pp. 82-115.

6. (a) Eldredge N. 1995. Reinventing Darwin: the great debate at the high table of evolutionary theory. New York: John Wiley and Sons, Inc.; (b) Hoffman A. 1989. Arguments on evolution: a paleontologist's perspective. New York and Oxford: Oxford University Press, p. 93; (c) Kerr RA. 1995. Did Darwin get it all right? Science 267:1421, 1422.
7. We will consider this further in chapter 11.
8. For a good introduction to the concept, see: (a) Kimura M. 1979. The neutral theory of molecular evolution. Scientific American 241(5):98-126. For a more technical discussion, see: (b) Kimura M. 1983. The neutral theory of molecular evolution. Cambridge, London, and New York: Cambridge University Press.
9. Kimura M. 1968. Evolutionary rate at the molecular level. Nature 217:624-626.
10. King JL, Jukes TH. 1969. Non-Darwinian evolution. Science 164:788-798.
11. Zuckerkandl E, Pauling L. 1965. Evolutionary divergence and convergence in proteins. In: Bryson V, Vogel HJ, editors. Evolving genes and proteins: a symposium. New York and London: Academic Press, pp. 97-166.
12. Baba ML, Darga LL, Goodman M, Czelusniak J. 1981. Evolution of cytochrome *c* investigated by the maximum parsimony method. Journal of Molecular Evolution 17:197-213.
13. Ayala FJ. 1986. On the virtues and pitfalls of the molecular evolutionary clock. Journal of Heredity 77:226-235.
14. (a) Easteal S. 1991. The relative rate of DNA evolution in primates. Molecular Biology and Evolution 8(1):115-127; (b) Goodman M, Koop BF, Czelusniak J, Fitch DHA, Tagle DA, Slightom JL. 1989. Molecular phylogeny of the family of apes and humans. Genome 31:316-335.
15. (a) Gillespie JH. 1984. The molecular clock may be an episodic clock. Proceedings of the National Academy of Sciences USA 81:8009-8013; (b) Gillespie JH. 1986. Natural selection and the molecular clock. Molecular Biology and Evolution 3(2):138-155.
16. Dayhoff MO. 1976. Atlas of protein sequence and structure, vol. 5, supplement 2. Washington, D.C.: National Biomedical Research Foundation, p. 129.
17. For 12 examples, see: Mills GC. 1994. The molecular evolutionary clock: a critique. Perspectives on Science and Christian Faith 46:159-168.
18. Wyss AR, Novacek MJ, McKenna MC. 1987. Amino acid sequence versus morphological data and the interordinal relationships of mammals. Molecular Biology and Evolution 4(2):99-116.
19. Fisher DC. 1990. Rates of evolution—living fossils. In: Briggs DEG, Crowther PR, editors. Paleobiology: a synthesis. Oxford: Blackwell Scientific Publications, pp. 152-159.
20. Lewin R. 1990. Molecular clocks run out of time. New Scientist (10 February), pp. 38-41.
21. Scherer S. 1990. The protein molecular clock: time for a reevaluation. In: Hecht MK, Wallace B, MacIntyre RJ. Evolutionary Biology, vol. 24. New York and London: Plenum Press, pp. 83-106.
22. See: Morell V. 1996. Proteins "clock" the origins of all creatures—great and small. Science 271:448.
23. Vawter L, Brown WM. 1986. Nuclear and mitochondrial DNA comparisons reveal extreme rate variation in the molecular clock. Science 234:194-196.
24. For a discussion and evaluation of pseudogenes, see: Gibson LJ. 1994. Pseudogenes and origins. Origins 21:91-108.
25. (a) Flam F. 1994. Hints of a language in junk DNA. Science 266:1320; (b) Nowak R. 1994. Mining treasures from "junk DNA." Science 263:608-610.
26. Ptashne M. 1989. How gene activators work. Scientific American 260(1):40-47.
27. Jacob F, Monod J. 1961. Genetic regulatory mechanisms in the synthesis of proteins. Journal of Molecular Biology 3:318-356.
28. See also: Ptashne (note 26).
29. For a semi-technical presentation, see: Radman M, Wagner R. 1988. The high fidelity of DNA duplication. Scientific American 259(2):40-46.
30. For technical discussions, see: (a) Grilley M, Holmes J, Yashar B, Modrich P. 1990. Mechanisms of DNA-mismatch correction. Mutation Research 236:253-267; (b) Lambert GR. 1984. Enzymic editing mechanisms and the origin of biological information transfer. Journal of Theoretical Biology 107:387-403; (c) Modrich P. 1991. Mechanisms and biological effects

of mismatch repair. Annual Review of Genetics 25:229-253.

31. Lambert (note 30b).
32. Shapiro JA. 1991. Genomes as smart systems. Genetica 84:3, 4.
33. See: Lovelock JE. 1987. Gaia, a new look at life on earth. Rev. ed. Oxford and New York: Oxford University Press.
34. Margulis L. 1990. Kingdom Animalia: the zoological malaise from a microbial perspective. American Zoologist 30:861-875.
35. See: Wills C. 1989. The wisdom of the genes: new pathways in evolution. New York: Basic Books, Inc.
36. See chapter 5.
37. A few references are: (a) Bak P, Chen K. 1991. Self-organized criticality. Scientific American 264:46-53; (b) Horgan J. 1995. From complexity to perplexity. Scientific American 272:104-109; (c) Kauffman SA. 1993. The origins of order: self-organization and selection in evolution. Oxford and New York: Oxford University Press; (d) Lewin R. 1992. Complexity: life at the edge of chaos. New York: Collier Books, Macmillan Pub. Co.; (e) McShea DW. 1991. Complexity and evolution: what everybody knows. Biology and Philosophy 6:303-324; (f) Oreskes N, Shrader-Frechette K, Belitz K. 1994. Verification, validation, and confirmation of numerical models in the earth sciences. Science 263:641-646; (g) Waldrop MM. 1992. Complexity: the emerging science at the edge of order and chaos. New York, London, and Toronto: Simon and Schuster.
38. See Horgan (note 37b).
39. For example: Dawkins R. 1986. The blind watchmaker. New York and London: W. W. Norton and Co.
40. Lewin, p. 101 (note 37d).
41. Horgan (note 37b).
42. Lewin p. 184 (note 37d).
43. Oreskes et al. (note 37f).
44. Grassé P-P. 1977. Evolution of living organisms: evidence for a new theory of transformation. Carlson BM, Castro R, translators. New York, San Francisco, and London: Academic Press. Translation of: L'Évolution du Vivant.
45. *Ibid.,* p. 246.
46. Behe MJ. 1996. Darwin's black box: the biochemical challenge to evolution. New York and London: Free Press.
47. Crick F. 1981. Life itself: its origin and nature. New York: Simon and Schuster.
48. Denton M. 1985. Evolution: a theory in crisis. London: Burnett Books.
49. *Ibid.,* p. 358.
50. Hitching F. 1982. The neck of the giraffe: where Darwin went wrong. New Haven and New York: Ticknor and Fields.
51. Ho M-W, Saunders P, editors. 1984. Beyond neo-Darwinism: an introduction to the new evolutionary paradigm. London and Orlando: Academic Press.
52. *Ibid.,* p. ix.
53. Løvtrup S. 1987. Darwinism: the refutation of a myth. London, New York, and Sydney: Croom Helm.
54. *Ibid.,* p. 422.
55. Ridley M. 1985. The problems of evolution. New York and Oxford: Oxford University Press.
56. Shapiro R. 1986. Origins: a skeptic's guide to the creation of life on earth. New York: Summit Books.
57. Taylor, GR. 1983. The great evolution mystery. New York: Harper and Row.
58. *Ibid.,* p. 15.
59. Dawkins R. 1989. The selfish gene. New ed. Oxford and New York: Oxford University Press, p. 1.
60. Mayr E. 1985. Darwin's five theories of evolution. In: Kohn D, editor. The Darwinian heritage. Princeton, N.J.: Princeton University Press, pp. 755-772.
61. See chapter 20 for a suggestion.

THE FOSSILS

CHAPTER 9

THE FOSSIL RECORD

How hard I find it to see what is
right in front of my eyes!
—Ludwig Wittgenstein[1]

I had just crawled up a steep cliff and into a hole in a lava layer above Blue Lake in the state of Washington. The view inside was amazing. I was inside the mold of a rhinoceros entombed in a lava flow. As the lava hardened, it made a cast of the rhinoceros's body. While no parts of the body remained, I was unmistakably in what had once been a rhinoceros, and it was fascinating to get the "inside story." When preserved, the animal was lying on its left side. The cavities where the short legs had been were clearly visible, and the molding of the rock was so detailed that I could easily recognize the eyes and folds of the skin. The bones of the rhinoceros had been found earlier in the cast and sent to a museum, confirming the cavity's identification.

We consider any evidence of life from the remote past to be a fossil. Thus either the mold of the rhinoceros or the bones inside it would qualify as fossils. Fossils have many forms, such as the actual body of an insect trapped and preserved in resin that oozed from a tree and later changed to amber, or they can be just a shell in a rock completely replaced by other minerals. In other cases they can be the skeletal remains of dinosaurs (Figure 9.1) or other unfamiliar animals such as a flying reptile that had a wingspan of 15.5 meters.[2] Also included would be just the footprint of a turtle preserved between layers of sandstone.

In this chapter we will look at some general information about fossils, including their formation and problems in identifying them. Especially important is the order of fossils in the geologic column. This information is essential for an understanding of the following two chapters.

FIGURE 9.1

Dinosaur bones in a sandstone layer of the Jurassic Morrison Formation. These bones are located in Dinosaur National Monument near Jensen, Utah. The longest bones are one and a half to two meters long. Their disorderly arrangement suggests some transport before final deposition.

THE FASCINATION OF FOSSILS

Part of the fascination of fossils no doubt comes from curiosity about what is sometimes called the "great history"—namely, the history of all life on earth. Fossils are highly important to the question of origins, for they provide the best scientific clues available about the nature of past life on earth. While fossil hunters deal with the dead, they like to think that, in a sense, each of them "resurrects"[3] as they interpret and reinterpret past life on the basis of what they see. This leads to a fascination difficult to explain, but which is well-demonstrated by the countless fossils found on display in private and public museums throughout the world. Scientists have described about a quarter of a million fossil species to date. This number is about one fifth the number of living species identified, but the comparison might not be very valid, since different experts classify by different criteria.

Many scientists have dedicated their entire lives to the study of fossils, and some so devotedly that their antics have become part of the often-humorous, and sometimes morbid, lore of *paleontology*—the term designating the study of fossils.

Edward Drinker Cope (1840-1897), who eventually joined the faculty of the University of Pennsylvania, and Othniel Charles Marsh (1831-1899), at Yale University, can be rightfully considered pioneers of American vertebrate (animals with backbones) paleontology. Each of them described many hundreds of fossil organisms they had either excavated or had others collect from the vast exposures of geological formations during the exploration of the American West. Cope and Marsh loved fossils much more than they loved each other and persistently tried to outdo each other in their "great bone rush." Unfortunately, the western United States was too small for both passionate collectors. In biology and paleontology the first person to describe an organism has priority in naming it, and his or her own name is often associated with the species designation. Cope and Marsh frequently competed at being the first to describe any new species found. Marsh had access to the *American Journal of Science* for rapid publication, and Cope owned and edited the *American Naturalist.*

One incident often recounted in the story of their infamous feud occurred at a meeting in Philadelphia that both attended. Cope announced the first discovery of Permian reptiles in the West. Reportedly Marsh left the meeting early, went to his laboratory, looked at some specimens, and quickly published a careless article claiming to be the first to report Permian vertebrates in the United States. In so doing, he totally ignored Cope's announcement. A disturbed Cope published his own report, claiming that he had distributed it three weeks earlier than was actually the case.[4]

In another incident, Cope hastily assembled a reptile skeleton, mixing up some of the neck and the tail bones. Marsh quickly accused him of putting the head on the tail, causing Cope to spend considerable effort in recalling the issues of the *Transactions of the American Philosophical Society* in which he had published the erroneous restoration.[5]

In 1890 the details of the warfare between the two scientists reached the pages of the New York *Herald.* Among Cope's many accusations was that Marsh had plagiarized from the Russian scientist Alexander Kowalevsky the famous evolutionary fossil-horse series that appears to this day in many textbooks of biology and paleontology. In a subsequent issue of the *Herald,* Marsh denied any such wrongdoing and accused Cope and Kowalevsky of being fossil predators of the museums of the world. Marsh went on to state: "Kowalevsky was at last stricken with remorse and ended his unfortunate career by blowing out his own brains. Cope still lives, unrepentant."[6]

After the exposure in the *Herald,* the feud subsided, but only a little. We must recognize that in a sense the competition was helpful for paleontology.

The amount of scientific work the two men accomplished was prodigious, although some of it was careless. In 38 years Cope alone published 1,400 scientific papers.[7]

HOW FOSSILS FORM

A footprint left in mud by a frog, or a grasshopper dying in a field, usually does not get preserved, because mechanical and chemical breakdown occurs long before an organism or its tracks can be buried. Fossilization is a rare event. "In general, the more rapidly an organism is buried and the tighter the seal of its sedimentary tomb, the better the chances of preservation."[8] Coral reefs are a notable exception, because new reef material grows over the coral skeltons, protecting and preserving them as they form the fossilized framework of the reef.

Fossils appear almost exclusively in sedimentary rocks such as limestone, shale, sandstone, or conglomerate. They are completely absent in many rock formations, and abundant in a few localities. Under unusual conditions they can get incorporated into volcanic deposits, and even more rarely they occur in granite.[9]

During the process of fossilization, changes often take place over time. Such changes can be minimal, as in the case of frozen mammoths, but most frequently only hard parts remain, as is common with fossil bones or shells. Some fossils, such as wood or bones, might hardly be altered at all. Sometimes the original small "pore" spaces of the once living organism fill with minerals, while in other cases the original shell, bone, or wood gets completely replaced by minerals. Much of the hydrogen, oxygen, and nitrogen of the original organic matter (tissue) escapes. On occasion the organic matter leaves a thin carbon film in the form of an imprint.

Many fossils are well preserved, some not so well, and for some we cannot be sure if they are really fossils at all.

THE PSEUDOFOSSIL PROBLEM

I marvel at those paleontologists who can point out a wide variety of fossil forms on what appears to be a plain piece of rock. However, I have always maintained a healthy skepticism about some claims. Accusations by paleontologists that others do not have a "trained eye" have not always alleviated questions of doubt concerning some of their claims. Determination of whether a peculiar form in a rock is a bona fide fossil can, in some cases, be extremely difficult. Preserved mud curls caused by drying have sometimes been interpreted as crab parts; drag marks caused by movement of objects during storms

FIGURE 9.2

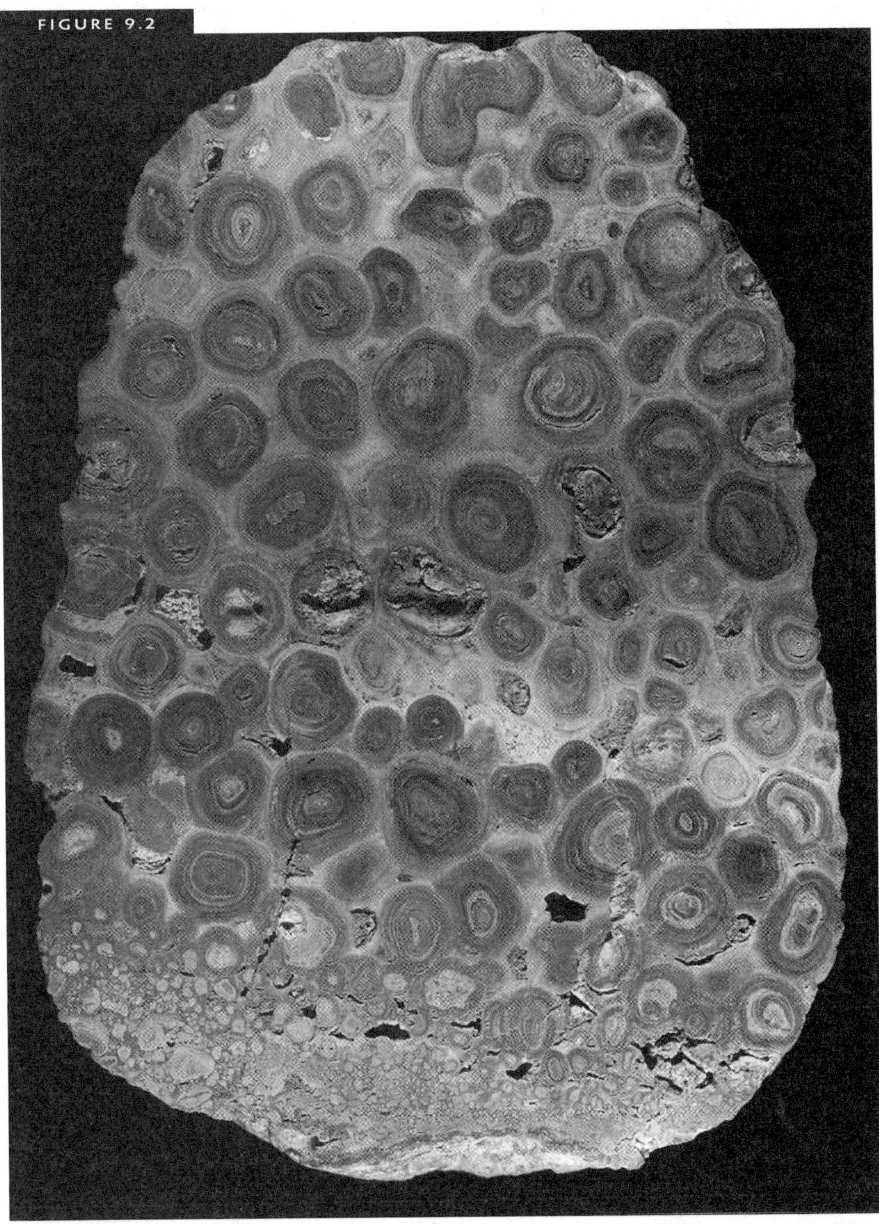

A pseudofossil. This polished slab of rock—called a pisolite—is from the Permian Yates Formation in Walnut Canyon, New Mexico. The concentric layers forming the spherical bodies were once thought to be formed like a stromatolite by microorganisms living on the surface of the pebble-like pisoliths. According to newer interpretations, they are the result of inorganic chemical precipitation taking place below the surface of the ground but above the water table. Evidence includes the way the pisolith growth patterns are sometimes flattened against each other, and laminae that grow around several pisoliths. Specimen is 12 centimeters long. See text for further details.

can resemble worm tracks; chemical precipitation, in roselike shapes, of the mineral pyrite have been interpreted as jellyfish, as have gas-bubble markings;[10] and some spongelike organisms (archeocyathids) have turned out to be forms produced by inorganic crystallization.[11] Paleontologists use the terms *pseudofossil* and *dubiofossil* to describe false or dubious fossils. The venerable *Treatise on Invertebrate Paleontology*[12] lists 69 published descriptions of "fossil organisms" originally identified as coral, algae, fungi, sponges, snails, etc., that are most likely of nonbiological origin. Such misidentified objects appear to have resulted from unusual depositional conditions. *Brooksella canyonensis* is a "fossil" that resembles a star-shaped crack. It has an impressive pedigree of interpretations, including: (1) the body fossil of a jellyfish, (2) the reverse imprint of an inorganic fracture system produced by gas evasion, (3) the result of compaction, (4) the imprint of a starlike feeding burrow, or (5) possibly the work of a worm.[13] While we should not ignore these examples, one also must keep in mind that there are many excellent fossils.

The problem of pseudofossils is particularly acute in the lowest parts of the geologic record, where evolutionists expect the earliest, simple life forms. Finding the earliest forms of life has almost become an obsession with some paleontologists. The professional literature has reported many likely candidates. On the other hand, several investigators have been able to simulate the shape of these simple life forms by inorganic precipitation or by special depositional conditions. Spherical, tubelike, or coiled shapes, characteristic of fossil forms, can be easily reproduced from simple inorganic chemicals in the laboratory.[14] It is to the credit of paleontologists that a number of them express considerable caution toward the authenticity of most claims concerning fossils in what geologists consider to be the oldest sediments, the Archean (see Table 9.1). Two specialists in this field, William Schopf and Bonnie Packer, discussing microfossils reported from at least 28 Archean localities, state: "However, virtually all have recently been reinterpreted . . . as dubiofossils or as nonfossils: pseudofossils, artifacts, or contaminants."[15] Paleontologist Richard Cowen comments: "Only a few reports of fossil Archean cells seem to be genuine, out of fifty or more claims."[16] Roger Buick at Harvard refers to a host of problems with the identification of most of these primitive fossils found at North Pole, Australia.[17] (It is called North Pole because, like the real North Pole, it is a notably desolate area.) An old geological dictum stating that "I never would have seen it if I hadn't believed it" seems to apply to many of these cases.

The pseudofossil problem comes into closer focus in the case of stromatolites, which are finely laminated sedimentary structures, usually in the centimeter to meter range, often having a mounded or wavy form. Stromatolites develop underwater as thin mats of microscopic organisms living on their surface trap or precipitate minerals, which then become incorporated into a layered structure. The question arises as to whether what appears to be a fossil stromatolite may have formed biologically, or whether it is just the passive accumulation of fine layers of sediment subjected to geological deformation. The sedimentologist Robert Ginsburg points out that "almost everything about stromatolites has been, and remains to varying degrees, controversial."[18] Stromatolite specialist Paul Hoffman notes: "Something that haunts geologists working on ancient stromatolites is the thought that they might not be biogenic at all."[19] By way of illustration he cites the example of the "algal pisolites" (rock composed of layered pea-size spheres) of the Permian in western Texas (Figure 9.2). Paleontologists originally thought they had formed biologically in a similar way to stromatolites, but they turned out to have developed by chemical precipitation.[20] The well-known paleontologist Charles Walcott, who for 20 years directed the U.S. Smithsonian Institution, described five new genera and eight new species of stromatolites believed to be of biological origin. Each has since been reinterpreted as of nonbiological origin by at least one investigator.[21] Even presently forming "stromatolites" can be enigmatic. Researchers have more recently reinterpreted a number of "stromatolites" described in various parts of Scandinavia as being of nonbiological origin.[22] Many unquestionable living stromatolites, however, do exist across the earth's surface.

THE GEOLOGIC COLUMN

The "geologic column" refers to a composite columnar representation of what would be the complete sequence of rock units in earth's crust.[23] It is somewhat analogous to a map. In such representations the oldest layers are at the bottom. One can think of the geologic column as a thin, vertical slice through thick layers of rock, such as those visible in the Grand Canyon region of Arizona (Figure 13.1). At that locality only part of the lower portion of the geologic column is represented. The terms used for the various major divisions of the column appear on the left side of Table 9.1. The sequence is not complete at any one place on earth, although parts of all the major divisions do occur in a number of localities. Geologists assemble the composite column by correlating information from many different areas. Minor variations in interpretation with respect to the idealized sequence are common, but the general arrangement appears reliable. Detailed correlation between parts often rests on the fossils found in them and/or the kind of rock of the various layers, while the

TABLE 9.1

	DIVISIONS		DOMINANT KINDS OF ORGANISMS	ABUNDANCE
PHANEROZOIC	**CENOZOIC**	QUATERNARY	Flowering plants abundant, some conifers, man, birds, mammals, fishes, and insects abundant	Fossils relatively abundant
		TERTIARY	Same as above, other mammals, plants as in the upper Cretaceous	
	MESOZOIC	CRETACEOUS	Cycads, conifers, flowering plants, reptiles, mammals, and small marine organisms	
		JURASSIC	Cycads, conifers, dinosaurs, and other reptiles	
		TRIASSIC	Horsetails, seed ferns, conifers, reptiles, and some amphibians	
	PALEOZOIC	PERMIAN	Horsetail trees, seed fern trees, lycopod trees, sea lillies, fishes, amphibians, reptiles	
		CARBONIFEROUS	Coal "forests" of horsetail trees, seed fern trees, lycopod trees, sharks, clams, amphibians, small marine organisms	
		DEVONIAN	Small land plants, jawless fish, armored fish, bony fish, sharks, small marine organisms	
		SILURIAN	Jawless fish, small marine organisms, unusual land plants	
		ORDOVICIAN	Many marine organisms, including trilobites, lamp shells, and sea lilies	
		CAMBRIAN	Trilobites, lamp shells, and other small marine organisms, the Cambrian explosion	
PRECAMBRIAN	**PROTEROZOIC**		Ediacaran (odd marine organisms) Acritarchs (algae?) Bacteria Stromatolites Acritarchs (algae?) Bacteria	Fossils very rare
	ARCHEAN		Assumed photosynthetic bacteria and eukaryotes Filamentous forms? Stromatolites? Many pseudofossils	Fossils extremely rare or nonexistent

DOMINANT TYPES OF ORGANISMS IN THE GEOLOGIC COLUMN

general picture is based on both radiometric-age dating and the relationship of the fossil layers to each other. Sometimes correlation is good, and sometimes it is tenuous. A lower layer would, of course, be deposited first and be older.

The order of the fossils found in the geologic column is crucial to any interpretation of past life. Fossils can give us clues regarding the environment in which they lived and the origin of the organisms they represent. The dimension of time and the age of the fossils enters the broader picture of origins—whether it be a few thousand years, as interpreted by creationists, or thousands of millions of years, as suggested by evolutionists.

A BRIEF CLIMB THROUGH THE GEOLOGIC COLUMN

Those who search for fossils frequently find different kinds of fossils in different geologic layers. Table 9.1 gives a general picture of the *dominant types* of life found in the geologic column as represented by the fossils, while Figure 10.1 shows the *distribution* of major fossil types in the geologic column. Readers can consult both illustrations when they have questions about the terminology and arrangement of the geologic column.

The great difference that exists between the two main divisions of the column—the Precambrian, which lies below the important Cambrian division, and the Phanerozoic, which extends upward from the Cambrian—can hardly be overemphasized. For centuries no one found fossils in the Precambrian, while many thousands turned up in the layers immediately above. Recently researchers have described a number of Precambrian fossils, but the great abundance and variety in the Phanerozoic remain a striking contrast. Any model of the history of life on earth must take this disparity into account.

The search by evolutionists for the earliest evolving forms of life in the Archean (the lowest layers) has concentrated in the Swaziland Supergroup sediments of South Africa and the Warrawoona Group near North Pole, Australia. Both are considered to be around 3,500 million years old. Researchers have described small filamentous types of fossils from both regions. Because of their possible authenticity, they are of considerable interest.[24] Some evolutionists consider them to be the earliest known forms of life.

The Proterozoic (upper half of the Precambrian), has relatively abundant stromatolites. We should make special mention of the Gunflint Chert of the Great Lakes region of the United States. This chert, from the lower part of the Proterozoic, has well-preserved filamentous fossils that greatly resemble the modern *Lyngbya* and *Oscillatoria* cyanobacteria (blue-green algae).[25]

Special spherical fossils called acritarchs occur in the upper half of the

FIGURE 9.3

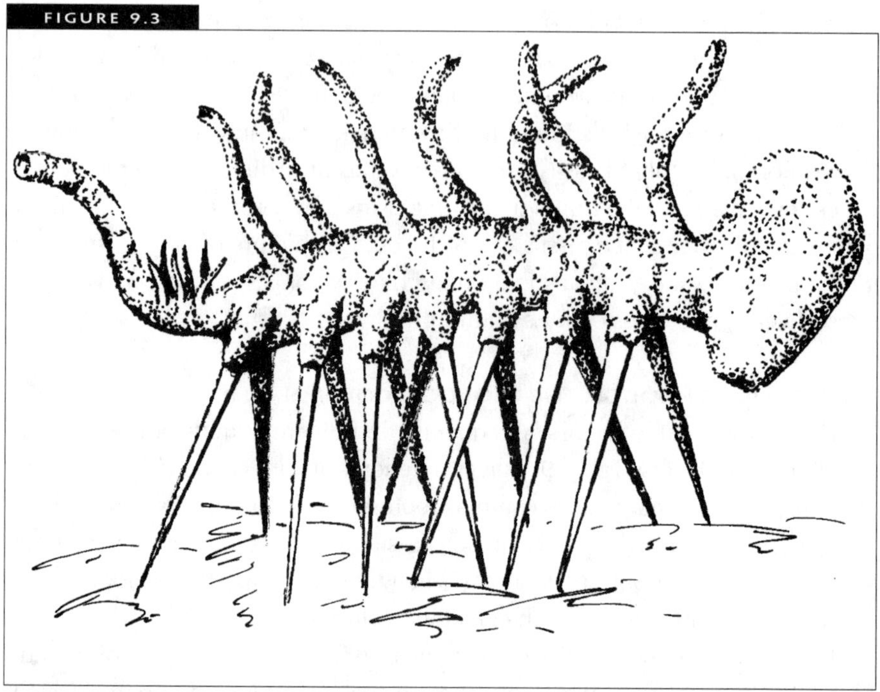

An early interpretation of the enigmatic animal *Hallucigenia* from the Cambrian Burgess Shale of Canada. Newer interpretations place the spines on top.

Proterozoic. Commonly about 0.05 millimeter in diameter, they are thought to be some form of algal cysts.[26] They show both greater diversity and size increase near the top. Paleontologists regard acritarchs as a more advanced form of life (eukaryotes) because they have a nucleus in their cells, though some have disputed this interpretation. Eukaryotes include most kinds of organisms, from microscopic amoeba to the huge kauri trees of New Zealand. By contrast, evolutionists consider bacteria, which have no nucleus (prokaryotes), to have evolved earlier. Several other minor fossil types have been described in the Proterozoic, including small vase-shaped objects (0.07 millimeter) of unknown affinity.

In the very top of the Proterozoic, very close to the Cambrian, we find peculiar multicellular types of animals (Ediacaran fauna),[27] especially in Australia and Russia. Some resemble ferns, worms, spoked wheels, etc., and are not easily associated with known living forms. Thus far none of the more advanced (multicellular) kinds of animals has turned up below this level, where only a few simple sometimes ill-defined forms possibly related to algae are present.[28]

Despite all the problems in identifying Precambrian fossils, we do encounter some good unquestionable examples. These include the Gunflint Chert cyanobacteria, the acritarchs, the Bitter Springs cyanobacteria, and the Ediacaran animal fauna, all of which derive from the upper half of the Precambrian (Proterozoic). To this we can add some more dubious filamentous forms from the Fig Tree (Africa) and North Pole (Australia) areas that belong to the lower Precambrian (Archean).

Directly above the almost-wasteland of the Precambrian comes the sudden appearance of all the major forms of animals (see Table 9.1 and Figure 10.1). Scientists commonly refer to this abrupt transition as the Cambrian explosion. Depending on the classification scheme used, about 30 to 40 or more animal phyla (the major categories of the animal kingdom) appear in this part of the geologic column. Few or no new basic types show up above this level. This sudden appearance challenges any idea of a long, gradual evolutionary process.

We should make special mention of the intriguing fossils of the famous Cambrian Burgess Shale of the Canadian Rockies, where researchers have collected more than 73,000 specimens.[29] Similar types have shown up in China and Greenland. These largely soft-bodied fossil organisms are famous for their excellent preservation. Some are so unique that researchers have proposed that a number of new animal phyla cover their classification. One organism is so puzzling that it has been given the fitting scientific name of *Hallucigenia*. Scientists first reconstructed it as an elongated body walking on seven pairs of spines with tentacles above the body (Figure 9.3). Others have proposed the reverse position with the spines extending up. It might be related to velvet worms (Onychophora), which have lobelike legs but no spines.[30] Another suggestion is that it might represent part of a much larger animal.[31]

Several varieties of terrestrial (land) plants and animals, such as ferns and insects, appear in rock strata above the Cambrian explosion. Mammals first turn up in the lower Mesozoic, while flowering plants do not appear until higher in the Mesozoic. Reptiles dominate in the Mesozoic, while mammals and flowering plants monopolize the Cenozoic strata. In general, marine organisms flourish in the lower Paleozoic, while terrestrial organisms dominate many of the portions above. We do not have good, authenticated human fossils until the last $\frac{1}{10,000}$ of the assumed geologic timescale. Of special interest is the position of various members of the phylum Chordata, which includes the animals with backbones, such as fish or humans. The Chordata seem to provide a general increase in complexity with ascending strata. Many consider this feature to be good evidence for evolution. We will look at alternative explanations in the next chapter.

Mass extinctions appear at a number of levels in the Phanerozoic. A mass-

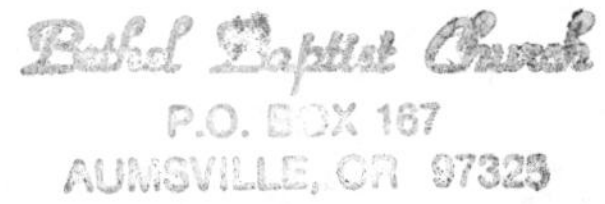

extinction horizon occurs when major proportions of fossil species present at one level no longer appear in overlying layers. The disappearance of the dinosaurs is a famous but debated example. The major extinctions take place at the top of the Cambrian, Ordovician, Devonian, Permian, Triassic, and Cretaceous periods, as well as the middle of the Tertiary.[32] Scientists have suggested both earthbound causes, such as flooding and volcanoes, and extraterrestrial causes, such as large meteorites.[33] Regardless of cause, the fossil record does witness to significant catastrophic activity in the past.

THE TURMOIL OVER THE ORIGIN OF FOSSILS

Several centuries ago few attempted to distinguish between fossils that resembled living organisms and other unique structures found in rocks, such as large inorganic crystals. People believed that both came from some kind of concentrating fluid or the action of some kind of special power or spirit. Later, during the last part of the seventeenth century, the debate centered on whether the fossils were of inorganic (nonliving) or organic (living) origin.

As time went on, questions concerning the biblical flood increasingly entered into the debate over fossils. Scholars generally accepted the flood as having occurred a few thousand years earlier, and considered it to be the major fossil-producing event. Some questioned how such an event sorted fossils into their respective beds. A number of thinkers suggested that the sorting resulted from density differences (the heavier fossils sinking deeper). Others questioned why some fossils were so different from any known living organisms. And some wondered whether there could be enough floodwater to cover the Alps of Europe. Ideas of major mountain uplift after the flood were not in vogue then. Nevertheless, in the mid-eighteenth century people widely accepted the biblical flood as a historical event and considered fossils to be the remains of ancient organisms buried by that flood.

The nineteenth century witnessed radical changes in thinking, not especially about the origin of the fossils themselves, but about the sources of the organisms that had produced them. Concepts of long ages for the development of rocks and for the development of life by evolution introduced many questions regarding the interpretation of the fossils. Were the fossils the result of the biblical flood described in Genesis, or were they the consequence of millions of years of evolution? We will consider these views of the origin of fossils in detail in the following two chapters.

CONCLUSIONS

Fossils are fascinating and have much to say about the origin of life and its history. Their interpretation relates to key concepts of evolution and creation. They lie near the core of the science-and-Scripture controversy.

The study of fossils is a challenge and has been marked by significant controversy. Caution is warranted. While many fossils are well preserved, some are partially or highly decomposed and difficult to identify. Sometimes we cannot be sure if a particular form is a genuine fossil.

The geologic column has simple organisms in its lower portions. Most animal types appear suddenly in the "Cambrian explosion," then in succeeding rock layers various plant types, reptiles, mammals, and flowering plants appear.

Over the centuries thinkers have considered a variety of concepts about the origin of fossils. Some have suggested that fossils form by the action of concentrating fluids. Many believed fossils to represent organisms buried by the biblical flood, while others regarded them as the remains of evolving organisms.

REFERENCES

1. Wittgenstein L. 1980. Culture and value. Winch P, translator; Wright GHv (with Nyman H), editor. Chicago: The University of Chicago Press, p. 39e. Translation of: Vermischte Bemerkungen.
2. Lawson DA. 1975. Pterosaur from the latest Cretaceous of west Texas: discovery of the largest flying creature. Science 187:947, 948.
3. Simpson GG. 1983. Fossils and the history of life. New York: Scientific American Books, p. 2.
4. I am indebted to AS Romer for the details of this incident. See: Romer AS. 1964. Cope *versus* Marsh. Systematic Zoology 13(4):201-207.
5. For Marsh's detailed account, see: (a) Shor EN. 1974. The fossil feud: between E. D. Cope and O. C. Marsh. Hicksville, New York: Exposition Press, pp. 184-186. For further details, see also: (b) Plate R. 1964. The dinosaur hunters: Othniel C. Marsh and Edward D. Cope. New York: David McKay Co.
6. Shor, p. 174 (note 5a).
7. For accounts of this famous feud, as well as the extensive reports given in the *Herald,* see: Shore, p. 174 (note 5a).
8. Beerbower JR. 1968. Search for the past: an introduction to paleontology. 2nd ed. Englewood Cliffs, N.J.: Prentice-Hall, p. 39.
9. Malakhova NP, Ovchinnikov LN. 1969. A find of fossils in granite of the central Urals. Doklady Akademii Nauk SSSR 188:33-35. Translation of: O nakhodke organicheskikh ostatkov v granitakh Srednego Urala.
10. Cloud P. 1973. Pseudofossils: a plea for caution. Geology 1(3):123-127.
11. Glaessner MF. 1980. Pseudofossils from the Precambrian, including "Buschmannia" and "Praesolenopora." Geological Magazine 117(2):199, 200.
12. Häntzschel W. 1975. Treatise on invertebrate paleontology, Part W: Miscellanea, supplement 1. 2nd ed. Boulder, Colo.: Geological Society of America, and Lawrence, Kans.: University of Kansas, pp. W169-179.
13. *Ibid.,* p. W146.
14. (a) Glaessner MF. 1988. Pseudofossils explained as vortex structures in sediments. Senckenbergiana lethaea 69(3/4):275-287; (b) Gutstadt AM. 1975. Pseudo- and dubiofossils from the Newland Limestone (Belt Supergroup, late Precambrian), Montana. Journal of Sedimentary Petrology 45(2):405-414; (c) Jenkins RJF, Plummer PS, Moriarty KC. 1981. Late Precambrian pseudofossils from the Flinders Ranges, South Australia. Transactions of the Royal Society of South Australia 105(2):67-83; (d) Merek EL. 1973. Imaging and life detection.

BioScience 23(3):153-159; (e) Pickett J, Scheibnerová V. 1974. The inorganic origin of "anellotubulates." Micropaleontology 20(1):97-102; (f) Service RF. 1995. Prompting complex patterns to form themselves. Science 270:1299, 1300.

15. Schopf JW, Packer BM. 1987. Early Archean (3.3-billion to 3.5-billion-year-old) microfossils from Warrawoona Group, Australia. Science 237:70-73.
16. Cowen R. 1995. History of life. 2nd ed. Boston, Oxford, and London: Blackwell Scientific Publications, p. 39.
17. Buick R. 1990. Microfossil recognition in Archean rocks: an appraisal of spheroids and filaments from a 3,500-million-year-old chert-barite unit at North Pole, Western Australia. Palaios 5:441-459.
18. Ginsburg RN. 1991. Controversies about stromatolites: vices and virtues. In: Müller DW, McKenzie JA, Weissert H, editors. Controversies in modern geology. London, San Diego, and New York: Academic Press, pp. 25-36.
19. (a) Hoffman P. 1973. Recent and ancient algal stromatolites: seventy years of pedagogic cross-pollination. In: Ginsburg RN, editor. Evolving concepts in sedimentology. Johns Hopkins University Studies in Geology, No. 21. Baltimore and London: Johns Hopkins University Press, pp. 178-191. See also: (b) Grotzinger JP, Rothman DH. 1996. An abiotic model for stromatolite morphogenesis. Nature 383:423-425. (c) Lowe DR. 1994. Abiological origin of described stromatolites older than 3.2 Ga. Geology 22:387-390.
20. (a) Hoffman (note 19a). See also: (b) Estaban M, Pray LC. 1975. Subaqueous, syndepositional growth of in-place pisolite, Capitan Reef Complex (Permian), Guadalupe Mountains, New Mexico, and west Texas. Geological Society of America Abstracts With Programs 7:1068, 1069; (c) Thomas C. 1968. Vadose pisolites in the Guadalupe and Apache Mountains, west Texas. In: Silver BA, editor. Guadalupian facies, Apache Mountains area, west Texas. Symposium and guidebook 1968 field trip, Permian Basin Section, Society of Economic Paleontologists and Mineralogists Publication 68-11:32-35.
21. Gutstadt (note 14b).
22. Bjærke T, Dypvik H. 1977. Quaternary "stromatolitic" limestone of subglacial origin from Scandinavia. Journal of Sedimentary Petrology 47:1321-1327.
23. For an insightful review of the development of the geologic-column concept, see: (a) Ritland R. 1981. Historical development of the current understanding of the geologic column: Part I. Origins 8:59-76; (b) Ritland R. 1982. Historical development of the current understanding of the geologic column: Part II. Origins 9:28-50.
24. (a) Schopf JW. 1993. Microfossils of the Early Archean Apex chert: new evidence of the antiquity of life. Science 260:640-646; (b) Schopf and Packer (note 15); (c) Walsh MM, Lowe DR. 1985. Filamentous microfossils from the 3,500-million-year-old Onverwacht Group, Barberton Mountain Land, South Africa. Nature 314:530-532.
25. Stewart WN, Rothwell GW. 1993. Paleobotany and the evolution of plants. 2nd ed. Cambridge and New York: Cambridge University Press, pp. 35, 36.
26. Mendelson CV. 1993. Acritarchs and prasinophytes. In: Lipps JH, editor. Fossil prokaryotes and protists. Boston, Oxford, and London: Blackwell Scientific Publications, pp. 77-104.
27. The exact position of these organisms is under discussion. See: (a) Grotzinger JP, Bowring SA, Saylor BZ, Kaufman AJ. 1995. Biostratigraphic and geochronologic constraints on early animal evolution. Science 270:598-604; (b) Kerr RA. 1995. Animal oddballs brought into the ancestral fold? Science 270:580, 581.
28. (a) Bengtson S, Fedonkin MA, Lipps JH. 1992. The major biotas of Proterozoic to Early Cambrian multicellular organisms. In: Schopf JW, Klein C, editors. The Proterozoic biosphere: a multidisciplinary study. Cambridge and New York: Cambridge University Press, pp. 433-534; (b) Han T-M, Runnegar B. 1992. Megascopic eukaryotic algae from the 2.1-billion-year-old Negaunee Iron Formation, Michigan. Science 257:232-235; (c) Shixing Z, Huineng C. 1995. Megascopic multicellular organisms from the 1,700-million-year-old Tuanshanzi Formation in the Jixian area, north China. Science 270:620-622.
29. For a general summary, see: (a) Briggs DEG, Erwin DH, Collier, FJ. 1994. The fossils of the

Burgess Shale. Washington, D.C., and London: Smithsonian Institution Press; (b) Gould SJ. 1989. Wonderful life: the Burgess Shale and the nature of history. New York and London: W. W. Norton and Co.

30. Cowen, pp. 83, 84 (note 16).
31. Gould, p. 157 (note 29b).
32. The classic publication is: (a) Newell ND. 1967. Revolutions in the history of life. In: Albritton CC, Jr., editor. Uniformity and simplicity: a symposium on the principle of the uniformity of nature. Geological Society of America Special Paper 89:63-91. See also: (b) Cutbill JL, Funnell BM. 1967. Numerical analysis of *The Fossil Record.* In: Harland WB, Holland CH, House MR, Hughes NF, Reynolds AB, Rudwick MJS, Satterthwaite GE, Tarlo LBH, Willey EC, editors. The fossil record: a symposium with documentation. London: Geological Society of London, pp. 791-820; (c) Raup DM, Sepkoski JJ, Jr. 1984. Periodicity of extinctions in the geologic past. Proceedings of the National Academy of Sciences, U.S.A. 81:801-805.
33. (a) Hallam A. 1990. Mass extinction: processes. Earthbound causes. In: Briggs DEG, Crowther PR, editors. Paleobiology: a synthesis. Oxford and London: Blackwell Scientific Publications, pp. 160-164; (b) Jablonski D. 1990. Mass extinction: processes. Extraterrestrial causes. In: Briggs and Crowther, pp. 164-171.

CHAPTER 10

THE GEOLOGIC COLUMN AND CREATION

There is enough light for those who desire only to see, and enough darkness for those of a contrary disposition.

—Pascal[1]

The two views—creation and evolution—could hardly be more different. Creation proposes a recent origin of life a few thousand years ago by God, and a subsequent destruction of that creation in the great deluge (flood) of Genesis. Because no life existed before creation, all of the fossil record would have formed after creation. Evolution, on the other hand, proposes a spontaneous origin of life[2] several thousand million years ago, and its gradual development into advanced forms, including the relatively recent evolution of human beings. The fossil record should have much to say about which view is correct.

Creationists and evolutionists view the fossil record from contrasting perspectives. Evolutionists see the record as representing the gradual development of life forms, while creationists view it as a record of burial during the deluge. To the former, the record represents evolutionary advancement, but to the latter it depicts sudden destruction. As we evaluate interpretations, we need to keep these contrasting perspectives in mind.

In this chapter we will evaluate important creationistic interpretations of the geologic column and compare them with some evolutionistic perspectives.

THE FOSSIL SEQUENCE AND CREATION

Evolutionists often consider the fossil record to be one of the strongest arguments for their theory. Without doubt, many evolutionists would have abandoned their belief in evolution if they did not see a very general picture of increase in complexity of organisms from bottom to top in the geologic column, and also a significant uniqueness of fossils at different levels. Fossil kinds are not at all mixed up as some would expect to have happened during the deluge. Furthermore, within the vertebrate group (animals with backbones, such as snakes and goats), one likewise sees a kind of increase in complexity from bottom to top in the Phanerozoic portion of the geologic column. Fish are the first vertebrates to appear, followed by amphibians, reptiles, mammals, and birds. This reflects a general trend toward advancement. The group represented (vertebrates) is small and comprises only about three percent of all our living species. However, vertebrates are the animals most familiar to us. Many consider such data as good evidence for evolution, but alternative explanations do exist. The remaining organisms (bacteria, protists, invertebrates, and plants) do not exhibit such good evolutionary sequences.[3]

Some creationists attempt to meet the challenge of the geologic column by pointing out that at some localities the column is out of order, with older fossils and rocks resting above younger ones. They argue that such anomalies invalidate the whole concept of the geologic column. George McCready Price, the leading creationist during the early part of the twentieth century, championed this view.[4] Many other creationists have followed him.[5] Favorite examples of the out-of-order fossils and/or layers include the Lewis overthrust in Montana and Canada, the Heart Mountain thrust sheet in Wyoming, and the Matterhorn in Switzerland. In the case of the Lewis overthrust, Precambrian rocks overlie Cretaceous rocks, which, according to standard geological interpretations, are believed to be around 900 million years *younger.* It appears that geological forces thrust (pushed horizontally) the older overlying layers from the west over the younger rocks for a distance of at least 50-65 kilometers. Some creationists deny any evidence of thrusting action, thus attempting to negate the validity of the geologic column. It has been a much-debated issue involving misidentification of the contact zone of the thrusting[6] and other reinterpretations. I have examined the Lewis overthrust contact zone, and the grooves and scratches evident in the rocks indicate that at least some thrusting has taken place.

One must recognize that all the outstanding examples of fossils in wrong sequence come from mountainous areas containing ample evidence of crustal disturbance, which often includes thrusting. More important is the fact that in many parts of mountainous areas and in the widespread, less-disturbed, flatter parts of continents, the fossils generally follow a consistent order. This needs to be taken into account. We cannot ignore the general picture, and the overall general sequence of fossils in the geologic column appears authentic. I shall proceed with explanations from that premise.

LIFE IN THE DEEP ROCKS

The lowest parts of the geologic column, sometimes called the Precambrian (Archean and Proterozoic; Figure 10.1, Table 9.1), usually lie deep in the earth. However, uplift and erosion do sometimes expose them at the surface of the earth. Oil well drilling operations that often reach depths of several kilometers can also retrieve samples. In recent decades paleontologists have placed a great deal of emphasis on the scarce fossil finds in these lower rocks. Such fossils represent the simplest of organisms. An exception is the more complex Ediacaran fossils. They are very close to the Cambrian (Figure 10.1) and appear more closely related to Cambrian kinds. For the purposes of this discussion we can consider them with the abundant Phanerozoic (Cambrian to Recent) fossil types. But what about the simpler organisms found lower in the column? Do they not represent early forms of life on their way to evolving into more complex types? The creationist may not need to accept this evolutionary idea, because simple forms of life live even at present in these deeper rocks and could easily become fossilized there.

We are all familiar with the animals and plants on land, as well as plankton, fishes, and whales of the world's oceans. But a new biological realm is coming into focus—that of life in the deep rocks. The rocks of earth's crust, especially the deeper ones, are relatively inaccessible. "Out of sight, out of mind" certainly applies here. And it is not surprising that although we have known of some life in deep rocks for decades, only recently have scientists given serious attention to this hidden biological realm.

It has long been known that organisms such as bacteria, worms, and insect larvae abound in the top meter of earth's soils. Below this level the number of organisms decreases dramatically, but persists in surprising numbers to great

---

*Based on (a) Benton MJ, editor. 1993. The fossil record 2. London, Glasgow, and New York: Chapman and Hall; (b) Boardman RS, Cheetham AH, Rowell AJ, editors. 1987. Fossil invertebrates. Palo Alto, Oxford, and London: Blackwell Scientific Publications; (c) Cutbill JL, Funnell BM. 1967. Numerical analysis of *The Fossil Record.* In: Harland WB, Holland CH, House MR, Hughes NF, Reynolds AB, Rudwick MJS, Satterthwaite GE, Tarlo LBH, Willey EC, editors. The fossil record: a symposium with documentation. London: Geological Society of London, pp. 791-820; (d) Eicher DL, McAlester AL. 1980. History of the earth. Englewood Cliffs, N.J.: Prentice-Hall; (e) Gould SJ. 1989. Wonderful life: the Burges Shale and the nature of history. New York and London: W. W. Norton and Co. (f) Knoll AH. 1992. The early evolution of eukaryotes: a geological perspective. Science 256:622-627; (g) Knoll and Rothwell (note 32); (h) Lipps JH, editor. 1993. Fossil prokaryotes and protists. Boston, Oxford, and London: Blackwell Scientific Publications; (i) Moore RC, editor. 1955-1981. Treatise on invertebrate paleontology, Parts F, I, K, O, S. Boulder, Colo.: Geological Society of America, and Lawrence, Kans.: University of Kansas Press; (j) Simonetta AM, Conway Morris S, editors. 1991. The early evolution of Metazoa and the significance of problematic taxa. Cambridge and New York: Cambridge University Press; (k) Simpson GG. 1983. Fossils and the history of life. New York: Scientific American Books; (l) Stanley SM. 1989. Earth and life through time. 2nd ed. New York: W. H. Freeman and Co.; (m) Stewart WN, Rothwell GW. 1993. Paleobotany and the evolution of plants. 2nd ed. Cambridge and New York: Cambridge University Press, pp. 510, 511. ⟶

FIGURE 10.1

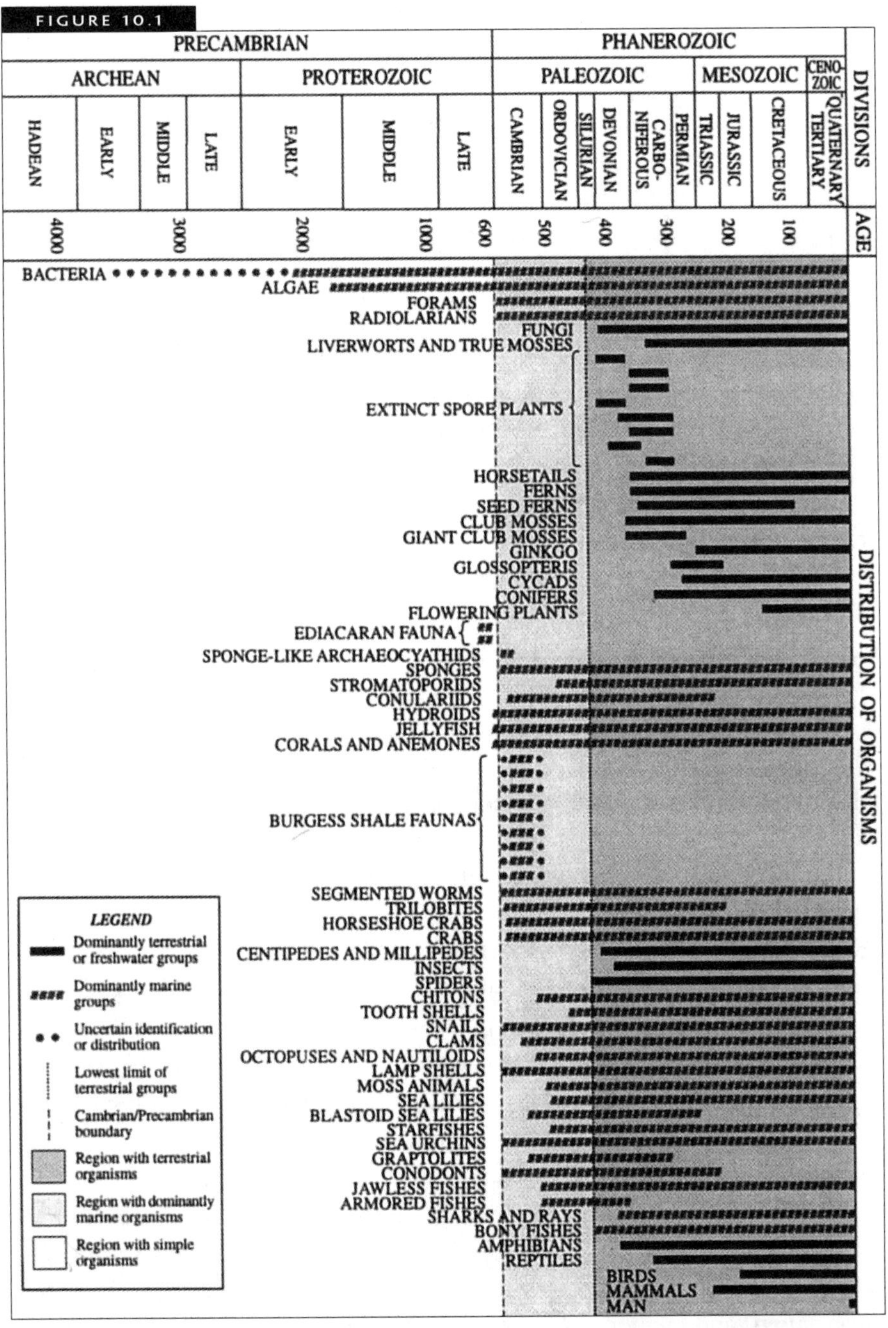

Distribution of main types of organisms in the geologic column. Age given in millions of years in Column 4 is based on the standard geologic timescale and is not endorsed by the author. Note that the timescale is not linear. The Phanerozoic is expanded five times compared to the Precambrian. See references on page 164.*

depths. The only kind of life that flourishes at these depths is various microorganisms. Examples abound.[7] Sulfur-reducing bacteria are abundant in aquifers (water-bearing sedimentary layers) at depths of 800-1,000 meters in the Baku district of Azerbaijan (former U.S.S.R.). There they impart a pink color to water coming from oil well drilling operations. One well produced some 5,000 liters of pink water daily for six months.[8] A coal seam in Germany, lying at a depth of 400 meters, harbors about 1,000 bacteria per gram of coal. About the same concentration of bacteria lives in groundwater more than one kilometer below the surface, in the Madison limestone of the northwestern United States.[9]

Extensive studies have been conducted in South Carolina in three holes drilled to depths as great as 500 meters. Typically researchers found 100,000 to 10 million bacteria per gram of sediment, and isolated more than 4,500 different strains. In less-permeable clay sedimentary layers that lie between aquifers, the numbers of bacteria were much fewer, usually less than 1,000 per gram.[10] Protozoa (one-celled animals, now classified as protists) and fungi were also found, but in significantly lower concentrations than bacteria.[11] Protozoa and bacteria also have turned up in a number of other deep subsurface sediments.[12] Surprisingly, at the South Carolina sites live filamentous green algae that usually require light for growth have appeared at several levels, reaching depths of 210 meters.[13] Researchers explained their presence at such great depths as possibly indicating some sort of connection to the surface, or a very long viability for the algae. Another study demonstrated the presence of the kind of viruses that live in bacteria at a depth of 405 meters.[14]

Microorganisms probably exist in all sedimentary rocks[15] and are most abundant in aquifers. Investigators have also discovered them in granite. Thomas Gold[16] provides evidence of their activity at a depth of 6 kilometers in an exploration oil well drilled in Sweden's Siljan impact crater (44 kilometers diameter). Furthermore, he reports the isolation of several strains of living bacteria found at depths greater than 4 kilometers at the same locality. He even suggests that the volume of living organisms in the rocks may be comparable to that of all organisms living on earth's surface.[17] Considering the thickness of the rock layers, there appears to be an abundance of life below our feet.

The capability of microorganisms to live in the rocks partially results from their small size, permitting them to exist in tiny pore spaces between mineral granules. Bacteria are commonly around 1/1,000 millimeter in diameter. Protozoa, algae, fungi, and cyanobacteria (bacteria that have photosynthetic capability) are generally 10-100 times larger, but can fit easily between particles of coarser sediments such as sand. Moisture is essential for their survival, but water is commonly available at depths of one kilometer, and often much deeper. The slow lateral and vertical movement of water in aquifers favors the passive spread of microorganisms.

The various microorganisms found at great depths possess a multitude of biochemical systems that permit them to survive under unusual conditions.[18] Some appear to thrive at temperatures above 150°C, but this information is debatable. Many require oxygen, while some cannot survive in its presence. Others can exist either way. Often the waters at these depths contain a moderate amount of oxygen, while pockets with no oxygen are not uncommon. The organisms obtain their energy from both organic and inorganic compounds.

From the above it is evident that a previously unknown world of life dwells in the rocks. Unfortunately these "secretive" organisms are relatively inaccessible. Their presence poses some interesting questions regarding the fossil record of microorganisms found in the deeper rocks.

CREATION AND LIFE IN THE DEEP ROCKS

We can often interpret data in more than one way. The hypothesis that the fossils of simple life found in the deeper rocks represent the early forms of life on their way to evolving into more advanced forms is one interpretation. The recent discoveries of life in deep rocks also permit the suggestion that such fossils represent organisms that normally live in or have infiltrated these deep rocks. The demonstrated presence of life in the rocks today would suggest that we should at least consider such an interpretation before we regard simple, one-celled Precambrian fossils as evidence for evolution. The fact that live filamentous algae have been found in these deep layers might represent a source for filamentous fossils postulated to be 3,500 million years old. Also the catastrophic Genesis flood could have facilitated the transport of microscopic algae as surface waters infiltrated permeable or cracked deep rocks.

Stromatolites[19] also occur in the deep rocks. Their interpretation is more equivocal from both the creationist and evolutionist perspectives. Stromatolites are an important part of the evolutionary scenario of early life (Table 9.1) but, like many of the fossils in the deeper rocks, their identification is problematic. Some scientists have reinterpreted some widely accepted examples of ancient stromatolites as precipitation and soft sediment deformation.[20] Paleobotanist A. H. Knoll of Harvard points out that "no Early Archaean stromatolites are known to contain microfossils. Thus, abiological alternatives must be considered."[21]

The correct identification of fossil stromatolites in deep rocks is important to the question of the origin of life. The recent discovery of living stromatolites actively forming in rock cavities such as in coral reefs complicates estimating of their ages. These special stromatolite deposits are called endostromatolites. Bacteria that do not require light as an energy source facilitate sediment accumulation on an endostromatolite. Claude Monty, a biosedimentologist from the University of Liège in Belgium, suggests that endostromatolites can form in rock cavities at depths of at least 3 km.[22] This raises the question as to whether some stromatolites in the deeper rocks, possibly growing in caves, might be endostromatolites of recent origin. Our knowledge regarding such stromatolites is still inadequate, and thus we cannot draw firm conclusions.

It appears that the evidence from deep rocks for the early evolution of life faces alternative interpretations. We must carefully consider three factors: (1) the problem of the valid identification of simple microscopic fossil types, (2) the fact that the fossilized life forms may represent created forms that lived in the rocks and have subsequently become fossilized, rather than early stages in the evolution of life, and (3) infiltration of microscopic surface organisms into deep rocks, especially during catastrophic events.

CREATION AND THE PHANEROZOIC FOSSIL SEQUENCE

The relative abundance of well-preserved fossils in the upper part of the geologic column—called the Phanerozoic (Cambrian to Recent; Figure 10.1 and Table 9.1)—provides a different frame of reference and interpretation than the rare and often-questionable fossils in lower layers (Precambrian).

Here, as mentioned earlier, we observe suggestions of an increasing complexity of fossils from the lower to higher layers of the geologic column. We shall discuss several alternatives that creationists have proposed to explain this pattern. They include sorting by (1) motility, (2) buoyancy, and (3) ecology. Any model of the deluge should consider all three factors as having some effect. No single factor could exist by itself and be solely responsible for the fossil sequence, and doubtless several other factors would be involved. We must remember that because we are dealing with a past unique and complex event about which we do not have much data, explanations must of necessity be considered as conjecture.

THE MOTILITY FACTOR

Motility sorting would apply to animals as they sought to escape the gradually rising waters of a global flood. For instance, birds are rare in the fossil record. Well-preserved remains have not yet been found below the Jurassic. We would expect them to escape gradually to higher ground during the months of the flood, leaving only tracks in soft sediments. This could explain the apparent relative abundance of bird tracks in the Triassic *below* any good fossil bird bones.[23] Likewise, tracks of amphibia and reptiles tend to dominate at a lower level in the geologic column than their body fossils.[24]

Larger land animals would seem to be better able to escape to higher ground during the flood than would smaller ones. This may be the basis for Cope's Rule, which states that in evolution organisms tend to progress toward larger sizes.[25] This rule derives from Cope's observation of an increase in size of particular types of fossils as one ascends the geologic column. In the context of a flood, the larger organisms of the same type would have escaped to a higher level in the column than did their smaller counterparts. (This is the same famous Cope who vied with Marsh in the study of vertebrates in the western United States.)[26] While the role of motility in the distribution of animals in the geologic column during the deluge must remain speculative, Cope's rule and such data as track distribution fit well with the concept of some sorting according to motility.

THE BUOYANCY FACTOR

For centuries, a number of scholars have suggested sorting by density during the Genesis flood as a mechanism for explaining the fossil record. It so happens that many simpler organisms, such as coral, snails, clams, brachiopods (lamp shells), and other marine organisms, have a greater density and also better representation in the lower parts of the geologic column than do more familiar vertebrates, such as frogs and cats. Could the effect of density acting during the deluge be responsible for such a distribution? Possibly so on a local level, but it is highly doubtful that sorting according to live animal density could be a general explanation for the entire column. Heavier-shelled animals also appear higher in the geologic column.

The buoyancy of vertebrate carcasses is a more likely factor. After death, some vertebrates tend to float much longer than others. Preliminary experiments on recent organisms indicate that birds float an average of 76 days, mammals 56 days, reptiles 32 days, and amphibians five days.[27] We must recognize that the present-day representatives of these groups vary somewhat from their fossil counterparts, thus possibly yielding different figures for the same vertebrate types. Nevertheless, this sequence fits well with both the arrangement in the geologic column and with the time frame of the flood described in Genesis. Thus sorting by buoyancy might have been a factor in the Genesis flood.

THE ECOLOGICAL ZONATION THEORY

Another creationist explanation for trends in the fossil sequence of the geologic column rests on a proposed ecological distribution of organisms before the flood. It is reasonable to assume that before the flood the distribution of plants and animals varied from place to place, as it does now. Polar bears do not live in the tropics. We also easily note ecological differences in mountainous areas where the plants and animals at lower altitudes vary significantly from those higher up. For instance, frogs and snakes do not inhabit the tops of our higher mountains, though some mammals do survive there. One creationist explanation for the geologic column, called the "ecological zonation theory," proposes a preflood ecological distribution somewhat similar to the distribution of fossils in the geologic column. In other words, the sequence of fossils in the geologic column reflects in general the altitudinal arrangement of the preflood ecology. In this model, dinosaurs and human beings lived at the same time, but in different ecological environments. Humans inhabited higher elevations.

As we consider how the flood might have caused the sequence found in the fossil record, we should differentiate between the familiar, small local floods and an unfamiliar worldwide event as described in Genesis. Sometimes we think of a flood as washing sediment from a higher area into a lower one and mixing everything in a disorganized pattern. However, flood deposits are often well sorted, forming widespread flat layers. On a larger scale, mixing is even more difficult. A sequence of fossils would result as slowly rising floodwaters *sequentially* destroyed the various preflood landscapes along with their unique organisms, redepositing them in order in large depositional basins of the continents. Of itself, we would not expect rain to dislodge animals and trees, but great waves of the rising floodwaters would. Often rapid underwater mudflows called turbidity currents[28] would carry sediment and organisms into the deep basins. The order of the fossils in such sedimentary basins would reflect the order of the eroded landscapes destroyed by the gradually rising waters. Harold W. Clark,[29] who, unlike his mentor George McCready Price, accepted the evidence for a sequence of fossils in the geologic column, developed the zonation idea. Figure 10.2 illustrates a proposed preflood landscape. If a gradually rising flood, as described above, destroyed such a landscape, it would result in the general sequence now found in the fossil record. In this model, the sequence of fish, amphibians, reptiles, and mammals referred to above would result from the original preflood distribution of the various organisms.

Sometimes proponents of the ecological zonation theory oversimplify it by comparing present ecology too closely with preflood ecology. While our pres-

FIGURE 10.2

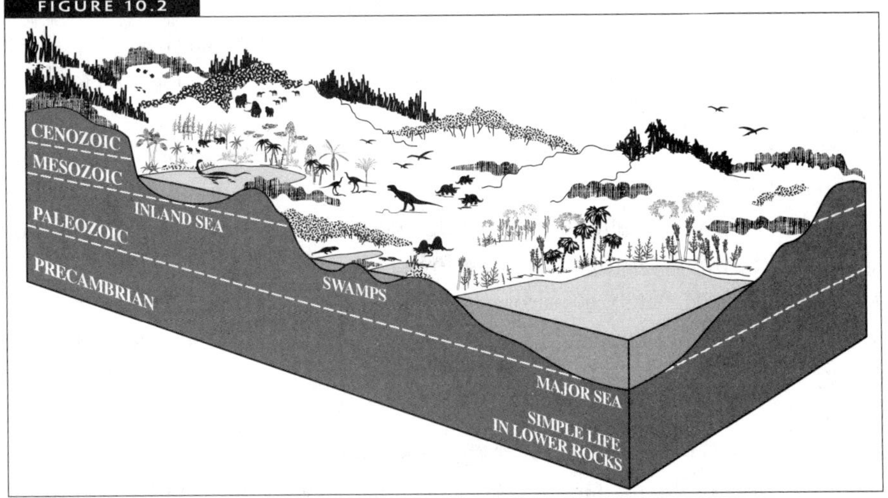

A suggestion of the general distribution of organisms before the Genesis flood. The ecological zonation theory proposes that the gradual destruction of these environments by the rising waters of the flood would produce the sequence of fossils now found in earth's crust.

ent ecology relates to the fossil sequence in a general way, we should not expect ecological patterns to survive in great detail through a worldwide flood, and we would expect any major catastrophe such as the Genesis flood to cause some changes in earth's ecological patterns. The precise distribution of organisms before such a catastrophe would most likely be different from the present. Furthermore, comparison of past and present ecology is complicated by the fact that we would expect both restricted and extensive lateral transport of sediments and organisms in any major flood. This transport along with uplift or subsidence of source and depositional areas would introduce further complications in the fossil sequence. Limited mixing, buoyancy, and motility of organisms could also modify the order of the fossils. The ecological zonation theory does not expect or propose exact parallels between preflood and present-day ecologies. It does suggest, however, a general ecological sequence resulting from the gradually rising waters.

Some general aspects of the fossil record do not relate easily to modern ecological sequences, and some have proposed a modified preflood world within the framework of the ecological zonation theory. For instance, present-day marine organisms live almost exclusively at sea level or lower. However, the fossil sequence has marine organisms abundant at several levels. Hence it has been proposed that before the flood major seas existed at different levels on the continents (Figure 10.2). These could be the sources of the main marine fossil levels in the geologic column. Such proposed seas would have been more extensive than modern-day saltwater seas, such as the Great Salt Lake, the Dead Sea, and the Caspian Sea, that now exist either above or below our present general worldwide sea level.[30]

The proposed preflood ecologic sequence (Figures 10.1 and 10.2) begins with simple life in the rocks in the lower regions. Many animal groups would dwell in the lowest preflood seas, while "coal" forests, amphibians, and reptiles would abound in hot, swampy lowlands. Flowering plants and warm-blooded animals, such as birds and mammals, including human beings, would occupy the higher and cooler regions. This general sequence fits the fossil record.

PROBLEMS WITH THE ECOLOGICAL ZONATION THEORY

The major problems facing the theory all relate to the extreme sorting of many organisms as found in the layers of the fossil record. Current ecological distributions only rarely reflect this. We might explain some of this sorting by extensive lateral transport of organisms from limited source areas during the flood, but the problem seems more general and is not limited to single source areas.

The scarcity or total absence of mammals, flowering plants, and their pollen[31] in the upper Paleozoic and lower Mesozoic are probably the most serious problems the ecological zonation theory must answer when we compare fossil distribution to present-day ecology. The ecological zonation model requires a more orderly (stratified) ecological distribution than now exists, with flowering plants, including grasses, and mammals only at higher elevations. A creation with a more orderly preflood ecology is certainly not out of the question. One can speculate as to possible causes: (1) Warm-blooded mammals could have been excluded from preflood lowlands because of too-warm temperatures there. Evidence for this will be given below; (2) Flowering plants could have been excluded from the lowlands because of an abundance there of a differently adapted flora. In the lower parts of the Phanerozoic fossil sequence we find evidence of vast forests composed of unfamiliar trees such as lycopods, seed ferns, and huge horsetails.[32] They grew as the famous Carboniferous coal forests (Table 9.1) and have formed some of our best coal reserves.

Some evidence from the rocks and fossils indicates that the earth's past ecology may have been somewhat different. Examples are not difficult to find. The middle of the Phanerozoic portion of the column (Permian-Triassic) contains many red rocks—the oxygen-bearing "red beds."[33] Below the "red beds" and also near the top of the column we find abundant black shales, indicating reduced oxygen conditions.[34] Both ecological conditions are unusual in present-day ecology. Some living organisms appear identical to their fossil counterparts,[35] but many, such as dinosaurs and some trees, are quite different, allowing for different ecological relationships.

Temperature averages also appear to have been significantly warmer in the past. We can estimate such averages on the basis of warm- or cool-climate fossil organisms or oxygen isotope ratios that are temperature-dependent. Near the top of the geologic column fossils of forest trees appear in both present-day Arctic and Antarctic regions.[36] Living forests do not exist there now. Close to the North Pole on Ellesmere Island[37] we find fossil salamanders, snakes, lizards, and alligators, which indicate a much warmer climate in the past. In Antarctica, forests from the middle of the Phanerozoic, assumed to have been only 5-10 degrees of latitude from the South Pole when they grew, also appear to have grown in a warmer climate. They do not even show frost damage rings.[38] In general, the evidence speaks of a warmer climate in the past than at present for most of the geologic column. Rough estimates suggest possibly 7-20°C warmer in the higher latitudes of both hemispheres.[39] Such evidence indicates that the past was somewhat different from the present, yet it was still sufficiently similar to support some of the very same kinds of organisms now living on earth.

EVIDENCE THAT AGREES WITH THE ECOLOGICAL ZONATION THEORY

While the past may have been somewhat different from the present, we would expect that the same general ecological relationships would have prevailed before the Genesis flood. On this basis some interesting comparisons between past and present are possible. Some of that data agrees well with the ecological-zonation theory.

1. As we examine the distribution of organisms on earth, we find simple organisms living down to great depths within the rock layers. In an ecological zonation theory interpretation of the fossil record, this would correspond to the rare simple fossils that we discover in the lower Precambrian layers (Figure 10.1; note especially the distribution of bacteria and algae in the Precambrian). Fossilization of these simple organisms could have occurred before, during, or after the Genesis flood in the deep rocks where they lived. Algae which require light but are occasionally found alive in deep rocks probably are transported there by the infiltration of surface waters.

2. The organisms found in the light-gray area between the dotted and dashed lines in Figure 10.1 are almost entirely marine. They would represent the organisms living in low preflood seas, which would have had an abundance

of marine life. This explains the evolutionary problem of the Cambrian explosion,[40] where most of the animal phyla, which happen to be almost entirely marine, appear suddenly without evolutionary ancestors. The ecological zonation theory readily explains the Cambrian explosion as reflecting the location of the low preflood seas.

3. Many kinds of terrestrial organisms first appear at about the same level in the geologic column. They include: fungi, many extinct plant groups, horsetails, ferns, seed ferns, club mosses, insects, centipedes, millipedes, spiders, and amphibians. Note the organisms above the dotted line in Figure 10.1. The appearance at about the same level of so many varied terrestrial groups seems unusual from an evolutionary standpoint. It is more in harmony with what we might expect when the rising waters of the flood destroyed the lowest land areas of the preflood world and preserved these terrestrial types as fossils.

4. The general fossil distribution pattern is similar to present ecology. The current sequence on earth shows small, single-celled organisms in the earth's deeper rocks, abundant marine organisms in the seas, and land forms at higher levels. The same general sequence occurs in the fossil record (Figure 10.1). According to the ecological zonation theory, grasshoppers and cows would not appear in the lowest geologic layers, because they would not have lived in the preflood seas. In the portion of the geologic column containing many fossils (the Phanerozoic) almost everything preserved in the lower portion (Cambrian to Silurian) are marine organisms, while in the upper portion (Tertiary) fossils dominantly represent terrestrial organisms, with varying proportions between. We would expect such a sequence from a single flood event in which the first disturbances would cause the burial of the lowest marine environments (Cambrian explosion), while only the highest terrestrial environments, which possibly had a cooler climate where the mammals lived, would be involved in the final stages, forming the top of the geologic column. The general suggestion of advancement of organisms as one ascends the geologic column may not represent evolution, but may reflect the preflood ecology of the earth.

Thus, as we have seen, a significant amount of data fits with the general expectations of the ecological zonation theory.

CONCLUSIONS

The discussion presented above is, to say the least, quite different from traditional interpretations. However, discoveries such as the Cambrian explosion challenge evolutionary interpretations of gradual development and suggest that we should consider other perspectives.

In general, when we look at the fossil sequence we find a significant uniqueness of organisms at different levels and a general suggestion of an ascending progression of life forms from simple to complex. Sometimes this pattern is considered to be compelling evidence for evolution. However, the limited progression need not reflect gradual development. Motility and buoyancy could cause some seeming progression in a global flood. Also significant is the fact that organisms at present live in and on earth's crust in a general ascending sequence from simple to complex. First single-celled organisms dwell in the deep rocks, then more complex organisms in the low marine environments, and further up the more complex land organisms. In the context of a gradually rising worldwide catastrophe such as the Genesis flood, we would expect such a general order in the fossil record—and that is what we find there.

REFERENCES

1. Pascal B. 1966. Pensées. Krailsheimer AJ, translator. London and New York: Penguin Books, p. 80.
2. A few evolutionists take exception to the idea that evolution includes the concept of the spontaneous origin of life. They prefer to limit evolution to development of life forms after life was organized. I will use the term more in the way it is usually understood in scientific journals and textbooks, where it includes both the evolution of simple life and the subsequent development of more complicated life forms.
3. However, as one compares living species to similar ones in the fossil record one sees an increasing proportion of strangeness (from present species) as one goes further down the geologic column. This has been interpreted as evidence of gradual change of species over time. However, that argument has to be evaluated against the expectation that in any major catastrophe such as the deluge one would expect those species that were buried the deepest in the geologic column to have the least chance to have representatives escape and survive the flood.
4. (a) Price GM. 1923. The new geology. Mountain View, Calif.: Pacific Press Pub. Assn., pp. 619-634. For an account of this, see: (b) Numbers RL. 1992. The creationists. New York: Alfred A. Knopf, pp. 72-101.
5. For instance, see: (a) Nelson BC. 1968. The deluge story in stone: a history of the flood theory of geology. Minneapolis: Bethany Fellowship, Inc.; (b) Rehwinkel AM. 1951. The flood in the light of the Bible, geology, and archaeology. St. Louis: Concordia Pub. House, pp. 168-274; (c) Whitcomb JC. 1988. The world that perished. 2nd ed. Grand Rapids: Baker Book House, pp. 86, 87; (d) Whitcomb JC, Jr., Morris HM. 1966. The Genesis flood: the biblical record and its scientific implications. Philadelphia: Presbyterian and Reformed Pub. Co., pp. 180-211.
6. Numbers, pp. 218, 219 (note 4b).
7. (a) Fliermans CB, Hazen TC, editors. 1990. Proceedings of the First International Symposium on Microbiology of the Deep Subsurface. WSRC Information Services Section Publications Group; (b) Fredrickson JK, Onstott TC. 1996. Microbes deep inside the earth. Scientific American 275(4):68-73; (c) Ghiorse WC, Wilson JT. 1988. Microbial ecology of the terrestrial subsurface. Advances in Applied Microbiology 33:107-172; (d) Pedersen K. 1993. The deep subterranean biosphere. Earth-Science Reviews 34:243-260; (e) Stevens TO, McKinley JP. 1995. Lithoautotrophic Microbial Ecosystems in Deep Basalt Aquifers. Science 270:450-454.
8. Ivanov MV. 1990. Subsurface microbiological research in the U.S.S.R. In: Fliermans and Hazen, pp. 1.7-1.15 (note 7a).
9. Ghiorse and Wilson (note 7c).
10. Balkwill DL. 1990. Density and distribution of aerobic, chemoheterotrophic bacteria in deep

southeast coastal plain sediments at the Savannah River Site. In: Fliermans and Hazen, pp. 3.3-3.13 (note 7a).

11. (a) Sinclair JL. 1990. Eukaryotic microorganisms in subsurface environments. In: Fliermans and Hazen, pp. 3.39-3.51 (note 7a); (b) Sinclair JL, Ghiorse WC. 1989. Distribution of aerobic bacteria, protozoa, algae, and fungi in deep subsurface sediments. Geomicrobiology Journal 7:15-31.
12. Sinclair JL, Ghiorse WC. 1987. Distribution of protozoa in subsurface sediments of a pristine groundwater study site in Oklahoma. Applied and Environmental Microbiology 53(5):1157-1163.
13. (a) Sinclair (note 11a); (b) Sinclair and Ghiorse (note 11b).
14. Bradford SM, Gerba CP. 1990. Isolation of bacteriophage from deep subsurface sediments. In: Fliermans and Hazen, p. 4.65 (note 7a).
15. Ourisson G, Albrecht P, Rohmer M. 1984. The microbial origin of fossil fuels. Scientific American 251(2):44-51.
16. Gold T. 1991. Sweden's Siljan ring well evaluated. Oil and Gas Journal 89(2):76-78.
17. Gold T. 1992. The deep, hot biosphere. Proceedings of the National Academy of Sciences, U.S.A. 89:6045-6049.
18. For an example, see: (a) Kaiser J. 1995. Can deep bacteria live on nothing but rocks and water? Science 270:377; (b) Stevens and McKinley (note 7e).
19. See chapter 9.
20. Lowe DR. 1994. Abiological origin of described stromatolites older than 3.2 Ga. Geology 22:387-390.
21. Knoll AH. 1990. Precambrian evolution of prokaryotes and protists. In: Briggs DEG, Crowther PR, editors. Paleobiology: a synthesis. Oxford and London: Blackwell Scientific Publications, pp. 9-6.
22. (a) Monty CLV. 1986. Range and significance of cavity-dwelling or endostromatolites. Sediments down under. Abstracts of the twelfth International Sedimentological Congress, Canberra, Australia, p. 216; (b) Vachard D, Razgallah S. 1988. Survie des genres Tharama et Ranalcis (Epiphytales, algues problématiques) dans le Permien supérieur du Djebel Tebaga (Tunisie). Comptes Rendus de L'Académie des Sciences Paris 306(Ser 2):1137-1140.
23. Lockley MG, Yang SY, Matsukawa M, Fleming F, Lim SK. 1992. The track record of Mesozoic birds: evidence and implications. Philosophical Transactions of the Royal Society of London B 336:113-134.
24. Brand L, Florence J. 1982. Stratigraphic distribution of vertebrate fossil footprints compared with body fossils. Origins 9:67-74.
25. For a discussion of Cope's Rule, see: Benton MJ. 1990. Evolution of large size. In: Briggs and Crowther, pp. 147-152 (note 21).
26. See chapter 9.
27. Brand LR. Personal communication.
28. See chapter 13.
29. Clark HW. 1946. The new diluvialism. Angwin, Calif.: Science Publications, pp. 37-93.
30. See chapter 12 for an alternative suggestion of the transport of marine sediments. Note especially Figure 12.2A, B.
31. Some consider the paucity of flowering plant pollen in the lower geologic layers as a serious problem for the ecological zonation theory, since pollen would be expected to be widely distributed. But the Bible suggests no rain ([a] Genesis 2:5) before the flood, which implies a different climatic system that may have also excluded high winds. Without rain and high winds, pollen distribution may have been limited until the floodwaters destroyed local accumulations. However, we would expect some transport of pollen from the rain of the flood, and there are a few references to plant tissues unusually low in the geologic column and to spores or pollen from layers considered to be older than the layers in which the plants which produced them are found. E.g., (b) Axelrod DI. 1959. Evolution of the psilophyte paleoflora. Evolution 13:264-275; (c) Coates J, Crookshank H, Gee ER, Ghosh PK, Lehner E, Pinfold ES. 1945. Age of the

Saline Series in the Punjab Salt Range. Nature 155:266, 267; (d) Cornet B. 1989. Late Triassic angiosperm-like pollen from the Richmond Rift Basin of Virginia, U.S.A. Paleontographica, Abteilung B 213:37-87; (e) Cornet B. 1986. The leaf venation and reproductive structures of a Late Triassic angiosperm, *Sanmiguelia lewisii*. Evolutionary Theory 7(5):231-291; (f) Cornet B. 1979. Angiosperm-like pollen with tectate-columellate wall structure from the upper Triassic (and Jurassic) of the Newark Supergroup, U.S.A. Palynology 3:281, 282; (g) Gray J. 1993. Major Paleozoic land plant evolutionary bio-events. Paleogeography, Paleoclimatology, Paleoecology 104:153-160; (h) Leclercq S. 1956. Evidence of vascular plants in the Cambrian. Evolution 10:109-114; (i) Sahni B. 1944. Age of the Saline Series in the Salt Range of the Punjab. Nature 153:462, 463; and references therein; (j) Wadia DN. 1975. Geology of India. New Delhi: Tata McGraw-Hill Pub. Co., Ltd., pp. 135-137. Such information, which fits well with a creation-flood model but not with a slow gradual evolutionary model, where we would not expect spores and pollen before the plants that produce them had evolved, is of course highly controversial and has often been subjected to reinterpretation.

32. E.g.: Knoll AH, Rothwell GW. 1981. Paleobotany: perspectives in 1980. Paleobiology 7(1):7-35.
33. The red beds are especially abundant in the Permian and Triassic. Scientists have much debated their origin. See for example: (a) Krynine PD. 1950. The origin of red beds. American Association of Petroleum Geologists Bulletin 34:1770; (b) Weller JM. 1960. Stratigraphic principles and practice. New York: Harper and Brothers, pp. 133-135.
34. Widespread black shales in the Cretaceous are especially considered peculiar. See: (a) Arthur MA. 1994. Marine black shales: depositional mechanisms and environments of ancient deposits. Annual Review of Earth and Planetary Sciences 22:499-551; (b) Schlanger SO, Cita MB. 1982. Introduction to the symposium "On the Nature and Origin of Cretaceous Organic Carbon-Rich Facies." In: Schlanger SO, Cita MD, editors. Nature and origin of Cretaceous carbon-rich facies. London and New York: Academic Press, pp. 1-6. See also rest of the volume.
35. See chapters 8 and 9.
36. For a review of some of the data, see: Axelrod DI. 1984. An interpretation of Cretaceous and Tertiary biota in polar regions. Paleogeography, Paleoclimatology, Paleoecology 45:105-147.
37. Estes R, Hutchison JH. 1980. Eocene lower vertebrates from Ellesmere Island, Canadian Arctic Archipelago. Paleogeography, Paleoclimatology, Paleoecology 30:325-347.
38. Taylor EL, Taylor TN, Cúneo NR. 1992. The present is not the key to the past: a polar forest from the Permian of Antarctica. Science 257:1675-1677.
39. See: (a) Allègre CJ, Schneider SH. 1994. The evolution of the earth. Scientific American 271(4):66-74; (b) Brooks CEP. 1949. Climate through the ages: a study of the climatic factors and their variations. New York and Toronto: McGraw-Hill Book Co.; (c) Emiliani C. 1987. Paleoclimatology, isotopic. In: Oliver JE, Fairbridge RW, editors. The encyclopedia of climatology. Encyclopedia of Earth sciences, vol. 11. New York: Van Nostrand Reinhold Co., pp. 670-675; (d) Frakes LA. 1979. Climates throughout geologic time. Amsterdam, Oxford, and New York: Elsevier Scientific Pub. Co., p. 261; (e) Goudie AS. 1987. Paleoclimatology. In: Oliver and Fairbridge, pp. 660-670 (note 39c); (f) Karhu J, Epstein S. 1986. The implication of the oxygen isotope records in coexisting cherts and phosphates. Geochimica et Cosmochimica Acta 50:1745-1756; (g) Menzies RJ, George RY, Rowe GT. 1973. Abyssal environment and ecology of the world oceans. New York and London: John Wiley and Sons, pp. 349, 350.
40. See chapter 9 for a brief description of the Cambrian explosion.

CHAPTER 11

WHAT FOSSILS SAY ABOUT EVOLUTION

One keeps forgetting to go right down to the foundations. One doesn't put the question marks deep down enough. —*Ludwig Wittgenstein*[1]

Fossils have much to say to us about the lingering question of Scripture versus science. They have been hailed as "the final court of appeal when the doctrine of evolution is brought to the bar."[2] What do fossils really have to tell us about evolution? Is their purported support for evolution really that good? We will examine two major questions: rates of evolutionary change and the linking of the fossil groups.

RATES OF EVOLUTIONARY CHANGE AND THE FOSSIL RECORD

Some important fossil finds, such as very simple forms for most of the Precambrian that lie just below a variety of complex animals, including the peculiar Ediacaran and Burgess Shale[3] (Figure 10.1) organisms, challenge the common supposition of general evolutionary progress over time. At best we would have to consider evolution highly irregular in its rate of operation.

According to the evolutionary model, life evolved at least 3,500 million years ago, but remained in a relatively simple unicellular state for nearly 3,000 million years. Then suddenly in less than 100 million years, almost all the phyla (about 40 of them)[4] of the animal kingdom resulted from the so-called Cambrian explosion, and virtually no animal phyla evolved thereafter. The figure of 100 million years for the Cambrian explosion is generous for evolution. Some suggest only 5-10 million years for the majority of the phyla, which is less than 1/300 of the time postulated for all of evolution. Samuel Bowring of the Massachusetts Institute of Technology comments: "And what I like to ask my biologist friends is, How fast can evolution get before they start feeling uncomfortable?"[5] Researchers also report notable increases in algae in the Cambrian region.[6] In general, plants, which represent only one fourth of presently living species, appear higher up with various groups at different levels (Figure 10.1). Further up in the column the record continues to show sudden appearances. For instance, most of the mammalian orders presumedly appeared in only 12 million years (lower Tertiary). The evolutionist Steven M. Stanley points out that since the average fossil mammal species persists more than 1 million years, there is time for only 10 or 15 successive species generations (chronospecies) to evolve into mammals as varied as whales and bats. He states: "This is clearly preposterous"[7] and suggests alternatives such as rapid changes in regulatory genes and small populations in which mutations would manifest themselves more rapidly to help account for the sudden emergence of a great variety of mammal types in such a short period of time. An "extraordinarily explosive evolution" has also been reported for birds with all the living orders evolving in "some 5-10 million years."[8] Earlier we pointed out that the punctuated equilibrium model is not a solution.[9] It deals with changes around the species level and does not address the problem of the rapid origin of larger groups such as orders, classes, phyla, and divisions.

Actually, the fossil record suggests a *reduction* in basic types of both plants and animals since the lower Phanerozoic. Stephen J. Gould points out that significantly more basic kinds of animals existed in the Cambrian deposits than do now. He proposes that the traditional evolutionary tree pattern (Figure 11.1) of starting from a single original type (the trunk) and proceeding to increasingly diverse organisms (the branches and leaves) should be reversed, since we find fewer anatomical plans now than in the past.[10] The paleobotanists Wilson Stewart and Gar Rothwell list 31 "major plant groups" for the lower Paleozoic compared to only 23 for the present.[11] We can see the greater variety of major kinds of organisms in the lower Paleozoic in Figure 10.1, where 67 groups appear in the Paleozoic and only 42 higher in the Cenozoic. This difference may be even greater, because the figure leaves out several smaller plant groups in the Paleozoic. The higher strata in the geologic column may have more species,[12] but this involves only minor variations in the basic types. In other words, more basic themes appear lower in the column, but more variation on fewer themes predominates in the higher regions. Because of extinctions, fewer basic anatomical plans survive higher in the column, while we would expect that evolution would gradually produce more as time progressed.

An irregular rate of evolutionary change would mean that when changes occurred, they must have been rapid. The fossils indicate little evolutionary ac-

FIGURE 11.1

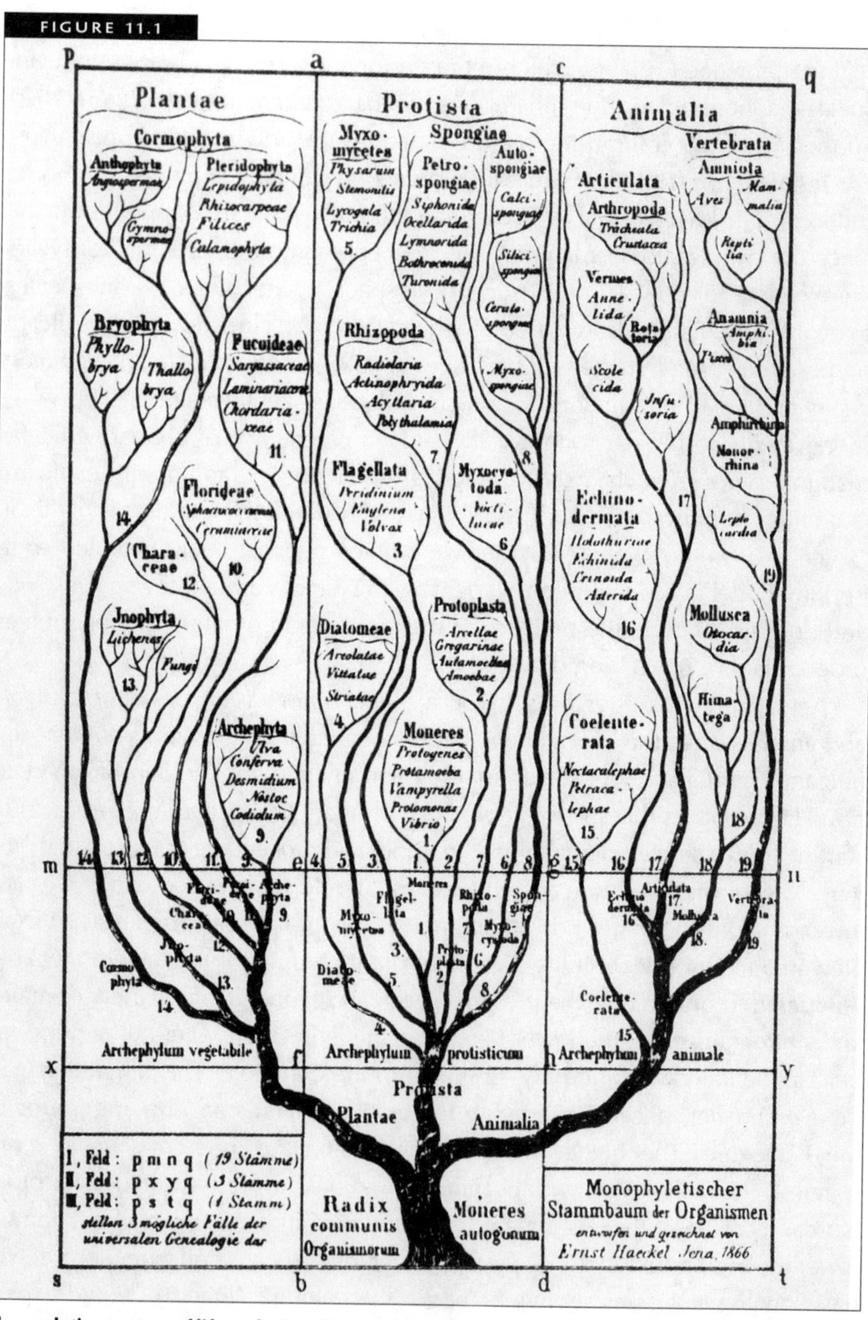

The evolutionary tree of life as depicted by Ernst Haeckel more than a century ago. Note that the solid main trunk and branches are all connected. Groups of organisms form the leaves of the tree, but there are few or no representatives from either living or fossil organisms for the branches or trunks of the tree. The labels for these represent mostly classification categories. Compare with Figure 11.2.

tivity during the first five sixths of geologic time below the Cambrian. Subsequent evolution would have followed an intermittent pattern, including punctuated equilibrium with frequent periods of stasis between rapid evolutionary changes. This leaves relatively little time for the actual process of evolutionary change—probably less than 1 percent of the geologic timescale, according to some evolutionary models. Such patterns in the fossil record significantly reduce the thousands of millions of years proposed for the full evolutionary process. Because of lack of time, these considerations increase even more the severe improbabilities that evolution faces.[13]

While the fossil record would require that major evolutionary changes occur rapidly, other data from the fossils suggest that evolutionary changes would have been extremely slow. Some living organisms are remarkably similar to their fossil counterparts. Lower Devonian mites, assumed to have evolved about 400 million years ago, closely parallel modern species.[14] J. William Schopf has found several fossil specimens of blue-green algae (cyanobacteria) from the Bitter Springs rocks of central Australia, with a putative age of 850 million years, that appear identical to present living species. He also reports about some 90 ancient species of varying assumed ages that have modern lookalikes.[15] Wilson Stewart and Gar Rothwell, commenting on similar organisms from Late Archaea to the Middle Proterozoic times (1,200-2,700 million years), state: "Although little can be determined about the rates of evolution of their biological systems, it is apparent that their morphotypes [shape] have remained fairly constant through the Precambrian to the present."[16]

Some forms in the Gunflint Chert of the Great Lakes region of North America, strata assumed to be nearly 2,000 million years old, are also closely similar to their living counterparts. Speaking more generally, Andrew Knoll states: "Many Late Proterozoic prokaryotes [no nucleus] differ little in morphology, development, or behaviour from living cyanobacterial populations."[17] Evolutionists try to explain this lack of change on the basis of an episodic (irregular) rate of evolutionary change, or internal evolutionary changes that cannot be seen, but in a creation context these similarities might also be the result of infiltration into rocks of recently living organisms.[18]

The fact that evolution now postulates extremely slow to extremely rapid rates of evolution to fit the fossil record illustrates how the general theory of evolution readily adapts to varied data. Highly varied rates of evolution challenge the traditional view of a slow, gradual evolutionary process, and one can wonder why some bacteria or similar simple organisms evolve all the way into human beings in 600 million years, while other organisms do not appear to change for 2,000 million years?

At best for the evolutionary model, the fossils reveal highly irregular evolutionary rates. The prolonged periods of slow or no evolution indicated by the fossils leave little time in the geologic past for highly improbable complex evolutionary changes.

THE GAPS IN THE FOSSIL RECORD

When I was a graduate student, the professor of evolution informed me that the faculty of the Department of Zoology was concerned about my creationistic beliefs. He wondered if I could explain them. I responded that I could see how a certain line of thought could lead to a belief in evolution, but that I had several questions about the theory. He was interested. One of the arguments I presented was that I could not understand how the turtle could have evolved from some other reptile without leaving fossil intermediates. The turtle is a unique organism, and in evolving this uniqueness—especially a shell—many intermediates would be involved, yet there is no such evidence in the fossil record. Paleontologists have found thousands of fossil turtles, some almost four meters long. They supposedly evolved more than 200 million years ago, and in the layers below where they first appear, we see no gradual sequence of the evolution of their peculiar shell.[19] After discussing some other considerations, the professor seemed satisfied with my answers and agreed that evolutionary theory had some problems. Later I was told that the only reason the faculty allowed me to graduate was that they could not agree on what to do with me!

Questions such as the origin of the turtle can be repeated hundreds of times. In each succeeding portion of the geologic column we find many sudden appearances of new kinds of organisms. A search for their ancestors in the layers below has been quite unsuccessful. Charles Darwin was fully aware of the problem. In *The Origin of Species,* he states, "But just in proportion as this process of extermination has acted on an enormous scale, so must the number of intermediate varieties, which have formerly existed, be truly enormous. Why then is not every geological formation and every stratum full of such intermediate links? Geology assuredly does not reveal any such finely graduated organic chain; and this, perhaps, is the most obvious and gravest objection which can be urged against the theory."[20] Darwin went on to attribute the problem to the "extreme imperfection" of the geologic record. However, as he himself acknowledged, the leading authorities on fossils of his day, such as "Agassiz, Pictet, and by none more forcibly than by Professor Sedgwick," opposed his view.[21]

The general picture of the missing intermediates has not changed significantly since Darwin's time. One hundred and twenty years later, David M.

Raup, curator of geology at the Field Museum of Natural History in Chicago and past president of the Paleontological Society, observed that "instead of finding the gradual unfolding of life, what geologists of Darwin's time, and geologists of the present day actually find is a highly uneven or jerky record; that is, species appear in the sequence very suddenly, show little or no change during their existence in the record, then abruptly go out of the record."[22]

And just a few years earlier the paleontologist David B. Kitts at the University of Oklahoma also admitted: "Despite the bright promise that paleontology provides a means of 'seeing' evolution, it has presented some nasty difficulties for evolutionists the most notorious of which is the presence of 'gaps' in the fossil record. Evolution requires intermediate forms between species and paleontology does not provide them."[23]

Stephen Jay Gould echoes the same: "The extreme rarity of transitional forms in the fossil record persists as the trade secret of paleontology. The evolutionary trees that adorn our textbooks have data only at the tips and nodes of their branches; the rest is inference, however reasonable, not the evidence of fossils."[24]

The patterns in the fossil sequence have compelled evolutionists to suggest that evolution occurs by rapid bursts. They also postulate that the changes occurred in small populations in which the chances of preservation of intermediates as fossils would be less likely, i.e., the punctuated-equilibrium model.[25] Such an explanation might account for the lack of intermediates between closely related species, but it fails to address the much more significant problem of the absence of intermediates between the major groups of organisms.

Living and fossil organisms fall into major categories called phyla and divisions. These are the distinct major groups of the hierarchal classification scheme. The more than a million different living species form less than 80 major groups (phyla and divisions). Why are the groups so distinct? And when we look at the fossils, why haven't we found the evolving intermediates between these distinct major groups? Here the evolutionary model fails one of its most crucial tests. The hope for some kind of evolutionary marvel that will transform one basic kind into another remains undemonstrated. Paleontologists will likely find many new species of fossils in the future, but as has been the case for centuries, we can expect them to belong to isolated major groups.[26] One might suggest, as Darwin did, that the fossil record is imperfect, but many millions of fossils have been collected. That they should consistently divide into major groups, while the large gaps between remain unrepresented, remains difficult for evolutionists to explain. It does not seem possible that the catastrophes or accidents favoring fossil formation and preservation would occur only when no evolution was occurring between major groups.

The venerable Harvard paleontologist George Gaylord Simpson has delineated the problem of the decreasing number of intermediates as one ascends the classification scheme. Table 11.1 outlines his evaluation.[27] According to the evolutionary model, we would expect the greatest number of intermediates between major groups, just where they are notably absent.

A few examples will illustrate the problem of the missing links.[28] The Cambrian explosion is not just a case of all the major animal phyla appearing at about the same place in the geologic column. It is also a situation of no ancestors to suggest how they might have evolved. Paleontologists have thoroughly studied the rocks just below the Cambrian explosion, in which we would expect to find the intermediates. It has been a virtually futile search. In the absence of fossil evidence, paleontologists have been in a quandary as to how the groups might be related to each other. Frederick Schram at the Scripps Institute of Oceanography comments: "Probably no subject has ever been marked by so much subjective speculation as that concerning relationships of invertebrate phyla. Hardly any two authorities agree. Furthermore, the abundance of rival interpretations of individual aspects of invertebrate anatomy and the confusing array of names applied to all manner of 'hypothetical ancestors' or paper animals is intimidating."[29]

Questions concerning the evolution of plants are not much different (Figure 10.1). Harold C. Bold, at the University of Texas, and his coauthors have stated that they, "after carefully weighing the current available evidence of comparative morphology, cytology, biochemistry, and fossil record, are *at present* unwilling to amalgamate any two or more of the 19 divisions in which they have tentatively classified the organisms of the plant kingdom."[30]

As an example, the flowering plants appear suddenly, fully formed and in abundance in the fossil record. Darwin called the origin of flowering plants

TABLE 11.1

Classification Level	Abundance of Intermediate Forms
Phyla	None
Classes	A few
Genera	Many
Species	A multitude

INTERMEDIATES IN THE CLASSIFICATION SCHEME*

*From Simpson (note 27).

"an abominable mystery." More than a century later some of the leading paleontologists (Axelrod, Bold, Knoll, and Rothwell) still call the problem "abominable."[31]

Flying organisms fall into four main groups: insects, pterosaurs (a flying reptile), birds, and bats (my apologies to humanity and its airline industry!). Flying is a highly specialized function requiring many features besides wings. For instance, the structure of a small airplane is distinctly different from that of an automobile. We would naturally expect the gradual evolution of flight to leave some evidence in the fossil record. But when fossil insects first appear in the geologic column, flying is fully developed.[32] The flying pterosaurs, birds, and bats also show up suddenly as fully functional flying organisms. The anatomical changes needed to develop flight, including transformations in bone, musculature, feathers, respiration, and nervous system, would take a long time, and the organisms undergoing such changes would surely leave some fossil record of intermediate stages. The feather of the bird supposedly evolved from the scales of some ancestral reptile. Anyone who has examined feathers under a microscope realizes that they are intricate and highly specialized structures. Would not the extended process of creating all these parts from reptile scales by undirected evolution, including unsuccessful lines of development, have made some record in the rocks? Thus far, none is apparent.

THE MISSING LINKS

Despite the fact that the fossil record is basically discontinuous, a few organisms do appear to represent "missing" links. These organisms are considered to be intermediate steps in a gap along an evolutionary lineage. Understandably, evolutionists want to make sure that others do not ignore such examples. The most famous is the reptile-bird *Archaeopteryx,* described in most texts of biology and paleontology. Discovered in Germany two years after Darwin published his *Origin,* it served to confirm the idea of evolution because it was both anatomically intermediate and at the right place in the geologic column. *Archaeopteryx* has some reptilian characteristics, such as teeth, a long tail, claws on its wings, and some reptilian bone features. It also has birdlike characteristics, such as fully developed feathers, a wishbone, and a grasping thumb.[33] Some of the main reptilian characteristics of *Archaeopteryx* are not unique to reptiles. A number of fossil birds have teeth, and claws occur on the wings of some living birds. A full retinue of fully developed flight feathers in *Archaeopteryx* establishes it as a bird.[34] *Archaeopteryx* was probably a bird with some reptilian characteristics. There have been two more recent discoveries of ancestral "birds." However, no feathers have turned up with either. One was found at about the same level in the geologic column as *Archaeopteryx,* the other a little lower. The evidence is much disputed.[35]

Textbooks often picture the famous fossil series that illustrates a gradual evolution of the horse. Creationists have not paid much attention to the argument, probably because the proposed changes are small and do not address the problem of intermediates between major kinds of created organisms. Nevertheless, it is interesting to note that evolutionists are now questioning the validity of the traditional arrangement of the horses as worked out by O. C. Marsh.[36] Simpson states: "The most famous of all equid [horse] trends, 'gradual reduction of the side toes,' is flatly fictitious."[37]

Raup states further that "the record of evolution is still surprisingly jerky and, ironically, we have even fewer examples of evolutionary transition than we had in Darwin's time. By this I mean that some of the classic cases of darwinian change in the fossil record, such as the evolution of the horse in North America, have had to be discarded or modified as a result of more detailed information—what appeared to be a nice simple progression when relatively few data were available now appears to be much more complex and much less gradualistic."[38]

The original display of the horse evolution at the American Museum of Natural History has been removed from public view.[39] Researchers are considering newer ideas about the evolution of the horse. A recent opinion is that the whole issue requires more study.[40]

Evolutionists often refer to a set of extinct intermediate organisms between reptiles and mammals called the synapsids. They have related a variety of skeletal features of one group to the other, and certain features of the jaws make an interesting, although very limited, example of a purported evolutionary sequence between reptiles and mammals. The paleontologist T. S. Kemp at Oxford states that this is "indeed . . . the only such major transition in the animal kingdom that is anything like well documented by an actual fossil record."[41] The group is highly varied. Some features of a particular type of synapsid fit some criteria of one proposed mammal ancestor, while other features do not. Although some of the features are intermediate, they do not provide a convincing line of descent between reptiles and mammals. The paleontologist Robert Carroll at McGill University states that "we cannot yet recognize the specific lineage that led to mammals."[42]

Evolutionists have proposed other examples of missing links. Some suggest a sequence for the origin of whales. However, in general the number of suggested missing links is extremely small compared to the hundreds of thousands needed to connect the gaps between the major groups of organisms. The emphasis on the very few that do exist witnesses to their paucity. Even those fossils claimed to be evolutionary links are not between the phyla and divisions where the largest gaps occur. When one realizes that paleontologists have identified more than 250,000 fossil species that as mentioned above divide into less than 80 major groups and many more subgroups, but have discovered very very

FIGURE 11.2

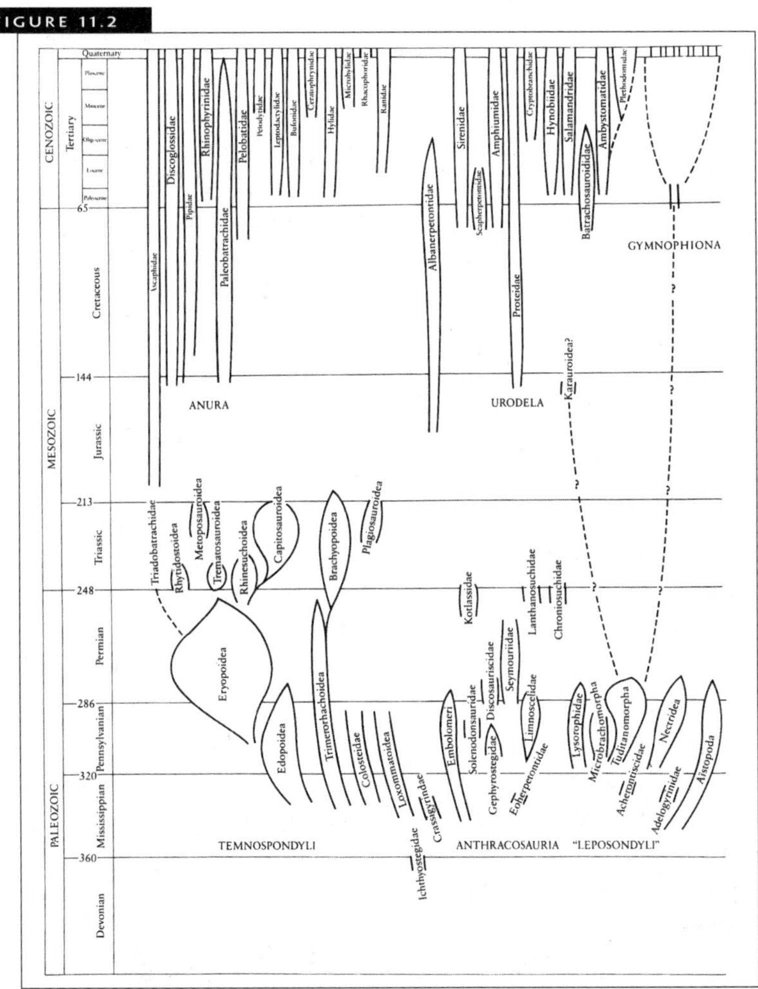

A recent representation of part of the evolutionary tree of life based on fossil amphibians. Note the almost total absence of proposed intermediates, reflecting the acceptance of the fact that the fossil record does not provide them. There are many more families of amphibians in the Paleozoic than in the Cenozoic. The Eryopoidea group illustrated includes 12 families, compared to single representation for the Cenozoic groups.†

†From Carroll, p. 157 (note 19a). Copyright © 1988 by W. H. Freeman and Co. Used with permission.

few organisms that can be considered as intermediates, evolution appears to have a serious problem.

Earlier we referred to the trees that evolutionists construct to depict the pathway that organisms have supposedly followed as species evolved from simple to complex. However, the ubiquitous gaps between fossil groups permit numerous arrangements, and seldom do any two comprehensive proposals for an evolutionary tree agree. Such trees are notorious for not having real organisms to represent the trunk and branches. Paleontologists have become more cautious recently and frequently identify as uncertain the unrepresented portions of evolutionary trees.

Figure 11.1 is an 1886 evolutionary tree based on the pioneer work of Ernest Haeckel, an ardent advocate for evolution on the European continent. Observe that everything is well-connected. Figure 11.2 is a 1988 representation of the fossil record of amphibians. Note how disconnected most of the groups are. The discontinuity of the fossil groups favors creation and not evolution. With evolution we would expect the major groups to be connected. Figure 10.1 shows many of the major groups into which biologists have classified organisms. If evolution had taken place, the groups should be connected with intermediates found lower in the fossil record, but again the intermediates are absent.

COMPLETENESS OF THE FOSSIL RECORD

Sometimes evolutionists will suggest that fossils of intermediate organisms are missing because they were soft-bodied and would not be as easily preserved as organisms with hard parts.[43] Such an argument does not appear to be significant because many soft-bodied organisms are well-preserved as fossils. One of the greatest problems for the evolutionary theory is the Cambrian explosion. The Ediacaran organisms below the Cambrian and the Burgess Shale organisms in the Cambrian are mainly soft-bodied, and many are excellently preserved, yet the expected intermediates below the Cambrian explosion are missing.

Evolutionists have also suggested that the record is imperfect because conditions for fossilization are rare.[44] However, the fossil record may be more complete than previously thought. The chances of an individual organism becoming fossilized are low, but the total population of a species is so large that representation of a species over evolutionary time by some well-preserved fossils is highly probable. Various recent studies comparing living species with those preserved as fossils in the same region, along with other less direct estimates, show a high proportion of species (not individual) preservation. In mollusks, the general level of fossil representation is estimated at 83-95 percent; clams and snails are at the 77-85 percent level;[45] and ostracods (a shelled crustacean) are at 60 percent.[46] The larger categories of organisms, which consist of many smaller groups, are, of course, better represented: the fossil record preserves orders of terrestrial vertebrates at the 98 percent level, and families at the 79 percent[47] level. Such figures suggest that the fossil record is fairly complete and not extremely imperfect, as Darwin proposed. This implies that the gaps seen between fossil types are real.

THE PREVAILING IMAGE

When the popular media discuss the topic of evolution, scientific hypotheses too often acquire an authority and reality that they do not actually have. The cautions expressed by the professional paleontologist seem to be missing. An example is the problems the fossils raise concerning the origin of fishes, since the expected intermediates are missing. Yet, in what is an all-too-typical "just-so story" presented to the public, the well-known BBC television guide for the *Zoo Quest* series, Dave Attenborough, states:

"During this immensity of time, the corals arrived and began to build reefs, and the segmented animals developed into forms that soon would leave the sea and establish a bridgehead on land. Important changes also took place among the proto-fish. The slits in the sides of their throats, which had originated as filtering mechanisms, were walled with thin blood vessels so that they also served as gills. Now the pillars of flesh between them were stiffened with bony rods and the first pair of these bones, slowly over the millennia, gradually hinged forward. Muscles developed around them so that the front ends of the rods could be moved up and down. The creatures had acquired jaws. The bony scales in the skin which covered them grew larger and sharper and became teeth. No longer were the backboned creatures of the sea lowly sifters of mud and strainers of water. Now they could bite. Flaps of skin grew out of either side of the lower part of the body, helping to guide them through the water. These eventually became fins. Now they could swim. And so, for the first time, vertebrate hunters began to propel themselves with skill and accuracy through the waters of the sea."[48]

However, we have virtually no evidence in the fossil record or elsewhere for any of the changes proposed during this "immensity of time"; but the public hears nothing about this problem. Some defenders of evolution are even more assertive. Ronald Ecker writes: "It is certainly correct to say that the fossil record is imperfect and contains a great many gaps. However, this in no way discredits evolutionary theory."[49] Such examples well illustrate how paradigms survive in spite of the evidence.

CONCLUSIONS

Instead of being a final court of appeal for the evolution of life, the fossils might be more a final court of appeal for creation. Scientists often suggest that we should put new ideas to what they call the falsification test. In other words, search for any data that will show that the concept is false. One way to falsify the evolutionary hypothesis would be to see if the fossils do not show a continuous sequence through the geologic column, especially between major groups. If evolution had taken place, we should expect a mostly continuous series of fossil organisms from simple to all the major types of present life forms. We should find all major groups connected with each other in lower fossil layers, instead of appearing abruptly. As is well known, the record is abysmally lacking in intermediates. The problem extends beyond the phyla and division level to the sudden appearance of hundreds of smaller isolated groups throughout the column. To this must be added the question of highly erratic rates of evolution that leave little time for evolutionary changes. Very complex, improbable major developments such as the Cambrian explosion are restricted to a few dozens of million years. The data suggests that the general model of evolution has been essentially falsified.

REFERENCES

1. Wittgenstein L. 1980. Culture and value. Winch P, translator; Wright GHv (with Nyman H), editor. Chicago: University of Chicago Press, p. 62e. Translation of: Vermischte Bemerkungen.
2. Lull RS. 1935. Fossils: what they tell us of plants and animals of the past. 2nd ed. New York: University Society, p. 3.
3. See chapter 9 for a description of these groups, and Figure 10.1 for their distribution.
4. Apparently some optimistic paleontologists have suggested that there may be as many as 100 phyla in the Cambrian explosion. See: Lewin R. 1988. A lopsided look at evolution. Science 241:291-293.
5. (a) Bowring SA, Grotzinger JP, Isachsen CE, Knoll AH, Pelechaty SM, Kolosov P. 1993. Calibrating rates of Early Cambrian evolution. Science 261:1293-1298. The quotation is from (b) Nash M. 1995. When life exploded. Time 146(23):66-74.
6. Kerr RA. 1995. Timing evolution's early bursts. Science 267:33, 34.
7. Stanley SM. 1981. The new evolutionary timetable: fossils, genes, and the origin of species. New York: Basic Books, p. 93.
8. Feduccia A. 1995. Explosive evolution in Tertiary birds and mammals. Science 267:637, 638.
9. See chapter 8.
10. (a) Gould SJ. 1989. Wonderful life: the Burgess Shale and the nature of history. New York and London: W. W. Norton and Co., pp. 39-50. As expected, the concept has not entirely escaped criticism. See: (b) Briggs DEG, Fortey RA, Wills MA. 1992. Morphological disparity in the Cambrian. Science 256:1670-1673; and later discussion by: (c) Foote M, Gould SJ, and Lee MSY. 1992. Cambrian and recent morphological disparity. Science 256:1816, 1817, with a

response by Briggs, Fortey, and Wills in Science 256:1817, 1818.

11. Stewart WN, Rothwell GW. 1993. Paleobotany and the evolution of plants. 2nd ed. Cambridge and New York: Cambridge University Press, pp. 510, 511.
12. It has been suggested that species diversity among invertebrates is highly correlated with the volume and area of sedimentary rocks. See: (a) Raup DM. 1976. Species diversity in the Phanerozoic: an interpretation. Paleobiology 2:289-297; (b) Raup DM. 1972. Taxonomic diversity during the Phanerozoic. Science 177:1065-1071. Because the volume and exposure of sediments is greater in the higher parts of the geologic column, this could bias conclusions toward greater numbers of reported species higher in the column. The basic types are fewer.
13. See chapters 4-8 for examples.
14. Bernini F. 1991. Fossil Acarida. In: Simonetta AM, Conway Morris S, editors. The early evolution of Metazoa and the significance of problematic taxa. Cambridge and New York: Cambridge University Press, pp. 253-262.
15. (a) Pennisi E. 1994. Static evolution: is pond scum the same now as billions of years ago? Science News 145:168, 169; (b) Schopf JW. 1968. Microflora of the Bitter Springs Formation, Late Precambrian, central Australia. Journal of Paleontology 42:651-688.
16. Stewart and Rothwell, p. 44 (note 11).
17. Knoll AH. 1990. Precambrian evolution of prokaryotes and protists. In: Briggs DEG, Crowther PR, editors. Paleobiology: a synthesis. Oxford and London: Blackwell Scientific Publications, pp. 9-16.
18. See chapter 10.
19. (a) Carroll RL. 1988. Vertebrate paleontology and evolution. New York: W. H. Freeman and Co., p. 207. For an attempt at explaining the turtle evolution on embryological grounds but not paleontological data, see: (b) Petto AJ. 1983. The turtle: evolutionary dilemma or creationist shell game? Creation/Evolution 3(4):20-29. For an attempt at explaining the anatomy based on bones, see: (c) Lee MSY. 1993. The origin of the turtle body plan: bridging a famous morphological gap. Science 261:1716-1720.
20. Darwin C. 1859. The origin of species by means of natural selection, or the preservation of favoured races in the struggle for life. London: John Murray. In: Burrow JW, editor. 1968 reprint. London and New York: Penguin Books, pp. 291, 292.
21. *Ibid.,* p. 309.
22. Raup DM. 1979. Conflicts between Darwin and paleontology. Field Museum of Natural History Bulletin 50:22-29.
23. Kitts DB. 1974. Paleontology and evolutionary theory. Evolution 28:458-472.
24. Gould SJ. 1980. The panda's thumb: more reflections in natural history. New York and London: W. W. Norton and Co., p. 181.
25. See chapter 8.
26. Cowen suggests that all the phyla of well-skeletonized shallow marine animals have been discovered. Cowen R. 1995. History of life. 2nd ed. Boston, Oxford, and London: Blackwell Scientific Publications, p. 97.
27. Simpson GG. 1967. The meaning of evolution: a study of the history of life and of its significance for man. Rev. ed. New Haven and London: Yale University Press, pp. 232, 233.
28. Evolutionists, creationists, and others have written much about these gaps. A few examples that recognize a problem include: (a) Denton M. 1985. Evolution: a theory in crisis. London: Burnett Books; (b) Grassé P-P. 1977. Evolution of living organisms: evidence for a new theory of transformation. Carlson BM, Castro R, translators. New York, San Francisco, and London: Academic Press. Translation of: L'Évolution du Vivant; (c) Hitching F. 1982. The neck of the giraffe: where Darwin went wrong. New Haven and New York: Ticknor and Fields; (d) Hoffman A. 1989. Arguments on evolution: a paleontologist's perspective. New York and Oxford: Oxford University Press; (e) Johnson PE. 1993. Darwin on trial. 2nd ed. Downers Grove, Ill.: InterVarsity Press; (f) Løvtrup S. 1987. Darwinism: the refutation of a myth. London, New York, and Sydney: Croom Helm; (g) Pitman M. 1984. Adam and evolution. London, Melbourne, and Sydney: Rider and Co.

29. Schram FR. 1991. Cladistic analysis of metazoan phyla and the placement of fossil problematica. In: Simonetta and Conway Morris, pp. 35-46 (note 14).
30. Bold HC, Alexopoulos CJ, Delevoryas T. 1987. Morphology of plants and fungi. 5th ed. New York and Cambridge: Harper and Row, p. 823.
31. (a) Axelrod DI. 1960. The evolution of flowering plants. In: Tax S, editor. The evolution of life: its origin, history and future. Evolution after Darwin: The University of Chicago centennial, vol. 1. Chicago: University of Chicago Press, pp. 227-305; (b) Bold HC. 1973. Morphology of plants. 3rd ed. New York and London: Harper and Row, p. 601 (the 4th and 5th editions of this text were coauthored by two other authors, and the word "abominable" was no longer used; however, the idea still prevails in the book); (c) Knoll AH, Rothwell GW. 1981. Paleobotany: perspectives in 1980. Paleobiology 7(1):7-35.
32. Wootton RJ. 1990. Flight: arthropods. In: Briggs and Crowther, pp. 72-75 (note 17).
33. For a more extensive discussion, see: Gibson LJ. Are the links still missing? Unpublished paper distributed by the Geoscience Research Institute, Loma Linda University, Loma Linda, California.
34. There has been a dispute over the authenticity of the *Archaeopteryx* fossils, but they appear authentic. See: (a) Charig AJ, Greenaway F, Milner AC, Walker CA, Whybrow PJ. 1986. *Archaeopteryx* is not a forgery. Science 232:622-626; (b) Clausen VE. 1986. Recent debate over *Archaeopteryx*. Origins 13:48-55.
35. (a) Wheeler TJ. 1993. Were there birds before *Archaeopteryx?* Creation/Evolution 13(2):25-35; (b) Zimmer C. 1992. Ruffled feathers. Discover (May), pp. 44-54.
36. See chapter 9 for the disputed origin.
37. Simpson GG. 1953. The major features of evolution. New York and London: Columbia University Press, p. 263.
38. Raup 1979 (note 22).
39. Milner R. 1990. Horse, evolution of. The encyclopedia of evolution. New York: Facts on File, p. 222.
40. MacFadden BJ. 1992. Fossil horses: systematics, paleobiology, and evolution of the family equidae. Cambridge and New York: Cambridge University Press, p. 330.
41. Kemp TS. 1982. Mammal-like reptiles and the origin of mammals. London and New York: Academic Press, p. 296.
42. Carroll, p. 398 (note 19a).
43. Patterson C. 1978. Evolution. London: British Museum (Natural History), and New York: Cornell University Press, p. 133. Patterson lists this explanation but does not especially defend it.
44. *Ibid.*
45. Kerr RA. 1991. Old bones aren't so bad after all. Science 252:32, 33.
46. Paul CRC. 1990. Completeness of the fossil record. In: Briggs and Crowther, pp. 298-303 (note 17).
47. (a) Denton, p. 190 (note 28a). Denton's data are based on: (b) Romer AS. 1966. Vertebrate Paleontology. 3rd ed. Chicago and London: University of Chicago Press, pp. 347-396.
48. Attenborough D. 1979. Life on earth: a natural history. London: William Collins Sons and the British Broadcasting Corporation, p. 112.
49. Ecker RL. 1990. The dictionary of science and creationism. Buffalo: Prometheus Books, p. 94.

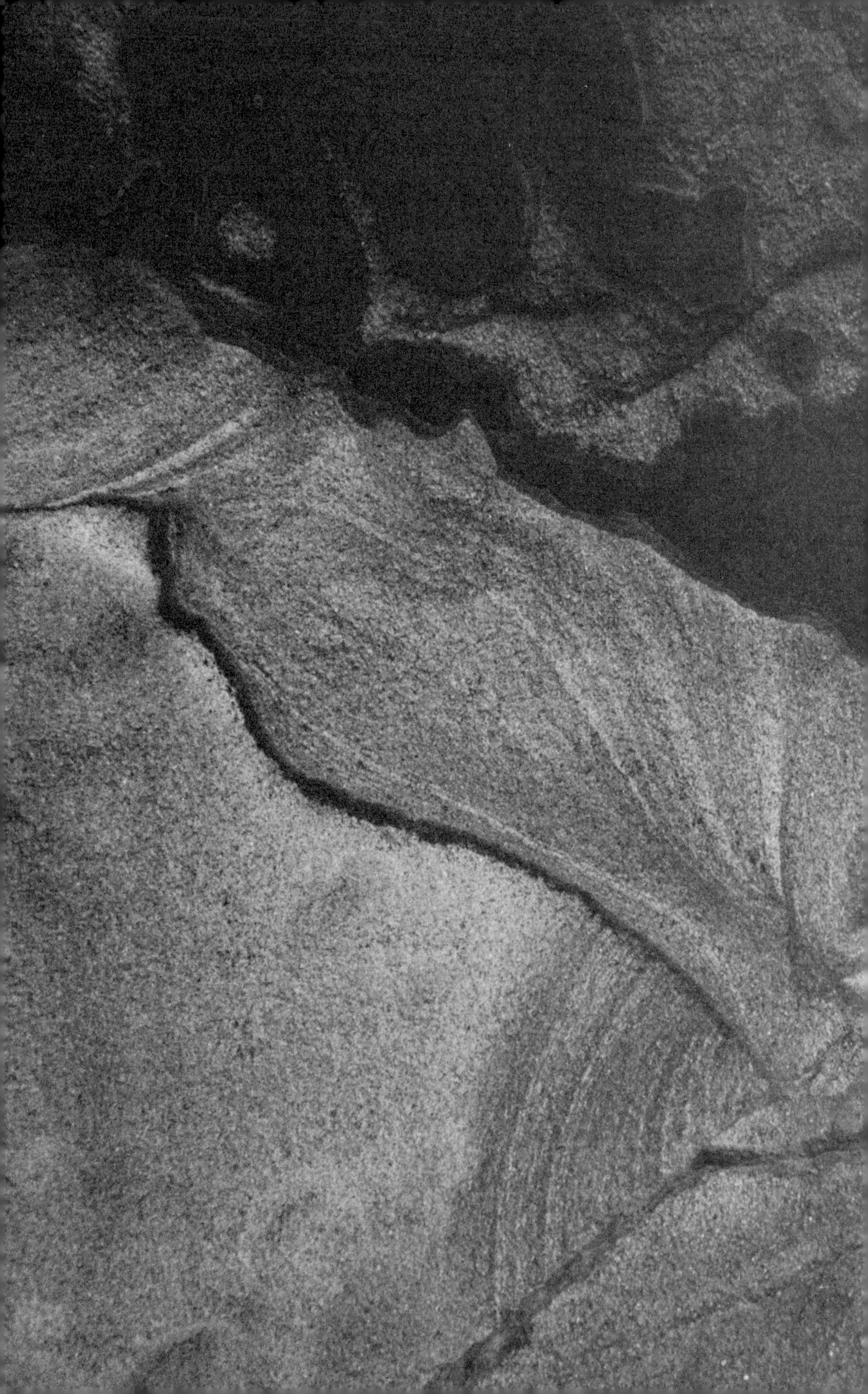

CHAPTER 12

CATASTROPHES: THE BIG ONES

There are times when truth
hardly seems probable.
—Nicolas Boileau[1]

Major world catastrophes are extremely unusual, and we have difficulty incorporating them into our thinking. In this chapter, we will follow the history of the acceptance, rejection, and then reacceptance of concepts of major catastrophes. We will also consider some examples, including the deluge (Genesis flood) of Scripture.

A CASE HISTORY

In 1923 the independent-minded geologist Harlen Bretz described one of the most unusual landscapes to be found on the surface of our planet. Covering some 40,000 square kilometers in the southeastern region of the state of Washington, it contains a vast network of huge dry channels, sometimes many kilometers wide, forming a maze of buttes and canyons cut into stark, hard volcanic rock. Unlike ordinary river valleys that generally have a broad **V** shape in cross-section, these channels often display steep sides and flat floors. In addition, huge mounds of stream gravel occur at various elevations. Evidence of hundreds of ancient waterfalls, some as high as 100 meters with large eroded plunge pools at their base, witnesses to something very unusual. How did such an odd landscape ever form? Bretz had an idea, but it was outrageous enough to spark a geological controversy that lasted for 40 years.

In his first publication on the topic, Bretz did not express his suspicion of a major catastrophic flood, but only indicated that it would require prodigious amounts of water.[2] However, in that same year he published a second paper fully expressing his view that a truly vast but short-lived catastrophic flood had produced the landscape. This flood had scoured the area, eroded the channels, and deposited the immense gravel bars.[3]

At that time the geological climate of thought strongly opposed any explanation associated with catastrophes, and Bretz knew this. *Uniformitarianism*—the idea that geological changes proceed slowly over long periods of time—was the accepted view. Geologists recognized the activity of volcanoes and earthquakes, but considered them unimportant. Other geologic changes were to be interpreted as proceeding extremely slowly. *Catastrophism*—the idea of sudden major catastrophic changes—was anathema. It was in the same category as creation finds itself in many scientific circles now—totally unacceptable. The geologic community had to deal with the young upstart Bretz, who was completely out of line. Bretz's heretical ideas were also uncomfortably close to the rejected idea of the biblical flood.[4] To adopt his ideas would mean a return to catastrophism, which implied retreating into "the Dark Ages."[5]

As Bretz, who was professor of geology at the University of Chicago, continued his study and publication, some geologists decided to apply some persuasion on their wayward colleague. The Geological Society of Washington, D.C., invited him in 1927 to present his views. The meeting had a special agenda—"a veritable phalanx of doubters had been assembled to debate the flood hypothesis."[6] After Bretz's presentation, five members of the prestigious United States Geological Survey presented objections and offered alternative explanations such as glaciation and other slow changes.[7] Two of the geologists had not even visited the area! In answering them, a weary Bretz commented that "perhaps, however, my attitude of dogmatic finality is proving contagious."[8] One major problem for Bretz's idea remained unanswered: Where did all the water come from so suddenly? Apparently the meeting changed no minds. To most the idea of a catastrophic flood was preposterous.

During the following years the geological community concentrated on developing alternatives to Bretz's model. In Bretz's words, the "heresy must be gently but firmly stamped out."[9] Nevertheless the field evidence from the rocks continued to generate ideas favorable to a catastrophic interpretation, and moderation of the conflict began. Bretz and others found a source for the floodwaters. Ancient Lake Missoula to the east once harbored 2,100 cubic kilometers of water. Some evidence indicated that ice had dammed the lake. A sudden break in the ice would release the volume of water needed to explain the rapid erosion seen to the west. The best support for such an explanation came later when geologists found giant ripples both in Lake Missoula and the channel region to the west. You are probably familiar with the parallel ripple lines frequently seen on sandy streambeds. They are usually just a few centimeters from crest to crest. The ripples on the floor of Lake Missoula and to the west were gigantic, with heights of 15 meters and spanning 150 meters from crest to crest.[10] Only vast quantities of rapidly moving water could produce such an effect. More recent studies have concentrated on details. Some suggest that as many as eight or more flood episodes might have happened.[11] A volume of water estimated at 7.2 cubic kilometers flowed at 108 kilometers per hour, and geologists have proposed mechanisms for eroding the deep channels in the hard volcanic rock in a few hours or days.[12]

Eventually most of the geological community accepted Bretz's masterful interpretations based on careful study of the rocks themselves. In 1965 the International Association for Quaternary Research organized a field trip to visit the region. At the conclusion of the conference, Bretz, who was unable to attend, received a telegram from the participants, sending him their greetings and closing with the sentence: "We are now all catastrophists."[13] In 1979 Bretz received the Penrose Medal, the United States' most prestigious geological award. Bretz had won—and so had catastrophism. This modern-day "Noah" and his likewise unwanted flood had been vindicated.

CATASTROPHISM AND UNIFORMITARIANISM

The idea of rapid, unusual major geological events—*catastrophism*—and the contrasting concept of slow changes—*uniformitarianism*—have played a major role in the interpretation of the past history of our world. The long ages required for slow uniformitarian changes would demand that we discard the biblical account of a recent beginning when explaining the huge geological layers found on earth. On the other hand, the biblical flood represents a prime example of catastrophism, in which major events occur rapidly. Sometimes uniformitarianism is expressed as "the present is the key to the past," meaning in part that the present slow rates of change represent how changes have always occurred. As expected, the definitions of both catastrophism and uniformitarianism have come under close scrutiny, with a resultant plethora of redefinitions and conflicting usages.[14] We will abide by the more general usage of the terms as given above.

Throughout most of human history catastrophism has been a well-accepted view.[15] It was a common motif in ancient mythology and in Greek and Roman antiquity. Interest waned during medieval times, although the Arabs closely followed Aristotle, who believed in catastrophes. The Renaissance brought a renewed interest, especially in the deluge (the Genesis flood). Scholars often explained the abundant marine fossils found on mountains as a result of that catastrophic event. Most of the seventeenth and eighteenth centuries witnessed attempts at harmonizing science with the biblical creation and flood accounts. However, some questioned the idea, such as René Descartes (1596-1650) who suggested the earth had formed by a cooling process. Others modified orthodox ideas, such as suggesting that the deluge might have resulted from natural causes and that it might not have formed all of the sedimentary rock layers. Georges Cuvier (1769-1832) in France proposed multiple catastrophes, and a few scholars advocated uniformitarianism, including M. V. Lomonosov (1711-1765) in Russia, and James Hutton (1726-1797) and his supporter John Playfair (1748-1819) in Scotland and England. The latter two did much to promote the idea. At the same time, also in England, strong support continued for the biblical flood, notably from such leading authorities as William Buckland, Adam Sedgwick, William Conybeare, and Roderick Murchison. In this milieu a book appeared that would have more influence on geological thought than any other.

Principles of Geology appeared in 1830. Written by Charles Lyell, it strongly emphasized uniformitarianism. Highly successful, going through 11 editions, it changed the prevailing climate of geological thought from catastrophism to the strict slow changes of uniformitarianism; specifically, "the permanent effects of causes now in action," as Lyell introduced it.[16] Not only did the book influence geology, but it had a significant effect on science as a whole. It is reported to have been one of Charles Darwin's "most treasured possessions"[17] while on his discovery voyage aboard the H.M.S. *Beagle.* By the middle of the century uniformitarianism was the dominant concept and catastrophism a dwindling view.

We can attribute part of the success of Lyell's book to his astute efforts to promote his views. Letters to his friend and supporter Poulett Scrope well illustrate this: "If we don't irritate, which I fear that we may . . . , we shall carry all with us. If you don't triumph over them, but compliment the liberality and candour of the present age, the bishops and enlightened saints will join us in despising both the ancient and modern physico-theologians [catastrophists]. It is just the time to strike, so rejoice that, sinner as you are, the Q. R. *[Quarterly Review]* is open to you. . . .

"If Murray [the publisher] has to push my vols., and you wield the geology of the Q. R., we shall be able in a short time to work an entire change in public opinion."[18]

As he had hoped, Lyell accomplished his entire change, if not in public opinion, certainly in the geological community. For more than a century geology refused to tolerate major catastrophic interpretations. Looking back at the establishment of this paradigm, Stephen J. Gould of Harvard comments: "Charles Lyell was trained as a lawyer, and his book is more a brief for gradualism than an impartial account of evidence. . . . Lyell denigrated catastrophism as an antiquated, last-ditch effort by miracle-mongers trying to preserve the Mosaic chronology of an Earth only a few thousand years old.

"I doubt that a more unfair characterization has ever been offered for a reputable scientific worldview."[19]

By the middle of the twentieth century some geologists had noticed that strict uniformitarianism conflicted with the data from the rocks themselves. Bretz, mentioned above, found evidence of very rapid geological action. Other scientists discovered sedimentary layers with both shallow- and deep-water components.[20] How could they ever get mixed together under quiet conditions? The resolution: catastrophic underwater mudflows, starting from shallow water and flowing down to deep water. Such fast flows, called *turbidity currents*, produce special deposits called *turbidites*. Turbidites have turned out to be surprisingly common over the world.[21] A few other daring souls suggested other catastrophic activities, such as mass extinctions caused by influxes of high-energy cosmic radiation[22] and the sudden spread of fresh arctic water over the world oceans.[23] All such theories indicated a growing departure from strict uniformitarianism.

The coup de grâce for the dominance of uniformitarian explanations did not, however, come from the study of the rocks themselves, but from the fossils they contained. Why did the dinosaurs disappear near the end of the Cretaceous, and why were other mass extinctions evident[24] at other levels of the fossil record?[25] Scientists had to find some reasonable cause. They had proposed various ideas for the extinction of dinosaurs, ranging from starvation to poisonous mushrooms or even hay fever. Nevertheless, most generally considered their disappearance a mystery. Then in 1980 Nobel laureate Luis Alvarez, from the University of California at Berkeley, and others[26] suggested that the unusual abundance of the element iridium found at a number of places throughout the world at the top of the Cretaceous layers might have come from an asteroid hitting the earth and killing off the dinosaurs at the same time. The idea engendered a mixed reaction. Some pointed out that the dinosaurs and other organisms did not seem to disappear that suddenly in the fossil layers. Others proposed widespread volcanic activity and global fires, or an impact from a comet instead of an asteroid.[27] The debate about details continues, but the door to catastrophic interpretations has swung wide open. The scientific literature now reports a wide range of sudden major changes.

Some of the newer catastrophic ideas propose that comets or asteroids could send ocean waves up to heights of eight kilometers[28] and plumes of volatiles hundreds of kilometers above earth's surface.[29] Others have suggested 500° C blasts of air at 2,500 kilometers per hour that would kill half of the life on earth, and global earthquakes with ground waves reaching heights of 10 meters. Other possibilities include the opening of cracks spanning 10-100 kilometers and rapid mountain building.[30] There is even a suggestion that such impacts could have initiated the breakup of earth's ancient supercontinent called Gondwanaland.[31]

Catastrophism has made a rapid return, but it is not exactly the classical catastrophism of two centuries ago that incorporated the biblical flood as a major geologic event. Interestingly, some geologists recently suggested that an extraterrestrial impact could be related to the Genesis flood account.[32] Geology currently accepts major rapid catastrophes, but in contrast to the biblical flood that took only one year, an abundance of time is introduced between many catastrophies. The term *neocatastrophism* (new catastrophism) seems to be gaining acceptance as geologists attempt to distinguish the newer concept from the older catastrophism. Likewise, the term *neodiluvialism* (new flood concepts) has been introduced to designate newer ideas of major flood activity during catastrophes.[33] Some have identified the return to catastrophic interpretations as "a great philosophical breakthrough,"[34] and it is acknowledged that "the profound role of major storms throughout geologic history is becoming increasingly recognized."[35] This latter view can fit well with the biblical model of the deluge as an extended series of storms during the year of the flood.

Neocatastrophism has stimulated reinterpretation of many geologic features. For instance, many sedimentary deposits once thought to have accumulated slowly are now regarded as the result of rapid turbidity currents, and a number of slowly forming fossil coral reefs have been reinterpreted as rapid debris flows.[36] Such newer interpretations by themselves fit well with the scriptural concept of the flood.

More important is the lesson we can learn from the history of these interpretations. For millennia thinkers accepted catastrophes, then for more than a century they virtually eradicated the concept from all geologic interpretations. Now they accept the idea again. We should be cautious about accepting paradigms based on opinion or restricted information.

EXAMPLES OF RAPID ACTION

Under normal quiet conditions, changes over earth's surface proceed extremely slowly. However, many examples of catastrophic activity permit us to conceive of major changes in a short time.

Erosion can occur very rapidly. In 1976 the newly built Teton Dam in Idaho sprung a leak that could not be stopped, and the rushing water cut through sediment to a depth of 100 meters in less than one hour.[37] While the dam consisted of soft sediment, geologists have also postulated rapid erosion to an equivalent depth in hard basalt in a few days, as in the case of Bretz's channels mentioned earlier. Research has determined that the carrying capacity of moving water increases as the third to fourth power of the velocity.[38] This means that if the speed of flow rises 10 times, the water can carry 1,000 to 10,000 times as much sediment.

Noncreationists sometimes point out that the geologic column is far too thick to have been deposited in the single year of the deluge.[39] But this may not be a significant argument. While most creationists would exclude the lowest (Precambrian) and highest portions of the geologic column from the flood (see below), some present rates of deposition are so rapid that it would be possible to deposit the whole column in a few weeks. Turbidity currents can deposit their sediment in any one locality in a few minutes or less, and over thousands of square kilometers in a few hours. Single megaturbidites found in Spain have thicknesses up to 200 meters, along with an immense volume of 200 cubic kilometers.[40] Several methods other than turbidity currents also exist for the rapid deposition of sediments. An intense deluge lasting a year could lay down a lot of sediment.

Geologists often assume that the accumulation of thick layers of tiny microscopic organisms such as the White Cliffs of Dover in England required lengthy periods of time. But such accumulation can occur rapidly. Along the coast of Oregon a three-day storm of high winds and rain deposited 10-15 centimeters of microscopic diatoms for a distance of 32 kilometers.[41] I have seen a well-preserved fossil bird and many fish in thick beds of microscopic diatoms near Lompoc, California. A whale was also found in this deposit. Such preservation would require rapid burial before disarticulation of the organism would occur. Evidently microscopic organisms can be deposited rapidly.

Another example of rapid action is the formation in 1963 of the volcanic island of Surtsey, located south of Iceland. In five days an island with a length of 600 meters formed where before there had existed only open ocean. It eventually reached a diameter of nearly two kilometers. Amazingly, when people visited the island, it looked as though it had been there for a long time. In about five months a mature-looking beach and cliff had developed (see Figure 12.1). One of the investigators comments that "what elsewhere may take thousands of years . . . may take a few weeks or even a few days here. On Surtsey only a few months sufficed for a landscape to be created which was so varied and mature that it was almost beyond belief."[42]

We seem to have difficulty thinking "catastrophically." It may be because catastrophes are both rare and unpleasant to contemplate. Such intellectual resistance may explain in part why people become trapped by these unusual events despite warnings of impending disaster. In the year 1902 on the island of Martinique, Mount Pelée exploded, producing a volcanic flow that overran a sugar factory and killed more than 150 people. This and other activity from the volcano caused apprehension among the inhabitants of the nearby town of St. Pierre, and some left for safer regions. In order to alleviate panic, government authorities kept assuring the inhabitants that they faced no immediate danger, and even the governor of the island and his wife moved to St. Pierre to encourage the people to remain in town. A major volcanic eruption on a neighboring island served to reassure the people, as they concluded that the explo-

FIGURE 12.1

The new island of Surtsey, south of Iceland. Note the beach, the cliff, and the men for scale. Five months and two days earlier, this area was open ocean. The small white objects on the beach in the foreground are krill. The rock stacks on the distant horizon are not part of the new island.*

*From Thorarinson, Figure 39 (note 42). Copyright © 1964, 1966 by Almenna Bokafelagid. Used by permission of Viking Penguin, a division of Penguin Books U.S.A., Inc.

sion had relieved the volcanic pressure on Mount Pelée. Many returned to St. Pierre. The next morning Mount Pelée suddenly exploded, sending a 700° C cloud of ash and steam (nuée ardente) that annihilated some 30,000 residents of St. Pierre in two minutes.[43] History records that only two to four individuals survived. One was a convict, protected because he was in an underground cell. After his rescue, the authorities immediately reincarcerated him.

We should keep in mind that other agents, such as earthquakes and wind, also cause rapid changes under catastrophic conditions. We have no shortage of examples showing that major geologic changes can occur quickly, yet because they are rare, we have some difficulty incorporating them into our thinking.

THE GENESIS FLOOD

A flood covering the entire surface of earth is highly unusual. However, the recent geological interpretations toward catastrophism involving rapid destruction of life suggest that the concept might not be that exceptional. Furthermore, the idea of a worldwide flood is not unique to the Bible. The fact that it is such a dominant feature of ancient legends[44] gives us ample reason to suspect it occurred, even if we completely disregard the biblical account. Nevertheless, among ancient documents the Bible gives the most comprehensive account of this event.[45] Unfortunately, geologic details in the Bible are sparse, but a review of related information is instructive.

The Bible describes an earth before the flood somewhat different from the present. There is a suggestion that there was no rain,[46] but there was an abundance of moisture, including rivers.[47] This suggests a different hydrologic system from the present.

The following chronology is implied for the flood:[48] Seven days after Noah entered the ark, subterranean waters erupted, accompanied by heavy rain that lasted at least 40 days. The floodwaters did not just rise suddenly—the biblical text suggests an extended process.[49] The period of 40 days appears to form part of the subsequently described period of 150 days, during which the waters either remained or more likely increased so that they covered the highest mountains. Since the biblical text seems to state that the "windows of heaven" and the "fountains of the deep" did not close until the end of the 150 days, it is more likely that the waters increased for 150 days,[50] as some Bible translators indicate.[51] A strong wind followed, then subsidence of the waters and drying for many months. When Noah left the ark 1 year and 17 days from the time he entered it, at least the higher areas in the immediate vicinity were dry,[52] and probably some new vegetation had already germinated. A number of significant geologic adjustments of the earth's crust no doubt followed, decreasing in intensity for succeeding centuries and even millennia.

Sometimes questions are asked about Noah's ark—especially how all the animals could fit into it. Creationists postulate fewer species at the time of the flood. Because of limited variation since the flood, most likely at the species level, more varieties now exist than the ark preserved. Furthermore, Noah took only terrestrial types of animals into the ark. One would expect marine organisms to survive the flood on their own. Some calculations indicate that within these restrictions there appears to have been ample room in the ark, possibly even two to three times the minimum requirements.[53]

Some wonder why certain unique animals such as the marsupials of Australia appear both in the fossil record and are presently living in the same region of the world. If they were in the ark that probably settled in the Middle East, how did they return to Australia? With the premise that the gathering of the animals into the ark would have involved special guidance, some creationists believe that it is not inconsistent to assume the same for the return to their home territory,[54] though the Bible makes no mention of it. It is sometimes suggested that homing instincts such as now seen in migrating mammals, birds, turtles, and fishes may have facilitated their return to their home region. The problem of return does not apply to most other continents of the world, where the congruence between fossils and living types is not so unique.

THE FLOOD AND CREATION WEEK

Few appreciate the importance of the flood to the creation account.[55] Unless most of the fossil record formed during the flood, an all-inclusive, six-day creation[56] seems out of the question. This is because the fossil layers contain different kinds of fossils at different levels in the geologic column. If the geologic column indicates millions of years between two basic kinds of fossils, then God did not create both in a single, six-day creation period. For example, if we assume a sponge was created 550 million years ago and a dinosaur 180 million years ago, then obviously God did not create both in a six-day creation event, as He states.[57] But there is no incongruity if these organisms originated during creation week and then were buried at different levels in the geologic column during the yearlong worldwide flood. The Genesis flood reconciles the geologic column to creation week. Without a flood, we also have difficulty fitting the thick layers of sediment with a recent creation. Sediments now accumulate on an average at rates of a few centimeters per thousand years. Sedimentary layers average many hundreds of meters in thickness, while a number of localities on earth have several kilometers of fossil-bearing Phanerozoic sediments. Without a worldwide flood to deposit such layers rapidly, the recent creation described in Scripture faces a serious challenge.

WAS THE GENESIS FLOOD A LOCAL EVENT?

The Genesis flood is frequently considered to have been a local event in Mesopotamia. For several reasons[58] it does not appear that we can reconcile this idea with the biblical record and the worldwide distribution of sediments and fossils:

1. The Genesis account repeatedly emphasizes a worldwide flood[59] with statements such as: "all the high mountains under the whole heaven were covered;" "all flesh died that moved upon the earth;" "everything on the dry land in whose nostrils was the breath of life died;" "He blotted out every living thing that was upon the face of the ground."[60]

2. After the flood God promised not to destroy the world again by this method.[61] Since local floods are fairly common, every subsequent local flood suggests that God does not keep His promises. Instead, the promise means that God would not destroy the entire surface of the earth again with water, and He has kept that promise.

3. Why would God ask Noah to build a big ark[62] to preserve the variety of animals on earth if the flood were only local? We would expect the animals to have had wide distributions, and a local event would not eliminate them.

4. The Genesis creation account appears to conflict with a local flood concept, because without a worldwide flood there does not seem to be a way to account for the thick layers of the geologic column found on all the continents. As mentioned previously, the flood is necessary to reconcile the geologic column to a recent six-day creation. Since the geologic column is quite well represented on all continents, this reconciliation is necessary for all continents. Denial of the worldwide flood implies rejection of a worldwide six-day creation. This is not the biblical model. The Bible seems to be speaking of both a worldwide creation and a worldwide flood.

MODELS OF THE FLOOD

Creationists have proposed a number of models for the flood.[63] However, much more work is needed, and caution would dictate that we consider each model as tentative. In general, the models fall into three broad categories: (1) exchange of continents with the oceans at the time of the flood; (2) contraction and expansion of the earth; and (3) subsidence of the continents during the flood with

FIGURE 12.2

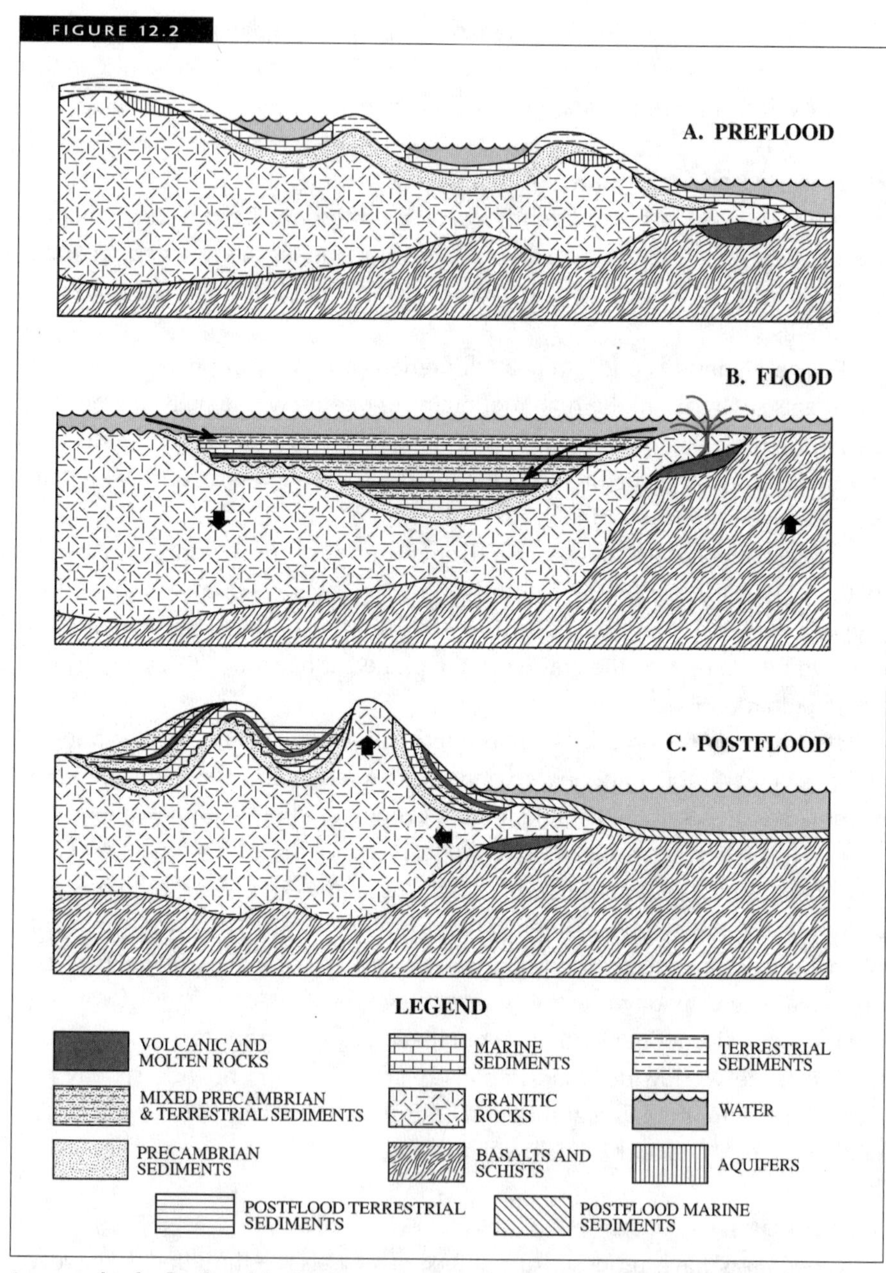

An example of a flood model. The diagram represents a cross section of part of a continent (left) and ocean (right). A: Preflood earth with major oceans at various levels; large granitic masses undergird the continent. B: Flood stage caused by sinking of the continents and uplift of the oceans (short arrows). Long arrows indicate movement of various sediments from their source area. C: Postflood stage following uplift and lateral compression of the continents with deformation, erosion, and redeposition of rock types.

subsequent uplift. Various combinations of these and other models are possible.

The configuration of the rock types of the crust of the earth is important to any consideration of a flood model. Sedimentary layers that usually have either a terrestrial (continental) or a marine origin, but sometimes both, cover today's continents. One can tell the origin by the terrestrial or marine organisms represented by the fossils. The sediments in our present oceans are quite thin compared to those on the continents (Figure 12.2C). A heavy-density basalt (volcanic type) of rock underlies current oceans, while the continents have a lighter density granitic-rock base. This arrangement keeps our continents literally floating above denser rock and thus maintains them above sea level so we have dry land to live on.

The exchange of continents with the ocean model proposes that the present continents were the preflood seas and vice versa.[64] During the flood major transfers of sediments from the preflood continents to the preflood seas occurred. This was accompanied by complex geochemical processes involving adjustments in rock types as well as consequent changes of earth's topography in response to load (isostatic adjustments). The shift produced our present continents. This model requires a large amount of flood sediments. A modification of this model suggests a collapse of extensive preflood continental aquifers, the resulting depressions or cavities thus creating our present ocean basins.

The idea of an expanding earth has been a persistent but minority view in contemporary scientific interpretations.[65] Credible evidence does support the concept. Some creationists have appropriated the concept to suggest a simple but elegant model. To bring on the flood, earth contracts, forcing the water over the continents. To end the flood, the earth expands as the continents separate and the waters return to the oceans. One problem is that there is no easy way of expanding and contracting the earth. Sometimes geologists suggest a change in the strength of gravity.[66]

Subsidence and uplift of the continents is the least dramatic of the models (Figure 12.2). In this example the flood would be caused by the flow of some of the soft, deeper layers of the earth (asthenosphere) moving from under the continents to under the oceans. This process would raise the ocean floors and lower the continents (short arrows in Figure 12.2B), resulting in inundation of the continents with the transport of some marine sediments onto the continents. Most geologists accept the movement of a partially molten asthenosphere as a means of shifting around the continents by the motion of their underlying plates.[67] During the Genesis flood the gradually rising waters would erode the preflood sediments, including some Precambrian sediments that would be redeposited along with living organisms that would become fossilized. The land-derived sediments would alternate with sediments from the preflood seas, as the flood currents transported sediment from different source areas into new depositional basins (note long arrows in Figure 12.2B). At the end of the flood the continents, made of a lighter density granitic rock, would rise, causing the waters to recede back to the ocean resulting in erosion of some of the flood deposits on the continents. One problem this model faces is the abundance of marine sediments on the continents with no land type of fossils below them. Possibly this type of arrangement could have originated from large preflood seas already on the continents (epicontinental seas) with additional marine sediments coming from larger oceans beyond the continents (longest arrow in Figure 12.2B). This pattern would complicate a simple ecological zonation theory interpretation (Figure 10.2) of the fossil record. However, few consider the flood to have been a simple event.

These flood models represent only introductory suggestions. Comprehensive investigation of such a complex event is needed. In this area study has just begun.

GEOLOGIC FACTORS RELATED TO THE FLOOD

The water for the flood was most likely already present on preflood earth. Most of it would have been in the preflood seas, some in "the fountains of the deep,"[68] and a small amount in the atmosphere. Geologists and others often criticize the Genesis flood concept because earth does not seem to have enough water to cover the top of Mount Everest,[69] while the Bible states that the flood covered the whole earth. Mount Everest is nearly nine kilometers above sea level. The criticism may not be that significant, though, since creationists often postulate a flatter preflood topography, requiring much less water to cover it (e.g., Figure 12.2B). If earth's surface were perfectly smooth, an ocean more than 2.44 kilometers deep would completely cover it.[70] Creationists postulate a significant uplift of mountains after the flood. Both flood and nonflood geologists agree that Mount Everest and many other mountains represent uplift after the deposition of their sedimentary layers. We should not use present topography to estimate the volume of water required for a worldwide flood.

People have often asked me why an event of such magnitude as a worldwide flood would not mix up everything. This is the "small bathtub model" in which everything can be easily stirred up. Actually, the sedimentary layers worldwide tend to be quite orderly and unique when viewed on a sufficiently large scale. For several reasons we should not expect the flood to have mixed everything up. Such mixing would be extremely difficult with sedimentary layers spread over thousands of square kilometers forming deposits sometimes having a thickness of several kilometers. It may be easy to stir up a few meters of mud, but it is not so easy to do the same thing with kilometers of mud. Once a layer gets deposited, it would tend to retain its integrity. The flood events extend over an entire year and would not produce instantaneous mixed-up deposition. Even our short floods produce well-ordered deposits. The deluge would gradually spread layers in a generally orderly sequence, a condition that would not favor mixing. Water is a good sediment-sorting agent and it usually deposits sediments in a near-horizontal pattern. Geologists call this pattern the "Law of Original Horizontality." In the laboratory scientists can rapidly deposit under water one soft turbidite layer above another soft layer without any significant disturbance to the lower layer. Some mixing events would be expected on a local level, and occasional local uplift would favor erosion of flood and preflood deposits, thus recycling the fossils and rocks they contained into stratigraphically higher layers of the geologic column as is occasionally found. However, to mix up most of the sedimentary layers of earth's crust would require extremely powerful convulsive events, a scenario we would not expect in a yearlong event.

Questions also arise as to how much of the geologic column should be attributed to the flood. This is a difficult question to answer because of the complexity of both the sedimentary and the fossil records. The variety of opinions among creationists on this topic implies that there isn't an accepted answer. Because water deposits most sedimentary strata, we would not expect a striking difference between flood layers and those laid down before or after the flood. Furthermore, the flood would not have started or ended at exactly the same place in the geologic column at every locality. As a first approximation, I would suggest that the flood deposits began in the region of the Cambrian and ended as a maximum in the upper region of the Tertiary (see Figure 10.1 for terminology). In some localities the flood may have ceased below this maximum. This may seem like an enormous amount of sediment—and it is! However, considering the size of the earth, it is a very thin veneer. Proportionately, on an ordinary 30-centimeter world globe the average thickness of these sediments would be less than a quarter of the thickness of an ordinary sheet of paper.

When traditional geologists began to accept the idea of continental drift and plate tectonics during the late 1960s and early 1970s, many creationists welcomed it, because such major changes on earth's surface suggested some possibilities for the same kinds of events during the deluge. Geology no longer interpreted the earth as solid and firm. Creationists generally propose rapid plate movement, especially during the later stages of the flood, producing mountain uplift and earth's present continents. Scientists in general do not fully understand the causes of plate motion, and creationist interpretations must also be tentative. We also need to remember that the standard scientific literature echoes a small but persistent note of doubt about the validity of the whole plate-tectonics concept.[71] We need more information before we can adequately address plate-tectonics theory in a flood model.

It is sometimes suggested that the many thousands of years required for numerous ice ages would challenge any recent creation-flood model. In addition to the obvious recent ice ages, other episodes of glaciation have been reported in the lower layers of the geologic column. Flood models usually include the fairly convincing data for recent ice activity as an aftermath of the flood. Plausible conditions that could produce and melt large quantities of ice within centuries instead of millennia have been proposed.[72] The general scenario is that volcanic activity during the flood blocked sunlight, causing a cooling trend. Moisture from warm oceans and the cool air would favor a short, intense period of post-flood ice activity.

The evidence for glaciation in the lower levels of the geological column is more debatable. As Robert P. Sharp of the California Institute of Technology points out: "Identifying ancient glaciations is not easy."[73] Some of the purported evidence can be easily confused with nonglacial activity. Another specialist points out that "numerous studies" have shown that so-called glacial deposits have turned out to be massive debris flows and related deposits.[74] Some striations (scratches) supposedly caused by glacial movement have been reinterpreted as sliding of rocks along a fault, or merely cable grooves left by tree-logging operations.[75] Many other examples of reported ancient glaciation have undergone reinterpretation.[76] Good reasons exist to maintain some skepticism about glaciation in the earlier parts of the geologic column.

CONCLUSIONS

Scientific interpretations of the past history of the world have changed a number of times. For centuries most thinkers accepted major catastrophes, then for more than a century there was almost complete rejection of catastrophes. Now science again recognizes their importance in geological history. Some recent reinterpretations of rapid action fit nicely with the biblical concept of a worldwide flood. Creationists now have to do less reinterpretation of accepted geologic views than in the past, because many newer catastrophic interpretations fit a flood model; but they still have plenty of work to do in developing their models. While a worldwide flood is foreign to our normal pattern of thought, strong evidence suggests that geologic changes can occur much more quickly than we suppose.

REFERENCES

1. Boileau N. 1674. L'Art poétique, I. Quoted in: Mencken HL, editor. 1942. A new dictionary of quotations on historical principles from ancient and modern sources. New York: Alfred A. Knopf, p. 1222.
2. Bretz JH. 1923a. Glacial drainage on the Columbia Plateau. Geological Society of America Bulletin 34:573-608.
3. Bretz JH. 1923b. The Channeled Scablands of the Columbia Plateau. Journal of Geology 31:617-649.
4. Allen JE, Burns M, Sargent SC. 1986. Cataclysms on the Columbia. Scenic trips to the Northwest's geologic past, No. 2. Portland, Oreg.: Timber Press, p. 44.
5. Bretz JH. 1978. The Channeled Scabland: introduction. In: Baker VR, editor. 1981. Catastrophic flooding: the origin of the Channeled Scabland. Benchmark papers in geology 55. Stroudsburg, Pa.: Dowden, Hutchinson, and Ross, pp. 18, 19.
6. Baker, p. 60 (note 5).
7. For a report of the presentations and discussions, see: Bretz JH. 1927. Channeled Scabland and the Spokane flood. In: Baker, pp. 65-76 (note 5).
8. Baker, p. 74 (note 5).
9. Bretz JH, Smith HTU, Neff GE. 1956. Channeled Scabland of Washington: new data and interpretations. Geological Society of America Bulletin 67:957-1049.
10. (a) *Ibid.;* (b) Pardee JT. 1942. Unusual currents in Glacial Lake Missoula, Montana. Geological Society of America Bulletin 53:1569-1600.
11. (a) Bretz JH. 1969. The Lake Missoula floods and the Channeled Scabland. Journal of Geology 77:505-543; (b) Parfit M. 1995. The floods that carved the West. Smithsonian 26(1):48-59.
12. (a) Baker VR. 1978. Paleohydraulics and hydrodynamics of Scabland floods. In: Baker, pp. 255-275 (note 5); (b) further details are reported by: Smith GA. 1993. Missoula flood dynamics and magnitudes inferred from sedimentology of slack-water deposits on the Columbia Plateau, Washington. Geological Society of America Bulletin 105:77-100.
13. Bretz 1969 (note 11a).
14. (a) Albritton CC, Jr. 1967. Uniformity, the ambiguous principle. In: Albritton CC, Jr., editor. Uniformity and simplicity: a symposium on the principle of the uniformity of nature. Geological Society of America Special Paper 89:1, 2; (b) Austin SA. 1979. Uniformitarianism—a doctrine that needs rethinking. The Compass of Sigma Gamma Epsilon 56(2):29-45; (c) Gould SJ. 1965. Is uniformitarianism necessary? American Journal of Science 263:223-228; (d) Hallam A. 1989. Great geological controversies. 2nd ed. Oxford and New York: Oxford University Press, pp. 30-64; (e) Hooykaas R. 1959. Natural law and divine miracle: a historical-critical study of the principle of uniformity in geology, biology and theology. Leiden: E. J. Brill; (f) Hooykaas R. 1970. Catastrophism in geology, its scientific character in relation to actualism and uniformitarianism. Amsterdam and London: North-Holland Pub. Co.; (g) Huggett R. 1990. Catastrophism: systems of earth history. London and NY: Edward Arnold, pp. 41-72; (h) Shea JH. 1982. Twelve fallacies of uniformitarianism. Geology 10:455-460.
15. For general reviews, see: (a) Ager D. 1993. The new catastrophism: the importance of the rare event in geological history. Cambridge and New York: Cambridge University Press; (b) Hallam, pp. 30-64, 184-215 (note 14d); (c) Huggett R. 1989. Cataclysms and earth history: the development of diluvialism. Oxford: Clarendon Press; (d) Huggett 1990, pp. 41-200 (note 14g).
16. Lyell C. 1857. Principles of geology; or, the modern changes of the earth and its inhabitants considered as illustrative of geology. Rev. ed. New York: D. Appleton and Co., p. v.
17. Hallam, p. 55 (note 14d).

18. Lyell KM, editor. 1881. Life, letters and journals of Sir Charles Lyell, Bart., vol. 1. London: John Murray, p. 271 (14 June 1830), 273 (20 June 1830).
19. Gould SJ. 1989. An asteroid to die for. Discover 10(10):60-65.
20. (a) Natland ML, Kuenen PhH. 1951. Sedimentary history of the Ventura Basin, California, and the action of turbidity currents. Society of Economic Paleontologists and Mineralogists Special Publication 2:76-107; (b) Phleger FB. 1951. Displaced foraminifera faunas. Society of Economic Paleontologists and Mineralogists Special Publication 2:66-75.
21. See chapter 13 for further discussion.
22. Schindewolf OH. 1977. Neocatastrophism? Firsoff VA, translator. Catastrophist Geology 2(1):9-21.
23. Gartner S, McGuirk JP. 1979. Terminal Cretaceous extinction scenario for a catastrophe. Science 206:1272-1276.
24. A classic paper on extinctions is: Newell ND. 1967. Revolutions in the history of life. In: Albritton, pp. 63-91 (note 14a).
25. For a listing, see chapter 9.
26. Alvarez LW, Alvarez W, Asaro F, Michel HV. 1980. Extraterrestrial cause for the Cretaceous-Tertiary extinction. Science 208:1095-1108.
27. For further review and discussion, see: (a) Ager DV. 1993. The nature of the stratigraphical record. 3rd ed. Chichester and New York: John Wiley and Sons; (b) Emiliani C, Kraus EB, Shoemaker EM. 1981. Sudden death at the end of the Mesozoic. Earth and Planetary Science Letters 55:317-334; (c) Gibson LJ. 1990. A catastrophe with an impact. Origins 17:38-47; (d) Hallam, pp. 184-215 (note 14d); (e) Sharpton VL, Ward PD, editors. 1990. Global catastrophes in earth history; an interdisciplinary conference on impacts, volcanism, and mass mortality. Geological Society of America Special Paper 247; (f) Silver LT. 1982. Introduction. In: Silver LT, Schultz PH, editors. Geological implications of impacts of large asteroids and comets on the earth. Geological Society of America Special Paper 190:xiii-xix.
28. Napier WM, Clube SVM. 1979. A theory of terrestrial catastrophism. Nature 282:455-459.
29. Melosh HJ. 1982. The mechanics of large meteoroid impacts in the earth's oceans. Geological Society of America Special Paper 190:121-127.
30. Clube V, Napier B. 1982. Close encounters with a million comets. New Scientist 95:148-151.
31. Oberbeck VR, Marshall JR, Aggarwal H. 1993. Impacts, tillites, and the breakup of Gondwanaland. Journal of Geology 101:1-19.
32. Kristan-Tollmann E, Tollmann A. 1994. The youngest big impact on earth deduced from geological and historical evidence. Terra Nova 6:209-217.
33. Huggett 1989, pp. 186-189 (note 15c).
34. Kauffman E. 1983. Quoted in: Lewin R. Extinctions and the history of life. Science 221:935-937.
35. Nummedal D. 1982. Clastics. Geotimes 27(2):22, 23.
36. For comments about turbidites, see: Walker RG. 1973. Mopping up the turbidite mess. In: Ginsburg RN, editor. Evolving concepts in sedimentology. Baltimore and London: Johns Hopkins University Press, pp. 1-37. See chapter 14 for further discussion of coral reefs.
37. For details from an eyewitness, see: Anonymous. 1976. Teton: eyewitness to disaster. Time (21 June), p. 56.
38. Holmes A. 1965. Principles of physical geology. Rev. ed. New York: Ronald Press Co., p. 512.
39. E.g., Ecker RL. 1990. Dictionary of science and creationism. Buffalo: Prometheus Books, p. 102.
40. Séguret M, Labaume P, Madariaga R. 1984. Eocene seismicity in the Pyrenees from megaturbidites of the South Pyrenean Basin (Spain). Marine Geology 55:117-131.
41. (a) Campbell AS. 1954. Radiolaria. In: Moore RC, editor. Treatise on invertebrate paleontology, Part D (Protista 3). New York: Geological Society of America, and Lawrence, Kans.: University of Kansas Press, p. D17. For further discussion of this topic, see: (b) Roth AA. 1985. Are millions of years required to produce biogenic sediments in the deep ocean? Origins 12:48-56; (c) Snelling AA. 1994. Can flood geology explain thick chalk layers? Creation Ex Nihilo Technical Journal 8:11-15.
42. Thorarinsson S. 1964. Surtsey: the new island in the North Atlantic. Eysteinsson S, translator.

New York: The Viking Press, p. 39. Translation of: Surtsey: eyjan nyja i Atlantshafi.
43. (a) Encyclopaedia Britannica, editors. 1978. Disaster! When nature strikes back. New York: Bantam/Britannica Books, pp. 67-71; (b) Waltham T. 1978. Catastrophe: the violent Earth. New York: Crown Publishers, pp. 36-38.
44. See chapter 18 for a discussion of flood legends.
45. Gen. 6-8.
46. Gen. 2:5.
47. Verses 6, 10-14.
48. See Gen. 7; 8.
49. See Gen. 7:17-19.
50. Gen. 8:2, 3, NKJV.
51. See Gen. 7:24, Goodspeed; NEB.
52. Gen. 8:14.
53. (a) Hitching F. 1982. The neck of the giraffe: Darwin, evolution, and the new biology. New York and Scarborough, Ont.: Meridian, New American Library, pp. 110, 111; (b) Morris JD. 1992. How could all the animals have got on board Noah's ark? Back to Genesis, No. 392. Acts and Facts 22. Santee, Calif.: Institute for Creation Research; (c) Whitcomb JC, Jr., Morris HM. 1961. The Genesis flood. Philadelphia: Presbyterian and Reformed Pub. Co., pp. 67-69; (d) Woodmorappe J. 1996. Noah's ark: a feasibility study. Santee, Calif.: Institute for creation research, pp. 15-21.
54. Gibson LJ. n.d. Patterns of mammal distribution. Unpublished manuscript distributed by the Geoscience Research Institute, Loma Linda University, Loma Linda CA 92350 U.S.A.
55. Numbers RL. 1992. The creationists. New York: Alfred A. Knopf, pp. 335-339.
56. Gen. 1; 2.
57. Ex. 20:11; 31:17.
58. For further elaboration, see: (a) Davidson RM. 1995. Biblical evidence for the universality of the Genesis flood. Origins 22:58-73. (b) Younker RW. 1992. A few thoughts on Alden Thompson's chapter: "Numbers, Genealogies, Dates." In: Holbrook F, Van Dolson L, editors. Issues in revelation and inspiration. Adventist Theological Society Occasional Papers, vol. 1. Berrien Springs, Mich.: Adventist Theological Society Publications, pp. 173-199 (especially pp. 187-193).
59. Hasel GF. 1975. The biblical view of the extent of the flood. Origins 2:77-95.
60. Gen. 7:19-23, RSV.
61. See Gen. 9:11-15 and Isa. 54:9.
62. Gen. 6:19-7:9.
63. For some significant investigations, see: (a) Austin SA, Baumgardner JR, Humphreys DR, Snelling AA, Vardiman L, Wise KP. 1994. Catastrophic plate tectonics: a global flood model of earth history. In: Walsh RE, editor. Proceedings of the Third International Conference on Creationism. Pittsburgh: Creation Science Fellowship, Inc., pp. 609-621. (b) Baumgardner JR. 1994. Computer modeling of the large-scale tectonics associated with the Genesis flood. In: Walsh, pp. 49-62 (note 63a). (c) Baumgardner JR. 1994. Runaway subduction as the driving mechanism for the Genesis flood. In: Walsh, pp. 63-75 (note 63a). (d) Molén M. 1994. Mountain building and continental drift. In: Walsh, pp. 353-367 (note 63a).
64. Flori J, Rasolofomasoandro H. 1973. Évolution ou Création? Dammarie les Lys, France: Editions SDT, pp. 239-251.
65. For a review and evaluation of the concept, see: (a) Mundy B. 1988. Expanding earth? Origins 15:53-69. Comprehensive advocacy is given by: (b) Carey SW, editor. 1981. The expanding earth: a symposium. Earth Resources Foundation, University of Sydney. Brunswick, Australia: Impact Printing; (c) Carey SW. 1988. Theories of the earth and universe: a history of dogma in the earth sciences. Stanford, Calif.: Stanford University Press; (d) Jordan P. 1971. The expanding earth: some consequences of Dirac's gravitation hypothesis. Beer A, translator/editor. In: ter Haar D, editor. International series of monographs in natural philosophy, vol. 37. Oxford and New York: Pergamon Press. Translation of: Die Expansion der Erde.

66. Smirnoff LS. 1992. The contracting-expanding earth and the binary system of its megacyclicity. In: Chatterjee S, Hutton N III, editors. New concepts in global tectonics. Lubbock, Tex.: Texas Tech University Press, pp. 441-449.
67. For example: (a) Gurnis M. 1988. Large-scale mantle convection and the aggregation and dispersal of supercontinents. Nature 332:695-699; (b) Gurnis M. 1990. Plate-mantle coupling and continental flooding. Geophysical Research Letters 17(5):623-626.
68. Gen. 8:2, RSV.
69. (a) Ecker (note 39); (b) Newell ND. 1982. Creation and evolution: myth or reality? New York: Columbia University Press, pp. 37-39; (c) Ramm B. 1954. The Christian view of science and Scripture. Grand Rapids: Wm. B. Eerdmans Pub. Co., p. 244; (d) Walker KR, editor. 1984. The evolution-creation controversy: Perspectives on religion, philosophy, science, and education. Paleontological Society Special Publication No. 1. Knoxville, Tenn.: University of Tennessee, p. 62.
70. Flemming NC, Roberts DG. 1973. Tectono-eustatic changes in sea level and seafloor spreading. Nature 243:19-22.
71. (a) For two volumes dealing with problems and alternatives, see: Beloussov V, Bevis MG, Crook KAW, Monopolis D, Owen HG, Runcorn SK, Scalera C, Tanner WF, Tassos ST, Termier H, Walzer U, Augustithis SS, editors. 1990. Critical aspects of the plate tectonics theory, 2 vols. Athens: Theophrastus Publications, S.A.; (b) Meyerhoff AA, Meyerhoff HA. 1972a. "The new global tectonics": major inconsistencies. American Association of Petroleum Geologists Bulletin 56:269-336; (c) Mayerhoff AA, Meyerhoff HA. 1972b. "The new global tectonics": age of linear magnetic anomalies of ocean basins. American Association of Petroleum Geologists Bulletin 55:337-359; (d) Smith N, Smith J. 1993. An alternative explanation of oceanic magnetic anomaly patterns. Origins 20:6-21; (e) for a score of papers by as many authors who question the standard view, see: Chatterjee and Hutton (note 66).
72. Oard MJ. 1990. A post-flood ice-age model can account for Quaternary features. Origins 17:8-26.
73. Sharp RP. 1988. Living ice: understanding glaciers and glaciation. Cambridge and New York: Cambridge University Press, p. 181.
74. Rampino MR. 1993. Ancient "glacial" deposits are ejecta of large impacts: the Ice Age paradox explained. EOS, Transactions of the American Geophysical Union 74(43):99.
75. (a) Crowell JC. 1964. Climatic significance of sedimentary deposits containing dispersed megaclasts. In: Nairn AEM, editor. Problems in paleoclimatology: proceedings of the NATO Paleoclimates Conference 1963. London, New York, and Sydney: John Wiley and Sons, pp. 86-99; (b) Dunbar CO. 1940. Validity of the criteria for Lower Carboniferous glaciation in western Argentina. American Journal of Science 238:673-675; (c) McKeon JB, Hack JT, Newell WL, Berkland JO, Raymond LA. 1974. North Carolina glacier: evidence disputed. Science 184:88-91.
76. For some other examples of reinterpretations of so-called glacial deposits, see: (a) Bailey RA, Huber NK, Curry RR. 1990. The diamicton at Deadman Pass, central Sierra Nevada, California: a residual lag and colluvial deposit, not a 3 Ma glacial till. Geological Society of America Bulletin 102:1165-1173; (b) Crowell JC, Frakes LA. 1971. Late Paleozoic glaciation of Australia. Journal of the Geological Society of Australia 17:115-155; (c) Dott RH, Jr. 1961. Squantum "tillite," Massachusetts—evidence of glaciation or subaqueous mass movements? Geological Society of America Bulletin 72:1289-1306; (d) Engel BA. 1980. Carboniferous biostratigraphy of the Hunter-Manning-Myall Province. In: Herbert C, Helby R, editors. A guide to the Sydney Basin. Department of Mineral Resources, Geological Survey of New South Wales Bulletin 26:340-349; (e) Lakshmanan S. 1969. Vindhyan glaciation in India. Vikram University Institute of Geology Journal 2:57-67; (f) Newell ND. 1957. Supposed Permian tillites in northern Mexico are submarine slide deposits. Geological Society of America Bulletin 68:1569-1576; (g) Oberbeck, Marshall, and Aggarwal (note 31); (h) Schermerhorn LJG. 1974. No evidence for glacial origin of late Precambrian tilloids in Angola. Nature 252:114, 115; (i) Schwarzbach M. 1964. Criteria for the recognition of ancient glaciations. In: Nairn, pp. 81-85 (note 75a); (j) Winterer EL. 1964. Late Precambrian pebbly mudstone in Normandy, France: Tillite or tilloid. In: Nairn, pp. 159-187 (note 75a).

CHAPTER 13

GEOLOGIC EVIDENCE FOR A WORLDWIDE FLOOD

Those who know the truth
are not equal to those
who love it.

—*Confucius*[1]

A geologist once offered $5,000 for "field evidence of a universal flood."[2] His offer reflects an often-echoed comment that no such evidence exists. The reader is invited to evaluate, on the basis of the information presented in this chapter, whether or not we have geologic evidence for the Genesis flood.

The scriptural model of the flood is not only intriguing, it is awesome, and not for the weak-minded! Creationists usually consider this event to involve much of the Phanerozoic portion of the geologic column, the part relatively rich in fossils. It represents an average of many hundreds of meters of sediment over the entire earth. One of the greatest differences between the evolution and the creation models is the amount of time proposed for the deposition of these Phanerozoic sediments. Evolution suggests hundreds of million of years, in contrast to the biblical account of one year for the flood.

Some good tests exist by which we can evaluate the two models. However, the renewed acceptance of catastrophic interpretations by the geologic community has reduced the contrast of some distinguishing features. Some of the evidences for the flood that creationists once used are no longer as pertinent, because they have been incorporated into neocatastrophism. For instance, creationists have sometimes cited the usually well-preserved quality of many fossils over the world as evidence of the rapid burial that we would expect from the deluge. However, because both creationists and noncreationists can now incorporate rapid burial into their catastrophic repertoires, the good preservation of fossils no longer serves as a valuable distinguishing feature between the two models.

In this chapter we will examine the data from the geologic layers and their fossils that indicate major flood activity or a brief time for their deposition as expected during a worldwide flood. Additional related information about the extent, time involved, and legends about the flood is discussed elsewhere.[3]

ABUNDANT UNDERWATER ACTIVITY ON THE CONTINENTS

Earth's continents consist of a lighter granitic-type rock that literally floats above heavier rocks (see Figure 12.2C), thus keeping the continents above sea level. Were it not for this, we might have a permanent flood over the world. As we trek over these continents, we find an unexpected abundance of rock layers with ocean-type fossils, such as marine coral, clams, and crinoids. We would expect marine fossils in the oceans. Geologist J. S. Shelton points out the dilemma: "Marine sedimentary rocks are far more common and widespread on land today than all other kinds of sedimentary rocks combined. This is one of those simple facts that fairly cry out for explanation and that lie at the heart of man's continuing effort to understand more fully the changing geography of the geologic past."[4] While some may feel that this is a "simple fact that cries out for explanation," it fits remarkably well with what we would expect of the deluge.

On November 18, 1929, an earthquake shook the New England coast and the Maritime Provinces of Canada. Known as the Grand Banks earthquake, it caused the slumping of a large mass of sediment lying in the ocean on the edge of the continental shelf. It also freed other sediments, forming loose mud that slid down the continental slope into the deeper part of the North Atlantic Ocean. The sediments spread over the abyssal plain at the foot of the slope. Some of the sediment traveled more than 700 kilometers.[5] One might think that a mass of loose mud flowing in the ocean would quickly mix with the seawater and lose its integrity as a separate unit, but that is not the case. The loose mud has a greater density than sea water, because it is a combination of water and an abundance of heavier rocks, sand, silt, and clay particles. Such mud flows beneath the lighter seawater in a manner somewhat comparable to the way water flows on land beneath air. Only a small amount of mixing takes place between the mud and the overlying water. The kind of flow that took place around Grand Banks was a *turbidity current,* which, as the flow stopped, deposited a unique and complex sedimentary layer called a *turbidite.*

Fortunately for science, but unfortunately for commercial telegraphy, 12 transatlantic cables lying in the path of the Grand Banks turbidity flow snapped in this catastrophe, some in two or three places. The first break of each cable was precisely timed by the interruption of the telegraphic transmission and its location determined by resistance and capacitance tests. Those cables closest to the epicenter of the earthquake near the top of the continental slope broke almost instantly, probably from the sudden slumping of sediments. Farther away an orderly sequence occurred as the turbidity current broke successive cables. Rates of travel were calculated to be sometimes greater than 100 kilometers per hour. The last cable, more than 650 kilometers from shore, broke a little more than 13 hours after the earthquake. The resulting turbidite from this mudflow covered more than 100,000 square kilometers and had an average thickness of a little less than one meter. The volume is estimated at 100 cubic kilometers.[6] The turbidity current also ran into the hulk of the *Titanic,* which sank in 1912.[7]

Turbidites are especially interesting as evidence of the flood. They form rapidly and only under water. One turbidite does not prove a flood, but their abundance in the sedimentary layers on the continents speaks of extensive underwater activity. Geology did not accept the turbidite concept until the middle of the century, but just two decades later it could be stated that "tens of thousands of graded beds stacked on top of one another have been interpreted as turbidity current deposits."[8] They are now considered "one of the commonest types of sedimentary rocks."[9] Even some rare rock types, such as gypsum, usually considered to have formed by evaporation of salt-laden waters, have been interpreted as turbidites.[10] Turbidites often turn up within larger depositional features called submarine fans. Abundant on the continents, they likewise form underwater.

Noncreationists explain the evidence for underwater geologic activity on the continents by suggesting that during most of the Phanerozoic, the sea level was substantially higher, sometimes more than a half kilometer higher than it is now.[11] They postulate flatter continents and higher oceans.[12] But in using this explanation, geologists inadvertently come close to a flood model (except for the time involved). Regardless, the abundance of marine fossils, turbidites, and submarine fans is evidence of widespread underwater activity on the continents.

Related to the evidence of underwater activity is the indication of a widespread directionality of water currents. When studying sedimentary rocks, geologists often find clues that indicate the direction of the current flow during deposition. Strengthening the concept of a single-flood catastrophe is the discovery of a dominant direction of current flow through major portions of the Phanerozoic of North America. Under ordinary conditions water flows in different directions, such as occurs in the various rivers on present-day continents. On the other hand, if the continents were submerged underwater during a worldwide flood, one might expect the current flow to tend in one direction. A comprehensive review of 15,000 locations in North America shows a strong pattern toward the southwest for the lower half of the Phanerozoic, with a gradual change toward the east in the layers above. The same pattern seems to apply to South America. This would represent the more intense forces during the major part of the flood. Near the top of the geologic column the rocks reveal no dominant pattern.[13] We can explain this later lack of direction as either the draining of the continents at the end of the flood or postflood activity, such as occurs today.

WIDESPREAD SEDIMENTARY DEPOSITS

In an event such as a worldwide flood, one would expect rather widespread deposition of sediments, and some remarkable examples exist.

Referring to the deposition of limestones, Norman Newell of the National Museum in New York speaks of "seas spread over immense and incredibly flat areas of the world."[14] Derek Ager, a geologist who strongly endorses catastrophism, describes rock units with thicknesses of 30 meters or less in the Permian of western Canada that persist over areas up to 470,000 square kilometers. He also refers to a thin layer "about a metre thick" that "can be found all around the Alpine chain"[15] of Europe. In the United States, the Dakota Formation of the western United States, with an average thickness of 30 meters, covers some 815,000 square kilometers.

The widespread nature of special sedimentary deposits with land-derived fossils offers evidence of a kind of catastrophic activity on the continents for which we have no contemporary analogs. An outstanding example is the Triassic fossil-wood-bearing Shinarump conglomerate, a member of the Chinle Formation found in the southwestern United States. This conglomerate, which occasionally grades into a coarse sandstone, usually has a thickness of less than 30 meters, but it spreads as an almost continuous unit over nearly 250,000 square kilometers.[16] Conglomerates and sandstones such as the Shinarump consist of sizable particles requiring considerable energy for transport. It would demand forces different from those with which we are familiar today to spread such an almost-continuous deposit over so wide an area. It is difficult to conceive of such continuity being produced by local sedimentary activities such as those of rivers, as is sometimes postulated. Any ordinary valley, canyon, or mountain forming over time would have easily broken the continuity. Basal conglomerates and other units found in many other geological formations present the same evidence. It is difficult to appreciate the thinness and breadth of some of these formations. As an example, if an area the size of this book page represented the Shinarump conglomerate, proportionately its thickness would average only about one fifth of the thickness of the paper. Such thin, unique, widespread deposits seem more reminiscent of sheetflood (broad, thin expanses of moving water) activity than local sedimentation.

The widespread, continuous, and significantly unique nature of many geologic formations indicates extensive distribution of sediments on a scale suggestive of a major flood. The reddish Chinle Group, which includes the Chinle Formation mentioned above, covers about 800,000 square kilometers.[17] The multicolored dinosaur-bearing Jurassic Morrison Formation of the western United States extends over 1 million square kilometers from Canada to Texas, in the southern part of the United States,[18] yet its average thickness is only about 100 meters. Such widespread formations reflect unusual and widespread depositional patterns. Perhaps these patterns are part of the reason fossil types tend to be much more widely distributed in the fossil record than are their living counterparts.[19]

Could these widespread deposits have resulted from such catastrophes as the meteoritic impacts envisioned by neocatastrophists[20] instead of the deluge? Earth's sedimentary layers are almost never the type of deposit produced by meteoritic impacts. For instance, at Meteor Crater in Arizona[21] the small local deposit caused by the meteoritic impact consists of mixed blocks of rocks, instead of the widespread, sorted sediments usually found on earth. Could asteroid impacts cause gigantic water waves that would produce widespread sedimentary layers? Such a scenario comes close to the events that may have occurred during the deluge. We must also remember that neocatastrophism has some implications that pose problems for the evolutionary model. Rapid catastrophic deposition of sediments would tend to eliminate the postulated millions of years required for the evolution of organisms within those formations. A persistent use of catastrophism by nonflood geologists reduces the vast time span postulated and approximates a flood model.

INCOMPLETE ECOSYSTEMS

If the Phanerozoic geologic column developed slowly over many hundreds of millions of years, the organisms found at any level should represent viable ecological systems that would be complete enough to permit their survival. In the basic food chain, animals require food from plants that in turn obtain their energy from the sun. The fossil record poses a problem when it yields evidence for animals without any corresponding indication of sufficient plants to provide them nourishment. What did the animals eat in order to survive through the millions of years of evolutionary development? The flood geologist believes this suggests that the animals were transported from their customary habitats and/or the plants were washed elsewhere, possibly forming some of the unusually thick coal beds, such as the Morwell (Australia) coal bed, with a depth of 165 meters.

The previously mentioned Morrison Formation of the western United States appears to represent a vast but incomplete ecological system. It has been one of the world's richest sources of dinosaur fossils (Figure 9.1), yet plants are rare, especially in the vicinity of dinosaur remains.[22] What did the behemoths eat? The paleontologist Theodore White comments that "although the Morrison plain was an area of reasonably rapid accumulation of sediment, identifiable plant fossils are practically nonexistent."[23] He further muses that by comparison to an elephant, an apatosaurus "would consume 3½ tons of green fodder daily." If dinosaurs were living there for millions of years, what did they eat if plants were so rare? Other investigators have also commented on this lack of plant fossils. One states that the Morrison in Montana "is practically barren of plant fossils throughout most of its sequence,"[24] and others comment that the "absence of evidence for abundant plant life in the form of coal beds and organic-rich clays in much of the Morrison Formation is puzzling."[25] These investigators also express their "frustration" because 10 of 12 samples studied microscopically were essentially barren of the "palynomorphs" (pollen and spores) produced by plants. With such a sparse source of energy, one wonders how the large dinosaurs could survive the assumed millions of years while the Morrison Formation was being deposited.

To explain the dilemma, some have suggested that plants existed but did not get fossilized. This idea does not seem valid, since a number of animals and a few plants are well preserved. Perhaps the Morrison was not a place where dinosaurs lived. Instead, it might have been a flood-created dinosaur burial ground with plants sorted and transported elsewhere.

Paleontologists report a similar situation for the dinosaur protoceratops found in the central Gobi Desert of Mongolia. Investigators studying various aspects of these Cretaceous deposits conclude that "the abundance of an unambiguous herbivore (protoceratops) and a rich trace fossil fauna [probably tubes made by insects] reflect a region of high productivity. The absence of evidence of well-developed plant colonization is, therefore, anomalous and baffling."[26]

Even more surprising are the data from the Coconino Sandstone, the light-colored unit seen near the top of the Grand Canyon in Arizona (Figure 13.1, just above the top arrow). This unit, which has an average thickness of 150 meters, spreads across many thousands of square kilometers. Hundreds of footprint trackways, probably made by amphibians or reptiles, occur in the lower half of the Coconino. Yet no plants appear to have been present. Aside from the footprints, field study reports only a few worm tubes and invertebrate tracks.[27] If it took millions of years to form the Coconino, what nourishment was available for the animals who made all these tracks? We find no evidence for the presence of plant food. If simple footprints are well preserved, we would also expect to find the imprints or casts of roots, stems, and leaves of plants.

Almost all the trackways in the Coconino indicate that the animals were going uphill,[28] and the same situation occurs in the De Chelly Sandstone formation to the east.[29] The animals that produced the tracks in the Coconino have not yet turned up in the fossil record, but their tracks are well preserved and abundant. Furthermore, we have strong evidence that the animals made their trackways underwater, instead of the usual interpretation that they left them on desert dunes.[30] Is it possible that animals seeking to escape the waters of the deluge left all those uphill tracks?

Some fossil assemblages appear to be complete ecosystems, while others

FIGURE 13.1

View of the Grand Canyon of the Colorado River in Arizona. The arrows from top to bottom point to three assumed gaps (missing layers) of about 6, 14, and 100 million years.

are not. How can a slow-sedimentation evolutionary model explain the incomplete fossil assemblages? Evolutionists assume that it took at least 5 million years to deposit the Morrison or Coconino formations. How did the animals represented in their layers survive without an adequate food supply? Sorting of organisms by a major flood can resolve the dilemma.

Ecological requirements infer that the Morrison and Coconino formations were deposited rapidly. This suggests the kind of activity expected during a worldwide flood.

THE GAPS IN THE SEDIMENTARY LAYERS[31]

When we look at major exposures of sediments on the sides of valleys and canyons, we are usually not aware that significant parts of the geologic column are often missing between some of the layers. The missing portions are not easily noticed unless we are well acquainted with the geologic column. As an illustration, we can represent a complete series of layers in the column by letters of the alphabet. If in one locality we find only a, d, and e, we would rightly conclude that b and c were missing between a and d. We would know this because layers b and c appear in their proper place in another locality. The layers above and below the gaps (i.e., a and d in our example) are often in a flat contact with each other. According to the standard geologic timescale, the amount of missing time represented at a gap reflects the time considered necessary to develop the missing layers, such as b and c found in the above example.

The Grand Canyon in Arizona is one of the great geological showcases of the world. The arrows in Figure 13.1 indicate significant missing portions (hiatuses or gaps) in the geologic column. From top to bottom the gaps represent approximately 6, 14, and more than 100 million years of layers absent from the standard geologic timescale. The lower arrow points to a gap that includes the entire Ordovician and Silurian periods (see Figure 10.1 for terminology). We know this gap exists because the Ordovician and Silurian deposits are present in other parts of the world. In an evolutionary context, these deposits would require a long time for their formation and for the evolution of the organisms forming the characteristic fossils found in them. Geologists determine missing portions mainly by comparing fossils in the sedimentary layers with complete sequences of the geologic column. They also use radiometric dating, especially in establishing the broad time framework of the layers.

Geologists have long been aware of these gaps and usually designate them as "unconformities," although they sometimes use the term in various ways in different countries. Several types of unconformities exist. If the layers above and below are at an angle to each other, the term *angular unconformity* is used. But if they are generally parallel but with some evidence of erosion between the layers, the contact is sometimes called a *disconformity.* And if the line of contact is not visible or there is no evidence of erosion, it is called a *paraconformity.* In this discussion we are especially interested in the latter two types.

The important question is: Why don't we see an irregular pattern of erosion of the lower layer at these gaps if they represent such extensive time periods? A lot of erosion should have occurred before the layer above the gap was laid down. As a very minimum, under normal circumstances we would expect a regional average of more than 100 meters of erosion in only 4 million years.[32] The geologist Ivo Lucchitta, who is not a creationist, and who has spent much of his life studying the Grand Canyon, which is well over a kilometer deep, suggests that "most of the canyon cutting occurred in the phenomally short time of 4 to 5 million years."[33] The lack of significant erosion suggests little or no time at the gaps. Figure 13.2A-D shows how uneven and complicated patterns would develop over geologic ages. However, the pattern we see is more like that of Figures 13.1 and 13.2E, with little or no erosion. We would expect some erosion from flood activity, but only rarely do we find ancient valleys and canyons within earth's sedimentary layers.

Perhaps we can obtain a better representation of these gaps if we display the sedimentary layers on the basis of the assumed standard geologic timescale. Figure 13.3 illustrates the layers to the northeast of the Grand Canyon region arranged on a timescale instead of thickness, although for sedimentary layers both categories tend to be related. In this figure the missing parts of the geologic column are in black. Note the standard geologic timescale in the second column. This diagram emphasizes the *time* to deposit the layers and the *time* missing between layers. Obviously the gaps (black) are common and represent significant parts of the geologic timescale. The graph shows only the major gaps. Many smaller gaps exist within the sedimentary layers illustrated (white portions).

The diagram has a vertical exaggeration of 16x. In other words, for the height represented, the lateral extent should be 16 times as wide as what is illustrated. The distance across the figure represents about 200 kilometers, while the thickness of the layers (white portions) is only about three and one half kilometers. This illustrates how flat and widespread these layers and gaps are, often spreading over several hundreds of thousands of square kilometers.

The lack of erosion at various gaps suggests that the sedimentary layers were laid down rapidly during the deluge. If long periods of time had occurred, we should see evidence of geological processes going on at the surface of the layers

FIGURE 13.2

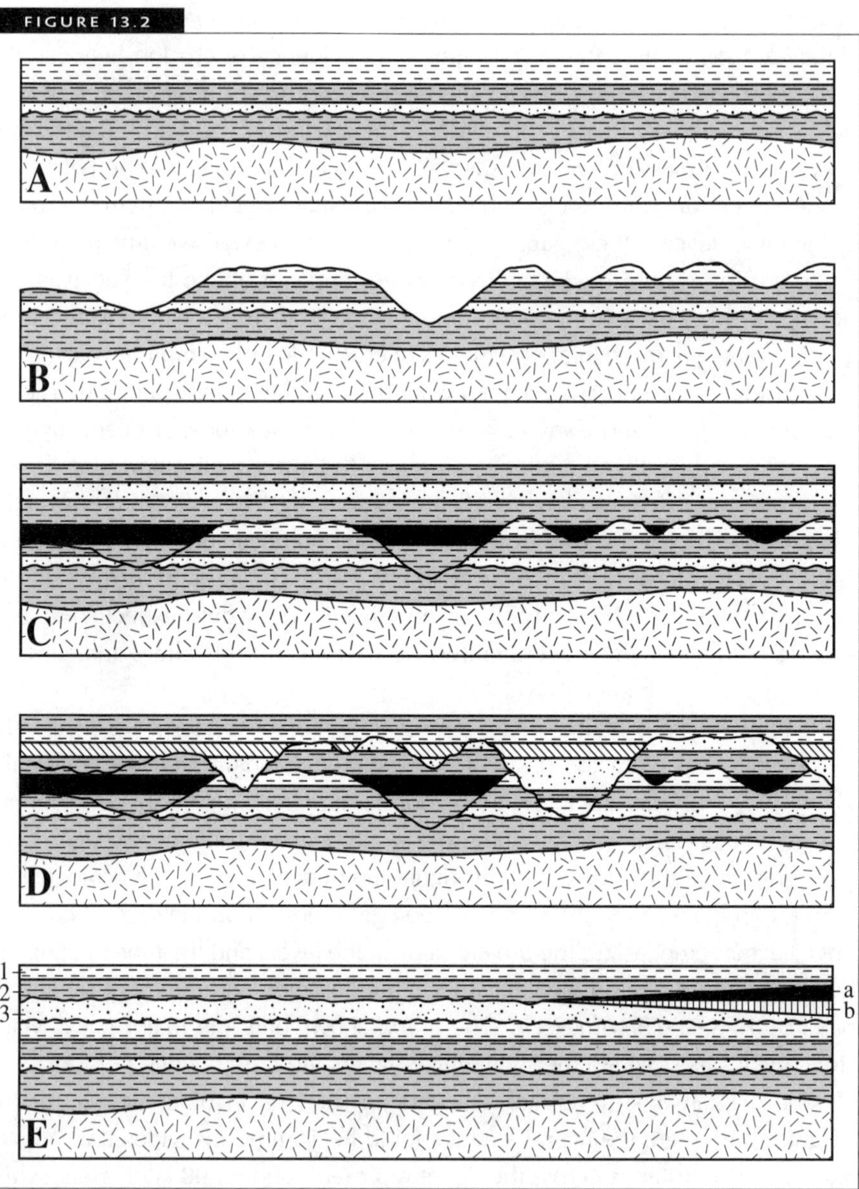

Deposition-erosion patterns. A: Pattern of continuous deposition. Sediments are usually laid down in a flat, horizontal pattern as shown. B: Erosion. C: Resumption of sedimentation. The old erosion surface is still visible. This pattern should be common within earth's sedimentary layers wherever significant parts of the geologic column are missing. D: A second cycle of erosion and deposition further complicates the pattern. E: The more normal pattern seen. In E we would expect significant erosion between layers 2 and 3 (left side), if extensive time was involved in depositing layers a and b wedged in on the right. Hypothetical diagram with variable vertical exaggeration depending on erosional conditions.

FIGURE 13.3

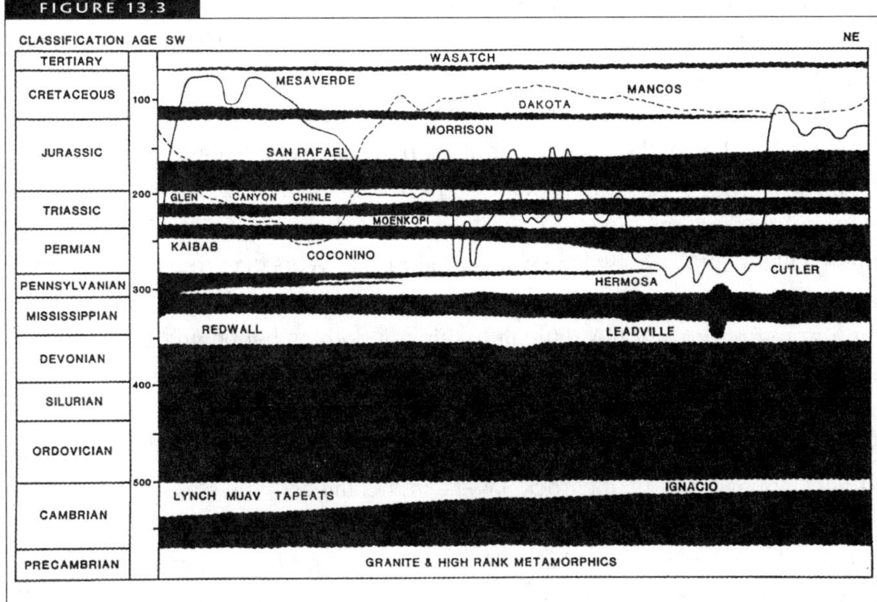

Representation of the sedimentary layers in eastern Utah and a little of western Colorado, based on the standard geologic timescale (instead of thickness, although the two are related). The clear (white) areas represent sedimentary rock layers, while the black areas represent the time for the main gaps (hiatuses) between layers where parts of the geologic column are missing in this region. The layers (white areas) actually lie directly on top of each other with flat contact planes. The black areas stand for the postulated time between the sedimentary layers. The irregular dashed and continuous lines through the upper layers represent two examples of the present ground surface in the region as carved by erosion. The dashed line (---) represents one of the flattest surfaces of the region as found along Interstate 70, while the smooth line (—) is in the hills farther south. This provides evidence for a flood model wherein the layers (white areas) were deposited rapidly in sequence without much time for erosion between. Erosion toward the end of the flood and afterward produced the irregular topography that exists today (dashed and continuous lines). If millions of years had elapsed between the layers (black areas), as postulated by the geologic timescale, we would expect patterns of erosion somewhat similar to the present surface pattern (dashed and continuous lines) between the white layers. The main divisions of the geologic column are given in the left column, followed by their putative age in millions of years. Names in the sedimentary units represent only the major formation or groups. Vertical exaggeration is about 16x. The horizontal distance represents about 200 kilometers while the total thickness of the layers (white part) is about three and one half kilometers.*

*Diagram based on (a) Bennison AP. 1990. Geological highway map of the southern Rocky Mountain region: Utah, Colorado, Arizona, New Mexico. Rev. ed. U.S. Geological Highway Map No. 2. Tulsa, Okla.: American Association of Petroleum Geologists; (b) Billingsley GH, Breed WJ. 1980. Geologic cross section from Cedar Breaks National Monument through Bryce Canyon National Park to Escalante, Capitol Reef National Park, and Canyonlands National Park, Utah. Torrey, Utah: Capitol Reef Natural History Assn.; (c) Molenaar CM. 1975. Correlation chart. In: Fassett JE, editor. Canyonlands country: a guidebook of the Four Corners Geological Society eighth field conference, p. 4; (d) Tweto O. 1979. Geologic map of Colorado, scale 1:500,000. Reston, Va.: U.S. Geological Survey.

just below the gaps. On the present surface of the land and seafloor today we can often see the effects of time as erosion washes away the continents and forms gullies, valleys, and canyons. Other effects of time, such as soil formation, weathering, and plant growth, leave marks that should also be evident at the gaps. However, the layers just below the gaps are usually flat and unweathered, suggesting that little or no time occurred before they were covered with other layers.

Figure 13.3 also illustrates the contrast between these flat assumed gaps and the present eroded topography of the earth. The fine wavy solid and dashed lines represent the present surface of the land in the same region in contrast to the much flatter contacts between layers. If millions of years occurred between each layer, why are the contacts between the assumed gaps so flat in comparison to earth's present surface? It is difficult to think of nothing happening at the surface of the gaps for millions of years on any kind of planet that would have a weather pattern normal enough to support life as evidenced in the fossil record.

As we stand on the edge of the Grand Canyon (Figure 13.1), the extremely parallel appearance of the rock layers immediately impresses us. This phenomenon contrasts rather sharply with the profile of the canyon itself, which illustrates the irregularity of erosion. Why don't we observe similar features at the gaps? Given the time postulated for these gaps, there would certainly be ample time for erosion. Present average rates of erosion are so rapid that the entire geologic column could have been eroded away many times[34] during the long ages postulated for the geologic past. Yet at the 100-plus-million-year gap (indicated by the lowest arrow in Figure 13.1), we notice only minor erosion, or the contact sometimes appears smooth, or it is invisible. Referring to one section along this gap, geologist Stanley Beus states: "Here, the unconformity, even though representing more than 100 million years, may be difficult to locate."[35] At the middle arrow (Figure 13.1), which represents an assumed gap of about 14 million years, another geologist points out that the evidence is so sparse that the contact line "can be difficult to determine, both from a distance and from close range."[36] If the postulated time had occurred, we should observe extensive irregular erosion.

The east coast of Australia has excellent exposures of coal seams (Figure 13.4). Between the overlying rocks and the Bulli Coal is a gap of around 5 million years.[37] This gap, which extends well beyond the Bulli Coal deposits, covers some 90,000 square kilometers in the region. Where the Bulli Coal is present, it is especially difficult to envision how the coal seam, or the vegetation producing it, remained there for 5 million years without being destroyed.

The European Alps in part consist of a complex of gigantic slides and folded layers called nappes. Between the layers within these nappes geologists postulate gaps that show the same lack of erosion noted elsewhere. Figure 13.5 shows part of the Morcles Nappe as seen from the Rhône valley

FIGURE 13.4

East coast of Australia in New South Wales. The arrow points to an assumed 5-million-year gap just above the black coal layer.

in Switzerland. The arrow points to an assumed gap of around 45 million years (Upper Cretaceous and more) that indicates little erosion. Incidentally, the sequence of the layers surrounding the arrow (upper portion of picture) is completely overturned, having been rolled over as a unit when the layers were thrust to the north during the formation of the Alps.

Some geologists have commented on the lack of evidence for the geological changes expected at these gaps. Referring to the kind of gaps called paraconformities, Norman Newell of the American Museum of Natural History in New York comments: "A remarkable aspect of paraconformities in limestone sequences is general lack of evidence of leaching of the undersurface. Residual soils and karst surfaces that might be expected to result from long subaerial exposure are lacking or unrecognized." "Speculating" on what causes these flat contacts, the author states further that "the origin of paraconformities is uncertain, and I certainly do not have a simple solution to this problem."[38]

In a subsequent publication Newell further comments: "A puzzling characteristic of the erathem boundaries and of many other major biostratigraphic boundaries [boundaries between differing fossil assemblages] is the general lack of physical evidence of subaerial exposure. Traces of deep leaching, scour, channeling, and residual gravels tend to be lacking, even where the underlying rocks are cherty limestones. . . . These boundaries are paraconformities that are usually identifiable only by paleontological [fossil] evidence."[39]

T. H. van Andel of Stanford University states: "I was much influenced early in my career by the recognition that two thin coal seams in Venezuela, separated by a foot of grey clay and deposited in a coastal swamp, were respectively of Lower Paleocene and Upper Eocene age. The outcrops were excellent but even the closest inspection failed to turn up the precise position of that 15 Myr gap."[40] It could well be that the 15 million years never occurred.

The intriguing question concerning the lack of evidence for the passage of time at these sedimentary gaps has sometimes given rise to alternative suggestions.[41] Some point to flat areas of the earth, such as the lower Mississippi Valley. However, this is not a gap, because water and other geological agents are currently depositing sediment there, and no gap will appear in the fossil record if those sediments continue to collect. Others suggest that erosion might not occur if the gaps were underwater. However, being underwater does not prevent either deposition or erosion, as we see well demonstrated by submarine sedimentation and the irregular erosion of large canyons found along the edge of the continental shelves. The Monterey Canyon, lying in the ocean off the coast of California, is about as deep and as wide as the Grand Canyon. Moving water can erode whether shallow or deep.

Some suggest that the contact surfaces of the gaps could be flat because of resistant rock layers just below them. This is not a solution, because soft sediments often form the layers just below the gaps. One example is the gap between the Chinle and the soft Moenkopi below (Figure 13.3). Others wonder if erosion might not produce a flat surface, but we have no good present examples to support such a suggestion, certainly not on the semicontinentwide scale of the gaps discussed in this chapter. In referring to such examples, the geomorphologist Arthur Bloom simply states: "None are known."[42] Other geologists wonder if there might actually be evidence of erosion at the gaps. Often we do observe a little erosion, but it is insufficient to support the lengthy time suggested for the gaps. The erosion is also minor compared to earth's present topography (Figure 13.3). And we would expect some erosion to occur during a worldwide flood. But Mount Everests and Grand Canyons seem conspicuously lacking from the record of a past that is well represented in earth's sedimentary layers. Certainly one has to acknowledge that the aphorism "the present is the key to the past" does not apply to these gaps where rapid activity is suggested. The past is definitely different.

FIGURE 13.5

Valley of the Rhône in Switzerland. The arrow points to an assumed gap in sedimentation of around 45 million years. All the upper layers from well below the arrow to the top are bottom side up, because of folding over as the layers slid from the south (right).

The difficulty with the extended passage of time proposed for various gaps in the sedimentary record is that we find neither deposition nor is much erosion evident. If there is deposition, there is no gap, because sedimentation continues. If there is erosion, one would expect abundant channeling and the formation of deep gullies, canyons, and valleys, yet the contacts (gaps), sometimes described as "continent-sized," are usually "nearly planar"[43] (flat). It is difficult to conceive of little or nothing happening for millions of years on our planet's surface. Over time either deposition or erosion will occur. The weather would have to cease in order to prevent either activity. Perhaps the proposed time for these gaps never occurred, and if time is missing in one place, it is missing earthwide.

The question of the flat assumed gaps in the sedimentary layers witness to a past that differed greatly from the present. We can easily reconcile that difference with catastrophic models such as the Genesis flood that propose rapid deposition of the layers with no extended time periods between them.

CONCLUSIONS

The great quantity of marine layers, turbidites, and submarine fans, as well as a strong depositional directionality exhibited by the sediments on the continents, substantiate great underwater activity on those continents in the past. Such evidence fits well with a flood model. The incredibly widespread deposits in earth's sedimentary layers also seem to support a flood model. Some other evidences for the flood relate primarily to time factors. What did the dinosaurs and other vertebrates eat during the assumed millions of years of Morrison and Coconino time, where plants appear sparse or absent? We can explain this by sorting during a worldwide flood. The scarcity of erosion at the gaps in the sedimentary layers, where significant portions of the geologic column are missing, infers rapid deposition, as we would expect during the flood, without long intervals of time between. Some of these data are difficult to explain if one denies a worldwide flood.

REFERENCES

1. Confucius. Analects XV. As quoted in: Mencken HL, editor. 1942. A new dictionary of quotations on historical principles from ancient and modern sources. New York: Alfred A. Knopf, p. 1220.
2. Roth AA. 1982. The universal flood debate. Liberty 77(6):12-15.
3. See chapters 12, 15, and 18 for information about the extent of the flood, the time involved, and flood legends respectively.
4. Shelton JS. 1966. Geology illustrated. San Francisco and London: W. H. Freeman and Co., p. 28.
5. For information on this event, see: (a) Heezen BC, Ewing M. 1952. Turbidity currents and submarine slumps, and the 1929 Grand Banks earthquake. American Journal of Science 250:849-873; (b) Heezen BC, Ericson DB, Ewing M. 1954. Further evidence for a turbidity current following the 1929 Grand Banks earthquake. Deep-Sea Research 1:193-202; (c) Heezen BC, Drake CL. 1964. Grand Banks slump. American Association of Petroleum Geologists Bulletin 48:221-233.
6. Kuenen PhH. 1952. Estimated size of the Grand Banks turbidity current. American Journal of Science 250:874-884.
7. Ballard RD. 1985. How we found *Titanic*. National Geographic 168(6):696, 697.
8. Walker RG. 1973. Mopping up the turbidite mess. In: Ginsburg RN, editor. Evolving concepts in sedimentology. Baltimore and London: Johns Hopkins University Press, pp. 1-37.
9. Middleton GV. 1993. Sediment deposition from turbidity currents. Annual Review of Earth and Planetary Sciences 21:89-114.
10. Schreiber BC, Friedman GM, Decima A, Schreiber E. 1976. Depositional environments of Upper Miocene (Messinian) evaporite deposits of the Sicilian Basin. Sedimentology 23:729-760.
11. (a) Hallam A. 1984. Pre-Quaternary sea-level changes. Annual Review of Earth and Planetary Sciences 12:205-243; (b) Hallam A. 1992. Phanerozoic sea-level changes. New York: Columbia University Press, p. 158; (c) Vail PR, Mitchum RM, Jr., Thompson S, III. 1977. Seismic stratigraphy and global changes of sea level, part 4: global cycles of relative changes of sea level. In: Payton CE, editor. Seismic stratigraphy—applications to hydrocarbon exploration. American Association of Petroleum Geologists Memoir 26:83-97.
12. (a) Burton R, Kendall CGStC, Lerche I. 1987. Out of our depth: on the impossibility of fathoming eustasy from the stratigraphic record. Earth-Science Reviews 24:237-277; (b) Cloetingh S. 1991. Tectonics and sea-level changes: a controversy? In: Müller DW, McKenzie JA, Weissert H, editors. Controversies in modern geology: evolution of geological theories in sedimentology, Earth history and tectonics. London, San Diego, and New York: Academic Press, pp. 249-277; (c) Hallam 1992 (note 11b); (d) Sloss LL, Speed RC. 1974. Relationships of cratonic and continental-margin tectonic episodes. In: Dickinson WR, editor. Tectonics and sedimentation. Society of Economic Paleontologists and Mineralogists Special Publication 22:98-119.
13. (a) Chadwick AV. 1993. Megatrends in North American paleocurrents. Society of Economic Paleontologists and Mineralogists Abstracts With Programs 8:58; (b) Chadwick AV. 1996 personal communication. For a more localized investigation, see: (c) Potter PE, Pryor WA. 1961. Dispersal centers of Paleozoic and later clastics of the Upper Mississippi Valley and adjacent

areas. Geological Society of America Bulletin 72:1195-1250.

14. Newell ND. 1967. Paraconformities. In: Teichert C, Yochelson EL, editors. Essays in paleontology and stratigraphy. R. C. Moore commemorative volume. Department of Geology, University of Kansas Special Publication 2:349-367.
15. Ager DV. 1993. The nature of the stratigraphical record. 3rd ed. Chichester and New York: John Wiley and Sons, p. 23.
16. Gregory HE. 1950. Geology and geography of the Zion Park region, Utah and Arizona. U.S. Geological Survey Professional Paper 220:65.
17. (a) Lucas SG. 1993. The Chinle Group: revised stratigraphy and biochronology of Upper Triassic nonmarine strata in the western United States. In: Morales M, editor. Aspects of Mesozoic geology and paleontology of the Colorado Plateau. Museum of Northern Arizona Bulletin 59:27-50. This paper reports 2.3 million square kilometers. This figure appears erroneous. There is debate over the nomenclature of the "Chinle Group." See (b): Dubiel RF. 1994. Triassic deposystems, paleogeography, and paleoclimate of the Western Interior. In: Caput MV, Peterson JA, Franczyk KJ, editors. Mesozoic systems of the Rocky Mountain region, U.S.A. Denver: Rocky Mountain Section of the Society for Sedimentary Geology, pp. 133-147.
18. Hintze LF. 1988. Geologic history of Utah. Brigham Young University Geology Studies Special Publication 7:51.
19. (a) Barghoorn ES. (1953) 1970. Evidence of climatic change in the geologic record of plant life. In: Cloud P, editor. Adventures in earth history. San Francisco: W. H. Freeman and Co., pp. 732-741; (b) Signor PW. 1990. The geologic history of diversity. Annual Review of Ecological Systems 21:509-539; (c) Valentine JW, Foin TC, Peart D. 1978. A provincial model of Phanerozoic marine diversity. Paleobiology 4:55-66.
20. See chapter 12.
21. (a) Kieffer SW. 1974. Shock metamorphism of the Coconino Sandstone at Meteor Crater. In: Shoemaker EM, Kieffer SW. Guidebook to the geology of Meteor Crater, Arizona. Center for Meteorite Studies, Arizona State University, Publication 17:12-19; (b) Shoemaker EM. 1974. Synopsis of the geology of Meteor Crater. In: Shoemaker, pp. 1-11 (note 21a).
22. (a) Dodson P, Behrensmeyer AK, Bakker RT, McIntosh JS. 1980. Taphonomy and paleoecology of the dinosaur beds of the Jurassic Morrison Formation. Paleobiology 6(2):208-232. (b) For further discussion see (b) Roth AA. 1994. Incomplete ecosystems. Origins 21:51-56.
23. (a) White TE. 1964. The dinosaur quarry. In: Sabatka EF, editor. Guidebook to the geology and mineral resources of the Uinta Basin. Salt Lake City: Intermountain Association of Geologists, pp. 21-28. See also: (b) Herendeen PS, Crane PR, Ash S. 1994. Vegetation of the dinosaur world. In: Rosenberg GD, Wolberg DL, editors. Dino fest. Paleontological Society Special Publication No. 7. Knoxville, Tenn.: Department of Geological Sciences, University of Tennessee, pp. 347-364; (c) Petersen LM, Roylance MM. 1982. Stratigraphy and depositional environments of the Upper Jurassic Morrison Formation near Capitol Reef National Park, Utah. Brigham Young University Geology Studies 29(2):1-12; (d) Peterson F, Turner-Peterson CE. 1987. The Morrison Formation of the Colorado Plateau: recent advances in sedimentology, stratigraphy, and paleotectonics. Hunteria 2(1):1-18.
24. Brown RW. 1946. Fossil plants and Jurassic-Cretaceous boundary in Montana and Alberta. American Association of Petroleum Geologists Bulletin 30:238-248.
25. Dodson, Behrensmeyer, Bakker, and McIntosh (note 22).
26. Fastovsky DE, Badamgarav D, Ishimoto H, Watabe M, Weishampel DB. 1997. The paleoenvironments of Tugrikin-Shireh (Gobi Desert, Mongolia) and aspects of the taphonomy and paleoecology of *Protoceratops* (Dinosauria: Ornithischia). Palaios 12:59-70.
27. (a) Middleton LT, Elliott DK, Morales M. 1990. Coconino Sandstone. In: Beus SS, Morales M, editors. Grand Canyon geology. New York and Oxford: Oxford University Press, pp. 183-202; (b) Spamer EE. 1984. Paleontology in the Grand Canyon of Arizona: 125 years of lessons and enigmas from the Late Precambrian to the present. Delaware Valley Paleontological Society. The Mosasaur 2:45-128.
28. Gilmore CW. 1927. Fossil footprints from the Grand Canyon: Second contribution.

Smithsonian Miscellaneous Collections 80(3):1-78.
29. (a) Lockley MG, Hunt AP, Lucas SG. 1994. Abundant ichnofaunas from the Permian DeChelley Sandstone, northeast Arizona: implications for dunefield paleoecology. Geological Society of America Abstracts With Programs 26(7):A374; (b) Vaughn PP. 1973. Vertebrates from the Cutler Group of Monument Valley and vicinity. In: James HL, editor. Guidebook of Monument Valley and Vicinity, Arizona and Utah. New Mexico Geological Society, pp. 99-105.
30. (a) Brand LR. 1978. Footprints in the Grand Canyon. Origins 5:64-82; (b) Brand LR, Tang T. 1991. Fossil vertebrate footprints in the Coconino Sandstone (Permian) of northern Arizona: evidence for underwater origin. Geology 19:1201-1204.
31. For additional information, see: (a) Roth AA. 1988. Those gaps in the sedimentary layers. Origins 15:75-92. See also: (b) Austin SA, editor. 1994. Grand Canyon: monument to catastrophe. Santee, Calif.: Institute for Creation Research, pp. 42-45; (c) Price GM. 1923. The new geology. Mountain View, Calif.: Pacific Press Pub. Assn., pp. 620-626; (d) Rehwinkel AM. 1951. The flood in the light of the Bible, geology, and archaeology. St. Louis: Concordia Pub. House, pp. 268-272.
32. Average present regional rates for North America are more than twice as fast as the suggested figure, and for the Grand Canyon region they are more than four times as fast as the figure used. See chapter 15 for further discussion.
33. Lucchitta I. 1984. Development of landscape in northwest Arizona: the country of plateaus and canyons. In: Smiley TL, Nations JD, Péwé TL, Schafer JP, editors. 1984. Landscapes of Arizona: the geological story. Lanham, Md., and London: University Press of America, pp. 269-301.
34. See chapter 15 for a discussion of erosion rates.
35. Beus SS. 1990. Temple Butte Formation. In: Beus SS, Morales M, editors. Grand Canyon Geology. New York and Oxford: Oxford University Press, pp. 107-117.
36. Blakey RC. 1990. Supai Group and Hermit Formation. In: Beus and Morales, pp. 147-182 (note 35).
37. Based on information from: (a) Herbert C, Helby R, editors. 1980. A guide to the Sydney Basin. Department of Mineral Resources, Geological Survey of New South Wales Bulletin 26:511; (b) Pogson DJ, editor. 1972. Geological map of New South Wales, scale 1:1 million. Sydney: Geological Survey of New South Wales.
38. Newell, pp. 356, 357, 364 (note 14).
39. Newell ND. 1984. Mass extinction: unique or recurrent causes? In: Berggren WA, Van Couvering JA, editors. Catastrophes and earth history: the new uniformitarianism. Princeton, N.J.: Princeton University Press, pp. 115-127.
40. Van Andel TH. 1981. Consider the incompleteness of the geological record. Nature 294:397, 398.
41. For a more extensive discussion of these alternatives, see: Roth 1988 (note 31a).
42. Bloom AL. 1969. The surface of the earth. Englewood Cliffs, N.J.: Prentice-Hall, p. 98.
43. *Ibid.*

TIME QUESTIONS

There are few problems more fascinating than those that are bound up with the bold question: How old is the earth? With insatiable curiosity men have been trying for thousands of years to penetrate the carefully guarded secret.

—*Geologist Arthur Holmes*[1]

What is time? We all know what it is! . . . or do we? Actually it is a concept we have some difficulty in really putting our hands on. We have no special sense organ for time as we have for seeing or hearing. This permits some innovative definitions, such as: Time is nature's way of keeping everything from happening all at once; or Time is that which we like to kill but ends up killing us. Is time a reality, or is it just an abstract concept of our mind? Can time be changed? Quantum mechanics theory suggests that it can be modified by space. Has time always existed? Will it always exist? What is the meaning of eternity? If time did not always exist, what happened before it began? Such intriguing questions have no easy answers.

The vast array of contraptions we have to measure time, such as calendars, London's Big Ben, or atomic clocks, all testify to the usefulness of the time concept. It is difficult to attach meaning to our existence without considering the past, present, and future—all bound to time. While the nature of time is elusive, it appears to be real. When you rush to the train station, only to see the last train of the day departing in the distance, you tend to be impressed with the reality of time.

Time poses one of the most contentious questions between the commonly understood scientific and scriptural viewpoints. We should expect this, because the marked differences are firmly entrenched. The Bible speaks of a recent creation most likely less than 10,000 years ago, while evolution suggests the development of life for many thousands of millions of years. The difference need not be as broad as often surmised, since little in the Bible precludes a very old universe.[2] However, according to Scripture, the creation of life on earth is a relatively recent event. Has life thrived on earth for thousands of millions of years, as purported in countless textbooks of science, or has it existed for just a few thousand years, as suggested by sacred history?

The evolution of all the various forms of life needs all the time it can get for all the highly improbable events postulated,[3] and evolutionary explanations rely heavily on long ages. If you transform a lancet fish spontaneously into an elephant, it is fantasy, but if you take millions of years to do it, it is called evolution. However, several studies indicate that the very old age of the universe is far too short to encompass the improbabilities of evolution.[4] On the other hand, creation with design by an all-knowing, all-powerful God does not need extended time.[5]

Throughout history ideas about the age of earth and the universe have varied widely. Ancient Greeks and Hindus often thought in terms of numerous cycles of time. The Hebrews and early Christians believed that only a few thousand years had elapsed since creation. The concept of a recent creation also prevailed in medieval times and was strengthened by the Protestant Reformation. To Martin Luther the Bible gave the supreme account of beginnings, and the flood described in Genesis was the most powerful factor in geologic history.[6] In general, the founders of modern science believed in a recent creation around 4000 B.C. Only from the middle of the eighteenth century onward did ideas of longer periods of time begin to take root, but little serious change occurred before the nineteenth century.[7] Thereafter a slow but steady increase in the perceived age of earth[8] and the universe developed in Western thought.

The question of earth's age has been approached from many perspectives. Some early estimates,[9] based on the rate of cooling of earth's surface and the sun, gave dates typically of less than 100 million years. Other studies were based on the time required for sodium to accumulate from rivers into the ocean, assuming there was none there initially. Such calculations gave about the same age as those based on rates of cooling, while slightly older values turned up when researchers evaluated rates of sediment accumulation over the earth's surface. Early this century, study of the slow rate of disintegration of unstable radioactive elements (radiometric dating) increased the estimate of the age of earth to 2,000 to 3,000 million years, and later to 4,600 million years.[10] Typical estimates place the age of the universe around 15,000 million years, although some suggest it is twice as old,[11] and others, only half that figure.[12]

In this chapter we will consider time arguments used against a recent creation, ranging from the huge coral reefs to the minute radioactive potassium-40 and carbon-14 atoms. Space precludes covering every problem that someone has raised; however, we will consider a sufficient number of them to permit a general evaluation of the time questions. Since probably at least 100 times as many scientists are at work interpreting data within a long-ages paradigm as compared to a recent-creation paradigm, it is not surprising that many questions have been asked about a recent creation. Arguments that question the validity of the long geological ages are discussed in chapters 13 and 15.

LIVING REEFS

On a quiet moonlit night in the year 1890 the British-Indian liner *Quetta* traveled through the Torres Strait near Thursday Island, north of Australia. Located at the northern end of the Great Barrier Reef, it is the world's most widespread coral reef complex. The ship suddenly hit a reef pinnacle that ripped through most of its hull, and sank within three minutes. Nearly half of the ship's 293 passengers perished. The strait had been carefully charted between 1802 and 1860, and the crew expected no reef where the ship foundered. Some have wondered if possibly a coral reef could have grown rapidly enough between the time of sounding and 1890 to cause the tragedy.[13]

Coral reefs result from the activity of a variety of organisms that remove lime (calcium carbonate) dissolved in seawater and slowly create the largest structures on earth made by living organisms. Mollusks, foraminifera, and bryozoa can provide substantial amounts of minerals for reef growth. However, biologists consider coral and coralline algae to be the most important contributors.

The rate of coral reef growth is of considerable interest not only because reefs are potential navigational hazards but also because of questions about the amount of time required to build them. Some wonder whether such huge structures could form in a few thousand years, as implied by the biblical model.

The enormous Great Barrier Reef of Australia does not appear to pose a very serious time problem for Scripture. While it is more than 2,000 kilometers long and up to 320 kilometers offshore, drilling operations down through the reef have encountered quartz sand (a nonreef type of sediment) at less than 250 meters,[14] indicating that it is a shallow structure not requiring a vast amount of time for development. On the other hand, drilling operations on Enewetak (Eniwetok) Atoll in the Western Pacific have penetrated 1,405 meters of apparent reef material before reaching a volcanic (basalt) rock base.[15] The rates of growth assumed by most investigators would dictate that it would take at least scores of thousands to hundreds of thousands of years to form a reef this thick. Criticizing the biblical model, one author points out that the Eniwetok reef would have to grow at the rate of 140 millimeters per year to have formed in less than 10,000 years. He states: "Such rates have been shown to be quite impossible."[16]

Researchers face many problems in determining how rapidly reefs grow. The fact that some estimates are more than 500 times faster than others (Table 14.1) indicates that we know extremely little about such complex and delicate ecological systems. The sparse distribution of coral in some studies reflects less-than-ideal reef conditions. The best growth rates seem to take place a little below the surface of the ocean.[17] Reefs cannot grow above sea level, and researchers sometimes use ancient reef surfaces to determine past sea levels. Since sea level limits the growth of reefs, estimates of growth near the surface of the ocean may be strongly influenced by growth-limiting circumstances. Low tides can kill the reef-forming coral by exposing them too long to the air. Silting and pollution from land can also be detrimental. Furthermore, a number of present-day reefs are now dying or dead.[18] Less-polluted conditions when earth was not so populated could have favored more rapid growth of the delicate organisms that build reefs.

One must also remember that coral reef growth ceases below a certain depth because of lack of light. Therefore, scientists assume that the volcanic base of Eniwetok Atoll, now 1,405 meters below sea level, would have been near sea level when coral growth began on its surface. The base gradually subsided, and coral growth kept up with this.

Some of my graduate students and I have studied reef-building organisms of Eniwetok and several other reef localities to determine how various environmental factors affect growth. A moderate rise in temperature of a few degrees favors more rapid growth, while ultraviolet light at the ocean surface inhibits

---

* References for the section entitled "Estimates of Rates of Reef Growth" are: (a) Adey WH. 1978. Coral reef morphogenesis: a multidimensional model. Science 202:831-837; (b) Chave KE, Smith SV, Roy KJ. 1972. Carbonate production by coral reefs. Marine Geology 12:123-140; (c) Davies PJ, Hopley D. 1983. Growth fabrics and growth rates of Holocene reefs in the Great Barrier Reef. BMR Journal of Australian Geology and Geophysics 8:237-251; (d) Hubbard, Miller, and Scaturo (note 17); (e) Odum HT, Odum EP. 1955. Tropic structure and productivity of a windward coral reef community on Eniwetok Atoll. Ecological Monographs 25(3):291-320; (f) Sewell RBS. 1935. Studies on coral and coral formations in Indian waters. Geographic and oceanographic research in Indian waters, No. 8. Memoirs of the Asiatic Society of Bengal 9:461-539; (g) Smith SV, Kinsey DW. 1976. Calcium carbonate production, coral reef growth, and sea level change. Science 194:937-939; (h) Smith SV, Harrison JT. 1977. Calcium carbonate production of the *Mare Incognitum,* the upper windward reef slope, at Eniwetok Atoll. Science 197:556-559; (i) Verstelle (note 21). References for the section entitled "Maximum Growth Rate of Coral Reef Frame Builders" are: (j) Earle SA. 1976. Life springs from death in Truk Lagoon. National Geographic 149(5):578-613; (k) Gladfelter EH, Monahan RK, Gladfelter WB. 1978. Growth rates of five reef-building corals in the northeastern Caribbean. Bulletin of Marine Science 28:728-734; (l) Gladfelter EH. 1984. Skeletal development in *Acropora cervicornis.* III. A comparison of monthly rates of linear extension and calcium carbonate accretion measured over a year. Coral Reefs 3:51-57; (m) Lewis, Axelsen, Goodbody, Page, and Chislett (note 22b); (n) Shinn (note 20); (o) Tamura T, Hada Y. 1932. Growth rate of reef-building corals, inhabiting in the South Sea Island. Scientific Report of the Tôhoku Imperial University 7(4):433-455. The calculations for their research were reported by: Buddemeier and Kinzie (note 22a). →

TABLE 14.1

ESTIMATES OF RATES OF REEF GROWTH

METHOD OF EVALUATION	*RATE (MILLIMETERS/YEAR)*	*YEARS TO GROW A 1,400-METER REEF*	*AUTHOR(S) (DATE)*
Carbon-14 dating	6 -15	233,000 -93,300	Adey (1978)
Coral growth and potential estimate	0.9 -74	1,550,000 -18,900	Chave et al. (1972)
Carbon-14 dating	1 ->20	1,400,000 -<70,000	Davies and Hopley (1983)
Growth rings (and maximum)	0.7 (3.3)	2,000,000 -424,000	Hubbard et al. (1990)
Potential estimate	80	17,500	Odum and Odum (1955)
Soundings	280	5,000	Sewell (1935)
CO_2 system	2 -5	700,000 -280,000	Smith and Kinsey (1976)
CO_2 system	0.8 -1.1	1,750,000 -1,270,000	Smith and Harrison (1977)
Soundings	414	3,380	Verstelle (1932)

MAXIMUM GROWTH RATE OF CORAL REEF FRAME BUILDERS

SPECIES	*RATE (MILLIMETERS/YEAR)*	*YEARS TO GROW A 1,400-METER REEF*	*AUTHOR(S) (DATE)*
Antipathes sp	143	9,790	Earle (1976)
Acropora palmata	99	14,100	Gladfelter et al. (1978)
Acropora cervicornis	120	11,700	Gladfelter (1984)
Acropora cervicornis	264 -432	5,300 -3,240	Lewis et al. (1968)
Acropora cervicornis	100	14,000	Shinn (1976)
Acropora pucchra	226	6,190	Tamura and Hada (1932)

SOME MEASUREMENTS ON CORAL REEF GROWTH
(See references on page 236.*)

growth.[19] These and other factors can significantly affect rates of reef growth. While some of the hard "brain"-shaped coral and coralline algae grow slowly, the branching forms develop rapidly. A dense concentration (Figure 14.1) of healthy branching coral growing at optimal rates (second part of Table 14.1) could create rapid reef growth. Many corals frequently form branches above each other, compounding production rates. The potential is impressive, 10 branches each growing at the rate of 100 millimeters per year and subdividing into three branches each year would result in a total of 59 kilometers of single branches in 10 years.[20]

A number of investigators have studied rates of coral and coral reef growth. Some estimates appear in Table 14.1. The top section, entitled "Rates of Reef Growth," derives from observations of reefs as a whole, while the section entitled "Maximum Rate of Coral Reef Frame Builders" represents the fastest rate of growth of those corals that could provide a physical framework for the reef. This framework would also offer protection for other smaller reef-building organisms as well as serving for the entrapment of water-transported sediments. Note that the fastest rates for reefs[21] and for framebuilders[22] do allow for the

FIGURE 14.1

Reef coral growing on top of a pinnacle in the lagoon of Eniwetok Atoll, Marshall Islands. The highest corals are about 7 meters below the surface of the ocean.

growth of the Eniwetok reef, which has a thickness of 1,405 meters, in less than 3,400 years. These fastest rates for reefs are based on soundings, which are the most direct and simple measurements and are probably more reliable than the less-direct methods that give slower growth rates. Such data indicate that the rate of coral reef growth does not present as great a challenge to the biblical concept of creation a few thousand years ago as is sometimes claimed.

DAILY GROWTH LINES IN CORAL

Some coral produce daily growth lines as they grow. These lines form seasonal patterns that have been used to infer an ancient age for the coral. Some authors have noted that Devonian corals, assumed to have grown some 375 million years ago, show 400 daily growth lines per year. This is interpreted as evidence that earth rotated faster in the past.[23] Calculations also suggest it took several hundred million years for the earth to slow down to its present rate of about 365 days per year. However, the whole argument involves considerable uncertainty. Counting growth lines in coral is quite subjective, because they are often ill-defined. Some individuals will find twice as many as others on the same sample.[24] Also, environmental factors such as depth affect the number of growth lines formed.[25]

FOSSIL REEFS

Besides the living reefs discussed above, fossil reefs occur in earth's sedimentary layers. A well-known fossil reef,[26] the Nubrygin reef complex, is located inland near the village of Stewart Town in eastern Australia. Instead of being formed by coral, this reef has been built by algae. It is classified as Devonian with an assumed age of about 400 million years. In the arrangement of the layers of the geologic column, many fossil layers lie below and many above the Devonian. In other words, this reef lies well-entrenched in the midst of earth's fossiliferous layers. Because it takes a long time to develop a reef, such a fossil reef could not have grown during the year of the biblical flood. This is important to the question of whether the fossil record represents life developing over many millions of years, or if it resulted mainly from the Genesis flood following a recent creation.

When I first viewed the Nubrygin reef, I was surprised. This widely known example of an algal reef complex did not resemble a reeflike structure. It was a mixture of pieces of broken fossil algae and nonreeflike types of rocks literally floating in a matrix of fine sediments. I understood why some researchers had recently decided that it was a debris flow and not a reef.[27] Since debris flows can form rapidly, this so-called reef can no longer be considered an argument against the short time proposed by the biblical model of origins. However, a single example does not settle the question of time and reefs, since the scientific literature describes hundreds of other fossil reefs. Field investigators have reported them throughout the geologic column from the Precambrian upward.[28] With notable exceptions, these fossil reefs are usually very small compared to present living reefs, but if each of them grew as a true reef, they would collectively represent at least scores of thousands of years.

Authenticating fossil reefs requires overcoming many problems, reflected even in the confused definition of a reef. A true reef represents the slow buildup by marine organisms of a wave-resistant structure. Many so-called fossil reefs appear to be only an accumulation of sediments swept in by water, and could have formed rapidly.

One report describes a number of fossil "reefs" that researchers now reinterpret as rapidly accumulating debris flows,[29] and the classic fossil Steinplatte Reef of the Austrian Alps has been described as a "sandpile."[30] Some specialists in sedimentology point out that "closer inspection of many of these ancient carbonate 'reefs' reveals that they are composed largely of carbonate mud with the larger skeletal particles 'floating' within the mud matrix. Conclusive evidence for a rigid organic framework does not exist in most of the ancient carbonate mounds. In this sense, they are remarkably different from modern coral-algal reefs."[31] Skeletal particles floating in a mud matrix would likely have been deposited rapidly. Other investigators "have expressed frustration at using modern reefs to interpret their ancient counterparts."[32]

Researchers sometimes seek to determine whether an ancient "reef" represents an authentic biological entity by analyzing the orientation of its fossil components. If the corals are in an upright (growth) position, they assume that they have grown where found. The usual nonquantitative remarks about orientation in the scientific literature mean little, since transport of reef material could result in some components ending up in almost any position. A quantitative study has shown that in some fossil reefs the preferred orientation of reef-producing components is upward as expected if in position of growth.[33] Such data do not preclude the transport and deposition during catastrophes of massive reef cores formed earlier. Geologists sometimes report the transport of blocks of reef material, and in the Austrian Alps huge layers of sediments containing suggested fossil reefs have been thrust over other sedimentary layers for many hundreds of kilometers as the Alps formed.[34]

If fossil reefs represent transported units, the question of time for their formation at their present location in the geologic column becomes less significant. In the context of biblical history, the formation of some reefs between creation and the flood followed by their transport during the upheaval of the flood is plausible. Transport scenarios are not at all restricted to models of the flood, however. When we take into account the new trends in geological interpretations toward catastrophism and the movement of continents over earth's surface, the movement of a small reef is not that dramatic.

Also we need to consider that there could be fossil reefs that grew between creation and the flood and did not get transported elsewhere. They are still located in the surroundings where they grew. Reefs located on basement (Precambrian) rocks may especially fit such an interpretation.

As we examine the interpretations of both living and fossil reefs, the abundance of conjecture should impress us. While at present many coral reefs appear to grow slowly, others form rapidly. And while it has not been established that all ancient fossil "reefs" are the result of rapid transport, their identification as in situ structures is often questionable. Our present knowledge indicates that the reef-time question is not a good challenge to a recent creation.

DINOSAUR NESTS IN THE FOSSIL RECORD

Since creationists propose that most of the geologic column was deposited during the year of the Genesis flood, they should not expect to find there evidence of any processes that would require longer periods of time. A pertinent question is the presence of dinosaur egg nests in the fossil record, sometimes in superimposed layers. Each nest level is assumed to represent at least one year.

Paleontologists have reported groups of dinosaur eggs, likely representing nests, from a variety of places, including North and South America, Mongolia, China, India, France, and Spain.[35] An outstanding example is in Montana, where John Horner of the Museum of the Rockies at Montana State University has described at least 10 dinosaur egg nests,[36] each with from two to 24 eggs. One nest had carefully arranged, vertically oriented eggs. The nests occupy three levels within a vertical distance of three meters. Abundant fragments of eggs and other nests have been found in the vicinity. One nest had skeletal remains of embryos in the eggs. Hatchlings and young dinosaurs were also found, and one "nest" held 11 small dinosaurs about one meter in length, about three times the size of a hatchling.

The dinosaur nests occur in Cretaceous sediments, which most creationists would interpret as having been deposited during the Genesis flood. What should the creationist do with this evidence of slow, "normal" reproductive behavior located well within the geologic column? Some alternatives follow, but any discussion of dinosaur nests remains highly conjectural.

First, some caution in identifying dinosaur nests seems warranted. A nest made of sediments and covered with more sediment is not that distinctive. Just finding a few eggs in close proximity may not represent a nest, although this is often inferred. There may be significantly fewer nests than claimed. However, several nests with well-arranged eggs seem unquestionably genuine. In some localities we find widely distributed dinosaur eggshell fragments or even entire eggs, but these could have originated from eggs laid before the flood and may not represent the potential time problem posed by nests.

Some creationists have suggested that the nests could have been formed soon after the flood,[37] but their location in the geologic column may pose a problem. A highly important portion of the geologic column (the Cenozoic) lies above the layers containing the nests. For creationists who propose that part of the Cenozoic belongs to the flood, this approach really offers no solution.

The situation in Montana seems unusual and might be an isolated case, since developing dinosaurs in eggs are scarce over much of the rest of the world.[38] We could suggest some reinterpretation. For instance, a nest containing 12-15 juvenile dinosaurs (each being one meter in size) may reflect gregarious crisis behavior under catastrophic conditions, instead of the suggestion that they died of starvation. To just sit there and die seems unusual. The juveniles show no sign of predation—nothing had tried to eat them.[39] In Mongolia the discovery of a dinosaur preserved in apparent brooding position over about 22 eggs is a puzzling find[40] that might also reflect stress and catastrophic burial conditions.

We would expect that dinosaurs would lay some eggs during the months of the rising waters of the flood. Some dinosaurs are estimated to have laid as many as 100 eggs per year.[41] However, is it possible for advanced embryos or early juveniles, occasionally found in these nests, to form in, at best, several weeks during one event such as the Genesis flood? We would expect some development in the eggs after they were laid, and development might also take place before the mother dinosaur deposited them. Also some dinosaurs may have even been born alive. Certain lizards and snakes retain their embryos for development and protection. The alligator lizard along the West Coast of the United States lays eggs in the south, but farther north a similar species retains the embryos within thin membranes in the body of the female until their development is complete. Another species of lizard in Australia lays eggs in some regions, gives live birth in others, and retains embryos and provides incomplete shells in another locality.[42] Such examples suggest that retention of embryos for development may be an easy adaptation in reptiles. A dinosaur egg found in the Cleveland-Lloyd Dinosaur Quarry in Utah, containing a probable embryo, had a double shell attributed to retention in the oviduct of the female during stress.[43] Furthermore, dinosaur fossils often occur in groups. Is it possible that a group of them laid nests on top of each other as a series of deluge storms buried lower levels? A set of eggs could be laid quickly.

Dinosaur eggs exhibit several other puzzling facts. While most dinosaur eggs appear normal, pathological (abnormal) eggs occur in several regions, notably France, India, Argentina, and China.[44] A common abnormality is the double shell, attributed to unintentional retention of the egg by the female during egg production. Birds produce abnormal eggs when under stress or when ill, and some dinosaurs are thought to have important similarities with birds.[45] Until we can deduce more about dinosaur reproductive physiology, especially when under stress, as would be expected during the flood, we must be cautious in interpreting the evidence for dinosaur nests.

It might be significant that most of these eggs and nests occur in the restricted upper portion of the Cretaceous part of the geologic column,[46] while adult dinosaurs appear throughout the Mesozoic (see Figure 10.1 for terminology). Why aren't the nests distributed equally with the adults? Could the dinosaurs have laid their eggs during a quieter period (upper Cretaceous) of the Genesis flood, even allowing time in some places for some development? But why are developing embryos so rare in dinosaur eggs? From an evolutionary perspective one would expect that random catastrophic preservation events over geologic time would catch dinosaur embryos in many stages of development. In a creation context, the Genesis flood may provide an answer to this enigma. The flood may have interrupted embryo development soon after the eggs were laid.

Another surprise is the presence of protein in dinosaur eggs.[47] Researchers consider this "rather remarkable because they [proteins] are not very stable chemically."[48] Evolutionists assume the eggs have been laid some 60 million years ago. We would expect chemical degradation during such a long time period, especially as ground water filtered through the sediments surrounding the eggs. Possibly the eggs are not that old.

While dinosaur nests might seem to pose a problem through their deposition during the year of the flood, the various anomalies mentioned above raise interesting questions about standard "normal" interpretations. Furthermore, the fact that such nests are buried may reflect the kind of catastrophic conditions we should expect during the Genesis flood.

WORM TUBES

Some rocks contain fossil "worm tubes" and animal burrows. They are tube-like structures produced by a variety of organisms, including worms, or by the escape of fluids or gases from the sediments. Their formation by living organisms requires some time and has been considered a problem for a flood model. Actually, we should expect to find abundant evidence of biological activity by living organisms during the year of the flood. To challenge the flood model seriously, one should propose factors that would take longer than a few months to a year. Organisms can produce burrows as rapidly as 1,000 centimeters per hour, although the usual rate is much slower.[49]

Biological activity can occur so rapidly that in shallow marine environments the lack of such evidence may indicate rapid formation of some sedimentary layers. Once I lived on the floor of the ocean close to the coral reef organisms that I was studying. I was working at a depth of 15 meters, using the underwater Hydro-Lab then located in the Bahamas. One night I could not sleep because of a storm severe enough to rock our underwater laboratory. The next morning, to my surprise, I noted that the storm had left a neat pattern of ripple marks all over the sandy floor of the ocean. Three days later fish, crabs, clams, snails, and worms, which persistently forage on the sand, had erased the pattern. Researchers have reported this process of destruction to occur in two to four weeks in the Virgin Islands.[50] Such observations indicate that, given any significant time, fine layers will not survive the presence of foraging organisms and worm tubes. Because we find such structures frequently preserved in ancient layers of marine deposits, it suggests that they must have been buried rapidly enough to have avoided destruction by a variety of organisms.

LAMINAE

Another time question sometimes raised regarding a recent creation is the multitude of fine layers in earth's sedimentary layers. Commonly less than a millimeter thick and called laminae, the layers usually consist of sediments that gradually change from coarse to fine as one goes from the bottom to the top of each lamina, or they may be composed of two parts, such as a layer of fine, plain sediments coupled to a layer rich in organic matter. A lamina interpreted to have taken one year to form is called a "varve." Since the actual formation time is debatable, we shall use the less-restrictive term *lamina* in this discussion.

Investigators have reported about several million laminae in the fossil-fish-bearing Green River Formation of Wyoming. If, as is often interpreted, each layer took one year to form, we cannot reconcile the implied millions of years to a recent creation. Some lakes contain deposits of many thousands of laminae. Sometimes researchers have correlated the laminae of several ancient lakes with each other by matching the patterns of the varying thicknesses of the layers. Such correlations have sometimes resulted in combined sequences interpreted to be tens of thousands of years old. They also challenge the concept of a recent creation a few thousand years ago.

On the other hand, several studies challenge the interpretation that laminae represent annual events. Analysis of recent sedimentation in the Walensee of Switzerland reveals that on an average two laminae develop per year, while in some years as many as five laminae are deposited.[51] Another study counted the number of laminae between two widespread volcanic ash layers of the Green River Formation of Wyoming. If they represented annual events, we would expect the same number in different localities, yet the number between the two same ash layers varied in different localities from 1,089 to 1,566.[52] A 12-hour flood in Colorado deposited more than 100 laminae.[53] Field observations and laboratory experiments suggest they can form in as little as a few minutes, seconds, or almost instantaneously.[54] Other experiments also show that sediments can sort themselves into laminae at the rate of several per second.[55] However, some laminae are thought to form differently by a settling process in quiet water and not by lateral transport. Even here experiments suggest that several laminae can form in a few hours during a single sediment-suspension settling event.[56] While such rapid rates do not demonstrate the deposition of millions of layers of the Green River Formation within a creation time frame, they do indicate alternatives to the long ages proposed for such formations. Geology needs comprehensive experimentation along these lines.

Problems arise when we attempt to correlate the laminae from different localities.[57] Both in Sweden and in North America extensive studies attempting to combine sequences of a few hundred laminae, many of them considered to be annual glacial varves, have run into trouble. A suggested combined chronology of 28,000 years for North America underwent reinterpretation to little more than 10,000 years when rechecked with carbon-14 dating.[58]

Another lamina-related question challenging a recent creation involves the extensive lists of sometimes more than 30 carbon-14 dates that generally increase with depth through the lamina.[59] The lamina and carbon-14 dates sometimes extend to 10,000-13,000 years. But there are problems with the lamina-carbon-14 correlation, including: (1) The laminae are usually considered more reliable than the carbon-14 dates, and researchers use them to correct the carbon-14 dates—the two systems do not give the same results. (2)

Serious difficulties arise in counting the laminae, with sections sometimes assumed to be missing or found to be undefined, and some of the laminae are so fine that it is difficult to identify them; thus different investigators report different numbers. (3) Researchers acknowledge some selection of carbon-14 dates.[60] Until we have more and better examples, we must remain cautious.

SUCCESSIVE FOSSIL FORESTS

Questions sometimes arise about the time required to grow successive "fossil forests." With many trees in an upright position, several such forests can be found one on top of the other. The successive fossil forests in Yellowstone National Park would appear to have required tens of thousands of years to grow and be buried. However, some data indicate rapid volcanic activity for the burial of this entire fossil forest series,[61] and a number of sedimentary features of the Yellowstone deposits suggest that the fossil trees were not in a normal growing environment.[62] Also, thousands of trees floated upright in Spirit Lake after the 1980 volcanic explosion of Mount St. Helens in the state of Washington.[63] Such discoveries can suggest rapid burial of upright trees associated with the water and volcanic activity of the Genesis flood, instead of the slow growth of successive forests.

OTHER TIME QUESTIONS

Some question how rapidly trees can petrify, how rapidly coal can form, and how rapidly earth's magnetic field can reverse itself. Trees can petrify in a few years.[64] Under the right circumstances, especially higher temperatures, coal can form within a few hours to years,[65] and it has been proposed that major magnetic changes can occur within months or days.[66] One investigator suggests complete reversal within a day. On the basis of our present knowledge, these time questions do not appear to pose serious challenges for a recent-creation model.

THE CARBON-14 DATING SYSTEM

The slow rate of disintegration of some unstable radioactive elements has become the basis for several dating methods. Several hundred thousand age determinations based on this have been published.[67] While many of the dates conflict with standard geological interpretations,[68] many of them agree and are worthy of serious attention. We will consider very briefly two commonly used systems. In this section we examine carbon-14; potassium-argon will be discussed in the next.

How can atoms of carbon-14 (^{14}C) indicate how old a bone is? The basic principle is fairly simple. Carbon-14 is an unstable substance found in bone and other living materials that slowly changes to nitrogen-14. As a bone becomes older, the amount of ^{14}C remaining decreases. Thus the less ^{14}C left in the bone, the older it is. Carbon-14 dating, also called radiocarbon dating, is especially useful for remains of organic matter, such as wood and shells, that have a representative sample of carbon. The method can be used also for lime deposits, and even impure water, when the researcher accepts special assumptions.

Plants obtain their carbon mainly from atmospheric carbon dioxide which has an extremely small proportion of ^{14}C. When animals eat plants, they incorporate this same proportion of ^{14}C into their bodies. Such ^{14}C is radioactive and disintegrates at an average rate of 13.6 atoms per minute for each gram of total carbon. The average person has around 170,000 atoms of ^{14}C disintegrating in his or her body each minute. The proportion of ^{14}C stays the same throughout our lifetime, since we constantly replace carbon from the food we eat. When an organism dies, its body no longer acquires new carbon, and the proportion of ^{14}C begins to decrease. In about 5,730 years half of the ^{14}C atoms will have disintegrated, and in another 5,730 years half of the remaining ^{14}C atoms left will have changed into nitrogen, leaving one fourth the original amount. Hence, the less ^{14}C, the older the sample. Because of constraints in measuring the rare ^{14}C atoms and because of problems of contamination that become quite severe at low levels of ^{14}C in older samples, the method is hardly useful beyond 40,000 to 50,000 years.[69]

While ^{14}C dating seems simple enough, and dating to a few thousand years back often gives expected results, actually there are many complications. For instance some aquatic mosses now living in Iceland date around 6,000 to 8,000 years by the ^{14}C method.[70] Living snails in Nevada give apparent ages of 27,000 years,[71] and most living marine specimens from the world's oceans date at least several hundred years old.[72] Such examples illustrate what is sometimes called the "reservoir effect," which is probably the most serious problem ^{14}C dating faces. The reason that some living examples have an unreasonable ^{14}C age is that their environment has less than the normal amount of ^{14}C, so they "date" old even before they are dead. Other anomalies probably result from other factors, such as the exchange of ^{14}C atoms with other forms of carbon. For instance, the scalp muscle of a frozen musk ox from Alaska gave a ^{14}C age of 24,140 years, while its hair dated at 17,210 years.[73] Marine shells in Hawaii register younger dates if preserved in volcanic ash instead of limestone.[74]

To determine a ^{14}C date, one has to know what the proportion of ^{14}C was at the time of its incorporation into the organism being tested. Can we be sure that this proportion, especially that of the atmosphere, which provides carbon to organisms, has been sufficiently constant in the past to warrant confidence in the method? All agree that there is significant evidence of change. Creationists suggest major changes, while noncreationists attempt to correct for smaller discrepancies.

Still other less severe problems face ^{14}C dating. Soils are notoriously difficult to date[75] because of upward and downward migration of organic substances. Organisms select ^{12}C in preference to ^{14}C (fractionation—in biochemical activity), though the researcher can easily correct for this problem by fairly simple calculations. Nuclear explosions increase the ^{14}C concentration, while the Industrial Revolution has diluted ^{14}C by adding less radioactive carbon from fossil fuels to the atmosphere. Again we can also easily correct for these difficulties. However, these examples illustrate how readily changes in the environment can affect the data. Because of several possible uncertainties, "it is not surprising that some archaeologists throw up their hands in despair"[76] at the method. While ^{14}C dating has many problems, it survives because no simpler method seems more reliable for dating within the past 50,000 years. We can illustrate the difficulty of dating in this period by the dating of 11 early North American human skeletons. Early published dates based on several dating methods averaged more than 28,000 years. Reinvestigation produced revised dates that averaged less than 4,000 years, but the revised dates have also been challenged.[77]

Some discrepancy exists between ^{14}C dates and other time clocks. Willard F. Libby, who received the Nobel Prize for developing the ^{14}C dating system, noted some years ago the difference between the age of trees based on their annual growth rings and that obtained by ^{14}C. In order to correct for this, he suggested that trees sometimes produce more than one growth ring per year.[78] His idea has not prevailed, and at present researchers generally accept that ^{14}C is in error and that tree rings are a more accurate measurement of time. A number of lists have been published, indicating how to convert ^{14}C dates to what is considered real time based mainly on tree rings.[79] The discrepancy is usually less than 10 percent. During the past 3,000 years the difference is especially small, although tree rings around A.D. 600 date 150 years too old when dated by ^{14}C; by 2000 B.C. they date 300 years too young. We do not have living trees that go back to 3000 B.C.,[80] and beyond that the plot thickens considerably.

Samples of subfossil wood dated by tree-ring correlation at around 9000 B.C. are interpreted to date as much as 1,200 years too young by ^{14}C. However, determining the age of a wood sample of this age by correlating tree rings is problematic. It is usually done by trying to match series of tree-ring patterns marked by irregularities caused by changing environmental factors, such as the amount of rainfall. If the patterns of two pieces of wood match, it is assumed that the rings grew at the same time. Matching tree rings is often difficult and subjective. Sometimes the rings do not show enough variation to be useful, or two series of rings may show equally convincing matchings at several places, only one of which can be correct. One sample of Douglas fir matched at 113 places, grouped in 10 different regions, when compared by a simple statistical test to its master tree-ring chronology.[81] Statistical methods to correct for this problem are being developed, but the bristlecone pine and European oak tree-ring chronologies that form the backbone for ^{14}C corrections have been respectively characterized by some statisticians as "suspect" and as containing "spurious correlations."[82]

The calibration of ^{14}C dates also struggles with a problem of missing rings.[83] C. W. Ferguson at the tree-ring laboratory at the University of Arizona developed the basic tree-ring chronology for ^{14}C dating employing the bristlecone pines of the White Mountains of California. He used dead wood found in the area to extend beyond the living tree ring chronology by matching tree rings. However, sometimes 10 percent of the rings appear to be missing.[84] Furthermore, he points out: "I often am unable to date specimens with one or two thousand rings against a 7500-year master chronology, even with a 'ballpark' placement provided by a radiocarbon date." The fact that Ferguson never published the raw data for his master chronology has cast a pall over its validity. In Europe the use of ancient oak and pine specimens, stretching the chronology to more than 9000 B.C., has also proved difficult. Even though researchers have studied more than 5,000 specimens and ^{14}C dating is also used to assist in matching,[85] the results are not certain.[86] Individual specimens usually cover only a few centuries at best, and it requires many matches, which are often difficult to make, to calibrate the counts back to 9000 B.C. The matching between the oak and pine chronologies by those who have done it is characterized as "tentative."[87]

Furthermore, dating has an element of circular reasoning when it first uses ^{14}C to date the specimens, then after matching them, using that match as a basis for a refined calibration of the ^{14}C method. That procedure tends to question the argument that tree rings corroborate ^{14}C dating. One would have more confidence in the proposed corrections if the tree ring matchings were done completely independently. Proposed ^{14}C dating corrections reflect a general pattern of younger ^{14}C dates (more ^{14}C) compared to tree rings, especially in older specimens. The variations about the general trend are such[88] that in some cases a single ^{14}C date can give three or more different calibrated dates.[89] There have been attempts to extend the correction of ^{14}C dating to 30,000 years using thorium-230/uranium-234 dating system on corals.[90] Differences of a thousand years in both directions obtained by other investigators[91] make such calibrations somewhat unconvincing. The currently accepted system for correcting ^{14}C data appears to be a fragile structure.

Some of the ^{14}C data are obviously selected. A series of ^{14}C dates obtained for progressively deeper organic soil layers in New Zealand's South Island sediments gave the sequence of 9,900, 12,000, 27,200, 17,300, and 15,650 ^{14}C years.[92] A subsequent publication removed the obviously anomalous younger 17,300 and 15,650 determinations found for material below the older date of 27,200.[93] This kind of "purification" is done openly and in all honesty, because the investigators trust the assumptions of the dating system. However, in the above case we might wonder if some of the factors considered responsible for anomalies in the lower parts of the sequence may not also be cause for concern about accepting the other dates.

The biblical account of beginnings implies an origin of life a few thousand years ago. Carbon-14 dating has produced many dates back beyond that time. A number of them are in ordered sequence as mentioned above for laminae. There are alternative explanations for such dating sequences. The worldwide flood described in Genesis would unquestionably cause a major change in the carbon cycle of our planet. Creationists have generally assumed that a lower concentration of ^{14}C existed in the atmosphere and plants before that flood. Such an assumption agrees with the extremely low proportion of ^{14}C in coal and oil. Creationists then suggest that *gradual* adjustments after that catastrophe have produced a slow increase in ^{14}C.[94] The gradual rise for some 1,000-2,000 years after the flood could produce the older dates and sequences found in lamina and other deposits. Factors proposed by creationists for changes in the concentration of ^{14}C include some of the same explanations used by noncreationists for ^{14}C anomalies. We should make special mention of: (1) a larger carbon reservoir diluting ^{14}C before the flood; (2) a stronger magnetic field before the flood, deflecting the cosmic rays that produce the ^{14}C; (3) a rate of mixing of ^{14}C into the oceans after the flood that would affect both atmospheric and oceanic concentrations of ^{14}C; and (4) change in the intensity of the source of cosmic rays that create the ^{14}C.[95]

Both creationists and those who believe life developed over long ages assume different conditions in the past to explain and adjust the raw data of ^{14}C dating. The distinction is in the kind of changes envisioned and especially the rate of such changes. Because of the Genesis flood, the creationist postulates both major and rapid shifts in ^{14}C concentration.

THE POTASSIUM-ARGON DATING SYSTEM

Scientists use carbon-14 dating mainly to date the remains of living organisms. They employ several other systems for the rocks, the most prominent of which is potassium-argon (K-Ar). This system was particularly important in establishing the presently accepted general timescale of the geologic column.

It is helpful to keep in mind that the age of the rocks and that of the fossil organisms found in them can be quite different. If a person is buried in a cave, his remains will, of course, be younger—much younger—than the rocks forming the cave. Similarly, the age of the rocks need not in any way represent the age of fossils found in them, unless we can demonstrate that both formed at about the same time, as may occur during the explosion of a volcano.

Like ^{14}C dating, the basic principle of K-Ar dating is simple.[96] A portion of potassium-40 (^{40}K) changes extremely slowly to the gas argon-40 (^{40}Ar). By comparing the amount of ^{40}K with the ^{40}Ar in a rock, we can calculate how old it is. The more ^{40}Ar, the older it dates.[97] This system works for much older dates than ^{14}C. Half of the ^{40}K atoms will decay in about 1,280 million years. Only a few minerals, some fine-grained igneous rocks, and a few sediments, can be easily dated by this method.

There are a number of problems with the K-Ar dating technique. Because argon is a noble gas that remains chemically free, it can easily move in and out of a system whose age we are seeking to determine. Especially troublesome is the excess argon found in deeply buried rocks. Molten rock from earth's interior can carry this excess argon and cause anomalously old dates. For instance, a lava flow in Hawaii historically dated at 1801 A.D. gives a date of 1.1 million years by the K-Ar method.[98] Similarly, lava flows from Rangitoto volcano in New Zealand contain wood that registers ^{14}C dates of less than 1,000 years, while the lava provides K-Ar dates of several hundred thousand years.[99] Data from diamonds using a more sophisticated "isochron" method of analysis come up with an age of 6,000 million years,[100] which is 1,400 million years older than the generally accepted age of the earth. Researchers attribute these anomalies and many more to excess argon.

Because the argon gas can also easily escape, K-Ar dates may be anomalously young. Gunter Faure, a specialist in this area, lists seven different factors that might cause the escape of argon.[101] Researchers in the field believe that heat and breakdown of the rock due to pressure, such as occurs in the processes of mountain building, are frequent contributing factors. Although they sometimes employ the K-Ar method to date episodes of mountain building, they have to be reasonably confident that all previous argon has escaped. Loss or gain of potassium from the dating system is also considered a possible cause of anomalous dates.

Despite the potential for error, many published sequences of dates appear to agree with generally accepted geological ages. While there is no shortage of dates that do not match, creationists also need to consider the numerous dates that do agree.[102] The scientific literature acknowledges selection of dates. One scientist points out: "In conventional interpretation of K-Ar age data, it is common to discard ages which are substantially too high or too low compared with the rest of the group or with other available data such as the geological timescale."[103] He suggests using the more complex isochron determination to alleviate discrepancies. In advocating analysis of individual minerals so as to give more precise information, another scientist states: "In general, dates in the 'correct ballpark' are assumed to be correct and are published, but those in disagreement with other data are seldom published nor are discrepancies fully explained."[104] Despite this cloud of uncertainty over the method, it still seems to me that creationists should address the question of the dates that agree with the standard geologic timescale. Noncreationists freely propose explanations for dates anomalous to their model, and creationists are entitled to the same privilege. Some tentative suggestions based on scientific findings for reconciling K-Ar sequences to a recent creation follow.

1. The pressure of overlying water may prevent excess argon from escaping from deep rocks. Rocks in the deep ocean can contain high gas concentrations because of the hydrostatic pressure of the overlying water. Sometimes these gases cause rocks to explode when brought to the surface. In one instance the "popping rocks," obtained from a depth of 2,490 meters, kept exploding for three days after reaching the surface. Some fragments hurled up as high as one meter.[105] A similar pressure effect has been suggested for lava flowing into the ocean off the coast of Hawaii. The samples, considered to be only a few thousand years old, contain excess argon. They show a general trend in increasing K-Ar dates with depth. Some samples from these recent flows dated as old as 19.5 million years at a depth of 5,000 meters.[106] Researchers attributed the apparent increase in age with depth to the effect of the increasing hydrostatic pressure of the overlying water. One might wonder whether the hydrostatic pressure caused by the waters of the flood could result in sequences of increasing dates with depth.

2. Excess argon could come from earth's deep mantle. Some minerals from the lower parts of the geologic column contain extra amounts of both helium and argon.[107] One sample had more than 1,000 times the argon that would have

decayed from its potassium in 2,750 million years. Interestingly, the excess of both argon and helium was greatest with samples from the lowest parts of the geologic column, and researchers attributed it to transfer of these gases from earth's deeper mantle. Could a transfer process function during a worldwide flood and contribute to a sequence of dates running from old to young as one goes from deeper to shallower rocks?

3. Some features of volcanic activity could produce sequences of dates. Sometimes one finds a rise in the temperature of the extruded lava as a volcano continues to erupt.[108] It is also known that heat favors the expulsion of excess argon from molten lava.[109] Both factors operating together could create an ascending sequence of decreasing K-Ar dates in volcanic deposits, at least in a local region. The first-erupted and cooler lava forming the lower layers would retain more excess argon and would yield an older age.

A number of other dating systems are based on radioactive decay rates, each with their own peculiarities. When different systems give similar ages for a sample, some may point to them as evidence against a recent creation. One exceptional example is Asuka, a meteorite found in Antarctica that presumably came from the moon. Five different dating systems applied to this meteorite gave ages reported to vary only from 3,798 to 3,940 million years.[110] While such congruence is unusual, it does seem to validate some of the basic principles of radiometric dating, such as the constancy of decay rates. However, we should not ignore the many other modifying factors as illustrated earlier for the K-Ar method. For samples of obvious terrestrial origin, some of which are associated with fossils, we can often find both congruence and disparity between methods. Some creationists explain the older radiometric dates, which range in millions of years, as evidence that the matter of earth (not life on earth) and the moon, including Asuka, might have existed for a long time before creation week.[111] Such dates might only represent old rocks, or reworked products from the old rocks. We would expect the events of the flood to recycle (redeposit) a multitude of old rocks to form newer ones. For the creationist who believes that God created the inorganic matter of earth only recently, the best explanation may be proposing that the rate of radioactive decay may have changed. But the scientific data referring to any such a change is minimal and suggests only slight shifts.

In summary, radiometric dating methods as illustrated by ^{14}C and K-Ar are complex and influenced by a variety of factors. The confidence in such dates that we find in the popular literature and in basic science textbooks soon dissipates on examination of the research literature.[112] The abundance of anomalous and/or especially old dates reported poses problems that both noncreationists and creationists resolve by invoking various modifying factors. Creationists especially need to give further study to such modifying factors.

CONCLUSIONS

I have presented examples of what I consider to be the most difficult time problems for creation.[113] Two features predominate in most of these examples. First: The data face various interpretations and corrections. Attempting to reconstruct an unknown past is both difficult and subjective. Second: When one incorporates the Genesis flood into an earth model, and this is implicit in sacred history, a number of possibilities emerge that can resolve many of the time problems suggested for creation. We also need to keep in mind that serious problems challenge the long geologic dates.[114] We still have much to learn about dating methods. The last chapter on this topic has not yet been written.

REFERENCES

1. Holmes A. 1937. The age of the earth. Rev. ed. London, Edinburgh, and New York: Thomas Nelson and Sons, p. 11.
2. See chapter 19 for a discussion of various possibilities.
3. See chapters 4, 6, and 11.
4. (a) Foster D. 1985. The philosophical scientists. New York: Dorset Press, pp. 54-57; (b) Bird WR. 1987, 1988, 1989. The origin of species revisited: the theories of evolution and of abrupt appearance, vol. 1. New York: Philosophical Library, pp. 78-83, 301-308.
5. For a discussion of some alternatives, see: Yang S-H. 1993. Radiocarbon dating and American evangelical Christians. Perspectives on Science and Christian Faith 45:229-240.
6. Toulmin S, Goodfield J. 1965. The discovery of time. New York: Harper and Row, pp. 74, 75.
7. (a) *Ibid.*, p. 55; (b) Toulmin S. 1989. The historicization of natural science: its implications for theology. In: Küng H, Tracy D, editors; Köhl M, translator. Paradigm change in theology: a symposium for the future. New York: Crossroad Pub. Co., pp. 233-241. Translation of: Theologie—Wohin? and Das Neue Paradigma von Theologie.
8. For a graphic representation of this trend, see Figure 1 in: Engel AEJ. 1969. Time and the earth. American Scientist 57(4):458-483.
9. For a summary of various estimates of the age of earth, see Table 2.1 in: Dalrymple GB. 1991. The age of the earth. Stanford, Calif.: Stanford University Press, pp. 14-17.
10. For the presently accepted geologic timescale, see: Harland WB, Armstrong RL, Cox AV, Craig LE, Smith AG, Smith DG. 1990. A geologic timescale 1989. Rev. ed. Cambridge and New York: Cambridge University Press.
11. E.g.: Gribbin J. 1992. Astronomers double the age of the universe. New Scientist 133 (January): 12.
12. (a) Freedman WL, Madore BF, Mould JR, Hill R, Ferrarese L, Kennicutt RC, Jr., Saha A, Stetson PB, Graham JA, Ford H, and others. 1994. Distance to the Virgo cluster galaxy M100 from Hubble Space Telescope observations of Cepheids. Nature 371:757-762. However, see also: (b) Chaboyer B, Demarque P, Kernan PJ, Krauss LM. 1996. A lower limit on the age of the universe. Science 271:957-961.
13. Ladd HS. 1961. Reef building. Science 134:703-715.
14. (a) Flood PG. 1984. A geological guide to the northern Great Barrier Reef. Australasian

Sedimentologists Group Field Guide Series, No. 1. Sydney: Geological Society of Australia; (b) Stoddart DR. 1969. Ecology and morphology of recent coral reefs. Biological Reviews 44:433-498.

15. Ladd HS, Schlanger SO. 1960. Drilling operations on Eniwetok Atoll: Bikini and nearby atolls, Marshall Islands. U.S. Geological Survey Professional Paper 260Y:863-905.
16. Hayward A. 1985. Creation and evolution: the facts and the fallacies. London: Triangle (SPCK), p. 85.
17. This has been noted by several investigators, e.g.: Hubbard DK, Miller AI, Scaturo D. 1990. Production and cycling of calcium carbonate in a shelf-edge reef system (St. Croix, U.S. Virgin Islands): applications to the nature of reef systems in the fossil record. Journal of Sedimentary Petrology 60:335-360.
18. For some reports, see: (a) Anonymous. 1994. Coral bleaching threatens oceans, life. EOS, Transactions, American Geophysical Union 75(13):145-147; (b) Charles D. 1992. Mystery of Florida's dying coral. New Scientist 133 (11 January):12; (c) Peters EC, McCarty HB. 1996. Carbonate crisis? Geotimes 41(4):20-23; (d) Zorpette G. 1995. More coral trouble. Scientific American 273(4):36, 37.
19. (a) Clausen CD, Roth AA. 1975a. Estimation of coral growth rates from laboratory ^{45}C-incorporation rates. Marine Biology 33:85-91; (b) Clausen CD, Roth AA. 1975b. Effect of temperature and temperature adaptation on calcification rate in the hermatypic coral *Pocillopora damicornis.* Marine Biology 33:93-100; (c) Roth AA. 1974. Factors affecting light as an agent for carbonate production by coral. Geological Society of America Abstracts With Programs 6(7):932; (d) Roth AA, Clausen CD, Yahiku PY, Clausen VE, Cox WW. 1982. Some effects of light on coral growth. Pacific Science 36:65-81; (e) Smith AD, Roth AA. 1979. Effect of carbon dioxide concentration on calcification in the red coralline alga *Bossiella orbigniana.* Marine Biology 52:217-225.
20. Shinn EA. 1976. Coral reef recovery in Florida and the Persian Gulf. Environmental Geology 1:241-254.
21. Verstelle JTh. 1921. The growth rate at various depths of coral reefs in the Dutch East Indian Archipelago. Treubia 14:117-126.
22. (a) Buddemeier RW, Kinzie RA, III. 1976. Coral growth. Oceanography and Marine Biology: An Annual Review 14:183-225; (b) Lewis JB, Axelsen F, Goodbody I, Page C, Chislett G. 1968. Comparative growth rates of some reef corals in the Caribbean. Marine Science Manuscript Report 10. Montreal: Marine Sciences Centre, McGill University.
23. Wells JW. 1963. Coral growth and geochronometry. Nature 197:948-950.
24. See: (a) Clausen CD. 1974. An evaluation of the use of growth lines in geochronometry, geophysics, and paleoecology. Origins 1:58-66; (b) Crabtree DM, Clausen CD, Roth AA. 1980. Consistency in growth line counts in bivalve specimens. Paleogeography, Paleoclimatology, Paleoecology 29:323-340; (c) Liénard J-L. 1986. Factors affecting epithecal growth lines in four coral species, with paleontological implications. Ph.D. dissertation, Department of Biology, Loma Linda, Calif.: Loma Linda University.
25. Liénard (note 24c).
26. Percival IG. 1985. The geological heritage of New South Wales, vol. I. Sydney: New South Wales National Parks and Wildlife Service, pp. 16, 17.
27. Conaghan PJ, Mountjoy EW, Edgecombe DR, Talent JA, Owen DE. 1976. Nubrigyn algal reefs (Devonian), eastern Australia: allochthonous blocks and megabreccias. Geological Society of America Bulletin 87:515-530.
28. Heckel PH. 1974. Carbonate buildups in the geologic record: a review. In: Laporte LF, editor. Reefs in time and space. Society of Economic Paleontologists and Mineralogists Special Publication 18:90-154.
29. Mountjoy EW, Cook HE, Pray LC, McDaniel PN. 1972. Allochthonous carbonate debris flows—worldwide indicators of reef complexes, banks or shelf margins. In: McLaren DJ, Middleton GV, editors. Stratigraphy and sedimentology, section 6. International Geological Congress, 24th session. Montreal: International Geological Congress, pp. 172-189.

30. Stanton RJ, Jr., Flügel E. 1988. The Steinplatte, a classic Upper Triassic reef—that is actually a platform-edge sandpile. Geological Society of America Abstracts With Programs 20(7):A201.
31. Blatt H, Middleton G, Murray R. 1980. Origin of sedimentary rocks. 2nd ed. Englewood Cliffs, N.J.: Prentice-Hall, p. 447.
32. (a) Hubbard, Miller, and Scanturo (note 17). For further discussion, see: (b) Wood R, Dickson JAD, Kirkland-George B. 1994. Turning the Capitan Reef upside down: a new appraisal of the ecology of the Permian Capitan Reef, Guadalupe Mountains, Texas and New Mexico. Palaios 9:422-427; (c) Wood R, Dickson JAD, Kirkland BL. 1996. New observations on the ecology of the Permian Capitan Reef, Texas and New Mexico. Paleontology 39:733-762.
33. Hodges LT, Roth AA. 1986. Orientation of corals and stromatoporoids in some Pleistocene, Devonian, and Silurian reef facies. Journal of Paleontology 60:1147-1158.
34. (a) Giles KA. 1995. Allochthonous model for the generation of Lower Mississippian Waulsortian mounds and implications for prediction of facies geometry and distribution. Annual Meeting Abstracts, Houston, Texas. American Association of Petroleum Geologists and Society of Economic Paleontologists and Mineralogists 4:33A; (b) Janoschek WR, Matura A. 1980. Outline of the geology of Austria. Abhandlungen der Geologischen Bundesanstalt 34:40-46. See also portions of excursion guides in this same volume on pp. 142-144, 200-208; (c) Lein R. 1987. On the evolution of the Austroalpine realm. In: Flügel HW, Faupl P, editors. Geodynamics of the eastern Alps. Vienna: Franz Deuticke, pp. 85-102; (d) Polan KP. 1982. The allochthonous origin of "bioherms" in the early Devonian Stewart Bay Formation of Bathurst Island, arctic Canada. M.Sc. thesis, Department of Geological Sciences. Montreal: McGill University; (e) Tollmann A. 1987. Geodynamic concepts of the evolution of the eastern Alps. In: Flügel and Faupl, pp. 361-378 (note 34c). For a general review of the question, see: (f) Hodges LT. 1987. Fossil binding in modern and ancient reefs. Origins 14:84-91; (g) Roth AA. 1995. Fossil reefs and time. Origins 22:86-104.
35. (a) Andrews RC. 1932. The new conquest of central Asia: a narrative of the explorations of the central Asiatic expeditions in Mongolia and China, 1921-1930. Reeds CA, editor. Natural History of Central Asia, vol. 1. New York: American Museum of Natural History, pp. 208-211; (b) Carpenter K, Hirsch KF, Horner JR, editors. 1994. Dinosaur eggs and babies. Cambridge, New York, and Melbourne: Cambridge University Press; (c) Cousin R, Breton G, Fournier R, Watte J-P. 1989. Dinosaur egg-laying and nesting: the case of an Upper Maastrichtian site at Rennes-le-Chateau (Aude, France). Historical Biology 2:157-167; (d) Mateer NJ. 1989. Upper Cretaceous reptilian eggs from the Zhejiang province, China. In: Gillette DD, Lockley MG, editors. Dinosaur tracks and traces. Cambridge, New York, and Melbourne: Cambridge University Press, pp. 115-118; (e) Mohabey DM. 1984. The study of dinosaurian eggs from infratrappean limestone in Kheda district, Gujarat. Journal of the Geological Society of India 25(6):329-335; (f) Sanz JL, Moratalla JJ, Díaz-Molina M, López-Martínez N, Kälin O, Vlaney-Liaud M. 1995. Dinosaur nests at the seashore. Nature 376:731, 732; (g) Srivastava S, Mohabey DM, Sahni A, Pant SC. 1986. Upper Cretaceous dinosaur egg clutches from Kheda district (Gujarat, India): their distribution, shell ultrastructure and paleoecology. Paleontographica Abstracts A 193:219-233.
36. (a) Horner JR. 1982. Evidence of colonial nesting and "site fidelity" among ornithischian dinosaurs. Nature 297:675, 676; (b) Horner JR. 1984. The nesting behavior of dinosaurs. Scientific American 250(4):130-137; (c) Horner JR, Gorman J. 1988. Digging dinosaurs. New York: Workman Publishing; (d) Horner JR, Makela R. 1979. Nest of juveniles provides evidence of family structure among dinosaurs. Nature 282:296-298.
37. Mehlert AW. 1986. Diluviology and uniformitarian geology—a review. Creation Research Society Quarterly 23:104-109.
38. (a) Carpenter K, Hirsch KF, Horner JR. 1994. Introduction. In: Carpenter, Hirsch, and Horner, pp. 1-11 (note 35b). For further discussion of various views the reader should consult: (b) Oard MJ. 1997. The extinction of the dinosaurs. Creation ex Nihilo Technical Journal 11:137-154, and references therein.
39. Horner (note 36b).

40. Norell MA, Clark JM, Chiappe LM, Dashzeveg D. 1995. A nesting dinosaur. Nature 378:774-776.
41. Paul GS. 1994. Dinosaur reproduction in the fast lane: implications for size, success, and extinction. In: Carpenter, Hirsch, and Horner, pp. 244-255 (note 35b).
42. (a) Qualls CP, Shine R, Donnellan S, Hutchinson M. 1995. The evolution of viviparity within the Australian scincid lizard *Lerista bougainvillii*. Journal of Zoology (London) 237:13-26; (b) Stebbins RC. 1954. Amphibians and reptiles of western North America. New York, Toronto, and London: McGraw-Hill Book Co., pp. 299-301.
43. Hirsch KF, Stadtman KL, Miller WE, Madsen JH, Jr. 1989. Upper Jurassic dinosaur egg from Utah. Science 243:1711-1713.
44. (a) Erben HK, Hoefs J, Wedepohl KH. 1979. Paleobiological and isotopic studies of eggshells from a declining dinosaur species. Paleobiology 5(4):380-414; (b) Hirsch KF. 1994. Upper Jurassic eggshells from the western interior of North America. In: Carpenter, Hirsch, and Horner, pp. 137-150 (note 35b); (c) Zhao Z-K. 1994. Dinosaur eggs in China: on the structure and evolution of eggshells. In: Carpenter, Hirsch, and Horner, pp. 184-203 (note 35b).
45. For a discussion, see Carpenter, Hirsch, and Horner, pp. 1-11 (note 35b).
46. Carpenter K, Alf K. 1994. Global distribution of dinosaur eggs, nests, and babies. In: Carpenter, Hirsch, and Horner, pp. 15-30 (note 35b).
47. (a) Kolesnikov CM, Sochava AV. 1972. A paleobiochemical study of Cretaceous dinosaur eggshell from the Gobi. Paleontological Journal 6:235-245. Translation of: Paleobiokhimicheskoye issledovaniye skorlupy yaits melovykh dinozavrov Gobi; (b) Vianey-Liaud M, Mallan P, Buscail O, Montgelard C. 1994. Review of French dinosaur eggshells: morphology, structure, mineral, and organic composition. In: Carpenter, Hirsch, and Horner, pp. 151-183 (note 35b); (c) Wyckoff RWG. 1972. The biochemistry of animal fossils. Bristol: Scientechnica, p. 53.
48. Carpenter, Hirsch, and Horner, pp. 1-11 (note 35b).
49. (a) Howard JD, Elders CA. 1970. Burrowing patterns of haustoriid amphipods from Sapelo Island, Georgia. In: Crimes TP, Harper JC, editors. Trace fossils. Geological Journal Special Issue No. 3. Liverpool: Seel House Press, pp. 243-262; (b) Kranz PM. 1974. The anastrophic burial of bivalves and its paleoecological significance. Journal of Geology 82:237-265; (c) Stanley SM. 1970. Relation of shell form to life habits of the Bivalvia (Mollusca). Geological Society of America Memoir 125.
50. Clifton HE, Hunter RE. 1973. Bioturbational rates and effects in carbonate sand, St. John, U.S. Virgin Islands. Journal of Geology 81:253-268.
51. Lambert A, Hsü KJ. 1979. Nonannual cycles of varvelike sedimentation in Walensee, Switzerland. Sedimentology 26:453-461.
52. Buchheim HP. 1994. Paleoenvironments, lithofacies and varves of the Fossil Butte Member of the Eocene Green River Formation, southwestern Wyoming. Contributions to Geology, University of Wyoming 30(1):3-14.
53. McKee ED, Crosby EJ, Berryhill HL, Jr. 1967. Flood deposits, Bijou Creek, Colorado, June 1965. Journal of Sedimentary Petrology 37(3):829-851. Note especially Figure 12d.
54. Jopling AV. 1966. Some deductions on the temporal significance of laminae deposited by current action in clastic rocks. Journal of Sedimentary Petrology 36(4):880-887.
55. (a) Berthault G. 1986. Expériences sur la lamination des sédiments par granoclassement périodique postérieur au dépôt. Contribution à l'explication de la lamination dans nombre de sédiments et de roches sédimentaires. Comptes Rendus de l'Academia des Sciences Paris 303 (Ser 2):1569-1574; (b) Julien PY, Berthault G. n.d. Fundamental experiments on stratification (videocassette). Colorado Springs: Rocky Mountain Geologic Video Society. 1 videocassette: sound, color. For further discussion see: (c) Hernán AM, Havlin S, King PR, Stanley HE. 1997. Spontaneous stratification in granular mixtures. Nature 386:379-382, and references contained therein.
56. (a) Berthault (note 55a); (b) Mendenhall CE, Mason M. 1923. The stratified subsidence of fine particles. Proceedings of the National Academy of Sciences 9:199-202; (c) Twenhofel WH. 1950. Principles of sedimentation. 2nd ed. New York and London: McGraw-Hill Book Co., pp. 549-550; (d) Twenhofel WH. 1961 (1932). Treatise on sedimentation. 2nd ed. New York:

Dover Publications, Inc., vol. 2, pp. 611-613. I have seen up to 12 lamina form overnight in large laboratory cylinders.

57. For a review of this question see: (a) Oard MJ. 1992. Varves—the first "absolute" chronology. Part I—Historical development and the question of annual deposition. Creation Research Society Quarterly 29:72-80; (b) Oard MJ. 1992. Varves—the first "absolute" chronology. Part II—Varve correlation and the post-glacial timescale. Creation Research Society Quarterly 29:120-125.
58. Flint RF. 1971. Glacial and Quaternary geology. New York and London: John Wiley and Sons, p. 406.
59. (a) Stuiver M. 1971. Evidence for the variation of atmospheric C^{14} content in the late Quaternary. In: Turekian KK, editor. The Late Cenozoic glacial ages. New Haven and London: Yale University Press, pp. 57-70; (b) Hajdas I, Zolitschka B, Ivy-Ochs SD, Beer J, Bonani G, Leroy SAG, Negendank JW, Ramrath M, Suter M. 1995. AMS radiocarbon dating of annually laminated sediments from Lake Holzmaar, Germany. Quaternary Science Reviews 14:137-143; (c) Hajdas I, Ivey-Ochs SD, Bonani G. 1995. Problems in the extension of the radiocarbon calibration curve (10-13 kyr BP). Radiocarbon 37(1):75-79; (d) Hajdas I, Ivy SD, Beer J, Bonani G, Imboden D, Lotter A, Sturm M, Suter M. 1993. AMS radiocarbon dating and varve chronology of Lake Soppensee: 6000 to 12000 ^{14}C years BP. Climate Dynamics 9:107-116.
60. For details, see the references given in note 59. Also: Björck S, Sandgren P, Holmquist B. 1987. A magnetostratigraphic comparison between ^{14}C years and varve years during the late Weichselian, indicating significant differences between the timescales. Journal of Quaternary Science 2(2):133-140.
61. Webster CL. Personal communication.
62. Coffin HG. 1979. The organic levels of the Yellowstone petrified forests. Origins 6:71-82.
63. (a) Coffin HG. 1983. Erect floating stumps in Spirit Lake, Washington. Geology 11:298, 299; (b) Coffin HG. 1983. Mount St. Helens and Spirit Lake. Origins 19:9-17; (c) Coffin HG. 1971. Vertical flotation of horsetails *(Equisetum):* geological implications. Geological Society of America Bulletin 82:2019-2022.
64. Brown RH. 1978. How rapidly can wood petrify? Origins 5:113-115.
65. (a) Larsen J. 1985. From lignin to coal in a year. Nature 314:316; (b) Stutzer O. 1940. Geology of coal. Noé AC, translator/reviser; Cady GH, editor. Chicago: University of Chicago Press, pp. 105, 106. Translation of: Kohle (allgemeine kohlengeologie).
66. (a) Brown RH. 1989. Reversal of earth's magnetic field. Origins 16:81-84; (b) Coe RS, Prévot M. 1989. Evidence suggesting extremely rapid field variation during a geomagnetic reversal. Earth and Planetary Science Letters 92:292-298; (c) Coe RS, Prévot M, Camps P. 1995. New evidence for extraordinarily rapid change of the geomagnetic field during a reversal. Nature 374:687-692; (d) Huggett R. 1990. Catastrophism: systems of earth history. London, New York, and Melbourne: Edward Arnold, pp. 120-124; (e) Ultré-Guérard P, Achache J. 1995. Core flow instabilities and geomagnetic storms during reversals: The Steens Mountain impulsive field variations revisited. Earth and Planetary Science Letters 135:91-99.
67. Osmond JK. 1984. The consistency of radiometric dating in the geologic record. In: Walker KR, editor. The evolution-creation controversy: perspectives on religion, philosophy, science and education: a handbook. Paleontological Society Special Publication No. 1. Knoxville: University of Tennessee, pp. 66-76. The author estimates about 300,000 by 1984.
68. (a) Brown RH. 1983. How solid is a radioisotope age of a rock? Origins 10:93-95; (b) Giem PAL. 1997. Scientific theology. Riverside, Calif.: La Sierra University Press, pp. 111-190. This reference evaluates a number of radiometric dating methods.
69. For general reviews of ^{14}C dating, see: (a) Aitken MJ. 1990. Science-based dating in archaeology. Cunliffe B, editor. Longman archaeology series. London and New York: Longman Group, pp. 56-119; (b) Faure G. 1986. Principles of isotope geology. 2nd ed. New York: John Wiley and Sons, pp. 386-404; (c) Geyh MA, Schleicher H. 1990. Absolute age determination: physical and chemical dating methods and their application. Newcomb RC, translator. Berlin, Heidelberg, New York, and London: Springer-Verlag, pp. 162-180; (d) Taylor RE, Müller RA.

1988. Radiocarbon dating. In: Parker SP, editor. McGraw-Hill encyclopedia of the geological sciences. 2nd ed. New York, St. Louis, and San Francisco: McGraw-Hill Pub. Co., pp. 533-540; (e) Taylor RE. 1987. Radiocarbon dating: an archaeological perspective. Orlando, San Diego, New York, and London: Academic Press.

70. Sveinbjörnsdóttir ÁE, Heinemeier J, Rud N, Johnsen SJ. 1992. Radiocarbon anomalies observed for plants growing in Icelandic geothermal waters. Radiocarbon 34(3):696-703.
71. Riggs AC. 1984. Major carbon-14 deficiency in modern snail shells from southern Nevada springs. Science 224:58-61.
72. (a) Stuiver M, Braziunas TF. 1993. Modeling atmospheric ^{14}C influences and ^{14}C ages of marine samples to 10,000 B.C. Radiocarbon 35:137-189. See also: (b) Keith ML, Anderson GM. 1963. Radiocarbon dating: fictitious results with mollusk shells. Science 141:634-637; (c) Rubin M, Taylor DW. 1963. Radiocarbon activity of shells from living clams and snails. Science 141:637.
73. Stuckenrath R, Jr., Mielke JE. 1970. Smithsonian Institution radiocarbon measurements VI. Radiocarbon 12:193-204.
74. Dye T. 1994. Apparent ages of marine shells: implications for archaeological dating in Hawaii. Radiocarbon 36:51-57.
75. (a) Chichagova OA, Cherkinsky AE. 1993. Problems in radiocarbon dating of soils. Radiocarbon 35(3):351-362; (b) Scharpenseel HW, Becker-Heidmann P. 1992. Twenty-five years of radiocarbon dating soils: paradigm of erring and learning. Radiocarbon 34(3):541-549.
76. Aitken, p. 99 (note 69a).
77. (a) Taylor RE, Payen LA, Prior CA, Slota PJ, Jr., Gillespie R, Gowlett JAJ, Hedges REM, Jull AJT, Zabel TH, Donahue DJ, Berger R. 1985. Major revisions in the Pleistocene age assignments for North American human skeletons by C-14 accelerator mass spectrometry: none older than 11,000 C-14 years B.P. American Antiquity 50(1):136-140. Some of these conclusions have also been challenged by: (b) Stafford TW, Jr., Hare PE, Currie L, Jull AJT, Donahue D. 1990. Accuracy of North American human skeleton ages. Quaternary Research 34:111-120.
78. Libby WF. 1963. Accuracy of radiocarbon dates. Science 140:278-280.
79. For some recent examples, see: (a) Kromer B, Becker B. 1993. German oak and pine ^{14}C calibration, 7200-9439 B.C. Radiocarbon 35(1):124-135; (b) Pearson GW, Stuiver M. 1993. High-precision bidecadal calibration of the radiocarbon timescale, 500-2500 B.C. Radiocarbon 35(1):25-33; (c) Stuiver and Braziunas (note 72a); (d) Stuiver M, Pearson GW. 1993. High precision bidecadal calibration of the radiocarbon timescale, A.D. 1950-500 B.C. and 2500-6000 B.C. Radiocarbon 35(1):1-23; (e) Stuiver M, Reimer PJ. 1993. Extended ^{14}C data base and revised CALIB 3.0 ^{14}C age calibration program. Radiocarbon 35(1):215-230.
80. A suggestion has appeared that a tree in Tasmania may be 10,000 years old, but so far the evidence for this is very weak. See: News item. 1995. Living tree "8000 years older than Christ"(?). Creation ex Nihilo 17(3):26, 27.
81. (a) Yamaguchi DK. 1986. Interpretation of cross-correlation between tree ring series. Tree Ring Bulletin 46:47-54. For further discussion see: (b) Brown RH. 1995. Can tree rings be used to calibrate radiocarbon dates? Origins 22:47-52.
82. (a) Monserud RA. 1986. Time series analyses of tree ring chronologies. Forest Science 32(2):349-372; (b) Yamaguchi (note 81).
83. For further discussion of some tree-ring matching problems, see notes 81 and 82, and: (a) Baillie MGL, Hillam J, Briffa KR, Brown DM. 1985. Redating the English art-historical tree-ring chronologies. Nature 315:317-319; (b) Becker B, Kromer B. 1993. The continental tree-ring record—absolute chronology, ^{14}C calibration and climatic change at 11 ka. Paleogeography, Paleoclimatology, Paleoecology 103:67-71; (c) Sorensen HC. 1973. The ages of Bristlecone pine. Pensée (Spring/Summer), pp. 15-18; (d) Porter RM. 1995. Correlating tree rings (letter). Creation Research Society Quarterly 31:170, 171.
84. Sorensen (note 83c).
85. Becker B. 1993. An 11,000-year German oak and pine dendrochronology for radiocarbon calibration. Radiocarbon 35(1):201-213.

86. For instance, see: Becker, Figures 4 and 6 (note 85).
87. Kromer and Becker (note 79a).
88. See Figure 4 in: Becker and Kromer (note 83b).
89. Aitken, p. 100 (note 69a).
90. (a) Bard E, Hamelin B, Fairbanks sRG, Zindler A. 1990. Calibration of the ^{14}C timescale over the past 30,000 years using mass spectrometric U-Th ages from Barbados corals. Nature 345:405-410; (b) Bard E, Arnold M, Fairbanks RG, Hamelin B. 1993. ^{230}Th-^{234}U and ^{14}C ages obtained by mass spectrometry on corals. Radiocarbon 35(1):191-199.
91. (a) Fontes J-C, Andrews JN, Causse C, Gibert E. 1992. A comparison of radiocarbon and U/Th ages on continental carbonates. Radiocarbon 34(3):602-610; (b) Eisenhauer A, Wasserburg GJ, Chen JH, Bonani G, Collins LB, Zhu ZR, Wyrwoll KH. 1993. Holocene sea-level determination relative to the Australian continent: U/Th (TIMS) and ^{14}C (AMS) dating of coral cores from the Abrolhos Islands. Earth and Planetary Science Letters 114:529-547; (c) Hajdas et al. 1995 (note 59c).
92. Runge ECA, Goh KM, Rafter TA. 1973. Radiocarbon chronology and problems in its interpretation for Quaternary loess deposits—South Canterbury, New Zealand. Soil Science Society of America Proceedings 37:742-746.
93. Tonkin PJ, Runge ECA, Ives DW. 1974. A study of late Pleistocene loess deposits, South Canterbury, New Zealand. Part 2: Paleosols and their stratigraphic implications. Quaternary Research 4:217-231.
94. For suggested calculations, see: (a) Brown RH. 1990. Correlation of C-14 age with the biblical timescale. Origins 17:56-65; (b) Brown RH. 1992. Correlation of C-14 age with real time. Creation Research Society Quarterly 29:45-47; (c) Brown RH. 1994. Compatibility of biblical chronology with C-14 age. Origins 21:66-79.
95. (a) Brown RH. 1979. The interpretation of C-14 dates. Origins 6:30-44; (b) Brown RH. 1986. ^{14}C depth profiles as indicators of trends of climate and ^{14}C/^{12}C ratio. Radiocarbon 28(2A):350-357; (c) Clementson SP. 1974. A critical examination of radiocarbon dating in the light of dendrochronological data. Creation Research Quarterly 10:229-236; (c) Brown, 1994 (note 94c).
96. For reviews of the method, see: (a) Dalrymple GB, Lanphere MA. 1969. Potassium-argon dating: principles, techniques and applications to geochronology. San Francisco: W. H. Freeman and Co.; (b) Dickin AP. 1995. Radiogenic isotope geology. Cambridge: Cambridge University Press, pp. 245-276; (c) Faure, pp. 66-112 (note 69b); (d) Faure G. 1988. Rock age determination. In: Parker, pp. 549-552 (note 69d); (e) Geyh and Schleicher, pp. 53-74 (note 69c).
97. Space precludes discussing the ^{39}Ar-^{40}Ar method, which is based on the same principles. It is more complex and seeks to correct some temperature problems. The method faces the usual problem of excess ^{40}Ar and other complications. For some discussion, see references in note 96 and: (a) Ozima M, Zashu S, Takigami Y, Turner G. 1989. Origin of the anomalous ^{40}Ar-^{39}Ar age of Zaire cubic diamonds: excess ^{40}Ar in pristine mantle fluids. Nature 337:226-229; (b) Richards JP, McDougall I. 1990. Geochronology of the Porgera gold deposit, Papua New Guinea: resolving the effects of excess argon on K-Ar and ^{40}Ar/^{39}Ar age estimates for magmatism and mineralization. Geochimica et Cosmochimica Acta 54:1397-1415; (c) Ross JG, Mussett AE. 1976. ^{40}Ar/^{39}Ar dates for spreading rates in eastern Iceland. Nature 259:36-38.
98. Dalrymple and Lanphere, p. 133 (note 96a).
99. McDougall I, Polach HA, Stipp JJ. 1969. Excess radiogenic argon in young subaerial basalts from the Auckland volcanic field, New Zealand. Geochimica et Cosmochimica Acta 33:1485-1520.
100. Ozima et al. (note 97a).
101. Faure, p. 69 (note 69b).
102. There are many such lists: (a) Harland, Armstrong, Cox, Craig, Smith, and Smith (note 10); (b) Kulp JL. 1961. Geologic timescale. Science 133:1105-1114.
103. Hayatsu A. 1979. K-Ar isochron age of the North Mountain Basalt, Nova Scotia. Canadian Journal of Earth Sciences 16:973-975.
104. Mauger RL. 1977. K-Ar ages of biotites from tuffs in Eocene rocks of the Green River, Washakie, and Uinta basins, Utah, Wyoming, and Colorado. Contributions to Geology, University of Wyoming 15(1):17-41.

105. Hekinian R, Chaigneau M, Cheminee JL. 1973. Popping rocks and lava tubes from the Mid-Atlantic Rift Valley at 36°N. Nature 245:371-373.
106. Dalrymple GB, Moore JG. 1968. Argon-40: excess in submarine pillow basalts from Kilauea Volcano, Hawaii. Science 161:1132-1135.
107. Damon PE, Kulp JL. 1958. Excess helium and argon in beryl and other minerals. American Mineralogist 43:433-459.
108. Smith RL, Bailey RA. 1966. The Banderlier Tuff: a study of ash-flow eruption cycles from zoned magma chambers. Bulletin volcanologique 29:83-103.
109. (a) Dymond J. 1970. Excess argon in submarine basalt pillows. Geological Society of America Bulletin 81:1229-1232. See also: (b) Dalrymple and Moore (note 106).
110. Misawa K, Tatsumoto M, Dalrymple GB, Yanai K. 1993. An extremely low U/Pb source in the moon: U-Th-Pb, Sm-Nd, Rb-Sr, and ^{40}AR/^{39}Ar isotopic systematics and age of lunar meteorite Asuka 881757. Geochimica et Cosmochimica Acta 57:4687-4702.
111. See chapter 19 for discussion of this model.
112. Besides the radiometric dating techniques, several other methods of dating have been attempted, including electron spin resonance, thermoluminescence, the molecular clock, obsidian hydration, and amino-acid racemization. These are all more questionable methods whose validity are debated. For comments regarding some of these, see: (a) Lewin R. 1988. Mammoth fraud exposed. Science 242:1246; (b) Marshall E. 1990. Paleoanthropology gets physical. Science 247:798-801. For an evaluation of amino-acid racemization, see: (c) Brown RH. 1985. Amino acid dating. Origins 12:8-25.
113. A number of others, also with equivocal interpretations, could be mentioned. For a discussion of problems for creation, see: (a) Hayward (note 16); (b) Morton GR. 1994, 1995. Foundation, fall, and flood: a harmonization of Genesis and science. Dallas: DMD Pub. Co.; (c) Ross H. 1994. Creation and time: a biblical and scientific perspective on the creation-date controversy. Colorado Springs, Colo.: NavPress Pub. Group; (d) Wonderly DE. 1987. Neglect of geologic data: sedimentary strata compared with young earth creationist writings. Hatfield, Pa.: Interdisciplinary Biblical Research Institute; (e) Young DA. 1988. Christianity and the age of the earth. Grand Rapids: Zondervan Corporation. For views favoring creation, see: (f) Brown W. In the beginning: compelling evidence for creation and the flood. Phoenix: Center for Scientific Creation; (g) Coffin HG. 1983. Origin by design. Washington, D.C., and Hagerstown, Md.: Review and Herald Pub. Assn.; (h) Morris JD. 1994. The young earth. Colorado Springs, Colo.: Master Books Division of Creation-Life Publishers; (i) Van Bebber M, Taylor PS. 1994. Creation and time: a report on the Progressive Creationist book by Hugh Ross. Mesa, Ariz.: Eden Productions; (j) Whitcomb, JC, Jr., Morris HM. 1961. The Genesis flood. Philadelphia: The Presbyterian and Reformed Pub. Co.; (k) Woodmorappe J. 1993(?). Studies in flood geology: a compilation of research studies supporting creation and the flood. Distributed by the Institute for Creation Research, P.O. Box 2667, El Cajon, CA 92021; (l) chapters 12, 13, and 15 in this treatise.
114. See chapters 13 and 15.

CHAPTER 15

SOME GEOLOGIC QUESTIONS ABOUT GEOLOGIC TIME

We often discover what will do,
by finding out what will not do.
—Samuel Smiley[1]

We hear much about the great age of the earth and its fossils. Some dinosaur fossils are said to be more than 200 million years old. Geologists date rocks in the Inner Gorge of the Grand Canyon in Arizona at 1,800 million years, and early forms of life in South Africa are reported to have existed 3,500 million years ago. These and many other ancient dates are based on the standard geologic timescale (see column 2 of Figure 10.1). It postulates the formation of the earth around 4,600 million years ago, with the subsequent gradual formation of the sedimentary layers along with the evolution of life.

The present chapter raises some questions about such long geologic ages. At present, a number of geological changes are occurring so rapidly that they challenge the idea that the rock layers have existed for the eons of time postulated by the standard geologic timescale. These changes relate especially to the earth's sedimentary layers.[2] The strata can undergo many changes over time. Water can erode, transport, and redeposit their sediments. They can subside or be uplifted as a result of the movement of the rocks below them, and they can be augmented by precipitation or by the addition of volcanic or other materials.

While standard geology assumes the earth to be more than 4,000 million years old, it does not necessarily hold that its original conditions were the same as they are today. However, the majority of geologists agree that the major part of the continents formed before 2,500 million years ago.[3] While some geologists use older dates for the beginning of sedimentation,[4] we will use the figure of 2,500 million years, which is conservative with respect to this discussion.

Even if one considers the rates of change for only the Phanerozoic (570 million years), the discrepancies are still extremely large.

Information dealing with rates of geologic processes is not always as precise as one could hope for. Furthermore, it is dangerous to extrapolate too far into the past because conditions can change. Nevertheless, the incongruities we will outline below, that exist between present observations and standard geochronology (geologic time), are so great that any uncertainties hardly affect the conclusion that there appears to be a conflict between the two. Furthermore, the data are generally based on normal, noncatastrophic conditions. The addition of rapid, catastrophic changes would make the discrepancies all the more unfavorable for standard geochronology.

EROSION OF THE CONTINENTS

Each river has its drainage basin, the area that collects the rain that mostly ends up in the river. As this rainwater flows it often carries eroded (sedimentary) particles that eventually find their way to rivers and then to the world oceans. By the repeated sampling of river water at its mouth, we can make estimates of the amount of sediment carried away and the rate at which the drainage basin is eroding. Sedimentologists have made such estimates for a large number of the world's rivers. Some results appear in Table 15.1.

The rates may at first seem quite slow, but if extended over standard geologic time, no continents should remain. Geologists have recognized this inconsistency for many years. Using an estimated average erosion rate of 61 millimeters per 1,000 years,[5] a number of geologists point out that North America could be leveled in "a mere 10 million years."[6] In other words, at the present rate of erosion, the North American continent would have been eroded away about 250 times in 2,500 million years. Of course, we cannot take this analogy too literally. After continents have been eroded once, not much remains to be eroded again. The analogy does, however, permit one to ask the question: Why are the earth's continents still here if they are so old? The slowest rate given in Table 15.1 is 1 millimeter per 1,000 years. The continents average 623 meters above sea level. At an average rate of only 1 millimeter per 1,000 years, they would have been eroded to sea level in 623 million years. In a minimum 2,500 million years assumed for the existence of the earth's continents, this extremely slow erosion rate leveled the continents to sea level four times. But they are still here, and some rivers erode 1,350 times faster (Table 15.1). Referring to these rapid rates, the geologist B. W. Sparks, at Cambridge, comments: "Some of these rates are obviously staggering; the Yellow [Hwang-

TABLE 15.1

RIVER	AVERAGE LOWERING (millimeters/1,000 years)	RIVER	AVERAGE LOWERING (millimeters/1,000 years)
Wei-Ho	1,350	Yangtse	170
Hwang-Ho	900	Po	120
Ganges	560	Garonne and Colorado	100
Alpine Rhine and Rhône	340	Amazon	71
San Juan (U.S.A.)	340	Adige	65
Irrawaddy	280	Savannah	33
Tigris	260	Potomac	15
Isère	240	Nile	13
Tiber	190	Seine	7
Indus	180	Connecticut	1

EROSION BY SOME MAJOR RIVERS OF THE WORLD*

*Based on (a) Sparks, p. 509 (note7); also calculations from (b) Holleman JN. 1968. The sediment yield of major rivers of the world. Water Resources Research 4:737-747; and (c) Milliman and Syvitski (note 18d).

Ho] River could peneplain [flatten out] an area with average height that of Everest in 10 million years."[7]

The discrepancy is especially significant when one considers mountain ranges such as the Caledonides of western Europe and the Appalachians of eastern North America, which geologists assume are several hundred million years old. Why are these ranges still here today if they are so old?

Rates of erosion are faster in high mountains and slower in regions of less relief.[8] In the Hydrographers Range in Papua New Guinea, field researchers have noted erosion rates of 80 millimeters per 1,000 years near sea level and 520 millimeters per 1,000 years at an altitude of 975 meters.[9] Investigators report rates of 920 millimeters per 1,000 years for the Guatemala-Mexico border mountains,[10] while in the Himalayas, rates of 1,000 millimeters per 1,000 years have been noted.[11] In the Mount Rainier region of Washington rates can reach up to 8,000 millimeters per 1,000 years.[12] Probably the fastest recorded regional rate is 19,000 millimeters per 1,000 years from a volcano in Papua New Guinea.[13]

More significant than these rapid rates is the overall average rate, which reflects long-term effects on the continents. Another way of looking at the erosion rates is based on a dozen or so studies estimating how rapidly sediments from the continents reach the ocean. Rivers carry most of the sediments from the continents. Wind and glaciers transport a little as well as ocean waves as they pound the continental coastlines. Estimates for the world rest mainly on the total amount of sediment that the rivers carry as they enter the ocean. Calculations have varied from 8,000 million to 58,000 million metric tons per year (see Table 15.2). Many of the assessments do not take into account the bedload that represents the sediments rolled or pushed along the bed (bottom) of a river and which is not readily observed at river gauging stations. Sometimes the bedload is arbitrarily estimated at 10 percent because it is so difficult to measure.[14] The results reported are probably low, because normal measuring procedures do not account for the rare catastrophic events during which transport will increase considerably. The average rate for the dozen studies reported in Table 15.2 is 24,108 million metric tons per year. At this rate, the average height of the world's continents (623 meters) above sea level would erode away in about 9.6 million years,[15] a figure close to the 10 million year figure given earlier for North America.

Geologists often suggest that mountains still exist because the uplift is con-

TABLE 15.2

AUTHOR (Date)	MILLION METRIC TONS PER YEAR
Fournier (1960)	58,100
Gilluly (1955)	31,800
Holleman (1968)	18,300
Holmes (1965)	8,000
Jansen and Painter (1974)	26,700
Kuenen (1950)	32,500
Lopatin (1952)	12,700
McLennan (1993)	21,000
Milliman and Meade (1983)	15,500
Milliman and Syvitski (1992)	20,000
Pechinov (1959)	24,200
Schumm (1963)	20,500

SOME ESTIMATES OF THE RATE AT WHICH SEDIMENTS REACH THE OCEAN*

*(a) Holleman (Table 15.1); (b) Holmes A. Principles of physical geology. Rev. ed. New York: Ronald Press Co., p. 514; (c) Jansen JML, Painter RB. 1974. Predicting sediment yield from climate and topography. Journal of Hydrology 21:371-380; (d) McLennan (note 18c); (e) Milliman JD, Meade RH. 1983. Worldwide delivery of river sediment to the oceans. Journal of Geology 91:1-21; (f) Milliman and Syvitski (note 18d).

stantly renewing them from below.[16] Although mountains *are* rising (see below), the process of uplift and erosion could not continue long without eradicating the layers of the geologic column contained in them. Just one complete episode of uplift and erosion of the sedimentary layers, some of which however would have to be uplifted from their location below sea level, would eliminate them. Present erosion rates would quickly remove the sediments of the earth's mountain ranges as well as elsewhere, yet sediments from young to old are still well represented.[17] In the context of long geologic ages and rapid erosion rates, the renewal of mountains by uplift does not seem to be a solution.

Other attempts to reconcile present average erosion rates to geologic time include taking into account the fact that human activities, especially agricultural practices, have increased the rate of erosion, making present rates uncharacteristically rapid. Such an explanation does little to resolve the discrepancy. Studies suggest that agricultural pursuits have only doubled the rate of global erosion.[18] Nevertheless, the factor is significant. By eliminating man's agricultural practices, which would be less in the past, the continents would have eroded to sea level in about 20 million years instead of 10 million years. But this does not explain the presence of continents assumed to be 2,500 million years old; which, by analogy, without the presence of agriculture, could have been eroded to sea level 125 times in that period of time.

Still others have proposed that a drier climate in the past resulted in slower erosion rates. However, the lush vegetation evident in significant portions of the fossil record indicates at least some wetter conditions in the past, and estimates of global precipitation suggest variable but average or slightly wetter conditions over the past 3,000 million years.[19]

Also problematic for long geologic ages are some surfaces considered to be extremely ancient yet show little or no evidence of erosion. They extend over significant areas and give no indication of ever having had any other layers over them. An example is Kangaroo Island, (southeastern Australia), which is about 140 kilometers long and 60 kilometers wide. Its surface is estimated to be at least 160 million years old, an age based on both fossil and potassium-argon dating.[20] When I visited the island, I was impressed by the extreme flatness over most of the area. Figure 15.1 shows only a small region across from Kingscote Bay. How could such a surface exist for 160 million years without being eroded away?[21] In that suggested amount of time, corrected for agricultural practices, present rates of erosion would eliminate a layer of sediments five kilometers thick. Maybe Kangaroo Island is not 160 million years old.

FIGURE 15.1

View across Kingscote Bay showing part of Kangaroo Island, southern Australia. The general flatness of the island can be seen across the bay. The surface of this island is assumed to be at least 160 million years old and should have been eroded away long ago.

VOLCANIC ACTIVITY

Earth's sedimentary layers reveal much less evidence of volcanic activity than one would expect for the eons of geologic time postulated for the planet's age. Volcanoes release a variety of things, such as lava, ash, cinders, etc. Single eruptions produce anywhere from small volumes to many cubic kilometers of material. Several years ago, using the very conservative suggestion that all the volcanoes of the earth eject an average of one cubic kilometer of volcanic material per year, a geologist calculated that in 3,500 million years the entire earth should have a thick blanket of volcanic material reaching a height of seven kilometers. Since the actual figures indicate only a small fraction of that amount, he concluded that the rate of volcanic activity must be erratic.[22]

It appears that at present the earth's volcanoes release an average of about four cubic kilometers per year. Single major explosions can produce significant volumes. Tambora (Indonesia, 1815) ejected 100-300 cubic kilometers; Krakatoa (Indonesia, 1883), 6-18 cubic kilometers; and Katmai (Alaska, 1912), 20 cubic kilometers.[23] An estimate of only the major volcanic eruptions during four decades (1940-1980) suggest an average of three cubic kilometers per year.[24] This figure does not include a multitude of smaller eruptions such as occur periodically in Hawaii, Indonesia, Central and South America, Iceland, Italy, etc. An average volume of four cubic kilometers per year has been proposed.[25]

The classic work of the famous Russian geochemist A. B. Ronov suggests that the surface of the earth has 135 million cubic kilometers of sediment of volcanic origin, 14.4 percent of his estimate of the total volume of the earth's sediments.[26] While 135 million cubic kilometers of volcanic products is impressive, it is not much compared to what we would expect according to standard geological ages. At the current production rate extended over 2,500 million years, there should be 74 times as much volcanic material as we now find. This would be a layer of volcanic material with a thickness surpassing 19 kilometers over all of earth's surface. Removal of this material by erosion does not offer a good solution for those believing in the long geological ages. Erosion would only transfer the volcanic material from one place to another. One could also suggest removal by subduction into the earth according to the plate tectonics model, but even this does not appear to be a solution. Removal of volcanic material would also eliminate the other geologic layers containing it. Yet the geologic column, which contains this volcanic material, is still well represented worldwide. Perhaps volcanoes have not been erupting for 2,500 million years.

MOUNTAIN UPLIFT

The so-called solid ground we like to have under our feet is not as firm as we usually surmise. Careful measurements indicate that some areas of the continents are slowly rising and others are sinking. The major mountain ranges of the earth are rising slowly at the rate of a few millimeters per year. We can detect this through careful and precise direct measurement, noting the exact height of a mountain at a given time and remeasuring this height a few years later. It has been proposed that in general mountains are rising at a rate approaching 7.6 millimeters per year.[27] The Alps of central Switzerland rise more slowly at around 1 to 1.5 millimeters per year.[28] Field studies report rates of 0-10 millimeters and 1-10 millimeters per year for the Appalachians and the Rockies, respectively.[29]

I do not know of any precise direct measurements for the Himalayas; however, on the basis of the finding of fairly recent tropical plant and rhinoceros fossils that appear uplifted 5,000 meters, and on the basis of tilted beds, estimates of uplift rates of one to five millimeters per year have been proposed, assuming uniform conditions over long ages. It also appears that Tibet has risen at a similar rate. On the basis of mountain structure and erosion data, researchers have suggested an uplift rate of about three millimeters per year for the central Andes.[30] Parts of the Southern Alps in New Zealand are rising at the rate of 17 millimeters per year.[31] Probably the most rapid gradual (noncatastrophic) rise for mountains known is in Japan, where investigators have noted an uplift of 72 millimeters per year during a 27-year period.[32]

One cannot extend the present rapid rates of mountain uplift very far into the past without getting into difficulty. Using an average rate of five millimeters per year would result in mountains 500 kilometers high in just 100 million years.

Nor can we resolve the incongruence by suggesting that mountains erode just as rapidly as they are uplifted. The rate of uplift (around five millimeters per year) is more than one hundred times faster than estimates of average rates of erosion before the advent of agriculture (about 0.03 millimeters per year). As mentioned previously, erosion is faster in mountain regions and gradually decreases toward lower elevations; hence, the higher the mountains, the more rapidly they erode. However, calculations show that in order for erosion to keep up with what is called a "typical rate of mountain uplift" of 10 millimeters per year, a mountain would have to be 45 kilometers high.[33] This is five times as high as the world's highest mountain, Mount Everest. Several investigators have addressed the problem of relatively slow rates of erosion compared to faster rates of mountain uplift,[34] and they attempt to explain the discrepancy by proposing that we must now be in a period of unusually rapid mountain uplift (a form of episodism).

A further challenge to standard geochronology comes from the fact that if mountains have risen at current rates or even much slower, the geologic column, including its lower parts, which geologists consider to be many hundreds to thousands of millions of years old, should have been uplifted and eroded away long ago. Yet these older portions of the column, along with younger ones, are well-represented in the earth's mountains and continents, as cursory field study or examination of geologic maps will reveal. Mountains, where erosion and uplift are unusually rapid, do not seem to have gone through even one complete cycle of uplift and erosion, yet if present rates of erosion and mountain uplift operated in the past, we could by analogy expect at least a hundred cycles of uplift and erosion during the proposed geologic time.

CONCLUSIONS

Observed rates of erosion, volcanism, and mountain uplift seem to be too rapid to be accommodated into the standard geologic timescale of thousands

TABLE 15.3

FACTOR	Illustration of the Degree of Incongruence if Present Conditions Could Have Prevailed
Present rate of erosion of continents	Continents would be eroded to sea level 125 times in 2,500 million years.
Present rate of production of volcanic ejecta	In 2,500 million years, 74 times as much volcanic material would have been produced as is now found.
Present rate of uplift of mountain ranges	Mountain ranges would be 500 kilometers high in 100 million years.

FACTORS IN CONFLICT WITH STANDARD GEOCHRONOLOGY

of millions of years for the development of the earth's sedimentary layers and the evolution of the life forms represented in them. The discrepancies are not minor (see Table 15.3) and cannot be easily dismissed. It is not expected that conditions would necessarily remain sufficiently constant in the past to postulate the same rates over eons of time. Such rates of change could be faster or slower, but the figures of Table 15.3 serve to illustrate how severe the discrepancies are when we compare present rates to the geologic timescale. Geologists have suggested various explanations to reconcile the data, but they generally involve an unsatisfying degree of conjecture.

On the other hand, one can likewise argue that many of these rates are too slow to accommodate the apparent erosion, volcanism, and mountain uplift seen in less than the 10,000 years suggested by the creation model. This is not a very good argument, because inherent in the creation model is a catastrophic, worldwide flood that we would expect to dramatically increase the rates of each of these factors. Although it is unfortunate that our knowledge about this unique deluge is too meager to permit much quantification, the newer trend in geology toward catastrophic interpretations is giving some hints as to how rapidly some of these changes can occur.[35]

One can try to reconcile current rapid rates of change to geologic time by suggesting slower rates in the past or cycles of rapid and slow activity. However, some of these factors would have to operate scores to hundreds of times slower than at present. This is difficult to envision on an earth that is sufficiently similar to the present to support the kind of life found in the fossil record. For instance, fossil forests of the past would also require significant moisture as do their modern counterparts. Furthermore, slower changes in the past seem contrary to the general geologic scenario that the earth was more active during its early history.[36] Geologists consider heat flow and volcanic activity to have been much greater then. Can geological interpretations reverse this model and postulate that changes are much faster now? Unfortunately, such a trend is the opposite of what we would expect from the evolutionary model. That model calls for an original hot earth that cools to more stable conditions while rates of geologic change slow down over time on their way toward equilibrium.

One question that repeatedly comes to mind as we consider the present rates of erosion and mountain uplift is why so much of the geologic column remains if such processes have been occurring for thousands of millions of years. However, the current rates of geologic change can be fitted with the concept of a recent creation and a subsequent catastrophic flood. The receding waters of the deluge would have left significant portions of the geologic column in place. In a flood context the relatively slow rates of erosion, volcanism, and mountain uplift that we now observe may represent lingering remnants of that catastrophic event.

Current rates of geologic change seem to challenge the validity of the standard geologic timescale.

REFERENCES

1. Smiley S. n.d. Self-help, chapter 11. Quoted in: Mackay AL. 1991. A dictionary of scientific quotations. Bristol and Philadelphia: Institute of Physics Publishing, p. 225.
2. For a more comprehensive discussion of these and related factors, see: Roth AA. 1986. Some questions about geochronology. Origins 13:64-85. Section 3 of that article, which deals with the accumulation of sediments, needs updating.
3. (a) Huggett R. 1990. Catastrophism: systems of earth history. London, New York, and Melbourne: Edward Arnold, p. 232; (b) Kröner A. 1985. Evolution of the Archean continental crust. Annual Review of Earth and Planetary Sciences 13:49-74; (c) McLennan SM, Taylor SR. 1982. Geochemical constraints on the growth of the continental crust. Journal of Geology 90:347-361; (d) McLennan SM, Taylor SR. 1983. Continental freeboard, sedimentation rates and growth of continental crust. Nature 306:169-172; (e) Taylor SR, McLennan SM. 1985. The continental crust: its composition and evolution: an examination of the geochemical record preserved in sedimentary rocks. Hallam A, editor. Geoscience texts. Oxford, London, and Edinburgh: Blackwell Scientific Publications, pp. 234-239; (f) Veizer J, Jansen SL. 1979. Basement and sedimentary recycling and continental evolution. Journal of Geology 87:341-370.
4. I.e., Garrels RM, Mackenzie FT. 1971. Evolution of sedimentary rocks. New York: W. W. Norton and Co., p. 260.
5. Judson S, Ritter DF. 1964. Rates of regional denudation in the United States. Journal of Geophysical Research 69:3395-3401.
6. (a) Dott RH, Jr., Batten RL. 1988. Evolution of the Earth. 4th ed. New York, St. Louis, and San Francisco: McGraw-Hill Book Co., p. 155. Others using this same value are: (b) Garrels and Mackenzie, p. 114 (note 4); (c) Gilluly J. 1955. Geologic contrasts between continents and ocean basins. In: Poldervaart A, editor. Crust of the earth. Geological Society of America Special Paper 62:7-18; (d) Schumm SA. 1963. The disparity between present rates of

denudation and orogeny. Shorter contributions to general geology. U.S. Geological Survey Professional Paper 454-H.

7. Sparks BW. 1986. Geomorphology. 3rd ed. Beaver SH, editor. Geographies for advanced study. London and New York: Longman Group, p. 510.
8. (a) Ahnert F. 1970. Functional relationships between denudation, relief, and uplift in large mid-latitude drainage basins. American Journal of Science 268:243-263; (b) Bloom AL. 1971. The Papuan peneplain problem: a mathematical exercise. Geological Society of America Abstracts With Programs 3(7):507, 508; (c) Schumm (note 6d).
9. Ruxton BP, McDougall I. 1967. Denudation rates in northeast Papua from potassium-argon dating of lavas. American Journal of Science 265:545-561.
10. Corbel J. 1959. Vitesse de L'erosion. Zeitschrift für Geomorphologie 3:1-28.
11. Menard HW. 1961. Some rates of regional erosion. Journal of Geology 69:154-161.
12. Mills HH. 1976. Estimated erosion rates on Mount Rainier, Washington. Geology 4:401-406.
13. Ollier CD, Brown MJF. 1971. Erosion of a young volcano in New Guinea. Zeitschrift für Geomorphologie 15:12-28.
14. (a) Blatt H, Middleton G, Murray R. 1980. Origin of sedimentary rocks. 2nd ed. Englewood Cliffs, N.J.: Prentice-Hall, p. 36; (b) Schumm (note 6d).
15. The surface area of our continents is about 148,429,000 square kilometers. At an average height of 623 meters, we would have a volume above sea level of 92,471,269 cubic kilometers. Employing an estimated average density of 2.5 for the rocks, this would give us 231,171 x 10^{12} tons. This divided by 24,108 x 10^6 tons of sediment carried by the rivers of the world to the oceans in a year results in an average rate of erosion of the continents of 9.582 million years. By comparative analogy, in 2,500 million years this rate could erode the continents 261 (2,500 million divided by 9.582 million) times.
16. For example: Blatt, Middleton, and Murray, p. 18 (note 14a).
17. There should not be much, if any, of the old sediments remaining. All sediments (including a large proportion now below sea level) would be eroded many times. Total world sediments are 2.4 x 10^{18} tons. Rivers before agriculture carried approximately 1 x 10^{10} tons per year; so average cycles would be: 2.4 x 10^{18} tons divided by 10 x 10^9 tons per year, which would equal 240 million years or 10 full cycles of all sediments in 2,500 million years. This is conservative; some suggest recycling "three to ten times since late Cambrian" ([a] Blatt, Middleton, and Murray, pp. 35-38; [note 14a]). Furthermore, the residues of sediment per unit time are more abundant in some older periods (e.g., Silurian and Devonian) than more recent ones (Mississippian to Cretaceous) (see: [b] Raup DM. 1976. Species diversity in the Phanerozoic: an interpretation. Paleobiology 2:289-297). Because of this, some have suggested two cyclic series of changes in erosion rates in the Phanerozoic (e.g., [c] Gregor CB. 1970. Denudation of the continents. Nature 228:273-275). This pattern runs counter to suggestions that recycling is responsible for the smaller volume of older sediments. Also, our sedimentary basins tend to be smaller in their deeper regions which would, by default, restrict the volume of the lowest (oldest) sediments. One can also postulate that much more sediment than we now have has been produced in the past from granitic rocks, and that only a small portion remains. The sediments may have been recycled several times into granitic rocks. Probably the most serious problem this kind of model faces is the chemical mismatch between sediments and earth's granitic crust. Granitic-type (igneous) rocks have an average of less than half as much calcium compared to sedimentary rocks, three times more sodium, and less than one hundredth as much carbon. For data and further discussion, see: (d) Garrels and Mackenzie, pp. 237, 243, 248 (note 4); (e) Mason B, Moore CB. 1982. Principles of geochemistry. 4th ed. New York, Chichester, and Toronto: John Wiley and Sons, pp. 44, 152, 153; (f) Pettijohn FJ. 1975. Sedimentary rocks. 3rd ed. New York, San Francisco, and London: Harper and Row, pp. 21, 22; (g) Ronov AB, Yaroshevsky AA. 1969. Chemical composition of the earth's crust. In: Hart PJ, editor. The earth's crust and upper mantle: structure, dynamic processes, and their relation to deep-seated geological phenomena. American Geophysical Union, Geophysical Monograph 13:37-57; (h) Othman DB, White WM, Patchett J. 1989. The geochemistry of marine sediments, island arc magma genesis, and

crust-mantle recycling. Earth and Planetary Science Letters 94:1-21. Calculations based on an assumption of the origin of all sedimentary rocks from igneous rocks give results that are not correct. Those based on the actual measurement of sediment types should be used. It seems difficult to switch back and forth in recycling between granitic and sedimentary rocks with such a mismatch of these basic elements. One of the more serious problems is how to get limestone (calcium carbonate) from granitic rocks that are comparatively low in calcium and carbon. Furthermore, recycling of sediments within a localized region on the continents does not seem to answer the problem of rapid erosion, because the figures used for the calculations are based on the quantity of sediment going from the continents into the ocean and would exclude local recycling. Furthermore, usually major sections of the geologic column are exposed and eroded in earth's major river basins. This erosion occurs especially rapidly in the mountains which have an abundance of ancient sediments. Why are these ancient sediments still here if they have been recycled?

18. (a) Gilluly J, Waters AC, Woodford AO. 1968. Principles of geology. 3rd ed. San Francisco: W. H. Freeman and Co., p. 79; (b) Judson S. 1968. Erosion of the land, or what's happening to our continents? American Scientist 56:356-374; (c) McLennan SM. 1993. Weathering and global denudation. Journal of Geology 101:295-303; (d) Milliman JD, Syvitski JPM. 1992. Geomorphic/tectonic control of sediment discharge to the ocean: the importance of small mountainous rivers. Journal of Geology 100:525-544.
19. Frakes LA. 1979. Climates throughout geologic time. Amsterdam, Oxford, and New York: Elsevier Scientific Pub. Co., Figure 9-1, p. 261.
20. Daily B, Twidale CR, Milnes AR. 1974. The age of the lateritized summit surface on Kangaroo Island and adjacent areas of South Australia. Journal of the Geological Society of Australia 21(4):387-392.
21. The problem and some general suggestions for resolution are given in: Twidale CR. 1976. On the survival of paleoforms. American Journal of Science 276:77-95.
22. Gregor GB. 1968. The rate of denudation in post-Algonkian time. Koninklijke Nederlandse Academie van Wetenschapper 71:22-30.
23. Izett GA. 1981. Volcanic ash beds: recorders of upper Cenozoic silicic pyroclastic volcanism in the western United States. Journal of Geophysical Research 86B:10200-10222.
24. See listings in: Simkin T, Siebert L, McClelland L, Bridge D, Newhall C, Latter JH. 1981. Volcanoes of the world: a regional directory, gazetteer, and chronology of volcanism during the last 10,000 years. Smithsonian Institution. Stroudsburg, Pa.: Hutchinson Ross Pub. Co.
25. Decker R, Decker B, editors. 1982. Volcanoes and the earth's interior: readings from Scientific American. San Francisco: W. H. Freeman and Co., p. 47.
26. (a) Ronov and Yaroshevsky (note 17g); (b) For just the Phanerozoic, 18 percent volcanic materials is suggested in: Ronov AB. 1982. The earth's sedimentary shell (quantitative patterns of its structure, compositions, and evolution). The 20th V. I. Vernadskiy Lecture, Mar. 12, 1978. Part 2. International Geology Review 24(12):1365-1388. Ronov and Yaroshevsky's estimates of sediment volume are high compared to some others. The discrepancies hardly affected the conclusions. The total thickness expected is based on 2,500 x 10^6 years x 4 cubic kilometers per year = 10,000 x 10^6 cubic kilometers divided by 5.1 x 10^8 square kilometers for earth = 19.6 kilometers high.
27. Schumm (note 6d).
28. Mueller St. 1983. Deep structure and recent dynamics in the Alps. In: Hsü KJ, editor. Mountain building processes. New York: Academic Press, pp. 181-199.
29. Hand SH. 1982. Figure 20-40. In: Press F, Siever R. 1982. Earth. 3rd ed. San Francisco: W. H. Freeman and Co., p. 484.
30. (a) Gansser A. 1983. The morphogenic phase of mountain building. In: Hsü, pp. 221-228 (note 28); (b) Molnar P. 1984. Structure and tectonics of the Himalaya: constraints and implications of geophysical data. Annual Review of Earth and Planetary Sciences 12:489-518; (b) Iwata S. 1987. Mode and rate of uplift of the central Nepal Himalaya. Zeitschrift für Geomorphologie Supplement Band 63:37-49.

31. Wellman HW. 1979. An uplift map for the South Island of New Zealand, and a model for uplift of the southern Alps. In: Walcott RI, Cresswell MM, editors. The origin of the southern Alps. Bulletin 18. Wellington: Royal Society of New Zealand, pp. 13-20.
32. Tsuboi C. 1932-1933. Investigation on the deformation of the earth's crust found by precise geodetic means. Japanese Journal of Astronomy and Geophysics Transactions 10:93-248.
33. (a) Blatt, Middleton, and Murray, p. 30 (note 14a), based on data from: (b) Ahnert (note 8a).
34. (a) Blatt, Middleton, and Murray, p. 30 (note 14a); (b) Bloom AL. 1969. The surface of the earth. McAlester AL, editor. Foundations of earth science series. Englewood Cliffs, N.J.: Prentice-Hall, pp. 87-89; (c) Schumm (note 6d).
35. See chapter 12 for some examples.
36. (a) Kröner (note 3b); (b) Smith JV. 1981. The first 800 million years of earth's history. Philosophical Transactions of the Royal Society of London A 301:401-422.

AN EVALUATION OF SCIENCE AND SCRIPTURE

CHAPTER 16

SCIENCE: A MARVELOUS ENTERPRISE

"Let us examine our ways
and test them."
—Lamentations 3:40, NIV

As we attempt to harmonize science and Scripture, we need to evaluate both sources of information. In this chapter we will consider a few examples that illustrate the strengths of science. Unless identified otherwise, the term *science* as I use it in this chapter and the next refers to science as the process of finding truth and explanations about nature.

We live in an age of unprecedented scientific and technological advance, and most of us are grateful for all the conveniences of our modern age. Marvelous devices witness to the fact that the principles of science work. Daily we wait for the next scientific breakthrough, wondering what else science will discover that might enhance our lives. In this chapter we take a glimpse at some of science's impressive accomplishments.

GENETIC ENGINEERING

A recent set of complex experiments at the San Diego campus of the University of California has produced plants that glow in the dark. Never before has the phenomenon of light production by biological activity (bioluminescence) been observed in advanced plants. A variety of organisms, including the common firefly, and especially a number of marine animals, produce "cold light" (because little heat is generated) by biochemical means, but the phenomenon has been unknown in more complex plants and animals. Yet now we have a tobacco plant that glows in the dark. Researchers selected the tobacco plant because its genetic system is fairly well known, and it has a good carrier to transfer new information into its DNA.[1] They developed this new variety of plant by using the intriguing techniques of genetic engineering.

Genetic engineering is one of the many scientific advances that ought to impress us with its success. Basically, the methodology employs the powerful technique of inserting a gene from one organism into the hereditary mechanism of another. In the case of the glowing tobacco plants, researchers incorporated the gene for the enzyme luciferase, necessary for light production in the firefly, into the genetic system (DNA) of the tobacco plant. When watered with the proper chemicals (adenosine triphosphate and luciferin), the plants glowed faintly, confirming that they had incorporated the gene for luciferase. Other plants treated in the same way but without the gene did not glow. The glowing plants emitted light from most plant parts, but it was brighter in the roots, young leaves, and vascular tissues.

The process of transferring genes is a complex manipulation of the basic hereditary information found coded along the long molecules of DNA. Genetic engineering has provided techniques whereby biologists can isolate sections of DNA from one organism and transfer it to another organism in which it will reproduce and function. The transfer is accomplished by using a virus or plasmid (special DNA from a bacterium) as a carrier of the desired DNA. This combined DNA, called recombinant DNA, can carry information between a large variety of organisms. In the case of the "glowing success" with the tobacco plants described above, researchers combined the firefly gene for the light-producing enzyme luciferase with "promoter" DNA from a virus, inserted it into a plasmid, and finally into the tobacco plants, which then acquired the ability to glow. These are not simple procedures.

Such dramatic results have more significance than the novelty of an advanced form of plant life that glows. Since light is easily detectable, this system has provided a way of identifying and studying gene behavior. One can also imagine what it might be like to have more organisms that glow at night. Luminescent children might be easier to locate in a dark forest! Already biologists have reported some success with inserting the luciferase gene into monkey cells.[2] However, the promises of genetic engineering are less optimistic for complex forms of life since they have less genetic flexibility.

With simpler organisms, genetic engineering has already recorded an impressive list of successes. Several highly specialized molecules needed in medical treatment, previously obtainable only by expensive and laborious extraction from living organisms, can now be produced in large quantities by bacteria genetically altered to manufacture the substances. The protein interferon, which increases human resistance to virus infections, and the hormone insulin, which controls our blood sugar level, are examples. Through various techniques researchers have used growth hormone genes to make larger mice and pigs, and cows that produce more milk. Employing genetic engineering, scientists are creating new kinds of complex enzymes that function in governing chemical changes.[3]

One of the most dramatic developments promises relief for several immunodeficiency diseases. Individuals with these kinds of diseases cannot resist germs and must remain in strict sterile isolation, as was the case for the child who lived in a protective plastic bubble and became known as the "bubble boy." More recently, researchers removed cells from two girls with an immunodeficiency disease, genetically altered them, and reinjected them into the girls, thus providing the immunological resistance they needed. Dramatic accomplishments in agriculture produce genetically altered fruits that remain fresh for a longer time and plants more resistant to viruses and insects.

Such accomplishments, however, also raise concerns about what kind of possible negative impact the new varieties of organisms might have on the environment. This is a concern we cannot dismiss lightly. But genetic engineering tells us that science is a powerful tool.

DEVELOPMENT OF ORGANISMS

How do advanced organisms develop from a single cell to a complex adult? And why does one cell gradually develop into an earthworm and another into a shark? Although we don't have many answers, science has made some pertinent discoveries.

In theory, at least, each cell contains the DNA that has the instructions for producing all the parts of an organism, and each cell has the information for any function of the organism as a whole. Hence a cell that is part of the cortex of the brain, where we do our thinking, also contains the instructions to produce fingernails. Yet each part of our body has developed in its own specific way to produce heart muscle, liver, or a tooth as required for a functional organism. How does this specific orderly development take place?

Science has shown that as an organism develops through its early stages, different parts become more and more specific in their potential. Most organisms start as a single cell. In many animals the division of that first cell into two establishes the future right and left halves of the organism. Sometimes the two cells become separated and create two complete organisms instead of one. Since each has the same complete hereditary information, they produce highly similar offspring, such as identical twins. The armadillo normally produces identical quadruplets. Obviously each of the very early cells of an organism has the capability to produce a complete organism. Conversely, the few cells that form an early amphibian embryo can be separated into single cells that when rejoined can mature into a single complete normal embryo.

Some ingenious experiments have shed light on differentiation in development. Among the most impressive are those done on developing frogs.[4] Investigators have used the South African clawed frog with particular success. Among its peculiarities is the ability to regenerate lost limbs in the adult form. This causes problems when the method of toe clipping is used to identify experimental animals, because they soon regenerate a new toe. In experiments using these frogs, investigators removed the nuclei of the cells, which contain the controlling DNA, from eggs and replaced them with nuclei from cells from more developed forms. They did this to determine how well the older transferred nuclei would control development. It was found that nuclei from early embryonic stages were much more likely to be able to produce normal frog tadpoles than nuclei taken from more advanced stages, such as from a swimming tadpole.[5] In a few instances nuclei from the cells of the intestines of tadpoles reportedly produced fertile adult frogs; however, this result has been disputed.[6] Nuclei derived from the skin of adult frogs stimulated development only to the more rudimentary, nonfeeding tadpole stage.[7]

The science press has reported a major breakthrough in sheep. Most experts considered it impossible to clone a mammal. While the experiment involved some difficulty, it does attest to the progress of science. Researchers implanted the nucleus of a cell from the mammary gland of 6-year-old female sheep in an unfertilized egg from another sheep. They had previously removed the original nucleus from the unfertilized egg. Then they implanted the new "embryo" with the genetic information from the mammary gland into the uterus of another sheep, where it developed into an apparently normal sheep, having the identical genetic information of the mammary gland of its 6-year-old "mother."[8] The potential and variety of experiments which this kind of success implies are overwhelming.

Plants have been easier to work with. Plant physiologists at Cornell University[9] were able to culture cells from a mature carrot plant in coconut milk. In this culture the carrot cells form an amorphous mass of tissue. When the researchers transferred cells from these masses to a solid medium, they developed into a complete reproductively active adult carrot plant. Such results further confirm the hypothesis that every cell has the information necessary to produce a complete organism.

Another illustration of the skill of developmental biologists is the process of mixing the early developmental cells of two individual organisms to produce a single "mixed" one. For instance, the cells of extremely young mouse embryos (consisting of only a few cells) can be easily separated. When researchers do this for two different kinds of mice and then combine them, the cells from the two different embryos will fuse to form a single organism. When implanted into a foster mother, this mosaic embryo can develop and eventually become an adult with a mixture of cells from two embryos. Such organisms have four parents instead of the normal two. If the two original embryos have genes for different colors of coat, some of the offspring develop a mottled-coat color pattern, one color coming from each original embryo. If the two original embryos are of different sex, some of the offspring are hermaphroditic.[10]

One can also stimulate the embryonic development of unexpected parts of the body by transferring cells that induce the particular formation. Certain cells in more advanced embryos stimulate the formation of the head, trunk, and tail. Experiments on embryos of the salamander *Triturus* show that if researchers transfer a particular portion of one embryo to another, the part moved can stimulate the production of an extra head on the embryo. The intriguing part of this experiment is that the transferred part does not eventually become a head in a normal embryo, but is a part of the primitive gut of the organism.

A new area of study that is just beginning is that of the developmental function of homeotic genes (homeobox-containing genes).[11] Such genes influence development, and the kind of development they control is modified by the changing environment of the forming parts. So the process is complicated. Experimental removal or transfer of the genes can produce bizarre organisms, some with extra wings, eyes, or antennae. But such complicated findings promise exciting discoveries about the development process as a whole.

No less surprising are the advances in facilitating human fertility and development. The process of fertilizing one human ovum with a sperm in a laboratory dish has become a very common procedure. The developing organisms thus produced can then be transferred to a genetically unrelated person, who serves as a surrogate nine-month incubator for the baby. It is also possible to freeze and preserve an eight-cell stage of a human embryo for an indefinite period of time, and when convenient, technicians can implant it in a surrogate uterus.

Such advances along with the cloning of sheep raise the question of cloning human beings. Many popular-level writings have speculated about this possibility. Dictators could have themselves cloned *ad infinitum,* thus ruling forever! We can already directly clone carrots, sheep, and possibly frogs, and our present scientific data suggest that human beings can be cloned from developed

FIGURE 16.1

The landscape of Mars as seen from the lander Mars Pathfinder (ramp at the lower left, airbag at the lower right). The exploring rover Sojourner (left foreground) is equipped with an alpha proton X-ray spectroscope for analysis of the martian rocks. Such achievements witness to the success of both science and its associated technology. Photo courtesy of NASA/JPL/Caltech.

body cells. Another technology to produce human clones starting from the early embryonic level is now available and has been performed at the rudimentary level on flawed embryos. To obtain a clone, one could divide the very early embryonic stage of a human being into two—this actually occurs when identical twins form naturally. One half could be implanted for immediate development, the other half preserved by freezing for years. If a clone of the first individual were wanted, the frozen identical embryo could be implanted in a surrogate mother. However, we need to keep in mind that human beings are not just the product of their genetic formula. Our environment, freedom of choice, and other factors determine what we become. To clone a developed trained mind may be formidable, and the cloning of a whole human being may thus be much more difficult than that of ordinary animals. The sociological, moral, and ethical questions raised by cloning procedures are awesome—but so are the advances of science as a whole.

MANAGING THE ELECTRONS

One of the major accomplishments of this century has been the miniaturization of transistors and other electronic components, such as diodes, resistors, and capacitors, into a single tiny silicon chip producing a complex, coordinated integrated circuit containing millions of functional electronic units, each witnessing that the principles of science work.

Individuals developing ordinary integrated circuits on flat computer chips have been called "flatlanders" by a new generation of technologists who are building microscopic motors on those same flat chips. Incredibly, researchers at the University of California at Berkeley have constructed motors with diameters less than one tenth of a millimeter (3/1,000 of an inch). Unlike a conventional electric motor that works on the basis of magnetic forces, these motors use the attraction and repulsion of electrostatic forces. And again the principles of science work. A number of suggested uses for such motors include microscopic cleaning and exploring. It has even been proposed that they might act as tiny robots in the bloodstream of a person to clean away the cholesterol lining the arteries.

Evidences that the basic principles of science work are legion. In addition to those we mentioned above, we can add a host of products of technology based on scientific principles, such as television, personal computers, satellites, space exploration (Figure 16.1), nuclear reactors, etc. We need not devote more pages enumerating the value and successes of science. Science works.

CONCLUSIONS

Science is so successful that as humans we find ourselves surrounded by a technocracy that threatens to engulf us. In the experimental realm, science has accomplished much good. In this realm science deserves much respect. Any general rejection of science as urged by some is not warranted. However, this does not mean that science does not have some serious weaknesses.

REFERENCES

1. Ow DW, Wood KV, DeLuca M, de Wet JR, Helinski DR, Howell SH. 1986. Transient and stable expression of the firefly luciferase gene in plant cells and transgenic plants. Science 234:856-859.
2. De Wet JR, Wood KV, DeLuca M, Helinski DR, Subramani S. 1987. Firefly luciferase gene: structure and expression in mammalian cells. Molecular and Cellular Biology 7(2):725-737.

3. Flam F. 1994. Co-opting a blind watchmaker. Science 265:1032, 1033.
4. (a) Gurdon JB. 1968. Transplanted nuclei and cell differentiation. Scientific American 219(6):24-35; (b) Gurdon JB, Laskey RA, Reeves OR. 1975. The developmental capacity of nuclei transplanted from keratinized skin cells of adult frogs. Journal of Embryology and Experimental Morphology 34:93-112; (c) Gurdon JB. 1977. Egg cytoplasm and gene control in development. The Croonian Lecture, 1976. Proceedings of the Royal Society of London B 198:211-247.
5. McKinnell RG. 1978. Cloning: nuclear transplantation in amphibia. Minneapolis: University of Minnesota Press, p. 101.
6. For discussion, see McKinnell, pp. 110-112 (note 5).
7. Gurdon, Laskey, and Reeves (note 4b).
8. Wilmut I, Schnieke AE, McWhir J, Kind AJ, Campbell KHS. 1997. Viable offspring derived from fetal and adult mammalian cells. Nature 385:810-813.
9. (a) Steward FC, with Mapes MO, Kent AE, Halsten RD. 1964. Growth and development of cultured plant cells. Science 143:20-27; (b) Steward FC. 1970. From cultured cells to whole plants: the induction and control of their growth and morphogenesis. The Croonian Lecture, 1969. Proceedings of the Royal Society of London B 175:1-30.
10. (a) Mintz B. 1965. Experimental genetic mosaicism in the mouse. In: Wolstenholme GEW, O'Connor M, editors. Preimplantation stages of pregnancy. Ciba Foundation Symposium. Boston: Little, Brown, and Co., pp. 194-207; (b) Mintz B, Illmensee K. 1975. Normal genetically mosaic mice produced from malignant teratocarcinoma cells. Proceedings of the National Academy of Sciences U.S.A. 72:3585-3589.
11. See chapter 6 for a brief description of a DNA homeobox.

CHAPTER 17

SCIENCE AND TRUTH: SOME QUESTIONS

Values, life meanings, purposes, and qualities slip through science like sea slips through the nets of fishermen. Yet man swims in this sea, so he cannot exclude it from his purview.

—*Huston Smith*[1]

Science has been so successful that we may forget that it has limits. How could something that has brought us antibiotics, genetic engineering, space travel, and nuclear bombs not be all-powerful? Some scientists, deeply impressed with their discipline, believe that science has the answer to all major world problems, and that the sooner we adopt a scientific worldview, the sooner we will solve these problems. Occasionally people hold up the close cooperation between scientists from countries with widely differing political philosophies as an example of how we might use science to override political conflicts and bring about world peace. Such attitudes illustrate how powerful the scientific image has become. However, one only has to remember some of the wars fought within science or the crises of nuclear and chemical pollution to realize that, at least thus far, science has fallen short of being the solution to all our problems. Also, scientists, like other professionals, tend to look at reality through their specialized outlook. Such confined viewpoints can be a problem when we are looking for the whole truth. Will Rogers, a revered source of simple wisdom, reminds us that "there is nothing so stupid as an educated man, if you get off the thing that he was educated in."[2]

We considered some of the accomplishments of science in the previous chapter. Here we shall complement the picture by examining some of its limitations.

SCIENCE—WHAT IS IT?

We all know what science is—or do we? Science is what a person called a scientist does! Beyond that the question becomes both intriguing and difficult.

We can define science in many ways. A few of the major concepts include: (1) organized knowledge, (2) verifiable knowledge, (3) facts about nature, (4) explanations about nature, (5) a system of thought based on scientific principles (a definition that requires that we know which principles are scientific and which are not), (6) a methodology to discover truth about nature, and (7) a naturalistic philosophy that excludes the supernatural.

Actually, we don't know exactly what science is or how it operates, a sobering admission for such a successful enterprise. Peter Medawar, a Nobel Prize recipient and past president of the British Association for the Advancement of Science, describes the dilemma: "Ask a scientist what he conceives the scientific method to be, and he will adopt an expression that is at once solemn and shifty-eyed: solemn, because he feels he ought to declare an opinion; shifty-eyed, because he is wondering how to conceal the fact that he has no opinion to declare. If taunted he would probably mumble something about 'induction' and 'establishing the laws of nature,' but if anyone working in a laboratory professed to be trying to establish the laws of nature by induction we should begin to think he was overdue for leave."[3]

We recognize that science works, but in a certain sense a scientist does not know what he is doing. Part of the problem revolves around a complex of varied scientific procedures, many of which are ill-defined, and part from the fact that we really do not know what science is. This can bring us back to our initial definition: science is what a scientist does. However, we have a general idea of what science is: it is finding truth and explanations about nature.

SCIENCE DEALS ONLY WITH PART OF REALITY

One of the more obvious limitations of science, especially what we consider as naturalistic (mechanistic) science, is the fact that it leaves many things unexplained. An exclusively naturalistic scientific system of thought excludes many areas that, we suspect, are also part of reality. One only has to mention such concepts as the ultimate meaning of reality, morality, good and evil, freedom of choice, concern, conscience, consciousness, purpose, loyalty, or unselfish love to realize that there exists a vast realm beyond the simple naturalistic cause-and-effect explanations of science.

A number of thought leaders have testified in one way or another about the reality beyond science. Vannevar Bush, who had an illustrious career as a scientist and administrator and who has been called the "father of the modern computer," has stated that "science proves nothing absolutely. On the most vital questions, it does not even produce evidence."[4] The noted astronomer

Arthur Stanley Eddington, referring to the areas of meaning beyond science, observed: "Natural law is not applicable to the unseen world behind the symbols, because it is unadapted to anything except symbols, and its perfection is a perfection of symbolic linkage. You cannot apply such a scheme to the parts of our personality which are not measurable by symbols any more than you can extract the square root of a sonnet."[5]

The famous mathematician-philosopher Alfred North Whitehead also emphasized the limitations of scientific explanation by pointing out an inherent incongruity: "Scientists animated by the purpose of proving that they are purposeless constitute an interesting subject for study."[6] Physician-author Oliver Wendell Holmes described the relationship more graphically when he quipped, "Science is a first-class piece of furniture for a man's upper chamber, if he has common sense on the ground floor."[7] The philosopher Huston Smith expresses the problem more directly: "In envisioning the way things are, there is no better place to begin than with modern science. Equally, there is no worse place to end."[8] All these statements emphasize science's inherent incompleteness.

The question of the origin of morality within a scientific context also illustrates the partialness of science. Does science engender morality? The question has served as the topic of lengthy discussions.[9] Is science moral? Certainly scientists are. But one has real difficulty reconciling Darwinian evolution and its "reign of tooth and claw," along with competition and the resultant demise of all but the fittest, with our morally responsible society that has concern for fairness and the weak and deprived. The concept of evolutionary altruism does not easily explain human morality based on free will.[10] Scientists who follow a naturalistic philosophy may deny the existence of free will, but human beings have more moral concern than we can deduce from just the survival-of-the-fittest concepts of origin. From a purely naturalistic science perspective, the answers to the origin of moral rectitude are few and unconvincing. Science, which sometimes claims to be free of religious, moral, and political influences,[11] has trouble working such attributes into its explanatory menu.

The expression "scientific worldview" can suggest a contradiction in terms, because science gives only a partial view of reality. Science is not a complete worldview. Any wholistic worldview must account for those areas of experience beyond naturalistic explanations. We should not attempt to reduce truth to just our simplistic level of understanding, but must look beyond science for many explanations.

The partial view of reality exhibited by science is also evident when we consider questions about ultimate causes. Science works well in describing the physical world and its details and interrelationships, but does not do well with the underlying reasons for things. It tells us much about "how" things are, but not "why." Critics have accused scientific explanations of being a closed system that defines all terms in relation to each other. This is analogous to describing a pony as a small horse and a horse as a big pony. Such definitions do not tell us what a horse or a pony really is. Our current science contributes little toward ultimate explanations for our existence, consciousness, and moral responsibility. "If you ask science to make an atomic bomb, it will tell you how. If you ask science if you should really make one, it will remain silent."[12]

Related to the incompleteness of science is the fact that science does not work well in explaining the unique event. Science's success rests largely on repeatable situations that permit the discovery of consistent principles. If an event occurs only once, such as creation or the evolution of the first cell, science is unable to provide much analysis. It can only bring forth related peripheral information.

HISTORICAL SCIENCE

In the acrimonious controversy between creation and evolution, individual scientists sometimes state that the general theory of evolution is as much a fact as gravity. Naturally, such statements evoke varied reactions. Some feel comfortable with them, because both gravity and evolution are naturalistic concepts currently accepted by many scientists. Others see a significant difference in the possible degrees of validation. We can easily demonstrate gravity, while this is not the case for the general theory of evolution.

Many of us became acquainted with the realities of science by performing laboratory experiments that would lead to certain expected results. It gave us great confidence in the scientific method. We could predict the outcome of such experiments. Of course, occasionally the results did not come out as planned, and usually we explained the failure in terms of faulty procedure, inaccurate measurement, contamination, etc., but never as indicating that something could be wrong with science. Such basic experiments helped establish in our minds the idea that science is an absolute and that if things go amok, the fault is the result of anything except science itself.

Ample evidence supports the predictability of simple laboratory experiments. It is regrettable that the general public and even some trained scientists seldom appreciate the contrast between such well-tried experiments and the unknowns of original research. They see science as a simple, sure procedure. But difficult research can quickly teach us otherwise. We need to appreciate that what we glibly call the "advancing frontiers of knowledge" also represent the "edge of ignorance."

Some scientists have attempted to alleviate the confusion over degrees of confidence in science by isolating some of the less sure areas of science under the designation of *historical science.*[13] As with other broad concepts, we cannot define historical science in a simple manner. We should not confuse it with the historian's use of the same term to describe his or her methodology. As used by scientists, historical science refers especially to those aspects of science not easily testable and predictable because they are more unique—at least within the limits of practicality. They often involve concepts about the past, hence the historical connotation. Scholars usually consider physics and chemistry less historical, while many aspects of geology, biology, and paleontology are more so. This difference results in part from the complexity of the factors under consideration—physics and chemistry being the simplest and most predictable, while biology and paleontology, which deal with a vast complexity of interacting factors, present more uncertainties. Historical science, as contrasted to firmer experimental science, has more opportunity for speculation and demands more caution. Some aspects of historical science are more reliable than others. We can usually be more certain of the original shape of a fossil than what caused the death of the organism from which it came.

A significant number of major controversies in science have centered in historical science. For instance, a recently published volume entitled *Great Geological Controversies*[14] deals with seven topics, all conflicts over interpretations of the past. Examples include the age of the earth, mass extinction of life on earth, and the ice ages. The uncertainty of historical science facilitates controversy. Another outstanding example of the tentativeness of historical science relates to the European Alps. Every few years someone proposes a new major theory of how these complex and thoroughly studied mountains formed, and there seems to be no end in sight. Given the difficulty in testing the past, we should expect this.

EMOTIONALISM IN SCIENCE

The newspaper headline read: "Creationism Is Scientific Prostitution." It was only one of many similar statements that I had heard the previous day in New Orleans at a national meeting of the Geological Society of America. Still, it surprised me that it received such prominent publicity.

The statement quoted above came from a professor of geology at Oregon State University, who chaired one of two symposium sessions on creation and geology. He also declared that creationists "intentionally and cynically mislead well-intentioned citizens" and are "as crooked as a $3 bill" (United States currency has no such bill). A biologist from Boston University stated that "biblical catastrophism" is "dishonest, nasty." The same speaker also asserted that creationism as a science "represents political and religious mischief." A prominent scientist from the American Museum of Natural History referred to creationism as the "tyranny of a well-organized and strongly motivated minority." Another scientist from the same institution labeled both creation science and ecological zonation[15] as "a ruse." A scholar from Georgia State University pronounced creationism to be "erroneous pseudoscience they pass off as scholarship," and a geologist from the United States Geological Survey warned that one "should not let science fall to the fraud of creationists," and that "if you are a creationist, you are in the wrong place." This last statement became more obvious when at the end of one session an individual supporting creation was interrupted as he spoke and not allowed to continue because the conference considered his viewpoint inappropriate. While creation was at issue in each symposium, none of the 15 speakers scheduled was a creationist. The conference hardly represented a balanced approach.

The emotionalism demonstrated at these sessions far exceeded what I had observed at other scholarly meetings. Many of the scientists had moved from objectivity to name-calling. I wondered what had happened to the stereotype of the scientist as a white-coated, cool, unbiased appraiser of data. Evolutionists have been foremost in asserting that creation, in contrast to evolution, is not scientific. However, the behavior of several evolutionists at these meetings failed to convince me that evolution was a purely scientific concern.

Realistically, if creation is "nonsense," is it worthy of special concern? Why expend such emotional energy on something so obviously erroneous? The overabundance of ridicule, condescension, and deprecation of character I witnessed there made me wonder if creation is not a more substantial foe than the speakers were willing to acknowledge. Could Michel de Montaigne be right when he said "Since we cannot attain unto it, let us revenge ourselves with railing against it"?[16]

Lest creationists settle smugly into the comfort of self-righteousness, let me state that several speakers at the symposia presented well-documented examples of errors made by creationists. Such errors, including the often-repeated statement that no Precambrian fossils exist, were too numerous to be dismissed as totally unrepresentative. On the basis of personal acquaintance as well as the presentations at these symposia, I can vouch for the gentlemanliness, decorum, and scholarship of some of the evolutionists. Nevertheless, some of the deprecating comments I heard are difficult to forget.

Has the issue between creation and evolution become so polarized that science, reason, and understanding can no longer function? Given the accusations reported above, we must conclude that emotional reaction is interfering with scholarship. Such behavior lessens confidence in the scientific process. We should also remember that the negative emotional reaction of some scientists need not necessarily reflect on the integrity of the scientific process itself. However, it is probably impossible to separate the two.

All of us, including scientists, find ourselves easily swayed by subjective factors such as peer pressure. Using 123 college students, Solomon Asch conducted one of the classical studies[17] in this area. He asked the students in groups of seven to compare the lengths of lines on large cards held in front of them. They had to give their answers orally, and each student could hear the responses of the others. Unknown to one of the students in each group, the other students had been previously instructed to reply with certain wrong answers. The researchers then noted the effect of the pressure of the incorrect answers on the one individual who did not know that the others were deliberately falsifying their responses. The experiment showed that group pressure in the form of wrong answers caused the number of errors in judging the length of lines to increase from 1 percent to 37 percent. Only one quarter of the individuals in this experiment remained free from social pressure. Some aligned themselves with the majority even when there was as much as 17 centimeters of difference in the length of the lines on the cards held only a few meters from them. Asch states: "That we have found the tendency to conformity in our society so strong that reasonably intelligent and well-meaning young people are willing to call white black is a matter of concern. It raises questions about our ways of education and about the values that guide our conduct."

A number of studies on the scientific process itself have revealed the subjectivity of scientific evaluation. The controversial peer review process determining which ideas will be accepted or rejected for publication has been subject to several studies. One such experiment, conducted by Michael J. Mahoney[18] of the University of California at Santa Barbara, sent five different versions of an article to 75 "reviewers" for evaluation. The articles, which differed from each other only in data and interpretation, purported to give the results of experimental testing of the effect of extrinsic reinforcement on children's intrinsic interests. The reviewers, who did not know that the results were fabricated, rated methodology, data presentation, and recommendation for publication much higher in those versions that agreed with traditional views than those that opposed them. Obviously, it is difficult to get published if you don't follow the "party line." After the real nature of the study became known, about one quarter of the so-called reviewers expressed disapproval of the way they had been deceived into participating in the experiment. Three even tried to have Mahoney fired or censured by the American Psychological Association.

Sociologist Robert Merton[19] has shown that eminent scientists carry more influence in the scientific process because they receive disproportionate credit for discoveries and have an easier time getting published. Such circumstances stifle a fair evaluation and representation of what is actually being discovered.

Another example of peripheral pressure in science is the so-called discovery of N-rays by the French physicist René Blondlot. In 1902, while investigating the polarization of X-rays, Blondlot noticed that a spark seemed to be brighter under the influence of a new kind of radiation that appeared to behave differently than normal X-rays. He named the new rays "N-rays" in honor of his university and city, Nancy, France. His entire original system of identification and analysis rested upon his observations of the brighter appearance of a spark, and not on its length, which could have been more objectively evaluated. Blondlot was not the only person taken in by "appearances." Soon "at least 40 people" reported on the effects of the rays and "some 300 papers by 100 scientists and medical doctors between 1903 and 1906" analyzed them.[20] The studies found the rays to emanate from animal muscles, the digestion of albuminoids, and by plants in the dark. They also observed that intellectual activity increased the production of N-rays by the nervous system. This new radiation improved visual perception, and some used it to explain spiritualistic phenomena. The study of N-rays soon became "a minor industry."[21] Furthermore, in 1904 the French Academy of Sciences, the official voice of French scientists, bestowed its coveted Le Conte award on Blondlot.

However, several scientists were unable to reproduce the supposed results. Those who had seen the rays usually accused the skeptics of having eyes insensitive to the increase in spark intensity and other apparent luminous effects of the rays. Soon a growing group of scientists became doubtful. Their skepticism grew in 1904 when R. W. Wood of Johns Hopkins University, in the role of a sleuth, visited the laboratories at Nancy to investigate the authenticity of the rays. While Blondlot was demonstrating the spectral qualities of the rays in a darkened room, Wood surreptitiously removed a crucial aluminum prism from a spectroscope, yet Blondlot reported identical results after the prism was gone![22] During his visit Wood also found other unexplainable results, showing that the data could be readily contrived. This incident, though reported in English, French, and German science journals, did not immediately end the defense in support of N-rays. Research and discussion on the apparent effects continued for several years, although interest soon dwindled. It turns out that there are no N-rays. The episode is now of only historical interest and teaches us to be cautious even when many scientists agree on something.

THE QUESTION OF DECEPTION IN SCIENCE

The tragic story of Paul Kammerer[23] also warns us in an unusual way to be cautious when evaluating scientific interpretations. During the early part of this century Vienna-born Kammerer studied the effect of environmental factors on amphibians. His findings supported his leanings toward Lamarckism. He conducted experiments on the midwife toad, which has the peculiarity that the male carries the female eggs entwined around his legs until they hatch. When he forced the toads underwater, he noted that after a few generations the males developed (evolved) nuptial pads on the thumbs that would help in holding on to the females underwater. His discovery caused quite a sensation, and Kammerer gained a great deal of notoriety. Some, especially in England, characterized his findings as "perhaps the greatest biological discovery of the century" and that "Kammerer begins where Darwin left off."[24] Here was experimental evidence for evolution. Kammerer's fame won him a professorship at the State University in Moscow. But by 1926 only a single specimen supported Kammerer's claims and his assertions that dozens of scientists had seen the pads and were convinced.

G. K. Noble, a scientist from the American Museum of Natural History, went to Vienna to examine the male specimen. A thorough examination by him and others revealed that the nuptial pads had been produced by the injection of India ink into the specimen. A few weeks later Kammerer shot himself. He left letters asserting that he had never committed the scientific tricks of which he was accused. While he suggested that someone might have manipulated the specimen, he also said that he was too tired to repeat the experiments. He was only 46 years old. Under these circumstances, his death seems strange. Scholars have much debated the question of whether Kammerer actually perpetrated a hoax.

That other scientists found and corrected the error is commendable and reflects the basic integrity of science. However, we need to address other related questions. Why would anyone fraudulently inject India ink into a frog's thumb? If the discovery was so important, why didn't anyone else attempt to repeat the experiment? And especially, why would science hail the discovery as such a success when it was based on extremely scanty evidence?

A number of other examples of deception in science have been reported. Several books, including *Betrayers of the Truth: Fraud and Deceit in the Halls of Science*,[25] describe some of them. The authors of *Betrayers of the Truth* suggest that science is quite different from the conventional ideology granted it. The book portrays a world of science that has a long history of fierce competition and deliberate adjustment of data. The authors point out that many of the past luminaries of science would occasionally misrepresent their data to assure that their ideas prevailed. They likewise touch on the problem of self-deception, gullibility, and hoaxes in science, and detail some of the more recent and notorious cases of fraud in scientific research. Every scientist should read this book.

Fortunately, in spite of the previous examples, deliberate deception in science is extremely rare. However, we should not totally ignore it. Considering the voluminous output of scientific reports published at the rate of one every 35-40 seconds, the number of reported cases of falsification appears to be remarkably low.

Nevertheless, a related problem associated with the scientific enterprise is more important. The problem is self-deception. Lewis Branscomb, who was vice president and chief scientist for the IBM Corporation and is now at Harvard, has outlined the problem.[26] Simply stated, scientists tend to experiment and search until they find the results they expect, then they stop. Pressures to publish may prevent them from continuing their research to see if their results are really valid. This leads to what is called "intellectual phase locking." Such scientists gain confidence in their ideas because of the agreement with the expected results. This facilitates the perpetuation of error. The support given to Kammerer's nuptial pads, mentioned earlier, illustrates this. Branscomb states: "A revitalization of interest in scientific honesty and integrity could have an enormous benefit both to science and to the society we serve." Although we must keep in mind that the scientific enterprise is basically very honest, at the same time we need to be aware of the problem of "intellectual phase locking" (self-deception) that facilitates honest mistakes. This is the significant problem. Such phase locking is an important component in perpetuating paradigms.

PARADIGM DOMINANCE AND CHANGE

In chapter 2 we referred to dominant ideas called paradigms. While the concept of a paradigm developed from the study of science, it is helpful to keep in mind that science is not at all unique, because the paradigm thought pattern can permeate all areas of inquiry. In later chapters we have seen how science can revert back to an abandoned paradigm. For instance, scientists once believed in spontaneous generation of life. Then they rejected the idea, only to later reaccept it.[27] The same can be said for catastrophism, which science first accepted, rejected, then again accepted.[28]

Such patterns warn us of a grouplike behavior in the scientific thought process. Science is a human enterprise subject to the same vicissitudes as other human activity. While science occasionally changes paradigms, the humanness of the scientist can also resist such shifts. It is not always easy to give up cherished ideas that one has defended for years. The eminent German physicist Max Planck once candidly commented that a "new scientific truth does not triumph by convincing its opponents and making them see the light, but rather because its opponents eventually die, and a new generation grows up that is familiar with it."[29] Shifts in paradigms can sometimes require a long time.

We need to take all these factors into consideration as we try to evaluate the value of scientific consensus, which can change from time to time and be right or wrong.

CONCLUSIONS

The scientific process struggles with a number of well-recognized problems. (1) A number of areas of reality lie beyond science. (2) Historical science is not easily tested. (3) Scientists become emotionally involved in their science. (4) Paradigm acceptance influences the scientific community.

Though some would reject all scientific information as simplistic, biased, erroneous, and restricted, such a view is unwarranted. We must not forget that science has an impressive record of successes, especially in the experimental realm. We should not use the limitations and problems inherent to science in some areas as excuses to deny the value of science in its proper sphere. On the other hand, we should reject the simplistic worship of science as a whole. Science has brought us an abundance of new information, but we must remember that there is good science and there is poor science, and we need to distinguish between the two.

REFERENCES

1. Smith H. 1976. Forgotten truth: the primordial tradition. New York and London: Harper and Row, p. 16.
2. As quoted in: Durant W. 1932. On the meaning of life. New York: Ray Long and Richard R. Smith, Inc., p. 61.
3. Medawar PB. 1969. Induction and intuition in scientific thought. Jayne Lectures for 1968. Memoirs of the American Philosophical Society 75:11.
4. Bush V. 1967. Science is not enough. New York: William Morrow and Co., p. 27.
5. Eddington AS. 1929. Science and the unseen world. The Swarthmore Lecture, 1929. London: George Allen and Unwin, p. 33.

6. Quoted in: Sullivan JWN. 1933. The limitations of science. New York: Mentor Books, p. 126.
7. Holmes OW. 1892. The poet at the breakfast table. Boston and New York: Houghton Mifflin and Co., and Cambridge: Riverside Press, p. 120.
8. (a) Smith, p. 1 (note 1). For further discussion see: (b) Horgan J. 1996. The end of science: facing the limits of knowledge in the twilight of the scientific age. Reading, Mass., and New York: Helix Books, Addison-Wesley Pub. Co., Inc.
9. A few references include: (a) Appleyard B. 1992. Understanding the present: science and the soul of modern man. London: Picador, Pan Books; (b) Bowler PJ. 1993. Darwinism. Twayne's studies in intellectual and cultural history. New York: Twayne Publishers, pp. 8-13; (c) Bulger RE, Heitman E, Reiser SJ, editors. 1993. The ethical dimensions of the biological sciences. Cambridge: Cambridge University Press, pp. 1-63; (d) Mayr E. 1988. Toward a new philosophy of biology: observations of an evolutionist. Cambridge, Mass., and London: Belknap Press of Harvard University Press, pp. 75-91; (e) Proctor RN. 1991. Value-free science? Purity and power in modern knowledge. Cambridge, Mass., and London: Harvard University Press; (f) Rappaport RA. 1994. On the evolution of morality and religion: a response to Lee Cronk. Zygon 29:331-349; (g) Sorell T. 1991. Scientism: philosophy and the infatuation with science. International library of philosophy. London and New York: Routledge, pp. 74-97; (h) Stein GJ. 1988. Biological science and the roots of Nazism. American Scientist 76:50-58.
10. See Mayr (note 9d).
11. See chapter 20.
12. Chauvin R. 1989. Dieu des Fourmis Dieu des Étoiles. Paris: France Loisirs, p. 214. English translation mine.
13. For a discussion and references, see: (a) Bird WR. 1987, 1988, 1989. Philosophy of science, philosophy of religion, history, education, and constitutional issues. The origin of species revisited: the theories of evolution and of abrupt appearance, vol. 2. New York: Philosophical Library, pp. 109-111. Especially useful is: (b) Simpson GG. 1963. Historical science. In: Albritton CC, Jr., editor. The fabric of geology. Reading, Mass., and Palo Alto, Calif.: Addison-Wesley Pub. Co., pp. 24-48.
14. (a) Hallam A. 1989. Great geological controversies. 2nd ed. New York: Oxford University Press. A preponderance of disputed past events is also reported in: (b) Müller DW, McKenzie JA, Weissert H, editors. 1991. Controversies in modern geology: evolution of geological theories in sedimentology, Earth history and tectonics. London, San Diego, and New York: Academic Press.
15. See chapter 10 for a discussion of ecological zonation.
16. Montaigne M de. 1588, 1993. Essays, book 3, chapter 7. Of the incommodity of greatness. Fiorio J, translator. In: Andrews R, editor. Columbia dictionary of quotations. New York: Columbia University Press, p. 199.
17. Asch SE. 1955. Opinions and social pressure. Scientific American 193(5):31-35.
18. (a) Dickson D. 1986. Researchers found reluctant to test theories. Science 232:1333; (b) Mahoney MJ. 1977. Publication prejudices: an experimental study of confirmatory bias in the peer review system. Cognitive Therapy and Research 1:161-175.
19. Merton RK. 1968. The Matthew effect in science. Science 159:56-63.
20. Nye MJ. 1980. N-rays: an episode in the history and psychology of science. Historical Studies in the Physical Sciences 11:125-156.
21. Broad W, Wade N. 1982. Betrayers of the truth: fraud and deceit in the halls of science. New York: Simon & Schuster, p. 113.
22. Wood RW. 1904. The N-rays. Nature 70(1822):530, 531.
23. (a) Anonymous. 1926. Obituary: Dr. Paul Kammerer. Nature 118:635, 636; (b) Goran M. 1971. The future of science. New York and Washington, D.C.: Spartan Books, pp. 73-77; (c) Koestler A. 1971. The case of the midwife toad. London: Hutchinson and Co.; (d) Noble GK. 1926. Kammerer's Alytes, part 1. Nature 118:209, 210; (e) Przibram H. 1926a. Kammerer's Alytes, part 2. Nature 118:210, 211; (f) Przibram H. 1926b. Prof. Paul Kammerer. Nature 118:555; (g) Silverberg R. 1965. Scientists and scoundrels: a book of hoaxes. New York: Thomas Y. Crowell

Co., pp. 188-206; (h) Wendt H. 1956. In search of Adam: the story of man's quest for the truth about his earliest ancestors. Cleugh J, translator. Boston: Houghton, Mifflin Co., and Cambridge: Riverside Press, pp. 320-326. Translation of: Ich suchte Adam.

24. As quoted in Goran, p. 74 (note 23b).
25. (a) Broad and Wade (note 21); (b) Feder KL. 1990. Frauds, myths, and mysteries: science and pseudoscience in archaeology. Mountain View, Calif., and London: Mayfield Pub. Co.; (c) Kohn A. 1986. False prophets: fraud and error in science and medicine. Rev. ed. Oxford and Cambridge, Mass.: Basil Blackwell.
26. Branscomb LM. 1985. Integrity in science. American Scientist 73:421-423.
27. See chapter 4 for details.
28. See chapter 12 for details.
29. Planck M. 1949. Scientific autobiography and other papers. Gaynor F, translator. Westport, Conn.: Greenwood Press, pp. 33, 34. Translation of: Wissenschaftliche Selbstbiographie, mit Dokumentation zu ihrer Entstehungsgeschichte (1943-1948) ausgewahlt.

CHAPTER 18

SCRIPTURE: SOMETHING UNUSUAL

Alone at nights, I read my Bible more and Euclid less.

—Robert Buchanan[1]

The controversial German philosopher Friedrich Nietzsche (1844-1900) often stated that "God is dead." Nietzsche, a prolific and critical writer, was not only expressing his own opinion in stating that God is dead, he reflected the rising tide of nihilism—the denial of an objective basis for truth—that had infiltrated the thinking of his time. Also Nietzsche severely criticized Christianity and regretted the adverse effects it has had.[2] He did not hesitate to challenge the most sacred theme of the Bible: God and Christ's forgiveness as shown in the atoning sacrifice of Christ's death on the cross. Referring to Christ, Nietzsche categorically stated, "He died for *his* guilt. All evidence is lacking, however often it has been claimed, that he died for the guilt of others."[3] Though Nietzsche's influence as a philosopher was great, one must also recognize that a century later his famous statement "God is dead" has to be questioned. The philosopher seems to have preceded God into that terminal condition we call death.

A number of the world's leading intellects have directed their verbal switch-blades at the Bible and what it represents. Yet the Bible continues to be highly sought after and greatly respected. One of the reasons is that despite having been written by many authors over a period of centuries, it has remarkable internal consistency. Another reason is that numerous facts it mentions have been verified historically, archaeologically, and geographically. In this chapter we will examine some of the evidence, mainly from external sources, that authenticate the truthfulness of Scripture.

ACCEPTANCE OF THE BIBLE

While religion and religious adherents are difficult to define, it is clear that Christianity has made dramatic growth since its inception 2,000 years ago. A recent estimate is that Christians now number some 1,869,751,000, or 35 percent of the world population. Muslims comprise 18 percent, nonreligious 16 percent, Hindus 14 percent, Buddhists 6 percent, and atheists 4 percent.[4] In three years of public ministry Christ started a movement that has had no parallel. These Christians turn to the Bible as their guide for life.

No less remarkable is the publication record of the Bible. As mentioned earlier,[5] the Bible is many times more in demand than any other book. The Old Testament of the Bible or parts of it were translated into several languages several centuries before Christ. The whole Bible or at least one "book" of the Bible has been translated into more than 2,000 languages since then. By way of comparison the book *Lenin* has been translated into more than 222 languages, and *The Truth That Leads to Eternal Life* has been translated into more than 100 languages.[6]

HISTORICAL AUTHENTICATION

Many question the reliability of the Bible. Their questions often center on the credibility of the Bible as a whole, and on the genuineness of the central figure of Christianity: Jesus Christ. During the Enlightenment some scholars began to doubt the historicity of sayings attributed to Christ. Others went as far as rejecting the historicity of Jesus Christ Himself. Early in this century some scholars used "form criticism" to evaluate the four biblical Gospels, which give an account of the life of Christ. This approach suggests that the Gospels came from less-reliable oral traditions of the Christian community instead of the accounts of direct witnesses. This concept weakens the factual validity of the Gospels. Such argumentation continues to this day.[7]

Another critical approach has been to declare the biblical account as off limits for historical information. Many have pointed out that the Bible deals with theological interpretations, not with facts. F. F. Bruce, the world-renowned biblical scholar at the University of Manchester, rejected such a suggestion. He states: "We are frequently told today that the task of extracting historical data from the four Gospels is impossible, and in any case illegitimate. But the people who tell us that are for the most part theologians, not historians. Whether the task of extracting historical data from the Gospels is impossible or not is for the historian to discover, not for the theologian to tell him; and one thing that no self-respecting historian will allow himself to be told is that his quest is illegitimate. . . .

"There are other historical characters for whom our source material is scanty and problematical—even more so than the source material for the life of Jesus. But in these cases no scholar holds up his hand like a traffic policeman and says: The materials for reconstructing the historical career of this or that figure do not exist, and it is illegitimate to try to reconstruct them; that is not the purpose for which the available literature was composed. And if anyone were so foolish as to say so, we should simply reply: We know that is not the purpose for which the available literature was composed, but nevertheless that literature is available for the historian to use, with all proper critical safeguards, as source material for his work."[8]

To this we can add the testimony of some of the writers of the biblical Gospels themselves. Luke does not seem to indicate that his writings are just interpretations when he writes: "as one who has gone over the whole course of these events in detail, have decided to write a connected narrative for you, so as to give you authentic knowledge about the matters of which you have been informed."[9]

If one suggests that Scripture has an internal bias, one still has to face the external (i.e., extrabiblical) evidence that supports the truthfulness of the biblical record. Because of this, it has become difficult to suggest that the Bible, or at least the history contained in it, is the product of imagination.

In A.D. 64 a nine-day fire destroyed a major portion of the city of Rome. The Roman emperor of that time was the infamous Nero, who had his half-brother and mother murdered. Public opinion assumed that Nero ordered that fire so that he could rebuild the city on a more magnificent scale.

One of the greatest Roman historians, Cornelius Tacitus (c. A.D. 55-118), in his *Annals,* reports on this and at the same time authenticates both the existence of Christ and the circumstances of His death under the authority of Pilate as given in each of the four biblical Gospels. Tacitus, in commenting about Nero, states: "But all human efforts, all the lavish gifts of the emperor, and the propitiations of the gods, did not banish the sinister belief that the conflagration was the result of an order. Consequently, to get rid of the report, Nero fastened the guilt and inflicted the most exquisite tortures on a class hated for their abominations, called Christians by the populace. Christus, from whom the name had its origin, suffered the extreme penalty during the reign of Tiberius at the hands of one of our procurators, Pontius Pilatus."[10]

Many other nonbiblical references authenticate details of the biblical account of Christ's existence. F. F. Bruce and Josh McDowell list at least 10 examples.[11]

During the past two centuries there have been a number of attempts to mythologize Christ. However, in view of the extrabiblical references to Him, this is not taken very seriously at present. Present theological thinking concentrates on the meaning of Christ, and not on whether or not He existed. The extrabiblical evidence of His existence is difficult to deny. As Bruce points out: "The historicity of Christ is as axiomatic for an unbiased historian as the historicity of Julius Caesar. It is not historians who propagate the 'Christ-myth' theories."[12]

ARCHAEOLOGICAL AUTHENTICATION

Many archaeological findings have also substantiated the historical accuracy of the Old Testament of the Bible. An attitude of questioning almost everything developed during the Enlightenment of the eighteenth century. It carried over into the nineteenth century, during which important historians and theologians vigorously challenged biblical history. Probably the most famous biblical scholar of this school was Julius Wellhausen (1844-1918), who exerted considerable influence in developing and popularizing ideas of the mythical nature of the Bible. For instance, referring to biblical patriarchal accounts, he states: "It is true, we attain to no historical knowledge of the patriarchs."[13] Since then the opinion of the scholarly community has changed so dramatically that William Albright, who was considered one of the most famous orientalists of his day, could state as early as 1933, "Practically all of the Old Testament scholars of standing in Europe and America held these or similar views until very recently. Now, however, the situation is changing with the greatest rapidity, since the theory of Wellhausen will not bear the test of archaeological examination."[14] What has happened is that many archaeological discoveries made since the days of Wellhausen have substantiated the truthfulness of the Bible in a remarkable way.

A century ago many would have labeled a number of the ancient cities mentioned in the Bible as nonexistent because no trace of them had been found. Large centers such as Babylon or Nineveh were unknown otherwise. However, modern archaeology has discovered and excavated these and other cities, and no one can continue to deny their existence. Interestingly, Scripture also predicted their destruction.[15]

In 1868 F. A. Klein, a German missionary, found a remarkable archaeological stele (monument) on the tableland east of the Dead Sea. This stele was an inscribed slab of basalt rock now known as the Moabite stone. After its discovery the local Arabs broke it up into pieces for commercial purposes by heating it and then pouring cold water on it. Fortunately, before they did so someone made a poor cast of it. The pieces were recovered, and the stone is now in the Louvre museum in Paris. The inscription on the rock consists of 34 lines written about 860 B.C., describing the "victory" of King Mesha of Moab over the

Israelites.[16] This account substantiates the same event recorded in the Bible.[17]

Archaeological findings have confirmed that "even such trivial points as the names of midwives (Ex.1:15) are true for the middle centuries of the second millennium, despite previous assertions to the contrary."[18]

Another example has come to light with the discovery of the impressive palace of Sargon II, king of Assyria during much of the eighth century B.C. The walls of that palace, located in present-day Iraq, contained an inscription reporting the conquest of the Northern Kingdom of Israel (Samaria) by Sargon II in 722 B.C. He captured 27,290 inhabitants in the process. For more than two millennia this event was known only from the Bible.[19] Now an extrabiblical source confirms that biblical account. In commenting on this discovery the historian and statesman Moshe Pearlman has stated: "Equally suddenly, skeptics who had doubted the authenticity even of the historical parts of the Old Testament began to revise their views."[20]

The Bible makes some 40 references to a group of people called the Hittites. For a long time scholars did not know of their existence from any other source, and many criticized the biblical statements about them.[21] No longer does anyone doubt the existence of the Hittites. These people whose activities centered in the region of present-day Turkey have left a rich record whose study has become a minor archaeological industry.

The early part of the Bible, which includes the portion that deals with beginnings and is of special concern to this treatise, has frequently faced special criticism. One of the objections to its authenticity is that it must have been written much later than it purports, since no writing existed at that early time. Some consider oral tradition less reliable. The finding of documents written much earlier has refuted this objection.[22]

Along a similar line, some have suggested as inaccurate the more than a dozen references to camels in the book of Genesis. Since some scholars considered the domestication of camels to have taken place many centuries later than the time depicted in Scripture, they assumed that the biblical record must be referring to asses. This assumed anachronism has also turned out to be invalid. The discovery of a number of figurines of camels and references to camels[23] from a much earlier time than previously known has negated the supposed error.

We could cite many more examples.[24] Suffice it to say that the harsh skepticism toward the accuracy of the Bible that dominated theological thinking a century ago on both sides of the Atlantic Ocean has moderated. This is not to say that other questions aren't being raised—many are. But the lessons from the mistakes of the past have cautioned those who challenge the Bible's factuality. Early this century the historian James Shotwell could already state that "the Old Testament stands higher today than when its text was protected with the sanctions of religion."[25]

FLOOD STORIES

Accounts of an ancient devastating flood, often called the deluge, appear all over the world. They are of special interest as we seek to evaluate the relevance of the biblical record to earth's history. Such an event is unusual and thus provides a special external test of biblical accuracy.

The most important extrabiblical flood account occurs in the Gilgamesh Epic, the outstanding literary work from ancient Babylon. It was discovered during archaeological excavations at Nineveh in the famous library of the Assyrian king Ashurbanipal, which dates from the seventh century B.C. The epic appears on 12 clay tablets in cuneiform (wedge-shaped) script of the semitic Akkadian language. The hero of the story, Gilgamesh, searching for eternal life, seeks out Utnapishtim, who has been granted eternal life because he saved animal and human life at the time of the great flood.[26]

The actual flood account, recorded on Tablet No. 11 (Figure 18.1), is re-

FIGURE 18.1

The eleventh tablet of the Epic of Gilgamesh, which contains a flood story remarkably similar to the biblical flood account. The tablet, which dates from the seventh century B.C., was found at Nineveh.*

* Photo © British Museum. Used with permission.

markably similar to the Genesis narrative, and scholars generally agree that the two accounts are related. For instance, in both accounts: (1) the flood is brought on because of evil on earth; (2) the flood is divinely planned; (3) the hero is instructed to build an ark for the preservation of humanity and animals; (4) a select group of humans and animals enter the ark; (5) the event is universal;[27] (6) after the floodwaters subside, the hero releases a raven and a dove (the Gilgamesh account also recounts the release of a swallow, and the sequence is different) to test the dryness of the land; (7) and at the flood's end someone offers a sacrifice that the deity then accepts.

The ancient Greeks also had the concept of a deluge.[28] Their flood hero, Deucalion, received advice from his father to construct an ark because the god Zeus wished to destroy humankind. Deucalion and his wife entered into the ark after stocking it with provisions. Zeus caused such a great rain that in nine days it washed away the greater part of Greece. Most human beings perished, except a few who fled to high mountains. Deucalion also survived in his ark. Greece also has other stories of a deluge, although the one associated with Deucalion is the most famous.[29]

The Aztecs of Central America also had the concept of one or more deluges. The accounts antedate the sixteenth-century advent of missionaries, who brought the flood story from the Bible. The Aztec legend of beginnings[30] includes an original earth destroyed by a great flood caused by the rain god Tlaloc. One account indicates that after the creation of the world, a period of 1,716 years went by before its destruction by floods and lightning.[31] The time span is close to some biblical interpretations. Severe earthquakes followed. Tlazolteotl is "the woman who sinned before the deluge," while the flood heroes Nata and Nena escaped the ravages by building themselves a ship. Others escaped by seeking refuge in caverns or mountaintops. The Aztecs took the threat of subsequent deluges extremely seriously, and reportedly sacrificed large numbers of children to the rain god Tlaloc as appeasement.

In ancient times people did more than consider a major flood as plausible. They incorporated it into their thought system. For instance, they often divided early human history into preflood and postflood categories. Aristotle wrote about the ravages of the deluge in the time of Deucalion. Plato also mentions the flood that occurred in Deucalion's day.[32] Later in the second century A.D. the town of Apamea[33] in Asia Minor issued coins that depicted the ark, Noah and his wife, a dove, etc.[34] While it is likely that Jewish biblical ideas had begun to influence Greek thought by this time, issuing a coin to commemorate the deluge indicates the importance the people of the area gave to the event.

The accounts cited above represent a minute sample of the available flood stories. Instead of elaborating further on this theme, we will focus on some objections raised about the authenticity of such accounts.

One of the prevalent ideas is that the ubiquitous flood narratives all developed locally, possibly from regional floods,[35] and do not reflect a worldwide event such as described in the Bible. This position is difficult to substantiate. It is probable that some accounts have a local origin. Many of them vary in details, as the examples given above have shown. However, we would expect some variations if the story originated in Asia Minor, as seems to be the case,[36] and was passed on orally from generation to generation as humanity spread across the world.[37] On the other hand, certain themes, such as a favored family saved, a universal deluge, and birds sent out to test for dry land are well distributed around the world. Such global themes challenge the local-flood concept, because the similarities suggest a common origin.

In 1929 the British archaeologist Sir Leonard Woolley electrified the archaeological world when he announced the discovery of a sediment deposit from the biblical deluge in his diggings at Ur of the Chaldees in Mesopotamia. Woolley found about 12 meters down a three-meter layer of silt and sand containing no archaeological artifacts. This layer separated two layers of human occupation. Other excavators found a similar layer at Kish and at several other ancient Mesopotamian cities. Woolley interpreted the silt layer as originating during the flood of Noah, which he considered to be local, rather than worldwide. However, his concept has not survived careful scrutiny. His "deluge" deposit was too young to fit even with biblical dating for the flood. Besides, it did not extend even over the whole town of Ur.[38] Such highly localized deposits do not fit the cataclysm usually depicted in flood stories.[39]

Another objection raised against the validity of flood stories suggests that they may have resulted from the influence of missionaries as they disseminated biblical teachings, including the concept of a worldwide flood. While this has happened in a few instances, the objection is probably not very significant, since most deluge accounts predate the arrival of Christian missionaries.

Some suggest that the biblical flood account derives from Babylonian and earlier myths.[40] Without question the Babylonian and biblical accounts are related, since so many details are similar. Conversely, others have proposed that the Babylonian accounts had their basis on the biblical one. One could assume this for later versions, such as the Gilgamesh Epic, which probably dates from the seventh century B.C. However, the idea has not stood the test of more recent inquiry, since archaeologists have discovered Sumerian texts that precede the Babylonian texts and the earliest assumed time for the writing of the biblical text. The biblical book of Genesis was probably written about the fifteenth century B.C., while the Sumerian flood tablets probably originated many centuries earlier.[41] Sumerian writing is the oldest literature known, and it is of interest that here also we find a flood account.

To support the view that the biblical flood account had its origin in Babylonian myths, some scholars have attempted to show Babylonian influences on the biblical text. Such efforts make rather ineffective arguments, since the similarities of terminology purporting relationship between the two are not unique to these documents. The biblical account contains some fundamental uniquenesses.[42] It is the most detailed account available and is fiercely monotheistic (one God),[43] while the other accounts are strongly polytheistic (many gods). Thus it does not appear that the Bible originated in Mesopotamian mythology.

More significant to the question of the origin of flood stories is Alexander Heidel's proposal that all flood legends have a common origin.[44] Heidel, a respected scholar at the Oriental Institute of the University of Chicago, felt that while this point is not proven, it exhibits one factor that belies all other explanations—namely, how can one explain the worldwide dominance of stories about this kind of catastrophe if it did not have a common basis? A common origin[45] is consistent with biblical history. The few survivors of the flood as they repopulated the earth would have spread the story from Asia Minor.

Scholars have recorded some 270 flood stories from around the world.[46] The literature discussing them is voluminous.[47] While their geographical distribution is not uniform, it is generally worldwide. They most commonly appear in Asia, islands southeast of Asia, and the New World, being found from Tierra del Fuego to north of the Arctic Circle. Strangely they are not as common in Africa and Europe. Specific localities where they have turned up include Egypt, Greece, Persia, Syria, Italy, Wales, Scandinavia, Russia, India, China, Mexico, Indonesia, New Guinea, Melanesia, Polynesia, Micronesia, and Australia.

Many scholars testify to the fact that accounts of a deluge essentially coexist with nearly all of the human family.[48] What is more significant is their unusual abundance, a fact acknowledged even by those who do not believe in a universal flood. W. F. Albright speaks of the "extraordinary diffusion of Deluge stories over the earth."[49] T. H. Gaster states, "Legends of a primeval deluge . . . are a feature of almost all primitive mythologies,"[50] and F. H. Woods comments that these accounts "are remarkably frequent in the folklore of the ancient literature of peoples scattered over the greater part of the world."[51]

TABLE 18.1

CAUSES	NUMBER OF REFERENCES
Deluge (world flood)	122
Fire	19
Continuous winter	6
Large stones	2
Ogre	1
Earthworm	1
Objects (dead and alive)	1
Sunrise	1

REFERENCES TO WORLD CALAMITIES IN FOLK LITERATURE (exclusive of end-of-world calamities)*

*Based on classification and references in: Thompson (note 47i).

Stith Thompson has compiled and organized motifs in folk literature into a monumental six-volume treatise.[52] His listing includes some 33,000 specific motifs, all with referenced accounts. The literature dealing with past world calamities (exclusive of end-of-the-world legends) shows a definite preponderance of a deluge both in terms of motifs and references. The number of references for specific causes of past world calamities inferred from Thompson's Index (Table 18.1) is as follows: deluge (flood), 122; fire, 19; continuous winter, 6; large stones, 2; ogre, 1; sunrise, 1; objects, 1; earthworm, 1. It is surprising that common causes of calamities such as drought, pestilence, and earthquakes do not appear in the list. Such data testify to the remarkable commonness of flood traditions that have persisted from the time of some of our earliest writings to the present. One could hardly expect that accounts of major catastrophes from all over the world would be so selective toward one theme if they had not been based on an actual worldwide event. The dominance of flood stories strains the proposal that all the accounts arose locally. If the legends were derived from various local events, one would expect a greater mixture of causes, including many earthquakes.

The biblical flood story, while often denied at present, has ample authentication. Again external evidence supports the accuracy of the Bible.

PREDICTING THE FUTURE

The Bible with its affirmation of authority also claims to foretell the future. Much has been written about biblical prophecies. Some biblical prophecies are complex and poorly understood, while others are simple, direct, and quite remarkable in their fulfillment. Especially impressive are the Old Testament predictions about Christ, written before He lived on earth. Many of them involve things beyond His human control, so He could not have fulfilled them Himself to prove His divinity. Some examples follow.

1. He was to descend from the house of David (predicted in Isaiah and cited as fulfilled in Matthew).[53]

2. He was to be born in the town of Bethlehem (predicted by Micah and cited as fulfilled in Luke).[54]

3. The Messiah would be pierced at His death, and no bones would be broken (predicted in the Psalms and Zechariah and cited as fulfilled in John).[55]

4. His hands and feet would be pierced, and lots would be cast for His clothing (predicted in the Psalms and cited as fulfilled in Matthew and John).[56]

Some could claim that these fulfillments are coincidence and misinterpretations, but that all of these predictions should be fulfilled in the one Person of Christ seems beyond coincidence and misinterpretation. That it was a hoax perpetrated by Christ's disciples also seems extremely unlikely, since they suffered much for their beliefs, some even being martyred.[57] We can hardly expect such loyalty to a contrived hoax.

A half century ago a few argued that somebody had manufactured this whole series of prophecies about Christ, or twisted parts of it, to make it convincing, since the oldest significant manuscripts of the Bible dated nearly 1,000 years after the time of Christ. In 1947 shepherd boys discovered the first of the famous Dead Sea scrolls around the region of ancient Qumran northwest of the Dead Sea.[58] Before long the documents' antiquity and value captured the attention of both Christian and Jewish scholars. Thorough exploration of the region soon located a number of other manuscripts well preserved by the extremely arid climate of the region. Excavations found a variety of manuscripts, including major portions of the Old Testament. The manuscripts included portions of all the books of the Old Testament except the book of Esther.

At first considerable controversy raged over their authenticity and dating, but additional finds in the region and further dating convinced the scholars that they were not forgeries. Experts generally accept that the manuscripts date from the third century B.C. to the second century A.D. and as such represent the Old Testament at Christ's time. These new manuscripts have caused only minor revisions in the pre-Qumran versions of the Bible that had been based on more recent manuscripts. They testify to the accuracy of those who copied the Bible by hand over the centuries. Also they support the validity of the predictive capability of the Bible regarding the life of Christ.

However, as was the case for ancient biblical history, one does not have to stay within the confines of the Bible to find evidence of its predictive skills. One example particularly applies to the topic of this treatise and deals with a prediction of intellectual trends in that time the Bible calls the "last days." Christ describes the period before His return as a time of famine, war, pestilence, and moral decay.[59] These characteristics permit us to conclude that we have arrived at that time. A prediction regarding intellectual trends appears in the second letter written by Christ's apostle Peter. He states: "First of all, note this: in the last days there will come scoffers who live self-indulgent lives; they will mock you and say: 'What has happened to his promised coming? Our fathers have been laid to rest, but still everything goes on exactly as it always has done since the world began.' In maintaining this they forget that there were heavens and earth long ago, created by God's word out of water and with water; and that the first world was destroyed by water, the water of the flood."[60]

The intellectual traits Peter suggests for the last days are the specific trends of our current scientific age. The apostle states that in the last days people would lose sight of creation and the flood. As science has adopted the theory of evolution, the intellectual community of the world has forgotten creation, and as the idea of long geological ages with slow changes has gained approval, the concept of the destruction of the world by a worldwide flood has also virtually disappeared. It is rather remarkable that nearly 2,000 years ago the apostle Peter picked the very two themes that have led to major conflicts between the Bible and modern science. Peter could have selected hundreds of other ideas as themes of conflict in the "last days." Instead he chose the very ones that are the basis of the current conflict between naturalistic science and Scripture. All of this points to the reliability of Scripture.

CONCLUSIONS

The term *unusual* certainly characterizes the Bible. While it has been subject to extensive criticism, it remains as the world's most sought-after book. Most impressive are the findings of archaeology and history that provide external confirmation of the book's authenticity. We also must recognize that the Bible also exhibits some impressive predictive aspects.

Any investigation into the questions of beginnings would do well to take into account this unusual book.

REFERENCES

1. Buchanan R. n.d. An old dominie's story. Quoted in: Mackay AL. 1991. A dictionary of scientific quotations. Bristol and Philadelphia: Institute of Physics Publishing, p. 43.

2. Jaspers K. 1965. Nietzsche: an introduction to the understanding of his philosophical activity. Wallraff CF, Schmitz FJ, translators. Chicago: Henry Regnery Co., pp. 242-247. Translation of: Nietzsche: einfuhrung in das Verstandnis seines Philosophierens.
3. Kaufmann W. 1974. Neitzsche: philosopher, psychologist, antichrist. 4th ed. Princeton, N.J.: Princeton University Press, p. 339.
4. Trumbull CP, editor. 1994. 1994 Britannica Book of the Year. Chicago: Encyclopedia Britannica, p. 271.
5. See chapter 1 for details.
6. Figures are from: (a) McFarlan D, editor. 1990. Guinness book of world records 1990. 29th ed. New York: Bantam Books, pp. 195, 197; (b) Young MC, editor. 1994. Guinness book of records 1995. 34th ed. New York: Facts on File, p. 142.
7. For an extreme case, see: (a) Funk RW, Hoover RW, The Jesus Seminar, translators and commentators. 1993. The five gospels: the search for the authentic words of Jesus. New York: Macmillan Pub. Co. For an opposing view, see: (b) Johnson LT. 1996. The real Jesus: the misguided quest for the historical Jesus and the truth of the traditional gospels. San Francisco: Harper-Collins.
8. Bruce FF. 1966. History and the gospel. In: Henry CFH, editor. Jesus of Nazareth: Saviour and Lord. Contemporary Evangelical Thought Series. Grand Rapids: Wm. B. Eerdmans Pub. Co., pp. 87-107.
9. Luke 1:3, 4, NEB.
10. Tacitus CP. 1952. The Annals, Book 15:44. Church AJ, Brodribb WJ, translators. In: Hutchins RM, editor. Tacitus. Great books of the Western world, vol. 15. Chicago: Encyclopedia Britannica. Translation of: Annales.
11. (a) Bruce FF. 1960. The New Testament documents: are they reliable? 5th rev. ed. Grand Rapids: Wm. B. Eerdmans Pub. Co., pp. 113-120; (b) McDowell J. 1979. Evidence that demands a verdict: historical evidences for the Christian faith. Rev. ed. San Bernardino, Calif.: Here's Life Publishers (a Campus Crusade for Christ book), pp. 81-87.
12. Bruce, p. 119 (note 11a).
13. Wellhausen J. 1957. Prolegomena to the history of ancient Israel. Menzies A, translator. Gloucester, Mass.: Peter Smith, pp. 318, 319. Translation of: Prolegomena zur Geschichte Israels.
14. Albright WF. 1932-1933. The archaeology of Palestine and the Bible. New York, London, and Edinburgh: Fleming H. Revell Co., p. 129.
15. Isa. 13:19-22; Nahum 3:7. For the role of prediction as authenticating Scripture, see the section "Predicting the Future" later in this chapter.
16. J. Frederic McCurdy's translation of the stele is found in: Singer I, editor. n.d. Moabite Stone. Jewish Encyclopedia 8:634-636.
17. 2 Kings 3:4-27.
18. Albright WF. 1960. The archaeology of Palestine. 3rd rev. ed. Baltimore: Penguin Books, p. 237.
19. 2 Kings 17:6; Isa. 20:1.
20. Pearlman M. 1980. Digging up the Bible. New York: William Morrow and Co., p. 85.
21. (a) Prescott WW. 1933. The spade and the Bible: archaeological discoveries support the old book. New York, Chicago, and London: Fleming H. Revell Co., pp. 65-73; (b) Wright W. 1884. The empire of the Hittites. London: James Nisbet and Co., pp. vii-ix.
22. Archer GL, Jr. 1974. A survey of Old Testament introduction. Rev. ed. Chicago: Moody Press, pp. 172, 173.
23. For several examples, see: (a) Dayan M. 1978. Living with the Bible. Philadelphia: Jewish Publication Society of America and New York: William Morrow and Co., p. 39; (b) Hasel GF. 1985. Biblical interpretation today. Washington, D.C.: Biblical Research Institute, p. 26.
24. See: Archer, "Archaeological evidence for the antiquity of the Pentateuch," pp. 170-182 (note 22).
25. Shotwell JT. 1922. An introduction to the history of history. Records of civilization: sources and studies. New York: Columbia University Press, p. 80.
26. For an English rendition, see: Heidel A. 1949. The Gilgamesh Epic and Old Testament parallels. 2nd ed. Chicago: University of Chicago Press, pp. 80-93.

27. *Ibid.,* p. 249.
28. Frazer JG. 1918. Folklore in the Old Testament: studies in comparative religion, legend, and law. Vol. 1. London: Macmillan and Co., pp. 146-174.
29. Frazer JG. [1975.] Folklore in the Old Testament: studies in comparative religion, legend, and law. New York: Hart Publishing Co., p. 70.
30. Sykes E, compiler. 1965. *Everyman's* dictionary of nonclassical mythology. 3rd ed. London: J. M. Dent and Sons, p. 24.
31. Vaillant GC. 1962. Aztecs of Mexico: origin, rise and fall of the Aztec nation. Rev. ed. Garden City, N.Y.: Doubleday and Co., p. 56.
32. Frazer, p. 67 (note 29).
33. Teeple HM. 1978. The Noah's ark nonsense. Evanston, Ill.: Religion and Ethics Institute, Inc., p. 39.
34. Nelson BC. 1968. The deluge story in stone: a history of the flood theory of geology. 2nd ed. Minneapolis: Bethany Fellowship, p. 176.
35. Woods FH. 1959. Deluge. In: Hastings J, editor. Encyclopedia of religion and ethics, vol. 4. New York: Charles Scribner's Sons, pp. 545-557.
36. Teeple, p. 40 (note 33).
37. See Nelson, p. 169, Figure 38 (note 34).
38. (a) Albright WF. 1946, 1955. Recent discoveries in Bible lands. Young's analytical concordance to the Bible: supplement. New York: Funk and Wagnalls Co., p. 30; (b) Filby FA. 1970. The flood reconsidered: a review of the evidences of geology, archaeology, ancient literature and the Bible. Grand Rapids: Zondervan Pub. House, pp. 28-30.
39. See chapter 12 for an evaluation of the local flood concept.
40. For a comparison of these with the biblical text, see: Shea WH. 1984. A comparison of narrative elements in ancient Mesopotamian creation-flood stories with Genesis 1-9. Origins 11:9-29.
41. Heidel, p. 261 (note 26).
42. *Ibid.,* p. 264.
43. See: Hayes JH, Prussner FC. 1985. Old Testament theology: its history and development. Atlanta: John Knox Press, pp. 175, 176.
44. Heidel, p. 267 (note 26).
45. Teeple, pp. 11-40 (note 33).
46. Vos HF. 1982. Flood (Genesis). In: Bromiley GW, editor. International Standard Bible Encyclopedia, vol. 2, 3rd rev. ed. Grand Rapids: Wm. B. Eerdmans Pub. Co., p. 319.
47. See for instance the references already cited above: (a) Frazer (note 28); (b) Nelson (note 34); (c) Sykes (note 30); and (d) Woods (note 35). See also: (e) Andree R. 1891. Die Flutsagen. Braunschweig, Germany: Friedrich Vieweg und Sohn; (f) Gaster TH. 1969. Myth, legend, and custom in the Old Testament. New York and Evanston: Harper and Row (based mainly on Frazer [note 28]); (g) Huggett R. 1989. Cataclysms and earth history: the development of diluvialism. Oxford: Clarendon Press, Oxford University Press; (h) Riem J. 1925. Die Sintflut in Sage und Wissenschaft. Hamburg: Agentur des Rauhen Hauses; (i) Thompson S. 1955. Motif index of folk literature, vol. 1. Rev. ed. Bloomington, Ind.: Indiana University Press. For information related to evidence of the Genesis creation account, see: (j) Nelson ER, Broadberry RE. 1994. Genesis and the mystery Confucius couldn't solve. St. Louis: Concordia Publishing House.
48. See references already cited above: (a) Albright 1936, 1966, p. 30 (note 38a); (b) Filby, p. 41 (note 38b); (c) Frazer, vol. 1, p. 105 (note 29); (d) Gaster, p. xxix (note 47f); (e) Nelson, p. 165 (note 34); (f) Vos, p. 321 (note 46); (g) Woods, p. 545 (note 35). See also: (h) Rehwinkel AM. 1951. The flood in the light of the Bible, geology, and archaeology. St. Louis: Concordia Publishing House, p. 136; (i) Rudhardt J. 1987. The flood. Meltzer E, translator. In: Eliade M, editor. The encyclopedia of religion, vol. 5. New York: Macmillan Pub. Co., p. 356.
49. Albright 1936, 1955, p. 30 (note 38a).
50. Gaster, p. xxix (note 47f).
51. Woods, p. 545 (note 35).

52. Thompson (note 47i).
53. Isa. 9:6, 7; Matt. 1:2-16.
54. Micah 5:2; Luke 2:1-4.
55. Ps. 34:20 and Zech. 12:10; John 19:33-37.
56. Ps. 22:16-18; Matt. 27:35; John 20:25-27.
57. Acts 12:2.
58. Cross FM, Jr. 1961. The ancient library of Qumran and modern biblical studies. Rev. ed. Grand Rapids: Baker Book House.
59. Matt. 24:3-12.
60. 2 Peter 3:3-6, REB.

QUESTIONS ABOUT SCRIPTURE

Nature has some perfection to show that she is in the image of God, and some defects to show that she is only His image.

—Pascal[1]

Legions of books and articles discuss questions about Scripture. Since the Bible is the world's most popular book, we should not find this surprising. In this chapter we shall address biblical questions of special concern to the study of origins. Specifically, we will consider suffering in nature, creation week, and the origin of the creation and flood accounts. We have already explored some questions related to the biblical flood account.[2]

THE QUESTION OF SUFFERING

How could a good and loving God create a world exhibition containing so much pain and suffering? Charles Darwin, in a letter to his friend, the botanist Asa Gray, expressed his concerns about this: "There seems to me too much misery in the world. I cannot persuade myself that a beneficent and omnipotent God would have designedly created the Ichneumonidæ with the express intention of their feeding within the living bodies of Caterpillars, or that a cat should play with mice."[3]

Some consider the presence of moral evil, fear, pain, and other suffering as evidence that God does not really exist. Why do crocodiles and sharks eat human beings? Why do spiders build webs to trap insects and eat them? Did God create tapeworms and malarial parasites, to say nothing of deformed babies and cancer? While we have ample evidence of very complex design, beauty, and love in nature, all is not well. The question of God's goodness in the context of evil in nature has been the subject of extensive discussions.[4] The Bible also briefly addresses this problem and points to evil as the result of wrong choices, not by God, but by His creatures who have free will. Because of freedom of choice we have to cope with both good and evil. The Bible points out that humanity's decision to sin resulted in curses on nature,[5] and the human race has faced suffering ever since. The presence of evil challenges neither God's omnipotence nor His love if freedom of choice also exists. Most of us recognize this freedom. True freedom of choice requires that evil be permitted. Each of us can choose to pull the revolver's trigger. When God gives His creatures freedom to choose, He is not responsible for the consequences of wrong decisions any more than we should blame the builder of a house if an occupant decides to burn it down. To have God avoid the possibility of evil by creating inferior humanoid creatures who would have no freedom of choice would seem both dull and frustratingly confining.

Some suggest that suffering is helpful in the development of a good character. They base the idea on the premise that we remember acquired virtues better than innate ones. The suffering we experience helps us remember and improve. Sometimes it seems that we never learn without suffering, and the Bible indicates that suffering can be instructive.[6]

Still others argue that nature is not as evil as we perceive it to be. For instance, pain protects us by teaching us to not burn off our hands. Conversely, plants and simple forms of animals might not suffer at all when preyed upon. They might be part of an original, God-created food chain. Likewise, in the ideal garden of Eden the ants felt no pain when the elephants stepped on them! Some biologists are of the opinion that the bee-like Ichneumonidæ that Darwin expressed concern about and whose larva feed on caterpillars "are a factor of the first importance in the control of harmful insects; indeed, they are the most powerful barrier to their excessive propagation."[7] God might have created nature with some checks and balances.

Parasites such as tapeworms or roundworms have been a perennial topic when anyone discusses the issue of suffering. We can explain many parasites, especially the roundworms, as having degenerated from related free-living forms. However, some flatworms have complicated life cycles that might represent more than just degeneration. We just do not know. Living organisms are remarkably adaptable within narrow limits, and we cannot discount the possibility that harmless "parasites" (symbionts) may have been part of an original creation. God could have created some organisms to live together. Lichens, such as the familiar grayish-green leathery growth seen on rocks and trees, are a combination of an algae and a fungus living together and mutually helping each other. The coral that produce large coral reefs grow much better if a microscopic plant is present in their body. We must also recognize that each one of us, for approximately nine months before our birth, was, in every sense of the word, a parasite on our mothers. Parasitism could have somehow been part of God's original creation.

Some evil may represent degeneration and/or modification of behavior. This is not a matter of creative evolutionary development that requires foresight to form complex organisms. Rather it is simple degeneration. Biologically it is much easier to have degeneration than to develop new complex structures, the same way that it is much easier to ruin a watch than to make one. Behavioral modifications need not be that dramatic. Cats will play with a ball. It is not such a great change for them to play with a mouse, which also troubled Darwin. Also a fossilized plant-eating crocodile type has been discovered in China.[8] This leads us to muse about changes in diet in such fearsome creatures. All these explanations I offer only as suggestions.

In summary, we can note that we can explain the presence of suffering without the necessity of concluding that God does not exist. Suffering can be the result of a conflict between good and evil based in free will. At times suffering may also be useful in teaching and protecting us. Some experiences that we interpret as suffering in animals might not be such, or might result from degeneration. Such degeneration could include behavioral changes.

THE EVENTS OF CREATION WEEK

When the famous Scopes "monkey trial" took place in 1925,[9] two men emerged as the leading opponents: William Jennings Bryan, three-time candidate for the U.S. presidency, defending creation; and Clarence Darrow (Figure 1.1), a famous Chicago attorney, representing the evolutionist defendant. Bryan invited the prominent creation apologist George McCready Price, who was in England at the time, to attend the trial. Although Price declined, he suggested to Bryan that he not get involved in scientific argumentation![10]

One of the more poignant episodes of the trial occurred when Darrow asked Bryan about the biblical account of creation. How could there be an evening and a morning on the first four days of creation week before the existence of the sun, which, according to the text, God did not create until day 4? Bryan answered the objection by suggesting that the days of creation may have been very long periods of time. His argument did not resolve the peculiarity of having evenings and mornings without a sun.

It does seem, at least at first, quite incongruous to have an evening and a morning before the creation of a sun on day 4, as the sequence is chronicled in

Genesis. However, Genesis suggests that God also created light on day 1. A number of other questions have risen about the creation week account, and some question its factuality.[11] Yet the author of Genesis presents the narrative as simple factual information. (The reader may find it useful to read the account in the first two chapters of the Bible.)

Scholars have proposed several models of creation week. Some of the main differences involve when God created the various parts of the universe and what was the source of light during days 1-3 of creation week. For the sake of simplicity, I shall summarize only three main models.

1. **God made everything during creation week.**

God created the matter of the earth on day 1 and life on days 3, 5, and 6. He created the sun, moon, and all the rest of the universe on day 4. The Creator provided light for the first three days in an undisclosed manner, then the sun was the source afterward. The entire universe is only a few thousand years old.

2. **God created the solar system during creation week; the rest of the universe was created long ago.**

God made the stars and galaxies many millions of years ago, but the solar system is only a few thousand years old. The matter of the earth came into existence on day 1 and life on days 3, 5, and 6. The Creator brought the sun, moon, and planets into being on day 4. He provided light for days 1-3 in a special way and thereafter the sun illuminated the earth. Some modify this model by proposing that God made the sun on day 1, to provide some light, but it did not become distinctly visible until day 4, as proposed for the next model.

3. **God created life during creation week; all of the rest of the universe, including the solar system, was created long ago.**

Long ago God brought the universe into being, including the solar system and an empty, dark earth. He prepared the earth for life and created life on it a few thousand years ago during creation week. Light during creation week came from the sun, which already existed. The partial lifting of a dense cloud on day 1 of creation week illuminated the earth, but the sun, moon, and stars, while present, were not yet visible from its surface. The light was similar to that of an overcast day. The complete lifting of the cloud cover on day 4 made the previously existing sun, moon, and stars fully visible from the surface of the earth.[12] Hence, the scriptural account records their presence for that day.

A straightforward reading of the Genesis account clearly specifies each workday of creation week to be of approximately 24 hours' duration. Bryan's suggestion—the popular interpretation that the days of creation represent extended periods of time—does not appear in the biblical text itself. For each of the six days of creation the writer unambiguously states that they had an evening and a morning.

More debatable is the source of light on the first three days, since the text does not refer to the sun until day 4. As mentioned above, Genesis records the production of light on both days 1 and 4 of creation week.[13] While Scripture does not describe the source of the light on days 1-3, it would not be beyond the ability of a God who can create a universe of stars to provide light on days 1-3. If it were a localized source and if the earth was already rotating, we would have evening and morning in the conventional way. Some have also suggested that God Himself could have been the source of light, since the Bible elsewhere describes Him as a dazzling light[14] and as the source of light for a New Jerusalem, which has no need for the sun.[15]

One of the questions frequently raised about creation week concerns the length of time required for light to come from distant stars. On a clear night, even without a telescope, we can see the faint nebula of Andromeda (Figure 20.1), whose light takes some 2 million years to travel to our eyes. If God created the stars on day 4[16] a few thousand years ago, how can we already see the light from stars, some of which are so far away that it requires thousands of millions of years for that light to reach us? The proposal that God created the stars long before creation week is one way to resolve the problem. Another suggestion is that God could have made the stars recently, complete with their pattern of radiant light already reaching earth so humanity could see and enjoy them from the beginning.

Another question regarding the Genesis creation account pertains to the interpretation of the first two verses of Genesis. After stating that God created heaven and earth, the account follows with a description of a dark empty earth covered with water. Does that description apply to an earth that had already existed for an extended period prior to creation week, or does it refer to earth as first formed on day 1? Most translations of the Bible provide an equivocal statement, because the Hebrew of the biblical manuscripts is capable of more than one interpretation. A few translations favor an empty earth before creation week and begin the creation account with such statements as: "When God set about to create heaven and earth—the world being then a formless waste, with darkness over the seas and only an awesome wind sweeping over the water—God said, 'Let there be light.'"[17] Such translations definitely imply the earth's existence before creation week.

The description of an original dark, empty earth covered with water[18] could suggest that the earth existed in this state long enough to be worthy of description. This idea is strengthened when we consider similar descriptions in other Bible passages that speak of an original earth wrapped in "thick darkness"[19] with a cloud garment, and of an earth formed "out of water."[20] These three passages can imply the existence of something here before creation week. They suggest an original, dark earth covered with water, which could have been here for a long period of time before creation week. Scripture makes no specific mention of the creation of water in the creation-week account, but does clearly allude to its creation elsewhere.[21]

None of the three models proposed above for creation week challenge the concept of a literal six-day creation and God's rest on the seventh-day Sabbath, and all three can answer the apparent incongruity of a morning and an evening for the first three days of creation week before the sun appears on day 4.

Naturally a brief account of beginnings, such as that found in the book of Genesis, will leave many unanswered questions, and several interpretations are possible. We have little justification for being dogmatic on this topic.

DOCUMENTARY HYPOTHESIS

During the ongoing controversy as to whether the public schools of the United States should teach creation or not, I have frequently heard both scientists and theologians advocate that the account of beginnings given in the early part of the Bible represents a compilation from several different sources. Since the number of supposed sources has varied from speaker to speaker, I have remained unconvinced of the objectivity of such conclusions. The implication, however, is that the Bible combines ancient myths compiled by editors usually referred to as redactors (from the French word for editor). This contrasts with the biblical view that prophets inspired by God wrote Scripture.

The Protestant reformers adhered to the biblical model of its origins. However, early in the period of the Enlightenment there arose suggestions of multiple sources for various portions of the Bible previously attributed to one author. The scholars who suggested the concept considered each source as a separate *document* that the Bible editors combined with others to produce the Bible. This is the basis for calling this model of the origin of the Bible the "documentary hypothesis."

One example involves the account of beginnings given in the first two chapters of Genesis. Is this a single account with a special section at the end dealing with the relation of human beings to God, or does it represent two separate accounts put together by a redactor? The biblical account of beginnings, when divided, is sometimes designated as the Genesis 1 and the Genesis 2 accounts for convenience, although the separation between the two is often placed at the end of the first part of Genesis 2:4.

The Genesis 1 account invariably designates the name of God as Elohim in the ancient biblical manuscripts, while in Genesis 2 it is always Yahweh Elohim. This distinction has been an important basis for proposing two independent creation accounts. Some have also suggested that the sequence of creation events is different in the two accounts,[22] since the first has plants created before human beings but according to some views after humans in the second. The second account also chronicles the absence of some plants before humans. Interpretations favoring the idea that the sequence in both chapters represents one creation account include:

1. Since the first part (Gen. 1) is strongly chronological compared to the second (Gen. 2), which emphasizes the creation of humans and their relationship to God, sequence may not have been of special concern in the second account.

2. The suggested absence of plants before humans mentioned in Genesis 2 may refer only to agricultural crops and some other plants, since the biblical text seems to allude only to special plants and associates their absence with the statement that there was "not a man to till the ground."[23] It can be easily inferred that this is the case, since it appears that humans did not need to till the ground until after the fall. After the fall God told Adam, "By the sweat of your brow you will eat your food."[24] The assumed reference to no plants before humans in the second part may simply be an independent statement, not part of the creation narrative itself, but put there as a contrast to the original creation and later situation when human beings had to till the ground after their fall.[25]

3. The creation of plants alluded to after the creation of humans in the second part appears to be only the garden of Eden and not the original creation of plants mentioned in Genesis 1.

Scholars have especially applied the documentary hypothesis to the first five books of the Bible (the Pentateuch). Similar discussions have focused on the authorship of the book of Isaiah[26] and the four Gospels.[27] The late biblical scholar Gerhard Hasel, among others, has reviewed some of the problems of the hypothesis.[28] Scholars have suggested a wide variety of arrangements and sources and times of writing for the alleged different documents. Some eventually divided the book of Genesis itself into 39 fragments. The most influential scheme was the one developed by K. H. Graff, A. Kuenen, and Julius Wellhausen (the same Wellhausen mentioned in the previous chapter, who may have been the most influential biblical scholar of the nineteenth century). Those who advocate the documentary hypothesis often propose four major sources (J, E, D, P) for the first books of the Bible: a J source, i.e., "Jahwist," representing Yahweh Elohim as God's name; an E source, based on "Elohim" as God's name; a D source for the book of Deuteronomy; and a P source, based on an assumed document put together by the priestly source.

The unity of each source has varied with different scholars. Sometimes Yahweh or Elohim can end up in the wrong document. E has been divided into two and part changed to P; J has been split into two, and D into three sources. Points of division between sources vary. Scholars have proposed still other sources, and the assumed order and antiquity of the various sources has also varied.

The many different proposed schemes witness to the lack of evidence for a definitive model. Because of this, G. F. Hasel calls the documentary hypothesis "an exercise in imaginative subjectivity."[29] The biblical scholar Gleason Archer (also trained in law) points out that "it is very doubtful whether the Wellhausen hypothesis is entitled to the status of scientific respectability. There is so much of special pleading, circular reasoning, questionable deductions from unsubstantiated premises, that it is absolutely certain that its methodology would never stand up in a court of law. Scarcely any of the laws of evidence respected in legal proceedings are honored by the architects of this documentary theory. Any attorney who attempted to interpret a will or statute or deed of conveyance in the bizarre and irresponsible fashion of the source critics of the Pentateuch would find his case thrown out of court without delay."[30]

The internal evidence from the Bible itself is that Moses wrote most of the Pentateuch, since a number of texts allude to his role.[31] Christ Himself referred to Moses as the author of at least part of the Pentateuch,[32] and we have no evidence that He believed in the documentary hypothesis.

There is no direct mention of JEDP as editors in the Bible, and no serious external identity either. Some scholars have thoroughly devastated the documentary concept. Umberto Cassuto of the Hebrew University of Jerusalem has written extensively on the "pillars" that supposedly support the documentary hypothesis. He concludes: "I did not prove that the pillars were weak or that each one failed to give decisive support, but I established that they were not pillars at all, that they did not exist, that they were purely imaginary. In view of this, my final conclusion that the documentary hypothesis is null and void is justified."[33] Nevertheless, the concept still survives. It has received support in the United States and England, but has been less accepted among scholars on the European continent.[34]

Others have pointed out the similarities and expectations of single authorship for the two parts of the creation narrative. The biblical scholars William Shea, U. Cassuto, and Duane Garrett indicate that the type of parallel arrangement of literary units we find in the two parts of the creation account is fairly common in ancient writings and thus does not necessarily demand multiple authorship.[35] Jacques Doukhan and others emphasize that the second creation account can simply be the natural consequence of a progression of the Genesis narrative,[36] with the second part centering on human beings and their relationship to God. The more complex name for God in the second part emphasizes that aspect. Thus the two parts represent complementary and not contradictory descriptions of God. We also find numerous literary similarities for Genesis 1 and 2[37] as well as for the flood account of Genesis 6-11, which has also been divided into many fragments by the documentary hypothesis.[38]

Shea raises the provocative question as to why Assyriologists have not divided the Enuma Elish account of creation and the Gilgamesh Epic of the flood into various sources as others have done for the Bible.[39] Was the success of the documentary hypothesis the result of an overreaction in the emancipation from religion brought on by the Enlightenment? Was it an overreaction to the popularity and acceptance of the Bible? Other suggestions could be given.

CONCLUSIONS

A number of questions have risen about the reliability of Scripture. That, however, is also the case for science. We can explain the relationship of a loving God and the suffering we experience and observe in several ways. Especially important is the presence of freedom of choice. It is not reasonable to blame God for everything, including evil, as long as freedom of choice exists. While some have questioned the events of creation week as described in the Bible, several models reconcile suggested inconsistencies. The idea that the Bible and especially the creation and flood accounts consist of compilations from various documents does not have a sound factual basis. The Bible attracts unusual attention, because it is an unusual book.

REFERENCES

1. Pascal B. 1670. Pensées. As quoted in: Tripp RT, compiler. 1970. The international thesaurus of quotations. New York, Cambridge, and Philadelphia: Harper and Row, p. 616.
2. See chapter 12.
3. Darwin F, editor. 1888. The life and letters of Charles Darwin, vol. 2. London: John Murray, p. 312.
4. A few meaningful references include: (a) Emberger G. 1994. Theological and scientific explanations for the origin and purpose of natural evil. Perspectives on Science and Christian Faith 46:150-158; (b) Hick J. 1977. Evil and the God of love. 2nd ed. London: Macmillan Press,

Ltd.; (c) Lewis CS. 1957. The problem of pain. New York: Macmillan Co.; (d) Lewis CS. 1961. A grief observed. New York: Seabury Press; (e) Wilder-Smith P, translator. Costa Mesa, Calif.: TWFT, Publishers. Translation of the 6th German edition.

5. Gen. 3:14-19; Rom. 5:12-19; 8:18-23.
6. Rom. 5:3; 2 Cor. 4:17; Heb. 12:9-11.
7. Caullery M. 1952. Parasitism and symbiosis. Lysaght AM, translator. London: Sidgwick and Jackson, Ltd., p. 120. Translation of: Le parasitisme et la symbiose.
8. Wu X-C, Sues H-D, Sun A. 1995. A plant-eating crocodyliform reptile from the Cretaceous of China. Nature 376:678-680.
9. See chapter 1 for a discussion of the legal issues involved. For more details about the Scopes trial, see: (a) Allen LH, editor. 1925. Bryan and Darrow at Dayton: the record and documents of the "Bible-Evolution Trial." New York: Russell and Russell; (b) Cornelius RM. 1991. World's most famous court trial. Reprinted from: Broyles BJ, compiler. History of Rhea County, Tennessee. Dayton: Rhea County Historical and Geneological Society, pp. 66-70; (c) Ginger R. 1958. Six days or forever? Tennessee versus John Thomas Scopes. Boston: Beacon Press.
10. Numbers RL. 1992. The creationists. New York: Alfred A. Knopf, p. 98.
11. E.g.: (a) Skinner J. 1930. A critical and exegetical commentary on Genesis. 2nd ed. In: Driver SR, Plummer A, Briggs CA, editors. The international critical commentary on the Holy Scriptures of the Old and New Testaments, vol. 1. Edinburgh: T. and T. Clark, p. 1; (b) Van Till HJ. 1986. The fourth day. Grand Rapids: Wm. B. Eerdmans Pub. Co., p. 80.
12. For further details, see: Hoen RE. 1951. The Creator and His workshop. Mountain View, Calif.: Pacific Press Pub. Assn., pp. 17-21.
13. Gen. 1:3, 15.
14. Ps. 104:2; Eze. 1:27, 28; Dan. 7:9, 10; 1 Tim. 6:16.
15. Rev. 21:23; 22:5
16. Gen. 1:16-19.
17. Gen. 1:1-3, Anchor. See also verses 103, Goodspeed.
18. Gen. 1:2.
19. Job 38:9, NIV.
20. 2 Peter 3:5, NIV.
21. John 1:3; Col. 1:16; Rev. 14:7.
22. E.g., (a) Bailey LR. 1993. Genesis, creation, and creationism. New York and Mahwah, N.J.: Paulist Press, pp. 82-85; (b) Cuthbert AS, Bowie WR. 1952. Genesis. Interpreter's Bible, vol. 1. New York and Nashville: Abingdon Press, pp. 437-827 (see p. 465).
23. Gen. 2:5.
24. Gen. 3:19, NIV.
25. Cassuto U. 1989. A commentary on the book of Genesis. Abrahans I, translator. Part I: from Adam to Noah: Genesis I-V18. Jerusalem: Magnes Press, Hebrew University, pp. 100-103. Translation of: Perush 'al Bereshit.
26. For a succinct review of the developments, see: Hasel GF. 1985. Biblical interpretation today. Washington, D.C.: Biblical Research Institute, pp. 28-36.
27. Funk RW, Hoover TW, The Jesus Seminar. 1993. The five gospels: the search for the authentic words of Jesus. New York: Macmillan Pub. Co.
28. Hasel, pp. 7-28 (note 26); see also note 36.
29. Hasel, p. 16 (note 26).
30. Archer GL, Jr. 1974. A survey of Old Testament introduction. Rev. ed. Chicago: Moody Press, pp. 112, 113.
31. See Hasel, pp. 27, 28 (note 26).
32. Matt. 19:8.
33. Cassuto U. 1961. The documentary hypothesis and the composition of the Pentateuch: eight lectures. Abrahams I, translator. Jerusalem: Magnes Press, the Hebrew University, pp. 100, 101. Translation of: Torat ha-te'udot vesiduram shel sifre ha-Torah (transliterated; 1941 ed.).
34. Archer, p. 91 (note 30).

35. See: (a) Cassuto, pp. 90-92 (note 25); (b) Garrett DA. 1991. Rethinking Genesis: the sources and authorship of the first book of the Pentateuch. Grand Rapids: Baker Book House, pp. 22-25; (c) Shea WH. 1978. The unity of the creation account. Origins 5:9-38; (d) Shea WH. 1990. Genesis 1 and 2 paralleled in an Ancient Near Eastern source. Adventist Perspectives 4(3):30-35.
36. This and other aspects supporting the unity of the two parts of the creation account can be found in: (a) Doukhan JB. 1978. The Genesis creation story: its literary structure. Andrews University Seminary Doctoral Dissertation Series, Vol. V. Berrien Springs, Mich.: Andrews University Press; (b) Doukhan J. 1995. La Création de L'Univers et de L'Homme. In: Meyer R, editor. Cheminer avec Dieu. Lausanne: Editions Belle Reviére, pp. 7-17; (c) Garrett, pp. 13-31, 187-241 (note 35b); (d) Shea (note 35c).
37. Shea WH. 1989. Literary structural parallels between Genesis 1 and 2. Origins 16:49-68.
38. Shea WH. 1979. The structure of the Genesis flood narrative and its implications. Origins 6:8-29.
39. Shea WH. 1984. A comparison of narrative elements in ancient Mesopotamian creation-flood stories with Genesis 1-9. Origins 11:9-29.

SOME CONCLUSIONS

IS SCIENCE IN TROUBLE?

In nearly all matters the human mind has a strong tendency to judge in the light of its own experience, knowledge and prejudices rather than on the evidence presented. Thus new ideas are judged in the light of prevailing beliefs.

—*W.I.B. Beveridge*[1]

Two centuries ago the French mathematician-astronomer Pierre-Simon de Laplace developed the nebular hypothesis. It proposed that the solar system originated by condensation from vaporous matter. Laplace, who had become famous as a scholar, decided to present a copy of one of his books to the emperor Napoleon. Having been told in advance that the book made no mention of God, the emperor asked Laplace why he had not even mentioned the Creator of the universe in his book. Laplace replied tersely that "he had no need of that particular hypothesis."[2]

Too frequently science has manifested an attitude of exclusiveness that tends to isolate it from other areas of inquiry. Laplace's comment reflects a self-sufficient attitude. Too often scientists leave others with the impression that science is superior to all other areas of inquiry. They consider any powers and realities foreign to science to be both inferior and illegitimate.[3] Science recognizes the existence of religion and scholarship in other areas, but it is loath to incorporate them into its own theories.[4] Scientism, the worship of science, can be restrictive.

While science is powerful and, from a practical standpoint, highly successful, some serious problems challenge that success both from inside and outside the scientific community. The thesis of this chapter is that science has been too exclusive. It would make a better contribution toward our fund of knowledge if it recognized its limitations and were more open to the validity of other disciplines. As indicated earlier,[5] many views and definitions of science exist, and in this chapter we will be dealing repeatedly with several of them. As delineated earlier, we will use the term *science* as it is usually understood—namely, finding information and interpretations about nature. Occasionally we will use the term *naturalistic science* to designate that science which excludes the concept of a Designer in its explanatory menu. We will employ *methodological science* to refer to that science which is more open to a variety of explanations, including the concept of a Designer. During the past two centuries science has tended toward the naturalistic definition, with some recent indications of reversal.[6] This reversal includes some semimystical concepts that have little to do with Scripture.

SOME PHILOSOPHICAL CONSIDERATIONS

A few brief comments about the philosophical history of science may help us as we try to understand the difficulty science now faces. Many consider the fifth-century B.C. Ionian philosophical school to be the first serious attempt at emancipating the human mind from ancient mythology into a naturalistic philosophy. Although this school broached some biological and cosmological topics with a philosophy that reflects modern science, it does not fit our usual concepts of empirical science (science based on sense perception and experimentation).

The ancient Greeks (fourth and third centuries B.C.) had a mixture of philosophical themes, some of them favorable to modern science. But a naturalistic approach was not strong among them. Aristotle strongly believed in God as a guiding force, and Socrates was not the "infidel" that history has often portrayed him as being. Actually, he opposed some of the naturalism of the Ionian school.

Experimental science came more into its own with the Islamic science of the eighth to fifteenth centuries. Its impetus resulted in part from religious motivation. To know God, one must study His creation. However, some discussed whether truth lies in divine revelation or reason.

Modern methodological science with affinities to Judeo-Christian traditions[7] followed in the sixteenth to seventeenth centuries. Ideas anticipating evolution also appear at this time—not among scientists, but among theologians[8] and philosophers such as Francis Bacon, Descartes, Leibniz, and Kant.[9] The pioneer scientists of this era, such as Kepler, Pascal, Linné, Boyle, and Newton, strongly favored creation by God.

This period experienced extensive intellectual turmoil. The Protestant Reformation and the Catholic Counter-Reformation contributed to the intellectual unrest. The "Enlightenment" of the eighteenth century is particularly important. Such notable thinkers as Diderot, Voltaire, Hume, Kant, and Goethe dominated this period. Rational free thought became a solution to almost everything, while religious concerns took a secondary place. The French Revolution followed this radical period. The subsequent bloodbath of the Reign of Terror did more than behead thousands, including Louis XVI and Marie Antoinette—it put a damper on the Enlightenment. A religious revival followed. Nevertheless, in intellectual circles the trend toward secularism continued.

Explanations of origins that excluded God won further acceptance as naturalistic scientific interpretations gained acceptance. The French marine zoologist Félix Lacaze-Duthiers (1821-1901) had a sign on his laboratory stating "science has neither religion nor politics."[10] Later this century Harvard physicist Philipp Frank pointed out that "every influence of moral, religious, or political considerations upon the acceptance of a theory is regarded as 'illegitimate' by the . . . 'community of scientists.'"[11] More recently, Nobel Laureate Christian de Duve, discussing the troublesome problem of the spontaneous origin of life, indicated that "any hint of teleology [purpose] must be avoided."[12] Such statements illustrate the strong exclusiveness of science as a naturalistic philosophy. Many scientists believe in God or some form of overruling mind or principle, but are reticent to mention these concepts in their scientific publications. Such ideas are considered unscientific.

Early in the twentieth century many considered science to be the authoritative source of information with almost limitless potential. The work of the Vienna Circle, a group of philosophers, scientists, and mathematicians who met regularly in Vienna, Austria, during the 1920s and 1930s, further strengthened this mind-set. A related group met in Berlin. World War II, however, brought on the demise of both groups.

The Vienna Circle emphasized *positivism,* which in its most extreme form stipulates that the only valid kind of knowledge is scientific (i.e., *only* naturalistic science). Their famous "manifesto" stated: "We are struggling for order and clarity. We reject all hazy perspectives and bottomless depths. For in science there are no depths; everything in it is on the surface."[13]

Their statement implied the concept that metaphysics (the more abstruse aspects of philosophy, such as ultimate beginnings, religion, ethics, and esthetics) is unacceptable. As faith in the perfection of naturalistic science increased, its practitioners attempted to make all significant concepts fit into physical coordinates such as time and space. They elevated physico-mathematical information to the level of absolute truth.

Such ideas dominated scientific thinking for many decades to well past the middle of the twentieth century, even though some disturbing challenges such as quantum mechanics and the "uncertainty principle," had made their appearance earlier. Some aspects of mathematics and logic were also in trouble. In 1931 the mathematician Kurt Goedel at the University of Vienna published a short and unwelcomed paper that showed that any system large enough to be interesting would have some unprovable elements. Several other scholars developed other theorems along the same line called the limitative theorems. These dashed hopes of finding a fully consistent system of truth. Even mathematics, which is free of the limits of observations and other restrictions of science, lacked certainty. It turns out that belief in the consistency of mathematics is a matter of faith and not of logical proof. Likewise, no broad scientific statement can be free of uncertainties. All this ran counter to the hopes of the Vienna Circle, and "despite their claim to modernity, the scientist-philosophers of the Vienna Circle were, rather, the last spokesmen of the Enlightenment."[14]

Later other scholars addressed more directly the apparent unwarranted respect for science. One of the most vocal critics has been Theodore Roszak, who objected to the reductionist (oversimplification) tendencies of scientific interpretations. In particular he criticized science for oversimplifying reality and for "the turning of people and nature into mere, worthless things."[15] According to him, human beings are more than mere machines.

The noted, and sometimes controversial, philosopher of science Paul Feyerabend of the University of California at Berkeley has been one of science's most vocal critics.[16] He has interpreted science as an anarchist movement, and proposed that since there exists no one scientific method, hence no consistency in science, the success of science must depend not only on logic but also on persuasion, propaganda, subterfuge, and rhetoric.[17] Because of its subjectivity, he states, science should receive equal status with astrology and witchcraft. Bemoaning the authority and respect generally given to science and scientists, he once stated, "The most stupid procedures and the most laughable results in their domain are surrounded with an aura of excellence. It is time to cut them down to size, and to give them a more modest position in society."[18] While such extreme views are difficult to justify, they underscore the negative reactions engendered by the self-confidence and exclusiveness of science.

All of this witnesses to the decline of positivism. The eminent twentieth-century scientific philosopher Karl Popper has pointed out that "the old scientific ideal of epistēmē—of absolutely certain, demonstrable knowledge—has proved to be an idol. The demand for scientific objectivity makes it inevitable that every scientific statement must remain tentative for ever. It may indeed be corroborated, but every corroboration is relative to other statements which, again, are tentative. Only in our subjective experiences of conviction, in our subjective faith, can we be 'absolutely certain.'. . .

"Science never pursues the illusory aim of making its answers final, or even probable."[19]

On the other hand, Popper himself has helped science regain some confidence by emphasizing an approach to scientific investigation that has achieved a significant degree of acceptance. He suggests that science should not try to establish truth by induction or confirmation of consequences or the refutation of rival concepts, but by the more severe empirical tests of trying to falsify the hypothesis itself, and a hypothesis should be empirically falsifiable before we can consider it scientific. Too often we fail to recognize that this concept tends to limit science to a rather small segment of reality.

NEWER TRENDS

Thomas Kuhn's concept of paradigms in science,[20] first published in 1962, raised many questions and gave rise to a kind of revolution itself. Up to that time the philosophy of the past century had been dominated by the philosophy of science. Now its influence has been declining. Some have labeled the philosophy of science as being in a "crisis stage" due to a loss of confidence in objectivity and to the collapse of positivism, which has sometimes been described as "dead."[21] Even empiricism is being viewed with less reverence.

Scholars now perceive science more as a human activity, and some characterize the contrast between so-called objective truth and metaphysics as a "relic of a bygone philosophy of science."[22] For instance, the question is being raised as to why cosmology should not be reinstated to its former status as the combined realm of science, philosophy, and religion. More and more are now interpreting science as an activity with sociological dimensions. The focus is increasingly on factors that determine the origin and formulation of scientific questions rather than on the answers to those questions. Complex, holistic (broad-approach) methods are replacing reductionistic (simplifying) ones.

The moderation of confidence in science is, of course, of major concern to some scientists. Unfortunately, many of them are unaware of the changes occurring in the philosophy of their discipline and its resulting impact. Nevertheless, the primacy science once held in intellectual circles is facing strong challenges. Two British scientists in expressing their concern, state: "Having lost their monopoly in the production of knowledge, scientists have also lost their privileged status in society."[23] These authors bemoan the resultant decline of funding for science and the ascent of concepts such as creation.

They are concerned that by releasing a monopoly on truth, the exercise of science may be reduced to a pointless game.

No one knows where the philosophy of science is heading next. In the past few years it has moved well beyond Kuhn's original sociological diagnosis and appears to be going in diverse directions.[24] Some philosophers are only presenting old wine in new bottles, while others have made a complete reversal from empirical concepts to more subjective bases. In general, the philosophy of science appears to be abandoning the view that science can give us perfect knowledge. It has begun to consider other factors (sociological, psychological, etc.) to be important determiners of scientific questions and answers. While scientism (science as a form of religion) is still very alive among some scientists, others are viewing science more as one of many valid avenues of inquiry.

While major changes are going on in the philosophy of science, the practice of science still maintains its tendency toward primacy and exclusiveness. The affects of a dominant past still exert great influence. Despite the fact that scientists repeatedly change their views and that too often today's dogma is tomorrow's heresy, there still remains the general "feeling that this time we have it right, this time we are about to come into possession of a finished science, knowing almost everything about everything."[25] Such attitudes have resulted in trouble for science.

EVOLUTION: A TROUBLED THEORY

Most of the scientific community still strongly defends evolution. Theodosius Dobzhansky, one of the world's leading geneticists and one of the architects of the modern evolutionary synthesis, once stated that "nothing in biology makes sense except in the light of evolution."[26] His comment implies that all the centuries of careful biological studies before the acceptance of evolution were evidently nonsensical! Many no longer consider the general theory of evolution to be a theory. Sir Julian Huxley declared that after Darwin's *Origin*, "the fact of evolution had been established and was no longer in need of further proof."[27] Many other leading evolutionists have characterized evolution as a fact;[28] yet this "fact" is an outstanding example of a dominant scientific concept that is currently in difficulty. Without doubt scientific discoveries over the past decades have not been kind to evolution. Probably the most severe challenge evolution faces is the question of the origin of life itself. If naturalistic science had not thought itself to be self-sufficient and capable of providing most answers, it might not have been satisfied with less than adequate explanations. Other questions about evolution, such as the missing links in the fossil record, the lack of time and lack of a workable evolutionary mechanism, continue to challenge the concept.[29] To this list we can add questions about the meaning of life and the origin and implications of our consciousness. Lewis Thomas, who was chancellor of the Memorial Sloan-Kettering Cancer Center in New York, states well the dilemma: "I cannot make my peace with the randomness doctrine; I cannot abide the notion of purposelessness and blind chance in nature. And yet I do not know what to put in its place for the quieting of my mind. It is absurd to say that a place like this place is absurd, when it contains, in front of our eyes, so many billions of different forms of life, each one in its way absolutely perfect, all linked together to form what would surely seem to an outsider a huge, spherical organism. We talk—some of us, anyway—about the absurdity of the human situation, but we do this because we do not know how we fit in, or what we are for. The stories we used to make up to explain ourselves do not make sense anymore, and we have run out of new stories, for the moment."[30]

Such turmoil is symptomatic of the absence of a workable model for evolution and the limited explanatory value of a naturalistic philosophy. Despite this, scientific thought shies away from such alternatives as creation, since the concept of a God is unacceptable in naturalistic scientific explanations.

Others have wondered why evolution should persist when so few points support it. Phillip Johnson, professor of law at the University of California at Berkeley, echoes some of these concerns[31] as he examines the tenets of evolution from a trial lawyer's perspective. Given the shaky case for evolution, he wonders why the experts can be so blind.

The popular writer and Christian apologist Malcolm Muggeridge emphasizes some of the same concerns: "I myself am convinced that the theory of evolution, especially the extent to which it's been applied, will be one of the great jokes in the history books in the future. Posterity will marvel that so very flimsy and dubious an hypothesis could be accepted with the incredible credulity that it has."[32]

The theory of evolution is a prime example of the dominance of a paradigm that has persisted even though the evidence to support it is often difficult to find. In particular, this persistence points out that all is not well with science. Science often prides itself on being open and objective, but evolution brings into question both attributes. How did science get into the conundrum of defending an idea for which there is little support and for which one finds major scientific problems?

WHEN SCIENCE MADE ITS GREATEST ERROR

Science has great power in the experimental realm. Unfortunately, this same science too often appears self-satisfied with a naturalistic system of explanations and disregards other realms of reality when drawing its conclusions. Such exclusiveness makes naturalistic science vulnerable to accusations of simplistic understanding. Many sense more to reality than the simple cause-and-effect system of naturalistic science. As one scientist stated: "It is time to try to reestablish an equilibrium between science and spirituality, allowing humankind to find again a place in this universe."[33]

The problem is not just evolution. In a sense, evolution is only an important symptom of a more deep-seated issue. The real difficulty is more whether naturalistic science is going to persist in trying to provide answers to all questions within its own closed system of explanations. How did science get into this intellectual straitjacket?

Science made its greatest error when it rejected God and everything else except mechanistic explanations. By failing to recognize its limitations, science has attempted to answer almost everything within a purely naturalistic philosophy. Evolution then became the most plausible model of origins. Science would not now be facing apparently insurmountable challenges to evolution if it had not adopted such a strong exclusive, naturalistic stance. Concepts of the creation of life would still offer a possible explanation as they did for the pioneers of modern science.

In contrast, the Bible, although disavowed by naturalistic science, shows much more inclusiveness. It gives scientific types of information, such as the waters of the deluge rising 15 cubits above the mountains[34] and the sun's shadow retreating 10 steps.[35] It also promotes a scientific type of methodology, telling us to "test everything, hold fast what is good."[36] The Bible encourages investigation.[37] Scripture also uses nature as evidence, reminding us that "the heavens declare the glory of God; and the firmament sheweth his handiwork"[38] (Figure 20.1). It declares that we have no excuse for not believing in God's power when we can clearly see it in the things that He made.[39] While naturalistic science has rejected the Bible, the Bible does not reject methodological science as a means to find truth about nature. The Bible is also inclusive of religion, morality, ultimate purposes, history, and the meaning of existence. It represents a broader approach that includes more of the reality that we see about us. As such it seems more suitable to address the great questions of origin and meaning.

Exclusiveness in science developed gradually and, paradoxically, had its roots in the open free-thinking mode of thought of the eighteenth-century Enlightenment. Naturalistic science as a limiting philosophy became accepted

FIGURE 20.1

View of the great galaxy in the Andromeda constellation, one of the few galaxies visible to the naked eye. The galaxy has an estimated diameter of about 200,000 light-years and lies about 2 million light-years away. Many stars, star clusters, novae, and nebulae have been identified in this galaxy. It is one small example of the breadth of approach found in the Scripture that encourages us to look not only at the Bible but also at nature. Science, on the other hand, tends to accept only itself.*

*Photo courtesy of Hale Observatories, California Institute of Technology.

in the nineteenth century with the work of such notables as Laplace, Hutton, Lyell, Chambers, Darwin, and Huxley, among many others.

One can only speculate as to the cause of this exclusiveness. I will mention only two possibilities. The much-respected scientific philosopher Michael Polanyi suggested an overreaction to the constraints of medieval thinking. He states: "This is where I see the trouble, where a deep-seated disturbance between science and all other culture appears to lie. I believe that this disturbance was inherent originally in the liberating impact of modern science on medieval thought and has only later turned pathological.

"Science rebelled against authority. It rejected deduction [reasoning based on premises] from first causes in favour of empirical [sense perception] generalizations. Its ultimate ideal was a mechanistic theory of the universe."[40]

A second cause may have its roots in the success of experimental science. Science deals with firm factors such as matter and energy and produces impressive explanations such as those of celestial mechanics and genetics. It is difficult to argue with success, and if science is so successful in some realms, should it not also be successful when it adopts a naturalistic philosophy for all of reality? Unfortunately, one of the characteristics of authoritarianism is a failure to recognize itself. The success of science in some areas has encouraged scientists and even the general public to think that science is all-powerful and offers the only valid source of truth. That success can then eclipse other less-tangible, but more important, explanations of reality that give ultimate meaning and purpose to humanity and nature. The achievements of science can cause us to become satisfied with more perceivable but simpler explanations that may not fully reflect reality.

We could mention a host of other reasons for the strong naturalistic stance of science, and doubtless a complex of causes led to it.

CONCLUSIONS AND A SUGGESTION

While science is highly successful, the scientific process has inherent limitations. Of late it has become apparent that, among other problems, the evolutionary model of naturalistic science faces serious scientific obstacles. However, science has difficulty in working its way out of this quandary, because it has taken such a strong naturalistic stance and is not now open to such alternatives as creation. "To involve purpose is in the eyes of biologists the ultimate scientific sin."[41] Evolution is the best model that naturalistic science can provide. On the other hand, the large number of serious challenges to evolution originating within the scientific community[42] and the downgrading of positivism and even empiricism give hope that science may be emancipating itself from its restricted explanatory menu.

I would hope that naturalistic science would take a more inclusive stance toward other areas of inquiry and incorporate a broader realm of possibilities into its thought system. Science should return more toward the philosophy it had when Western civilization established science's foundations. At that time methodological science saw itself as the discovery of the principles of nature that God had Himself established in His creation. This perspective would help resolve some of the major questions naturalistic science now faces. It would also provide a broader base for arriving at truth and would give science an image of greater openness and understanding.

REFERENCES

1. Beveridge WIB. 1957. The art of scientific investigation. Rev. ed. New York: W. W. Norton and Co., p. 107.
2. As reported in: Dampier WC. 1949. A history of science and its relations with philosophy and religion. 4th ed., rev. Cambridge: Cambridge University Press; New York: Macmillan Co., p. 181.
3. Proudfoot W. 1989. Religion and science. In: Lotz DW, Shriver DW, Jr., Wilson JF, editors. Altered landscapes: Christianity in America, 1935-1985. Grand Rapids: Wm. B. Eerdmans Pub. Co., pp. 268-279.
4. Gibson RE. 1964. Our heritage from Galileo Galilei. Science 145:1271-1281.
5. See chapter 17.
6. See chapter 3.
7. *Ibid.*
8. Mayr E. 1982. The growth of biological thought: diversity, evolution, and inheritance. Cambridge, Mass., and London: Belknap Press of Harvard University Press, p. 309.
9. Dampier, p. 273 (note 2).
10. Quoted in: Nordenskiöld E. 1928. The history of biology: a survey. Eyre LB, translator. New York: Alfred A. Knopf, p. 426. Translation of: Biologins Historia.
11. Quoted in: Barber B. 1961. Resistance by scientists to scientific discovery. Science 134:596-602.
12. De Duve C. 1995. The beginnings of life on earth. American Scientist 83:428-437.
13. Quoted in: Zycinski JM. 1988. The structure of the metascientific revolution: an essay on the growth of modern science. Heller M, Zycinski J, editors. Philosophy in science library. Tucson, Ariz.: Pachart Pub. House, p. 49.
14. Toulmin S. 1989. The historicization of natural science: its implications for theology. In: Küng H, Tracy D, editors. Paradigm change in theology: a symposium for the future. Köhl M, translator. New York: Crossroad Pub. Co., pp. 233-241. Translation of: Theologie—Wohin? and Das Neue Paradigma von Theologie.
15. Roszak T. 1972. Where the wasteland ends: politics and transcendence in postindustrial society. Garden City, N.Y.: Doubleday and Co., p. 252.
16. Feyerabend P. 1988. Against method. Rev. ed. London and New York: Verso.
17. For examples of the use of rhetoric in science, see: Pera M, Shen WR, editors. 1991. Persuading science: the art of scientific rhetoric. Canton, Mass.: Science History Publications.
18. Feyerabend P. 1975. Against method: outline of an anarchistic theory of knowledge. London: New Left Books; Atlantic Highlands: Humanities Press, p. 304.
19. Popper KR. 1959. The logic of scientific discovery. New York: Basic Books, pp. 280, 281.
20. See chapters 2 and 17.
21. (a) Blackwell RJ. 1981. A new direction in the philosophy of science. The Modern Schoolman 59:55-59; (b) Durbin PT. 1986. Ferment in philosophy of science: a review discussion. Thomist 50:690-700.
22. Zycinski, p. 178 (note 13).
23. Theocharis T, Psimopoulos M. 1987. Where science has gone wrong. Nature 329:595, 598.
24. (a) Durbin (note 21b); (b) Gillies D. 1993. Philosophy of science in the twentieth century: four central themes. Oxford and Cambridge: Blackwell Publishers; (c) Smith H. 1982. Beyond the post-modern mind. New York: Crossroad Pub. Co., pp. 16-27.
25. Thomas L. 1980. On the uncertainty of science. Harvard Magazine 83(1):19-22.
26. Dobzhansky T. 1973. Nothing in biology makes sense except in the light of evolution. The American Biology Teacher 35:125-129.
27. Huxley J. 1958. Introduction to the Mentor edition of Charles Darwin: the origin of species by

means of natural selection, or the preservation of favoured races in the struggle for life. New York: New American Library of World Literature, p. xv.
28. For six other examples, see: Bird WR. 1987, 1988, 1989. Philosophy of science, philosophy of religion, history, education, and constitutional issues. The origin of species revisited: the theories of evolution and of abrupt appearance, vol. 2. New York: Philosophical Library, pp. 129, 159, 160.
29. See chapters 4-8, 11.
30. Thomas (note 25).
31. (a) Johnson PE. 1993. Darwin on trial. 2nd ed. Downers Grove, Ill.: InterVarsity Press; (b) Johnson PE. 1995. Reason in the balance: the case against naturalism in science, law, and education. Downers Grove, Ill.: InterVarsity Press.
32. Muggeridge M. 1980. The end of Christendom. Grand Rapids: Wm. B. Eerdmans Pub. Co., p. 59.
33. Mousseau N. 1994. Searching for science criticism's sources: letters. Physics Today 47:13, 15.
34. Gen. 7:19-21.
35. 2 Kings 20:10.
36. 1 Thess. 5:21, RSV.
37. Eccl. 1:13; Dan. 1:11-16.
38. Ps. 19:1.
39. Rom. 1:20.
40. Grene M, editor. 1969. Knowing and being: essays by Michael Polanyi. Chicago: University of Chicago Press, p. 41.
41. Hoyle F, Wickramasinghe NC. 1981. Evolution from space: a theory of cosmic creationism. New York: Simon and Schuster, p. 32.
42. See chapter 8.

ALTERNATIVES BETWEEN CREATION AND EVOLUTION

My people are destroyed for lack of knowledge.
—Hosea 4:6

The famous Englishman Thomas Huxley, Charles Darwin's able and valiant defender, once asserted that no man could be "both a true son of the Church and a loyal soldier of science."[1] Whether or not Huxley's 1871 statement is true, hosts of scholars have not followed his warning and have been trying to adjust both the biblical concept of creation and science's evolutionary theory so as to bring about some reconciliation.[2] Huxley's statement reflects his well-known aversion to religion. After he spoke at the opening ceremony of Johns Hopkins University in the United States, a critic wryly remarked: "It was bad enough to invite Huxley. It were better to have asked God to be present. It would have been absurd to ask them both."[3]

Our discussion in earlier chapters has generally focused on whether science or Scripture is correct. This is where the battle has been most intense, for here we find a sharp conflict between two respected sources of information. In this chapter we consider views that attempt to combine portions of both creation and evolution. Such interesting views are now quite popular among scholars in the Christian community. However, they are vague and because of this do not offer us much serious synthesis that we can put into testable models. Such intermediate views, compromising both naturalistic science and the Bible, have little to support them. Thus we find confusion both in the classification[4] and the terminology[5] of such alternatives. Nevertheless, many see in them the possibility of including some contemporary scientific interpretations along with some religion or Scripture. As has been the case for the creation-evolution debate, people have devoted considerable time, energy, and paper to such views.[6]

MODELS

I have outlined below a variety of intermediate views together with creation and evolution under eight main categories. Included are some of the questions each one raises. The geologic column[7] with its fossils telling us about past life is, or should be, a basic consideration of each view. Figure 21.1 gives a general image of the eight models and shows how each one relates to the geologic column. Time proceeds from bottom to top (not necessarily as a linear scale) as indicated in Model 1 by the arrow at the left. The heavy vertical line toward the left in each rectangle represents the geologic column. The lower and older geologic layers are at the bottom. The models are numbered in a general—although arguable—order that displays an increasing trend toward purely naturalistic interpretations and away from the Genesis account of beginnings.

1. Creation (also called Recent Creation, Special Creation, Young-earth Creation, or Fiat Creation)

Description of Model—This model reflects the most direct reading of Scripture.[8] God performed His creative acts in six literal days, each described

FIGURE 21.1

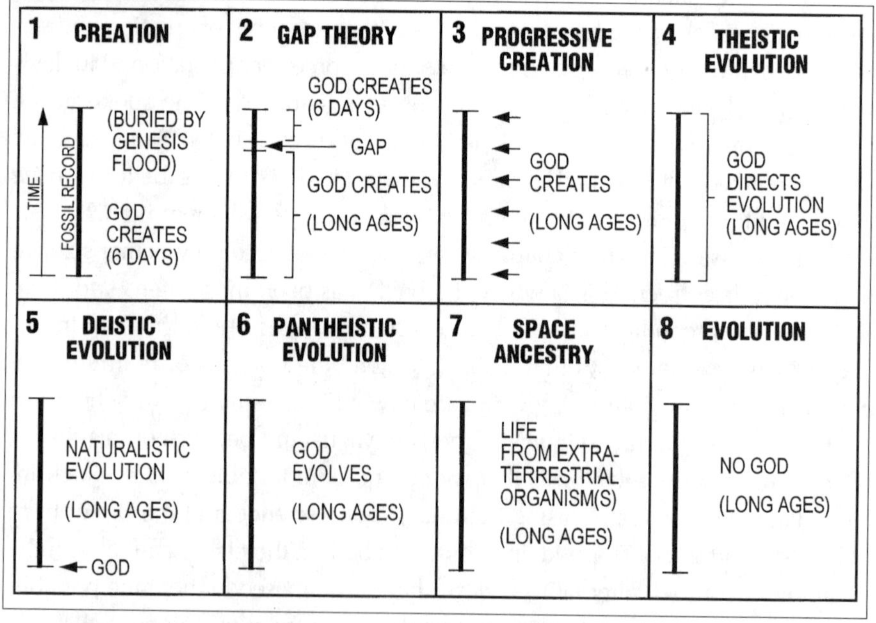

1 CREATION	2 GAP THEORY	3 PROGRESSIVE CREATION	4 THEISTIC EVOLUTION
TIME; FOSSIL RECORD; (BURIED BY GENESIS FLOOD); GOD CREATES (6 DAYS)	GOD CREATES (6 DAYS); GAP; GOD CREATES (LONG AGES)	GOD CREATES (LONG AGES)	GOD DIRECTS EVOLUTION (LONG AGES)
5 DEISTIC EVOLUTION	**6 PANTHEISTIC EVOLUTION**	**7 SPACE ANCESTRY**	**8 EVOLUTION**
NATURALISTIC EVOLUTION (LONG AGES); GOD	GOD EVOLVES (LONG AGES)	LIFE FROM EXTRA-TERRESTRIAL ORGANISM(S) (LONG AGES)	NO GOD (LONG AGES)

Representation of eight interpretations of the geologic column. The heavy bracketed line to the left in each rectangle represents the geologic column. The arrow in Model 1 shows the direction of time for all models, with the oldest layers being at the bottom.

with its own evening and morning.[9] Creation took place a few thousand years ago. After that creation evil became so rampant that God had to suppress it by a flood, the major catastrophe that produced most of the fossiliferous sedimentary layers on earth's surface. The Genesis flood event reconciles the fossil record to a six-day creation.[10]

The model fits well with scientific observations such as the lack of transitional fossils, the evidences for design, and the data suggesting rapid deposition of the sedimentary layers.

A variation of this model postulates that God created the fossils in place in the rocks.[11] Such an idea has little acceptance at present. One reason for its rejection is the contradiction it creates between the good and truthful God described in the Bible and the trickery implied in making fake fossils. Another alternative is that God created the matter of earth eons ago, but He prepared the earth for life and created life forms only a few thousand years ago in six days.[12] Sometimes called the soft-gap theory, this model has significant acceptance.

Questions—The model disagrees with those scientific interpretations that specify long ages for the deposition of the fossil layers and the evolutionary interpretation of the fossil sequence, as discussed in earlier chapters.[13]

In an attempt to preserve the integrity of the creation account, some have proposed a creation week a long time ago, much earlier than the few thousand years suggested by Scripture. This ancient-creation-week concept runs into some difficulty when we compare details of the fossil record with the Bible. Creation week is an all-inclusive event during which all the major kinds of organisms originate. If that week occurred long ago at the beginning of the fossil record and fossilization of the various living forms took place gradually over long ages, the major types of organisms should be well-represented from the lowest part to the top part of the fossil record. But, as we can see in Figure 10.1, many of the groups are unique at different levels. Deposition of the fossils in an ecological sequence or from different sources by the deluge[14] seems to be a better way to integrate creation week with the uniqueness of the layers of the fossil sequence.

2. The Gap Theory[15] (also called Ruin and Restoration, or Hard Gap)

Description of the Model—God created life on earth in the distant past. Later, following a judgment upon Satan, He destroyed that life. The creation described in Genesis 1 and 2 then followed. The *Scofield Reference Bible* has supported this interpretation by the tenuous comparison of Genesis, which says that earth was a waste place (ruined), with Isaiah, which reports that God did not create earth as a waste place.[16] Hence, earth must have become a waste place (ruined) subsequent to an ancient creation not described in Scripture.

Questions—We have no *direct,* scientific, scriptural, or other evidence for the idea itself. The fossil record contains no indication of a worldwide change in fossils (re-creation) and a gap. If there had been a gap, we would expect a distinct blank period (gap) on a worldwide basis prior to a subsequent re-creation.

Concepts such as this model are rationally unsatisfying because they lack external evidence. As an example, we can propose that we were all created only 15 minutes ago with a fully mature environment complete with developed minds and past memories. While we can use these kinds of models to answer many questions, we tend to reject them because they are so subjective. Our experience tells us that reality is not that capricious. The testable parts are not. We should look for good anchor points.

A somewhat related concept is that the fossil record and some of our living organisms are the results of experiments that Satan conducted on earth during long ages before creation week. This model also raises several problems. It is highly subjective. Scientific data do not indicate directly that such a scenario ever occurred, and Scripture has a different model of origins. The Genesis account describes an original earth that is both empty and dark at the beginning of creation week,[17] yet light is necessary for the life represented by fossils. The Bible does not support the concept of life before creation week. Also, Scripture repeatedly describes God—and not Satan—as the Creator.[18]

3. Progressive Creation[19] (the Day-Age and Revelation-Day concepts can fit under this classification)

Description of the Model—God performed multiple creation events spread over long periods of time. The degree of progression that we find from bottom to top in the fossil record reflects successive creative acts. This model fits with both the evidence of missing links in the fossil record, which supports creation, and the scientific interpretation of long ages for life in the geologic column.

The Day-Age modification proposes that each day of creation described in the Genesis account represents an extremely long period. The Revelation-Day concept suggests that creation required a long time, but God's disclosure of that creation to the author of Genesis took only seven days.

Questions—Neither scientific data nor Scripture suggests that creation occurred this way. The basic idea lacks support. It disallows the biblical concept of a six-day, all-inclusive creation as given in Genesis and the Ten

Commandments. In the progressive-creation model, the presence of rampant predation (e.g., the carnivorous dinosaurs) earlier than human beings in the fossil record suggests that evil, in the form of predation, appears before the advent of humanity. This negates the Genesis account of a good Creator and a perfect creation, followed by the fall and its consequent evil.[20] In the New Testament the apostle Paul also attests to the origin of evil by human transgression.[21] Progressive creation also implies many errors or failures by God over long periods of time before the advent of evil. Thousands of important groups of plants and animals at various levels in the fossil record no longer live on the earth's surface. The geneticist Theodosius Dobzhansky,[22] while criticizing belief in creation, emphasized the theological problem of extinction: "But what a senseless operation it would have been, on God's part, to fabricate a multitude of species ex nihilo and then let most of them die out!" Again, for the progressive-creation model this would have occurred before the appearance of human beings, their fall, and the consequences of sin on nature. Progressive creation raises this question without providing a good explanation. We can postulate a God who would create by this method, but He would not be the omniscient God portrayed in the Bible—a God whose creation Genesis describes as "very good."[23] Genesis provides an explanation for these extinct organisms by the subsequent worldwide deluge brought on because of human wickedness.

The Day-Age and the Revelation-Day modifications do not provide any improvement, since the sequence of the created kinds of organisms listed in Genesis does not fit the sequence of the fossil record. Genesis indicates that God created plants on day 3 and animals on days 5 and 6, while in the fossil sequence most animal groups appear before (lower than) most plant groups (see Figure 10.1). If the days of creation represent millions of years, how would plants created on day 3 requiring insects to pollinate them survive for millions of years waiting for animals created on days 5 and 6?

The idea of Revelation-Days faces the further incongruity that both in Genesis and in the Ten Commandments in Exodus[24] the texts speak of God *creating* on the days under consideration, not just God revealing information.[25]

4. Theistic Evolution[26] (sometimes referred to as Theological Evolution, Evolutionary Creationism, and Biblical Evolutionism)

Description of the Model—God directs in the continuous process of evolution from simple to complex. The idea fits fairly easily with many concepts of the general theory of evolution and still permits God's activity. Also, God is available to bridge some of the difficult barriers that evolution faces, e.g., the problem of the origin of life; the development of complex, integrated, biological systems; and the origin of humanity's higher mental faculties.

Questions—The missing links in the fossil record do not suggest a continuous process of evolution. The model seems demeaning to God, in contrast to the all-powerful Creator described in the Bible. Here He uses the crutch of evolution to produce advanced forms. The problem of numerous created errors implied by extinct groups (see Model 3), and the slow progress and competition implied in an evolutionary model, challenge the idea of God's creative power, knowledge, and goodness. Survival by competition and death of the weak seems especially out of character with the God of the Bible who has concern for the sinner,[27] does not forget the sparrow,[28] and whose ideal for life includes the lion and the lamb living peacefully together.[29] As in the case for progressive creation (Model 3), we also face the logical difficulty of the appearance of evil in nature before the fall of human beings.

5. Deistic Evolution[30]

Description of the Model—This ill-defined concept denies the revelation of Scripture but admits to some kind of God who was active mainly at the beginning. A usually impersonal God, not now active in human affairs, serves as a first cause. This Deity might resolve the most difficult problem evolution faces by originating life and possibly in some views guiding the formation of some complex biological systems.

Questions—The model faces many of the problems that evolution faces. One has to deny the evidence of the special nature of Scripture.[31] Since it eliminates the role of a personal God, it is more difficult to conceive of the origin of humanity's higher characteristics, such as love, morality, and concern, that seem to be founded in interpersonal relationships. We find little either scientifically or scripturally to *directly* authenticate such a model.

6. Pantheistic Evolution[32]

Description of the Model—God is all and all is God. He still exists. Nature is special, and God progresses with evolution itself. Some have related some Eastern cultures, New Age, and Gaia with this concept.

Questions—This model has some of the same problems as those given for the previous one. In addition, in the evolutionary process of survival God becomes both the destroyer and the victim of destruction. This is highly demeaning to the concept of God's greatness as depicted in the Bible. Neither Scripture nor nature offers any *direct* data indicating that this is God's past history.

7. Space Ancestry[33] (also refers to Cosmic Creation and Directed Panspermia)

Description of the Model—Under this heading we can include a variety of ideas that have gained some popularity in recent years. Basically they postulate extraterrestrial life forms originating or modifying terrestrial life. Some of the ideas propose that simple life, possibly traveling in a meteorite, passively reached earth. Others postulate that extraterrestrial beings deliberately brought them, or life came as a contaminant from refuse left on earth by a space traveler. This latter concept is the so-called "garbage theory." Some have even suggested hybridization between "superbeings" and earthly organisms to produce more advanced forms of life. Such models solve some of the problems of naturalistic evolution, especially regarding the origin of life on earth, by invoking organisms from outer space. One is no longer bound to terrestrial limitations.

Questions—Probably the most serious problem of this kind of model is the same as for many of the others presented above—namely, a lack of support for the ideas themselves. While they can solve some problems, the high degree of conjecture invoked makes them unattractive. Also, doubt exists about unprotected organisms surviving interplanetary space travel. Relegating the origin of complex life to some remote location in the universe does not help significantly in providing an adequate naturalistic explanation for its initial origin.

8. Evolution[34] (also called Mechanistic Evolution or Naturalistic Evolution)

Description of the Model—The concept of evolution suits those who limit the concept of reality to mechanistic causes. The various forms of life have developed as a result of the operation of natural law. It involves no intelligent design. Life originated first by the organization of the right molecules and developed thereafter. Advanced forms resulted from random mutations or mutations in combination with natural selection.

Questions—This model does not answer questions such as the following:[35] How do complex life systems originate on earth without a designer? How do inept, incomplete, still developing forms survive the competition of naturalistic evolution? How can one bridge across the missing transitional fossil forms? How can we reconcile the evidence for rapid geologic activity with the immensity of time required for highly improbable evolutionary events? How can humanity's higher characteristics, such as consciousness, free will, and love, originate in a purely mechanistic system?

There are other perspectives on the eight models given above, and other views intermediate to them. However, the examples given here serve to illustrate the variety of ideas being considered.

RELATION OF VARIOUS INTERPRETATIONS TO SCIENTIFIC INFORMATION

We have discussed much of the scientific information relating to these models in earlier chapters and need not repeat it here. Because we are considering so many different views, it is not easy to formulate a simple general statement.

Some scientific data helps us to differentiate between some of the models. The missing intermediates in the fossil record would seem to give preference for Models 1-3 over 4-8, (see Figure 21.1 for models) while scientific conclusions of long, gradual development for life would favor Models 2-8 over Model 1. Evidence to support a worldwide flood and a short time for the formation of the fossiliferous layers emphasizes Model 1. If we adhere strictly to a naturalistic interpretation of science, then we can accept only Model 8 and some versions of Model 7. By contrast, the concept of a personal God opens up the possibility of accepting Models 1-4, and some rare interpretations of Model 5.

RELATIONSHIP OF VARIOUS INTERPRETATIONS TO SCRIPTURE

None of the eight interpretations of origins discussed above, except the creation model (Model 1), have good biblical support. Models 2 through 8 suggest progress, while the Bible speaks of degeneration of nature since creation.[36] For several (Models 4-6), the concept of a God is their only serious link to Scripture. The Bible portrays the original earth as undeveloped, empty, and dark.[37] Since light is necessary for plants and animals require plants, the absence of light would seem to exclude any models with normal life before creation week.

Some suggest that the Bible supports the idea of long ages for each creation day. They use texts from both Psalms and 2 Peter,[38] which infer that to God 1,000 years is as a day, as support. However, such texts are really discussing the briefness of human existence and God's patience, and not creation week.[39] Also, as pointed out earlier, Scripture describes each creation day with its own evening and morning, something difficult to reconcile with millions of years.

Those who adopt one of the views intermediate to creation and evolution often assume the first part of Genesis to be allegorical.[40] Such an approach undermines the Bible as a whole, because the leading biblical personalities, either directly or by implication, refer to Genesis 1 through 11, which include both the creation and flood accounts, as factual history. Their testimony supports the truthfulness of the biblical account of beginnings.

The apostle Peter believed Genesis 1 through 11 to be factual. He stated that scoffers in the last days would be willingly ignorant of creation by God and destruction by the flood.[41] Peter also authenticates the account of Noah being saved by the ark during the flood.[42]

The apostle Paul did not consider Genesis 1 through 11 as allegorical. Several times he mentions the creation of Adam and Eve, or Adam as the first man.[43] He also appears to authenticate the flood and the existence of Abel, Cain, Enoch, and Noah[44] who lived between creation and the flood.

Christ refers to both the creation and the flood accounts in Genesis 1 through 11 as factual. He cites the Scripture describing God's creation of male and female,[45] mentions the evilness of Noah's time, and specifically refers to the day that Noah entered the ark.[46] Without question Christ believed in both creation and the flood described in Genesis.

God Himself authenticates both the creation and flood accounts. In the book of Isaiah He repeats His promise: "as I have sworn that the waters of Noah should no more go over the earth."[47] Likewise in the Ten Commandments[48] He authenticates the Genesis record of beginnings. All this runs counter to all the models for the development of life by an extended process over millions of years. In His own words, He created all in "six days." Such a thing could hardly be possible if each day represents millions of years. All of this substantiates the biblical model of a creation in six days. There is no suggestion in the Bible of the creation of life over an extended period of time.

If you believe in the biblical account of beginnings, you are in the good company of Peter, Paul, Christ, and God. It would be a strange God who would create over millions of years and then ask human beings to keep holy the seventh-day Sabbath as a memorial of His creating all in six days. Repeatedly Scripture tells us that the God of the Bible always speaks the truth and detests lying.[49] As God, He could order that the Sabbath be kept for a variety of other reasons. God personally gave the Ten Commandments, which state that He created in six days, and they represent His most authoritative communication to humanity. We cannot easily dismiss them. It would likewise be a strange God who would allow His prophets to be deceived for millennia on the all-important question of beginnings, only to wait for Charles Lyell and Charles Darwin to present the correct view. There does not seem to be any way to reconcile the biblical account of beginnings with long geological ages.

A linking of science and Scripture is not the same as a compromise of both views. One has to recognize that the Bible is not amenable to much compromise. Either it is the Word of God, as it claims, or it is a collection of human wisdom, posing as the Word of God. In the latter case we have a serious problem about the integrity of its writers. Scripture is more in an "all-or-nothing" mode than is science. Hence, dismissal of the Bible's "recent creation" model of origins tends more toward a rejection of Scripture as a whole than rejection of evolution is a discarding of science as a whole. Science, with its claims to be open to revision is, at least in principle, more amenable to change.

THEOLOGICAL TRENDS

Liberal theological views allegorize the biblical creation and flood accounts and generally yield in varying degrees to contemporary scientific interpretations. As they do so, they are following one of the weakest aspects of science, called historical science, which deals with the past and is more difficult to evaluate.[50] Possibly liberal theology has been so impressed by the success of experimental science that it does not recognize the limitations of historical science. Theologians may need to be more cautious in accepting a discipline unfamiliar to them. The philosopher of science Stephen Toulmin of Northwestern University and the University of Chicago warns theologians not to follow science too closely. He points out how this has gotten them into trouble in the past. As examples he mentions how in medieval times churchmen enthusiastically endorsed Aristotle and gave his views "an authority beyond their true strength." Likewise, later in dealing with cosmology they followed the mechanical ideas of Descartes and Newton. He states further: "In both cases, the results were unfortunate. Having plunged too deep in their original scientific commitments, the theologians concerned failed to foresee the possibility that Aristotle's or Newton's principles might not forever be 'the last word'; and, when radical changes took place in the natural sciences, they were unprepared to deal with them."

He also warns that to continue endorsing new scientific theories "will simply lay up fresh trouble for theology a century or two down the road, when scientists have rethought the problems of their own disciplines, to the point of making radical changes for which theologians would once again be ill prepared. . . . It will be better if they distance themselves from the ideas of science rather than embrace them too systematically and uncritically."[51]

By yielding the authority of the Bible to science, at least as far as interpretations of nature are concerned, liberal theology finds itself with a weakened basis for its own discipline. The Bible is no longer as authoritative. For liberal theologians, concepts of origins have moved well toward naturalistic evolution (Models 2-8). Once we abandon the authority of Scripture, we find ourselves on a slippery slide with few anchor points in sight. And when we reach a purely naturalistic philosophy, we discover many important questions unanswered. The challenge facing those who espouse intermediate views (Models 2-7) is to provide a better model than that offered by either science or Scripture. They especially need some authoritative sources for their models. But modern liberal theology is not contributing much to our knowledge about the important question of origins. The conservative "dean" of evangelical theologians, Carl F. Henry, puts the problem of priorities of authority into a different focus when he states: "Theology does not depend on an ordered universe: an ordered universe depends upon God."[52]

The physicist and Nobel Prize winner Steven Weinberg of the University of Texas has further concerns about liberal theological thinking. He states his case rather clearly: "Religious liberals are in one sense even farther in spirit from scientists than are fundamentalists and other religious conservatives. At least the conservatives like the scientists tell you that they believe in what they believe because it is true, rather than because it makes them good or happy. Many religious liberals today seem to think that different people can believe in different mutually exclusive things without any of them being wrong, as long as their beliefs 'work for them.' This one believes in reincarnation, that one in heaven and hell; a third believes in the extinction of the soul at death, but no one can be said to be wrong as long as everyone gets a satisfying spiritual rush from what they believe. To borrow a phrase from Susan Sontag, we are surrounded by 'piety without content.'. . .

"Wolfgang Pauli was once asked whether he thought that a particularly ill-conceived physics paper was wrong. He replied that such a description would be too kind—the paper was not even wrong. I happen to think that the religious conservatives are wrong in what they believe, but at least they have not forgotten what it means really to believe something. The religious liberals seem to me to be not even wrong."[53]

It would appear that Modern and Post-Modern theological trends could benefit by returning to the authority of the Bible.

THE DRIFTING PROBLEM

The intermediate views we have examined above have had a strong influence on the beliefs of many Christian churches. Since the popularization of the theory of evolution more than a century ago, many religious denominations have in some way accommodated to the various ideas of the progressive development of life during long ages. It is disappointing to see churches that once placed a high priority on biblical authority eventually change their beliefs; yet it occurs, often slowly and insidiously.[54] Erosion of membership often accompanies erosion of beliefs.[55] In recent years the mainline churches in the United States—who no longer believe in the biblical account of creation and many other traditional biblical concepts—have lost millions of members, while the more conservative evangelical churches have grown rapidly. It is particularly difficult to convince people that Christianity is for real when so many describe the Bible as in error, especially with respect to the important question of origins.

Theologian-sociologist H. Richard Niebuhr,[56] among others, has outlined the traditional history of a religious group. After its organization, the birth of a new generation soon changes the character of the sect. The new generation rarely has the fervor of its forebears, who fashioned their "convictions in the heat of conflict and at the risk of martyrdom." Succeeding generations find isolation from the world more difficult. Wealth and culture accrue as compromise of the original purposes brings in more accommodated beliefs and behavior. Soon the new group becomes a traditional church, more a social structure than the originally intended instrument for reform. Managerial requirements increasingly distract the church's efforts from religious pursuits.

Drifting away from the Bible and God is a common sociological pattern as has been repeatedly illustrated in biblical history. Repeatedly God had to use drastic means in an attempt to reverse such trends. Such incidents as the Genesis flood, the long sojourn of the Israelites in the desert, and the Babylonian captivity depict how difficult but important it is to resist such pressures.

Modern educational institutions also reflect the same tendency to drift.[57] A large number of institutions of higher learning in the United States (such as Auburn University, Boston University, Brown, Dartmouth, Harvard, Princeton, Rutgers, Tufts, the University of Southern California, Wesleyan University, Wichita State University, and Yale) began as religious institutions but have since moved well down the path of secularization and are no longer church-related. It is significant that (at least to this writer's knowledge) no institution has begun as secular and then become religious. Here also the trend seems to be away from God. And it is not entirely surprising. As long as the dominant climate of scholarly pursuits is secular, we can expect this to happen. Public and many private educational institutions seldom condone, let alone encourage, religious commitment.

The pattern of drifting away from God appears in modern churches, in biblical history, and in educational institutions. In my opinion, this is unfortunate. The eight models of interpretation of the fossil record given above, and a number of other intermediates that we could place between them, illustrate how one can easily and imperceptibly drift away from a belief in a recent creation by God to a naturalistic evolution where there is no God.

CONCLUSIONS

The many views between creation and evolution tend to be ill-defined. Such models have no basis in either Scripture or the data from nature and have little support from either source. One can endlessly suggest models, but until we can authenticate them, they should not command any firm support.

We can use some scientific data to indirectly support in varying degrees any of the models we have considered. For some the data are quite sparse. On the other hand, the Bible confirms only the creation concept. There is only one biblical model of beginnings. In God's own words, He created all in six days. Other leading Bible personalities also support the truthfulness of the creation account given in Genesis.

The intermediate views I have described can provide a way to gradually move from belief in creation toward naturalistic evolution. This drift can result in a gradual exclusion of God. While many traditional churches have tended in this direction, I would hope that they would exert efforts in the opposite direction: toward the Bible with its exceptional explanatory value, and toward God.

REFERENCES

1. Huxley TH. 1893. Darwiniana: essays. New York and London: D. Appleton and Co., p. 149.
2. See chapter 3 for some examples.
3. (a) Bibby C. 1959. T. H. Huxley: scientist, humanist, and educator. New York: Horizon Press, p. 236; (b) Bibby C. 1972. Scientist extraordinary: the life and scientific work of Thomas Henry Huxley 1825-1895. New York: St. Martin's Press, p. 97.
4. For a sample of the definitions and/or classification schemas of these various views, see: (a) Bailey LR. 1993. Genesis, creation, and creationism. New York and Mahwah, N.J.: Paulist Press, pp. 121-130; (b) Baldwin JT. 1994. Inspiration, the natural sciences, and a window of opportunity. Journal of the Adventist Theological Society 5(1):131-154; (c) Ecker RL. 1990. Dictionary of science and creationism. Buffalo: Prometheus Books, pp. 71, 208; (d) Johns WH. 1981. Strategies for origins. Ministry 54(May):26-28; (e) Key TDS. 1960. The influence of Darwin on biology. In: Mixter RL, editor. Evolution and Christian thought today. 2nd ed. Grand Rapids: Wm. B. Eerdmans Pub. Co., pp. 11-32; (f) Lewis JP. 1989. The days of creation: an historical survey of interpretation. Journal of the Evangelical Theological Society 32:433-455; (g) Maatman R. 1993. The impact of evolutionary theory: a Christian view. Sioux Center, Iowa: Dordt College Press, pp. 162-185; (h) Marsh FL. 1950. Studies in creationism. Washington, D.C.: Review and Herald Pub. Assn., pp. 22-55, 69-78; (i) McIver TA. 1989. Creationism: intellectual origins, cultural context, and theoretical diversity. Ph.D. dissertation, Department of Anthropology. Los Angeles: University of California at Los Angeles, pp. 403-541. Available from: Ann Arbor, Mich.: University Microfilms; (j) Mitchell C. 1994. The case for creationism. Grantham, England: Autumn House, Ltd., pp. 191-202; (k) Pinnock CH. 1989. Climbing out of a swamp: the evangelical struggle to understand the creation texts. Interpretation 43(2):143-155; (l) Roth AA. 1980. Implications of various interpretations of the

fossil record. Origins 7:71-86; (m) Thompson B. 1995. Creation compromises. Montgomery, Ala.: Apologetics Press, Inc.; (n) Wilcox DL. 1986. A taxonomy of creation. Journal of the American Scientific Affiliation 38:244-250; (o) Young DA. 1987. Scripture in the hands of geologists (parts 1 and 2). The Westminster Theological Journal 49:(Spring) 1-34, (Fall) 257-304.

5. For instance: (a) M. A. Corey's (1994. Back to Darwin: the scientific case for deistic evolution. Lanham, Md., New York, and London: University Press of America) use of "deistic evolution" seems to fit better with theistic evolution as used in this chapter, while (b) J. W. Klotz (1970. Genes, Genesis and evolution. 2nd ed., rev. St. Louis: Concordia Pub. House, p. 477) employs the expression "theistic evolution" for what appears to be deistic evolution.
6. For a review of some views, see: Young DA. 1995. The biblical flood: a case study of the church's response to extrabiblical evidence. Grand Rapids: Wm. B. Eerdmans Pub. Co., and Carlisle: Paternoster Press.
7. See chapter 9 for details.
8. Gen. 1 and 2. See also Ex. 20:11; 31:17. Some also consider Isaiah 45 and Job 38, 39, but they seem more concerned with God's attributes than creation.
9. For a comprehensive discussion of the evidence that they were ordinary 24-hour days, see: Hasel GF. 1994. The "days" of creation in Genesis 1: literal "days" or figurative "periods/epochs" of time? Origins 21:5-38.
10. For further discussion, see chapter 12.
11. See: McIver, pp. 461-473 (note 4i).
12. For a discussion of this alternative and related models, see chapter 19.
13. See chapters 9, 10, 14.
14. See chapters 10 and 12 for details.
15. See references in note 4, especially: (a) McIver, pp. 474-502 (note 4i). See also: (b) Fields WW. 1976. Unformed and unfilled: the gap theory. Nutley, N.J.: Presbyterian and Reformed Pub. Co.
16. Compare Gen. 1:2 with Isa. 45:18.
17. Gen. 1:2.
18. Gen. 1; 2; Ex. 20:11; 31:17; Neh. 9:6; Ps. 146:6; Isa. 40:26, 28; John 1:3; Acts 4:24; and Col. 1:16.
19. See references in note 4; also: (a) Baldwin JT. 1991. Progressive creation and biblical revelation: some theological implications. Origins 18:53-65; (b) Gedney EK. 1950. Geology and the Bible. In: American Scientific Affiliation, editors. Modern science and Christian faith: a symposium on the relationship of the Bible to modern science. Wheaton, Ill.: Scripture Press Foundation, pp. 23-57; (c) Pun PPT. 1987. A theology of progressive creationism. Perspectives on Science and Christian Faith 39:9-19; (d) Ramm B. 1954. The Christian view of science and Scripture. Grand Rapids: Wm. B. Eerdmans Pub. Co.; (e) Ross H. 1994. Creation and time: a biblical and scientific perspective on the creation-date controversy. Colorado Springs, Colo.: NavPress; (f) Spradley JL. 1992. Changing views of science and Scripture: Bernard Ramm and the ASA. Perspectives on Science and Christian Faith 44:2-9.
20. Gen. 3:14-19.
21. Rom. 5:12-19.
22. Dobzhansky T. 1973. Nothing in biology makes sense except in the light of evolution. The American Biology Teacher 35:125-129.
23. Gen. 1:31.
24. Gen. 1; Ex. 20:11.
25. See also Hasel (note 9).
26. See references in note 4. Also: (a) Bube RH. 1971. Biblical evolutionism? Journal of the American Scientific Affiliation 23:140-144; (b) Gibson LJ. 1992. Theistic evolution: is it for Adventists? Ministry 65(1):22-25; (c) Miller KB. 1993. Theological implications of an evolving creation. Perspectives on Science and Christian Faith 45(3):150-160; (d) Ramm, pp. 113, 280-293 (note 19d); (e) Teilhard de Chardin P. 1966. Man's place in nature: the human zoological group. Hague R, translator. New York: Harper and Row, pp. 61-63. Translation of: La place de l'homme dans la nature (possibly his views fit here); (f) Van Dyke F. 1986. Theological problems of theistic evolution. Journal of the American Scientific Affiliation 38:11-18.

27. Isa. 44:21, 22.
28. Luke 12:6.
29. Isa. 11:6; 65:25.
30. (a) Key, pp. 20, 21 (note 4e). Many varieties of deism exist. For a summary, see: (b) Aldridge AO. 1985. Deism. In: Stein G, editor. The encyclopedia of unbelief, vol. 1. Buffalo: Prometheus Books, pp. 134-137.
31. See chapter 18 for details.
32. (a) Key, p. 22 (note 4e); (b) Morris HM. 1992. Pantheistic evolution. Impact Series No. 234. El Cajon, Calif.: Institute for Creation Research.
33. (a) Arrhenius S. 1908. Worlds in the making. Borns H, translator. New York: Harper and Row. Translation of: Varldarnas ulveckling and Manniskan infor varldsgatan; (b) Brooks J, Shaw G. 1973. Origin and development of living systems. London and New York: Academic Press, pp. 354, 355; (c) Crick F. 1981. Life itself: its origin and nature. New York: Simon and Schuster; (d) Crick FHC, Orgel LE. 1973. Directed panspermia. Icarus 19:341-346; (e) Hoyle F, Wickramasinghe NC. 1981. Evolution from space: a theory of cosmic creationism. New York: Simon and Schuster; (f) von Däniken E. 1969. Chariots of the gods? Unsolved mysteries of the past. 2nd ed. Heron M, translator. Toronto, New York, and London: Bantam Books. Translation of: Erinnerungen an die Zukunft.
34. (a) Key, p. 20 (note 4e); (b) Marsh, p. 53 (note 4h); (c) Ramm, p. 113 (note 19d).
35. See chapters 4-8, 11.
36. Compare Romans 8:22, which speaks of degeneration in nature since the introduction of sin, contrasted with the very good, original creation described in Genesis 1:31.
37. Gen. 1:2.
38. Ps. 90:4; 2 Peter 3:8.
39. Hasel (note 9).
40. For some recent views, not all of which fit the allegory concept, see: (a) Bailey (note 4a); (b) Ross (note 19e); (c) Van Till HJ, Snow RE, Stek JH, Young DA. 1990. Portraits of creation: biblical and scientific perspectives on the world's formation. Grand Rapids: Wm. B. Eerdmans Pub. Co.
41. 2 Peter 3:3-6. See chapter 18 for further details of this prediction.
42. 1 Peter 3:20; 2 Peter 2:5.
43. Rom. 5:12-14; 1 Cor. 11:8; 15:22, 45; 1 Tim. 2:13, 14.
44. Heb. 11:4-7. That Paul is the author of Hebrews has been disputed for centuries, but he is the most likely candidate. We know of no other church leader of his time that could have set forth the profound arguments employed here.
45. Matt. 19:4-6; Mark 10:6.
46. Matt. 24:37, 38; Luke 17:26, 27.
47. Isa. 54:9.
48. Ex. 20:11; 31:17.
49. Num. 23:19; Ps. 119:163; Prov. 12:22; Isa. 45:19; Titus 1:2; Heb. 6:18; Rev. 21:8.
50. See chapter 17.
51. Toulmin S. 1989. The historicization of natural science: its implications for theology. In: Küng H, Tracy D, editors. Paradigm change in theology: a symposium for the future. Köhl M, translator. New York: Crossroad Pub. Co., pp. 233-241. Translation of: Theologie—Wohin? and Das Neue Paradigma von Theologie.
52. Spring B. 1985. A conversation with Carl Henry about the new physics. Christianity Today (1 February):26.
53. Weinberg S. 1992. Dreams of a final theory. New York: Pantheon Books, Random House, pp. 257, 258.
54. For an account of this in the United Methodist Church, see: Ching K. 1991. The practice of theological pluralism. Adventist Perspectives 5(1):6-11.
55. Kelley DM. 1972, 1977. Why conservative churches are growing: a study in sociology of religion. 2nd ed. San Francisco, New York, and Hagerstown, Md.: Harper and Row.
56. Niebuhr HR. 1957. The social sources of denominationalism. New York: Meridian Books, pp. 19, 20.

57. For instance, see: (a) Marsden GM. 1994. The soul of the American university: from Protestant establishment to established nonbelief. New York and Oxford: Oxford University Press; (b) Marsden GM, Longfield BJ, editors. 1992. The secularization of the academy. New York and Oxford: Oxford University Press; (c) Sloan D. 1994. Faith and knowledge: mainline Protestantism and American higher education. Louisville, Ky.: Westminster John Knox Press.

CHAPTER 22

A FEW FINAL WORDS

Truth is often eclipsed,
but never extinquished.
—Livy[1]

Why are we here?

This question is closely related to the lingering question we asked in the first chapter: Which is true, science or Scripture? Science in its modern naturalistic stance intimates that human beings have no purpose. Scripture intimates existence does have meaning, and humanity has a purpose, part of which is helping others. In the earlier chapters we have looked at the hard questions facing creation, evolution, and intermediate views. As we evaluate these questions as a whole, a brief summary of our earlier conclusions will be instructive.

RECAPITULATION[2]

Many seriously wonder which is correct: naturalistic science or Scripture. As we seek an answer, it is important to keep in mind that human thought patterns tend to follow the prevailing "climate of opinion." Hence we need to be careful to attach our anchor points for our worldviews on the firmest data. During our search for truth we should use as broad a base as we can, including both science and Scripture, which fundamentally are not as different from each other as many commonly surmise. A more important question is: what truths do I find when I look at both science (as a methodology) and Scripture?

Naturalistic science strongly endorses the evolutionary model of origins. Probably the most serious challenge to that model is the question of the origin of life. The simplest forms of life have hundreds of different, highly complex, information-laden, specialized, delicate molecules that could not arise by themselves, especially not in the concentrations needed to form any kind of living system. After two centuries of conjecture evolutionists have failed to find a satisfactory mechanism for their model. Explanations for the origin of living things are even more difficult when we consider advanced organisms. They have well-developed, complicated, interdependent physiological systems that will usually not function until all the basic parts are there. It does not seem plausible that such systems could all arise suddenly by a multitude of simultaneous random mutations whose direction of change has no foresight. Nor does it seem plausible, if such systems did form gradually, that nonfunctional developing parts could withstand the survival of the fittest pressure usually postulated for the evolutionary process. That process would tend to eliminate any useless parts. Furthermore, we do not seem to see new organs currently forming in contemporary organisms. When it comes to the origin of humanity, mechanistic explanations do not easily answer the question of our special mental faculties, such as consciousness morality and free will.

The problem of origins has become even more complicated with the discovery of "programmed" systems such as the genetic code, elaborate gene control systems, and the correcting systems for DNA replication. To the best of our knowledge, such complex kinds of programs do not arise spontaneously—they appear to represent intelligent design such as we would expect from a Creator.

The fossils found in the sedimentary layers of the earth reflect a general, but poor, trend from simple to complex. Evolutionists interpret this as gradual evolutionary development. However, the fossil pattern discovered would imply highly erratic rates of evolution with many major groups appearing extremely rapidly. Creationists see the general trend from simple to complex as the result of factors active during the Genesis flood as well as the distribution of organisms before the deluge. The present distribution of living organisms also broadly follows a simple to complex pattern as one begins below the sea floor and moves to higher altitudinal regions of earth's crust. We would expect to find a similar order in sediments originating from landscapes gradually eroded by the rising waters of the deluge. The "Cambrian explosion" of basic kinds of animals would represent the low preflood seas. The general lack of fossil intermediates (missing links) between the major categories of organisms indicates that evolution did not occur. Such gaps are especially conspicuous between the major categories (phyla and divisions) of plants and animals, areas in which we would expect to find the greatest number of intermediates if evolution were true.

Geology is again accepting catastrophic interpretations of earth history. Creationists propose that the worldwide flood described in Genesis produced a major portion of earth's sedimentary layers. This implies rapid deposition during the year of the flood. Evidence for this includes the unusually widespread nature of some of these deposits, as we would expect from major flood activity; the unusual but abundant indications of underwater activity on the continents; incomplete ecological systems; and a lack of support for the many millions of years of proposed elapsed time between some of these layers where we find major portions of the geologic column missing. Erosion should have been especially pronounced at such gaps, but field evidence shows that it is very minor or missing.

The slow rate of coral reef growth is considered a challenge to a recent creation but living reefs can sometimes grow quite rapidly, and many assumed fossil reefs have undergone considerable reinterpretation. Earth's fossil layers contain evidence of biological activity, such as trackways and worm tubes. Noncreationists view them as evidence of long periods of time, and creationists regard them as the result of activity by organisms during the year of the flood.

Radiometric dating is presented as a serious challenge to the recent creation described in Scripture. However, both creationists and noncreationists adjust carbon-14 dates to what they consider to be real time, but the time adjustments postulated by creationists are greater. Many radiometric dates are anomalous but many are not. Creationists suggest a variety of conditions during the Genesis flood that would alter radiometric dates. It is difficult to think that a worldwide catastrophe such as the Genesis flood would not affect these dating systems. Besides, the rate of a number of geologic changes occurring presently, such as erosion, volcanic activity, and mountain uplift, suggest much less time in the geologic past than proposed by the geologic timescale.

Experimental science as currently practiced is an extremely successful method for discovering truth about nature. But science is not as good when dealing with unrepeatable past events (historical science) and has little to contribute in the areas of morality, purposefulness, or religion. The Bible, on the other hand, covers these areas and also includes some scientific information. External geographical, historical, and archaeological evidence and some unusual predictive capabilities, including anticipating the present conflicts over creation and the flood, all authenticate Scripture.[3] The Bible explains the suffering in nature as the consequences of wrong decisions by those possessing freedom of choice. Although a number of questions have risen about the biblical account of beginnings, satisfactory answers do exist.

Naturalistic science faces a dilemma as more evidence emerges to pose insurmountable problems for evolution. Evolution is the best model that science can postulate while staying within the constraints of a naturalistic philosophy. Scientists are reluctant to give up this stance and yield to alternatives such as creation, which would resolve the dilemma.

Some suggest that God could have created over long periods of time, or that He only initiated primordial life, or that He used the process of evolution to create. Besides some of the problems mentioned above, such intermediate views between creation and evolution suffer from a lack of evidence. Neither scientific data nor Scripture directly suggest them. Their lack of supporting evidence is also reflected in their lack of definition. They are interesting, but have an inordinately high degree of conjecture.

To this writer, the creation model makes the most sense, as I will discuss further below.

THE SUPREMACY OF PREVAILING IDEAS

In 1712 two members of the House of Parliament in London—the duke of Hamilton and Lord Mohun—had a disastrous encounter. They had had a lawsuit pending for 11 years, and as a consequence were not the best of friends. While discussing their case with a legal court officer, the duke of Hamilton commented that one of the case witnesses who was favorable to Lord Mohun had neither truth nor justice in him. Lord Mohun reacted to the derogatory comment by suggesting that the witness had as much truth and justice as the duke of Hamilton. The duke made no reply to this quip, and in leaving he courteously saluted the lord. No one suspected the seriousness of the animosity. That evening a messenger from Lord Mohun twice tried to find the duke to challenge him to a duel. The man finally located him in a tavern and delivered the message. The duke accepted the challenge, and they set the encounter for two days later at 7:00 a.m. on Sunday, November 15, in Hyde Park. As was the usual practice, they appointed assistants (seconds) in the duel.

At the scheduled time the participants met in the part of the park called the Nursery and prepared for combat. When all was ready, the two leading opponents took up their swords and desperately attacked each other. Lord Mohun died on the spot, and the duke of Hamilton expired as his servants carried him away.[4] The argument was settled.

Such behavior may seem strange to us, but it was once very fashionable to protect one's honor by dueling. Duels of honor, which became dominant in medieval times, sought to rectify personal offenses. While duels did not always end in death, many times they did. The practice among the nobility of wearing swords as everyday dress aggravated such encounters. The slightest pretext, such as disputes at playing cards or dogfights, became a reason for a duel. The practice became very popular in France and was common in Italy, Germany, Russia, England, and Ireland. Historical accounts report as many as 23 duels a day in Ireland.[5] They were so common that people paid attention to them only when one or both of the combatants died. During the reign of Henry IV in France, more than 4,000 French "gentlemen" lost their lives from dueling in an 18-year period.[6] In the reign of Louis XIII the ordinary conversation in the morning was reportedly: "Do you know who fought yesterday?" and after dinner: "Do you know who fought this morning?" In a 20-year period the authorities issued 8,000 pardons for murders associated with duels.[7]

The mentality of the fad was not complex, but it is difficult to appreciate. Personal honor, pride, and revenge took precedence over other values, including life itself. As Joseph Addison commented in *The Spectator:* "Death is not sufficient to deter men who make it their glory to despise it."[8] In the minds of too many, pride and revenge for alleged affronts took precedence over all other values.

This devastating practice did not meet with everybody's approval, and many monarchs tried to suppress it, although some of them passively participated in it. In England, Francis Bacon perceived the difficulty of the problem. He pointed out that "the roots of this offence is stubborn: For it despiseth death, which is the utmost of punishments."[9] Bacon suggested that society attack those factors that led to dueling instead of the duel itself, but the practice continued.

Governments passed many laws against dueling, including death sentences in Poland, Munich, and Naples. The French monarchy especially opposed it, and executed many survivors of duels during the reign of Louis XIV; however, dueling outlived the French monarchy. In the United States the practice did not become popular until the beginning of the nineteenth century, when it spread rapidly, especially in the South.[10]

In the meantime, dueling began to lose its popularity and respect. Ridicule and embarrassing punishments for participants, such as hanging their bodies after they had died in a duel, began to moderate the practice. Much has been written about the implications of duels. Some, such as Jonathan Swift, suggested that there was no harm in rogues and fools shooting each other;[11] others labeled it as wild-animal behavior, murder, or suicide. Fortunately, the so-called duel of honor is no longer fashionable. This life-destroying paradigm has died.

Dueling well illustrates how strong a grip paradigms can have despite little logic to support them and dire consequences resulting from them. The practice endured for centuries. Earlier we mentioned the shrinking earth, witch-hunting, and alchemy as other dominant ideas that have also come and gone.[12] It should warn us not to base our worldviews merely on the accepted "climate of opinion," which can be here today and gone tomorrow.

EVALUATING MODELS OF ORIGINS

The dominance of paradigms raises the question as to whether creation and evolution are just temporary fashions in the continuing panorama of changing ideas. I would say no. Through all this there is truth, and we expect truth to survive error. The creation concept has a long endurance record, but endurance alone need not be the final test of truth. We could make a list of the arguments in favor of creation and another of those in support of evolution and see which is longer. A list of arguments that directly support concepts that lie between creation and evolution, such as theistic evolution and progressive creation, would be conspicuously short. But the length of lists might not be decisive, since some arguments are much better than others. In our evaluation we would do well to pay special attention to the quality of arguments as well as the quantity.

The recapitulation I have given above includes a number of scientific arguments favoring the biblical model of origins. It is significant that we can find biological, historical, archaeological, paleontological, and geological data that corroborate the Bible. Probably more important is the fact that even when hundreds of thousands of scientists are interpreting science under the evolutionary paradigm and only a handful under the creation paradigm, we still find so much evidence to support the Bible. What would the picture be if half the scientists were on one side of the question and half on the other? I would venture that the data examined and the conclusions drawn regarding origins would be vastly different than the present domination of evolution. Information that fits the biblical model is not that difficult to find.

Yet another lingering question still faces us: Can science, which is so successful in the experimental realm, be so wrong about the question of our origins? Success can easily blind us. Science is so successful in the experimental realm that it may be prone to overconfidence in other areas, such as historical science.

Despite the work of a vast multitude of scientists, firm evidence for the general theory of evolution is sparse. The philosopher Huston Smith, referring to evolution, expressed his concern: "Our personal assessment is that on no other scientific theory does the modern mind rest so much confidence on so little proportional evidence; on evidence, that is to say, which, in ratio to the amount that would be needed to establish the theory in the absence of the will to believe, is so meager."[13] The physicist Wolfgang Smith also worries about the quality of the scientific data supporting evolution: "The point, however, is that the doctrine of evolution has swept the world, not on the strength of its scientific merits, but precisely in its capacity as a Gnostic myth. It affirms, in effect, that living beings create themselves, which is in essence a *metaphysical* claim. This in itself implies, however, that the theory is scientifically unverifiable (a fact, incidentally, which has often enough been pointed out by philosophers of science). Thus, in the final analysis, evolutionism is in truth a metaphysical doctrine decked out in scientific garb."[14]

Is evolution a transient paradigm destined to oblivion? I will withhold speculation. But I would say that unless evolution can come up with more significant data to support it, its survival appears precarious. The more recent scientific discoveries in molecular biology make the question of its continuance particularly tenuous.[15] However, ideas with little foundation, such as alchemy or the duel of honor, can dominate for many centuries.

One further aspect needs mention as we evaluate the broad picture. The act of creation itself as a miraculous event is extremely difficult to evaluate scientifically, although the consequences of creation such as seen in the complexities of nature are not. The Genesis flood is somewhat more readily analyzable in the geologic layers, but here we are still dealing with historical science. Does this mean that creation is an irrational concept? I would say no. The hard data of molecular biology and the rock features indicating rapid deposition substantiate the rationality of creation. However, some of the significance of the evidence for creation lies not in direct observation, but in the failure of alternatives such as evolution to provide a plausible mechanism. These are all pertinent points important to the question of origins. We may not be as happy with indirect evidence as we would be with direct observation, but sometimes it is all that we have, and we should make the best of all the information available to us.

CONCLUSIONS

My personal evaluation follows: I cannot accept the idea that God does not exist. Nature is too complex and existence too meaningful for me to think that all the intricacies and delicate balances I see about me are just accidental. There has to be a Designer. If there is a Designer, I would expect some meaningful communication from Him. It would be an odd kind of Creator who would design our thinking, conscious minds and not communicate at all with us. I expect communication, and I look for that communication. Scripture is the best candidate. Written by more than two dozen authors claiming special revelation, it has unusual internal coherence and unusual external correspondence with history, archaeology, and nature. Not all questions find answers,[16] but among all the models considered, the creation described in Scripture makes the most sense. It answers the most questions.

When I examine models of origin by God over extended periods of time, such as deistic evolution, theistic evolution, or progressive creation, none of them are as convincing to me as the creation described in Genesis. Such models are too "dependent" on the absence of data. One reason to believe in creation is the evidence for the rapid deposition of the geologic layers.[17] Another is Scripture, which is no ordinary book.[18] If there is a God, and the Bible is His Word, it seems difficult to reconcile that word, which is clear about a recent creation, with different alternatives. If one is going to accept God as Creator, as many of the intermediate views do, one needs to keep in mind that the God described in Scripture could have created recently just as readily as over a long time. God had no need for an episodic creation process during eons of time. Finally, God Himself states that He created all in six days.[19]

Many who accept views intermediate between creation and evolution also readily accept the hope of eternal salvation extended by Jesus Christ, yet they effectively reject His endorsement of the biblical accounts of creation and the flood.[20] One could essentially be as consistent by accepting Christ's endorsement of creation and the flood and rejecting His salvation! Was Christ deceiving us when He treated creation and the flood as factual accounts? One might as well face the issue candidly: either Jesus Christ was the Son of God, or He was an impostor posing as God's Son. If He was an impostor, Christianity's salvation as well as the Bible and all its explanatory value are an illusion. We are back to naturalistic evolution and its many problems. If Jesus Christ was truly the Son of God, we would not expect Him to mislead us regarding the important question of origins.

It surprises me that the concept of evolution persists in view of the paucity of firm evidence to support it.[21] We can probably best explain such persistence on sociological grounds similar to other paradigms or trends that have endured sometimes for centuries but have little basis for support. Powerful science trying to answer the great questions of existence within its own limited naturalistic system of explanation encourages belief in evolution. Evolution is the best explanation for origins it can come up with, but in my opinion, it falls short of plausibility. Science may produce new interpretations that challenge creation, but until it can come up with a model that better explains the complexity of nature and the meaningfulness of existence, its approach cannot satisfy some of our most profound questions. As a pursuit of knowledge, science should become more cognizant of its limited sphere of expertise and accept the value of other disciplines, recognizing in its methodological stance that other areas have authoritative contributions to make to the search for truth. Then, and only then, can science significantly accord truth.

We began this chapter with the question Why are we here? My personal assessment is that creation answers that question better than do other models. Creation makes a significant, reasonable, and satisfying contribution to the great questions of truth, meaning, purpose, duty, and our personal destiny.

Some establish their worldview on the basis of science alone. While science is worthy of respect, it is an incomplete worldview. Others ground their worldview on the basis of Scripture alone. But even this is a restricted outlook, and Scripture encourages us to learn from God's creation.[22] To me, a more satisfactory approach is to link science and Scripture.

REFERENCES

1. Livy. *c* 10. History of Rome, XXII. Quoted in: Mencken HL, editor. 1942. A new dictionary of quotations on historical principles from ancient and modern sources. New York: Alfred A. Knopf, p. 1220.
2. This review is based on the material presented in the previous chapters. Supporting documentation appears in sequence in chapters 1-21.
3. 2 Peter 3:3-6.
4. As reported in: Mackay C. [1852.] 1932. Extraordinary popular delusions and the madness of crowds. New York: Farrar, Straus and Giroux, p. 681.
5. (a) Mackay, p. 686 (note 4). Other references on the historical development of dueling include: (b) Basnage M. 1740. Dissertation historique sur les Duels et les ordres de Chevaliere. Rev. ed. Basel: Jean Christ, p. 4; (c) Bataillard PC. 1829. Du duel, considéré sous le rapport de la morale, de l'histoire, de la législation et de l'opportunité d'une loi répressive. Paris, p. 14.
6. Mackay, p. 666 (note 4).
7. *Ibid.,* p. 668.
8. Addison J. [n.d.]. The spectator: religious, moral, humorous, satirical, and critical essays, vol. 2. New York: Hurst and Co., p. 210.
9. Bacon F. 1614. The charge of Sir Francis Bacon Knight. London: Robert Wilson, p. 18.
10. Kane HT. 1951. Gentlemen, swords, and pistols. New York: William Morrow and Co., p. x.
11. As reported in Mackay, p. 679 (note 4).
12. See chapter 2.
13. Smith H. 1976. Forgotten truth: the primordial tradition. New York, Hagerstown, Md., and San Francisco: Harper and Row, p. 132.
14. Smith W. 1988. Teilhardism and the new religion: a thorough analysis of the teachings of Pierre Teilhard de Chardin. Rockford, Ill.: Tan Books and Publishers, p. 242.
15. See chapter 8.
16. See chapters 10 and 14.
17. See chapters 13 and 15.
18. See chapters 1 and 18.
19. Ex. 20:11.
20. Matt. 19:4-6; 24:37, 38; Mark 10:6; Luke 17:26, 27. Chapter 21 discusses this and the endorsement by other authors of the Bible.
21. See chapters 4-8, 11.
22. E.g., Ps. 19:1-4; Rom. 1:19, 20.

GLOSSARY OF TECHNICAL TERMS

Alchemy: The pursuit, especially in medieval times, of trying to liberate substances. It comprised the transmutation of base metals into gold and the search for the "elixir of life."

Amino acid: Organic molecule with a nitrogen-bearing amino group. Amino acids are molecules (biomonomers) that combine to form proteins. Living organisms have 20 kinds of amino acids.

Basalt: Igneous rock dark in color with fine crystals, formed by the more rapid cooling of magma.

Base (of DNA): See *Nucleotide base*.

Bible: The Word of God as written by inspired prophets.

Biomonomer: A relatively simple organic molecule such as an amino acid or a nucleotide that will combine with many other similar molecules to form long biopolymers.

Biopolymer: A large chainlike molecule consisting of chemically bonded biomonomers. See *Biomonomer*.

Cambrian: The lowest division (period) of the Phanerozoic portion of the geologic column. It is the lowest unit with abundant fossils.

Cambrian explosion: A term applied to the fact that as one ascends through the geologic column, one suddenly finds almost all of the animal phyla in the Cambrian. The term refers to what evolutionists considered an "explosive" phenomenon of rapid evolution.

Catastrophism: Theory in which phenomena outside our present experience of nature have greatly modified earth's crust by violent, sudden, but short-lived events more or less worldwide.

Cenozoic: The highest of the three main divisions of the Phanerozoic. See *Phanerozoic*.

Class: See under *Classification of organisms*.

Classification of organisms: Biologists use the following hierarchial system. Each category below the first is a subdivision of the one above.

Kingdom
  Phylum (animals); Division (plants)
    Class
      Order
        Family
          Genus
            Species

Continental drift: The travel of continents to their present position caused by the movement of the underlying lithospheric plates. See also *Plate tectonics.*

Creation: The biblical concept of beginnings. God accomplished His creation in six literal days a few thousand years ago.

Debris flow: Mass movement of rock fragments, soil, and mud, with most of the particles larger than grains of sand.

Deistic evolution: The concept that God, usually considered to be impersonal, started the universe and possibly life sometime in the distant past, but He is not actively involved at present.

Deluge: See *Genesis flood.*

Disconformity: An unconformity with evidence of some erosion between the parallel layers that lie above and below the disconformity. See *Unconformity.*

Division (Plants): See under *Classification of organisms.*

DNA: Common abbreviation for deoxyribonucleic acid, which forms the long chain-like molecules that code the genetic information of an organism. DNA molecules can have millions of nucleotide bases attached to each other. See *Nucleotide.*

Ecological zonation theory: The theory that the sequence of fossils found in the geologic column results from the ecological distribution of the organisms before the Genesis flood. The gradually rising waters of the flood destroyed in sequence the preflood ecological zones. The preflood ecology is assumed to have been different from present ecology.

Ecosystem: A community of interacting organisms.

Empiricism: Belief that knowledge is derived from sense experience.

Enlightenment: The philosophical movement of Europe during the eighteenth century. It questioned traditional values and doctrines and emphasized individualism, reason, and human progress.

Epicontinental: Located on a continent or on the continental shelf, such as an epicontinental sea.

Episodic: A rate of change that fluctuates sporadically.

Evolution: Development from simple to complex. Biological evolution usually includes the origin of life from inanimate matter and the subsequent development of complex organisms from simple ones during eons of time.

Family: See under *Classification of organisms.*

Formation: A group of rock strata or a body of igneous or metamorphic rock that has certain unique characteristics common to the unit and differing from adjacent units, usually of mappable size.

Fossil: Remains or traces or evidence of ancient animals or plants.

Gaia: The hypothesis that the living matter of earth forms a collectively self-regulating system favoring the continuance of life.

Genesis: The first book of the Bible. The creation and flood accounts occur in the first 11 chapters.

Genesis flood: The worldwide catastrophe described in the first book (Genesis) of the Bible, when floodwaters destroyed the world. Sometimes called the deluge.

Genetic engineering: Manipulation of the genetic information of organisms so as to produce new kinds of organisms.

Genus: See under *Classification of organisms.*

Geologic column: A representation of the vertical arrangement and classification of the subdivisions of earth's rock layers, or sometimes just a portion of it.

Granite: Coarsely crystalline rock, consisting of light and dark interlocking crystals, not in layers; sometimes derived by the metamorphism of sedimentary rocks, also of igneous origin from the slow cooling of magma.

Hiatus: Gap, missing layers in a sedimentary sequence.

Historical science: The less testable and predictable aspects of science. Often associated with the study of the past, which is more subjective.

Homeobox: Sequences of DNA that are similar and are found in a variety of organisms. They appear to be associated with genes that control physical development.

Igneous: Rocks derived from molten material (magma).

Kingdom: See under *Classification of organisms.*

Lamina (plural: laminae): A sheet or layer of sedimentary rock with a thickness of less than 1 centimeter, commonly much thinner.

Limestone: Sedimentary rock containing more than 50 percent $CaCO_3$, often white to grayish, produced by precipitation of lime from seawater either inorganically or by living organisms.

Mesozoic: The middle of the three main divisions of the Phanerozoic. See *Phanerozoic.*

Methodological science: Used in this treatise to identify that science which is open to a broad spectrum of explanations, including creation by intelligent design. The pioneers of modern science understood nature as God's creation and would be methodological scientists. This contrasts with naturalistic science, which accepts only mechanistic explanations. See also *Science* and *Naturalistic science.*

Molecular clock: The concept that changes in nucleic acids occur at a constant rate and can thus be used to estimate the timing of evolutionary changes.

Morphology: A study of form and shape, especially of an organism or its parts.

Mutation: A more-or-less permanent genetic change.

Naturalism: The belief that only natural (mechanistic) explanations are valid. It excludes supernatural explanations.

Naturalistic science: Interpretations of nature that allow for only natural phenomena, thus excluding God's activity, or anything supernatural. See also *Methodological science.*

Nucleotide: A basic unit of DNA consisting of a nucleotide base in combination with phosphate and a five-carbon sugar. The order of the nucleotide bases determines the genetic information in DNA and RNA. See *Nucleotide base.*

Nucleotide base: A ringlike molecule containing nitrogen that serves as one of the basic units of nucleotides. The five different kinds found in DNA and RNA are adenine, guanine, cytocene, uridine (only in RNA), and thymine. See *Nucleotide.*

Order: See under *Classification of organisms.*

Orogeny: The process of forming mountains, especially uplift, folding, and thrusting.

Paleoanthropology: The division of anthropology that deals with fossil humans and their ancestors.

Paleontology: The study of fossil plants and animals.

Paleozoic: The lowest of the three main divisions of the Phanerozoic. See *Phanerozoic.*

Pantheistic evolution: The concept that God is nature and that God progresses with nature as it evolves.

Paraconformity: An unconformity in which we observe no erosional surface and the beds below and above are parallel, a nonsequence.

Paradigm: A broad concept accepted as true and that influences the interpretation of data.

Phanerozoic: The portion of the geologic column from the Cambrian up to the present. Containing abundant fossils, geologists divide it into the Paleozoic, Mesozoic, and Cenozoic eras.

Phylum (animals): See under *Classification of organisms.*

Plate tectonics: The concept of the movement of large plates that lie below the ocean floor and continents. See also *Continental drift.*

Positivism: Belief in the primacy of "positive" facts and phenomena, excluding any speculation. It stipulates that the only kind of knowledge is "scientific."

Precambrian: Rock layers below the Cambrian. The Precambrian is almost devoid of fossils, in contrast to rocks of the Cambrian and above, which contain many fossils.

Progressive creation: The concept that God created life on earth in a series of progressive steps spread over long periods of time.

Pseudofossil: A structure thought to be a fossil that later has turned out to be of inorganic origin.

Rational: Reasonable, sensible, agreeable to reason.

Reef: A projecting outcrop of rocks. See *True reef.*

Religion: Commitment or devotion to a set of beliefs. Often associated with, but not limited to, the worship of God.

RNA: Common abbreviation for ribonucleic acid, similar to DNA with a slightly different kind of sugar and a slightly different set of nucleotide bases. See *DNA* and *Nucleotide base.*

Science: The process of studying nature by gathering data and providing explanations and interpretations of it. See also *Methodological science* and *Naturalistic science.*

Scripture: See *Bible.*

Sediment: Any particles, of any size, transported or deposited after transport. Transport usually occurs by water, wind, or ice.

Sedimentary rock: Rock formed of fragments derived by transport, usually by water, etc., or by precipitation from solution. See *Sediment.*

Species: A group of similar organisms that interbreed and produce offspring with similar structures, functions, and habits.

Spontaneous generation: The development of living organisms from nonliving matter.

Stratum (plural: strata): A stratigraphic unit. A layer (or bed) of sediment limited by two surfaces that are approximately parallel, featuring sharp contacts (visually obvious) among the sediments.

Stromatolite: A sedimentary structure consisting of successive fine laminae. Stromatolites are often mounded but vary greatly in shape and size, being in the millimeter to meter range. They are produced by a thin layer of microorganisms on their surface which captures and/or precipitates the minerals that form the laminae. See *Lamina*.

Subsidence: Sinking of a large region of earth's crust.

Theistic evolution: The concept that life developed over long periods of time as the result of the work of God associated with an evolutionary process.

Theology: The branch of study that deals especially with God and His relation to the world.

True reef: Slow buildup by marine organisms of a wave-resistant structure. Sometimes called a bioherm or autochthonous reef. See *Reef*.

Truth: That which is in accord with fact or reality.

Turbidite: A sedimentary rock deposited by a turbidity current. See *Turbidity current*.

Turbidity current: A downhill, underwater density current consisting of suspended sediments. The current has a greater density than water and flows with a characteristic pattern, leaving a characteristic widespread deposit called a turbidite.

Unconformity: An interruption in deposition in a sedimentary sequence. A gap, or hiatus, in the layers forming the stratigraphic record.

Uniformitarianism: Theory stating that geologic processes operating today acted the same way and at the same speed in the past. This theory does not exclude some local catastrophes.

Varve: Layer of sediment usually consisting of a coarse and fine portion and thought to have been deposited during one year.

INDEX